JAPAN • THE VEGETARIAN COOKBOOK

NANCY SINGLETON HACHISU

LEGEND

VEGAN

DAIRY-FREE

GLUTEN-FREE

NUT-FREE

FEWER THAN 5 INGREDIENTS

LESS THAN 30 MINUTES

ITAMEMONO & YAKIMONO

STIR-FRIED & GRILLED

HON MIRIN

196

SHIRUMONO

SOUP

BUILDING A BOWL OF MISO SOUP

236

HANMONO

RICE

OKAYU: PORRIDGE TO HEAL
YOUR BODY AND SOUL

268

TSUKEMONO & HOZONSHOKU

PICKLED & PRESERVED

SUN-DRIED VEGETABLES

298

KANMI

SWEET

JAPANESE SUGAR

322

INTRODUCTION

~~~~~~

In the jingle, jangle of the world we live in, I seek quiet. My oasis can simply be an untroubled place I go to in my mind, shutting out the cacophony around me. Or it can be a peaceful nest in my bed, computer on my lap, kitty cat purring beside me.

I grew up in California, in a noisy house with five brothers and sisters and liberal '60s-era parents. Whoever shouted the loudest always won the argument. It was a bit of a wild ride.

I spent hours poring over my mother's extensive, and eclectic, cookbook collection. Perched on a stool at the corner of the counter, I watched with fascination as she prepped and cooked our dinner from *Sunset* magazine, enthralled by the tastes of the raw ingredients and the movements of her knife or smells of the sizzling food in the pan. At the age of ten I began baking bread, before moving on, by junior high school, to cooking full meals for the family. It was my passion for sushi and fascination with Japanese food that initially drew me to Japan in 1988, but another reason was to explore the peaceful elements I perceived in Japanese culture.

While I did dabble in *shojin ryori* (Japanese vegetarian temple food) and *zazen* (Zen meditation), neither stuck. Instead, the calming of my inner storms happened over decades and was hard-won. But always, the kitchen was where I could regain my equilibrium and find quiet.

I once said in an interview that "Food is how I look at life." It means that food or cooking is how I make sense of life and how I keep myself healthy, both in body and mind. For some it must seem like an obsession, and I suppose it is. But it is an obsession I have carried with me since I was a small child. Perhaps because I was not brought up with spirituality or religion, food became a centering part of my existence. Today, installed in our ninety-year-old farmhouse kitchen, I still feel a sense of spirituality in touching the just-picked vegetables as they naturally come together into simple, flavorful dishes.

The decision to marry a Japanese farmer meant finding a way to negotiate a smooth path through Japanese life without losing my American side. While I will never be Japanese, after spending more than half my life living in Japan, the lines between the Japanese influences and my inherent Americanness have blurred. And my position as a long-term foreigner in the food world in Japan has given me a voice here and beyond.

Although not vegetarian or vegan, I have always eaten a highly plant-focused diet, supplemented by sea or ranch. Vegetables are how I approach a menu, and given the long history of Japanese vegetarian food this makes sense for Japanese cuisine.

You do not have to be a Zen Buddhist or even be adhering to a plant-based diet to feel the attractiveness of this clean type of food or the approachability of these Japanese dishes, which are in tune with the seasons and a more natural way of life. After a meal we should not feel like groaning from being overstuffed—this is a singularly unpleasant sensation. Satisfied, refreshed, and in some way spiritually fulfilled is the goal.

Japanese vegetarian food is prepared with mindfulness. Even if you only make one dish, give that dish and its ingredients respect and appreciation, for in its simplicity lies its beauty. The main ingredient of dishes should be enhanced by the seasonings and other ingredients, but never obscured or overpowered. Beyond the spiritual roots, this is the single most important tenet. Restraint is paramount, and probably the most difficult aspect for Westerners when approaching this kind of elegantly spare cuisine. We need to consciously hold back. But eventually, this, too, will become second nature, and you will have evolved personally from the experience.

Some of the first dishes I cooked in Japan were from *The Heart of Zen Cuisine*, a *shojin ryori* cookbook written in the 1980s. (Years later I became close friends with the co-author, the late Kim Schuefftan, a veteran editor with fifty-plus years editing and writing on Japanese food, ceramics, and cloth.) I still remember trying (unsuccessfully) to follow the mindful advice on washing rice (something akin to being "one with the rice")—it took me about twenty years, but I did finally get it.

And in the process, I discovered that so much of the secular *shojin ryori* found in Japan is bastardized, commonly seasoned with MSG and a heavy hand with the sugar, rarely seasonal, and not necessarily homemade. This has been an eye-opening discovery and further deepened my resolve to write a book on Japanese vegetarian food that would be a valuable contribution for not only the world, but also for Japan—especially for young Japanese who are perhaps losing touch with their food traditions.

Appearing in Japanese media and publishing cookbooks throughout the world has given me a chance to give back to Japan. Advocating for Japanese food traditions and defending Japanese foodways has evolved into a deep personal responsibility. In this global climate of mixing food traditions between countries, native cuisines are in danger of losing ground. That is why I am not a fan of Westernized versions of miso or shoyu or other fundamental Japanese ingredients based on centuries-old methods. Artisanal Japanese seasonings in their purest form are perfect as they are and provide the essential backbone to all the dishes in this book.

Although rooted in hundreds of years of tradition, Japanese vegetarian food is timeless. It is unselfconsciously light, flavorful, deeply satisfying, and utterly delicious. Even meat and fish lovers will come away from a vegetarian meal not feeling the lack of meat or fish. It could be the perfect meal. And as you push away from the table, or pull yourself up off the floor, you will feel the healing properties of this food course through your body and you will feel satisfied and well-fed, both in mind and spirit.

The richness in the meal comes from the delicately fried morsels of vegetables, sesame- or walnut-dressed dishes, and all forms of tofu: fresh, fried, dried, or fermented. Sweet and sour are played off each other with rice vinegars, mirin, and sour "plum" (*ume*, see page 345) as the key components. Miso and shoyu add the fermented salt notes that give depth to the dishes. But it is in the variety of the dishes and the gorgeousness of the colors that Japanese vegetarian food is so deeply compelling. You can prepare one or two dishes, or get lost in a whole meal.

And in the end, it all comes back to the pure, seasonal ingredients as the basis for this clean, restorative food. Subtly introducing various flavors and seasonings to these ingredients enhances them, and thus the ingredients and seasonings enhance each other. Valuing and paying attention to the ingredients means, for instance, taking care not to allow grains of rice to escape when washing rice, or recycling the rice washing water for simmering root vegetables. Another deeply fundamental principle is that the humblest ingredients are treated with just as much care and respect as the more exalted or rare ingredients. If these ideas seem foreign or "put on" for you, I suggest just absorbing the food and philosophy gradually. Let the ideas seep into your life in a quiet, unobtrusive way.

Given the myriad distractions in our modern world, we all need a little peace, so it's best to choose the approach and path to this food that is best suited to your own life. In writing this book I realized that although I am not practicing Zen Buddhism in my own life, in my cooking I am exactly practicing the thoughtfulness and clear mind and spirit ideals set out by Zen Buddhism and *shojin ryori*.

Use these maxims to approach Japanese vegetarian cooking:

- TAKE YOUR TIME AND COOK WITH PRECISION.

- ENJOY THE INGREDIENTS.

- LOOK INTO YOUR HEART THROUGH THE FOOD.

HISTORY OF JAPANESE
VEGETARIAN CUISINE

Zen Buddhist priests were the primary conduits for bringing Chinese culture to Japan during the Medieval Age (1192–1568), and this included new foods and ways of cooking. The first mention of tofu in Japan was in 1183, and the method of skimming off soy milk skin for producing *yuba* (see page 352) came from China during the Kamakura period (1192–1336). The process of making *fu* (wheat gluten; see page 352) was also learned in China and brought back to Japan by Zen Buddhist monks. The use of *fu* then spread throughout the monasteries of Japan and also to the public at large. Tofu, *yuba*, and *fu* were not only important sources of protein, but these ingredients also added richness and texture to the temple food dishes. The customs of drinking tea and taking midday snacks also originated in the Zen temples and were not only precursors to the tea ceremony and *kaiseki* cuisine (elegant small-bite, traditional dishes), but eventually also spread to the lay public. The ruling class in this period was made up of *daimyo* (feudal lords) and samurai who embraced Zen Buddhism into their way of life and integrated the temple food (*shojin ryori*) into their banquets, thus influencing the later development of *kaiseki* cuisine.

Generally believed to have been developed in China during the Han dynasty (200 BCE–CE 200), the earliest mention of fermented soy products (miso, *kuki*, and *hishio*) being used in Japan was in the Taiho Code of 701. *Kuki* is similar to *tera natto* (see page 350)—dry fermented whole soybeans. *Hishio* is a liquidy paste fermented from soybeans, grain, and sake that people consider to be the precursor to shoyu (and is experiencing a bit of a revival among fermenters these days).

The taboo on meat-eating in Japan is as long-standing as it is convoluted. Although killing animals goes against the teachings of Buddhism, there is no express law prohibiting the consumption of flesh. And there is much variation regarding this among the different sects. Priests in some sects were vegetarian, while priests in others were not. There was also a concession that animal flesh could be consumed by priests if they had not actually killed the animal or if the animal had not been killed expressly for the priest. For the most part, lay people were exempt from this taboo on consuming flesh, but by custom there were specific days where the taboo was observed: for reasons of religion or respect for the death of ancestors.

More complicated are the decrees prohibiting meat, beginning with the one issued by Emperor Temmu in 675. The reasoning behind the various meat-related decrees that ensued over the next several centuries was not necessarily strictly based in Buddhist law. For instance, famine and the rise of consumption of beasts of burden needed to run farms were given as one reason to outlaw the killing and consumption of horses and cows. Included in these prohibitions were monkeys, dogs, and chickens, but Japanese considered monkeys, dogs, and chickens to be semi-deities or to have mythical qualities, so they were already in a protected class. Noteworthy is the fact that boar and deer, Japan's most important hunted game throughout history, were not included in the meat prohibition. Later, in the Nara period (710–794), government became based in Buddhist tenets, and so began a long period of governmental bans on the consumption of all meat.

Shintoism retained beliefs regarding the uncleanliness of blood but did not expressly forbid the consumption of animal flesh, though eventually also adopted the prohibition of meat. Fish, however, has been an integral part of Shinto ceremonies throughout the ages, and continues to be so today. Japan had no dairy industry to speak of, so there was no custom of raising animals, and eventually during the Kamakura period (1192–1336) the meat taboo spread to the general Japanese population. It was not until the beginning of the modern age, during the Meiji period (1868–1912), that the taboo on meat consumption dissipated. Yet still today, vestiges of this millennia-long history of low to no meat consumption in Japan is reflected in the daily cuisine.

Five alliums were forbidden in Buddhist cuisine because they were considered to stimulate sexual fantasy: garlic, red garlic, *nira* (garlic chive), *negi* (Japanese "leek"), and *rakkyo* (multiplying onion). The rules did not specifically prohibit onions, perhaps because they were not part of the diet at the time, but today no onions (or any allium) are used in Buddhist temple food. Historically, however, priests and nuns apparently did not always adhere to these regulations and thus became fodder for jocular stories that circulated around the public during the Edo period (1603–1868).

As the closed-door policy of the Edo period ended with the collapse of the Tokugawa shogunate regime in 1868, Japan entered the Meiji period, a time of modernization often called the Meiji Restoration.

Shinto priests had never been discouraged from consuming fish or alcohol and were allowed to marry. In contrast, most Buddhist sects prohibited the consumption of animal flesh and alcohol as well as sexual relations. With the Meiji Restoration came the separation of Shintoism and Buddhism. Registration of births, deaths, and marriage documentation were moved from the Buddhist temples to the Shinto shrines. The emperor became the highest Shinto priest in the land and Buddhism not only fell into disfavor, but priests and temples were subject to attacks by the surrounding laypeople. In consequence, to protect the clergy, the Meiji Decree of 1872 authorized Buddhist priests to live without restrictions regarding marriage, alcohol, and food. However, consuming sentient beings and alliums remained forbidden in Buddhist cuisine during meditative training and special ceremonies.

Obon is a Buddhist observance lasting several days in the middle of August when the spirits of ancestors "come back" on the smoke burned in front of the house and at the graves, then are "returned" in the same manner. During Obon, practicing Buddhists refrained from eating fish or meat in honor of the ancient customs of Buddhism, and vegetarian temple cuisine (*shojin ryori*) was commonly eaten on anniversaries of deaths in the family—though today that custom has mostly disappeared.

Shojin ryori originated in the Buddhist monasteries around Japan where the priests and nuns ate only vegetarian food as part of a daily discipline of selflessness and devotion to a pure approach to truth. But after World War II, foreign foods flooded into Japan and people began cooking less and less as the years went by.

Seasonality has been an inextricable cultural force throughout history in Japan and is still an essential way to approach art, poems, spiritual plant sculpting (bonsai), and food. Japan does not just have four seasons; there are seventy-two microseasons that catalogue the minute changes in land and sea. This profound connection to nature is awe-inspiring for most Westerners. And despite the prevalence of supermarkets selling produce from all seasons, and the popular phenomenon of convenience eating, the theory and reverence for seasonal eating is undeniable and certainly a desirable goal of all Japanese—though sometimes out of reach in busy urban Japan.

In 2003, Zen nun Harumi Kawaguchi wrote that she missed the taste of her mother's cooking and her hometown—Japanese food had always been known for *furusato no aji* (hometown taste), but now no longer. She feared for the future of Japan since the children were growing up eating fast food and convenience-store food. She noticed that seasons were virtually unknown since most fruits and vegetables are available year-round. At our first meeting in 2001, we had an immediate bond over food and our mutual concerns for preserving these deeply imbedded Japanese seasonal foodways. And since I first tasted Kawaguchi's beautiful food, she has been a crucial inspiration on my journey of discovering Japanese vegetarian dishes beyond the scope of our own farm life.

Since ancient times, Japan had followed a diet based on what was locally and seasonally available. While nowadays it is commonplace to eat what you want to eat without regard to locale or season, Buddhist cuisine still adheres to these ancient precepts and follows nature as its basic guide. And through this way of eating, Kawaguchi hopes we can bring about a revival in the true Japanese diet.

PREPARING AND EATING JAPANESE CUISINE

Each meal is a chance to feel gratitude for the earth and hands from which the food came, and in doing so we have the possibility of feeling humbleness, awe, and gratefulness for our own situation in life. Here are four elements to observe when eating Japanese food:

- Pick up your soup or rice bowl with two hands—this stance is much more pleasing to the eye and lends beauty to the appearance of eating.
- Put down your chopsticks in front of you while chewing—this will allow you to focus on the feel of the food in your mouth.
- Do not talk or make noise while eating—this allows a more gentle and harmonious eating environment that presents a nice appearance.
- Pour warm water or tea into your bowl after eating, and drink—this will allow you to partake of the very last lingering bits adhering to the bowl while warming your tummy, and it serves as a rinse to conserve water in the process of washing the dishes.

In formal settings, chopsticks are laid horizontally in front of a person on a rest, but at home and more casual settings, they are on the table. If using chopstick rests (which can be actual rests or something more creative such as origami shapes, shells, flowers, twigs, or pebbles), the rests should be large enough to lift the tips off the tabletop, and the chopstick tips should extend at least ½ inch (1 cm) from the rest. If serving dishes on an individual tray (*gozen*, see page 354), no chopstick rests are used.

Rules of thumb for chopsticks. Do not:

- leave chopsticks askew
- use your chopsticks to drag a plate or bowl closer to you—it will scrape the tray or table
- shovel food into your mouth aggressively with the chopsticks because this gives the impression that you are not enjoying the food—gently insert the chopsticks and deftly capture the morsel with your tongue
- hover your chopsticks over various dishes. Decide what to eat and go directly to that dish
- hold two chopsticks together like a stick and poke them into a piece of food to pick it up
- use chopsticks to pass food from one person to another
- stick chopsticks into your bowl of rice, because it is reminiscent of chopsticks that are stuck in ash and used at funerals to pick up the ash
- rest your chopsticks casually across your bowl. Use your non-dominant hand (the one not used for eating) to place them back on the table or tray between bites.

COOKING POINTS
ACCORDING TO
SHOYO YOSHIMURA,
ZEN BUDDHIST PRIEST

Based in Hiroshima, Shoyo Yoshimura is an important mentor, and here I have translated and paraphrased his approachable words on the Zen Buddhist philosophy toward food.

When preparing a Japanese vegetarian meal, take the time to make homemade dashi. Cut the vegetables thoughtfully, and bevel to create softly pleasing shapes. Even a simple simmered dish of vegetables will be adversely affected if you do not make the effort to put your heart into it.

Keep in mind how you should cut the vegetables when preparing a simmered dish, since the taste of the dish will change depending on the cutting style. For instance, *furofuki daikon* (simmered daikon with miso sauce) is best cut in thick rounds to make a strong statement, but these are difficult to eat with chopsticks. The trick is to make a ¼-inch (5 mm) deep crosscut on the underside of the daikon so the simmered piece will easily break into quarters when "cut" with chopsticks. However, if you are simmering the daikon in flavoring dashi, it is better to cut the daikon into rounded triangular shapes (*rangiri*) to enable the daikon to better absorb the simmering dashi.

Take the time to bevel (*mentori*) vegetables before simmering to create soft edges that do not bump against each other in the pan. The flavor of the dashi simmering liquid is of course extremely crucial, but do not discount the importance of this seemingly inconsequential step. Beveled simmered vegetables are gentle in the mouth and reach deep inside you to create a soft feeling in your heart.

If you get into the practice of treating vegetables with respect—using all their parts, including the peels, calyxes, and beveled trimmings—your days will brighten. Julienne the peels and stir-fry them as *kinpira* or add to country soup (*kenchinjiru*). Or chop the peels, fold into pressed, smashed tofu, pat into croquettes, and deep-fry in oil for *ganmodoki*. Dry the peels in the sun for half a day, add cold water, and bring just to a simmer for a flavorful vegetable broth. Get in the habit of preparing a bowl next to your kitchen workspace for the trimmings, providing both a neat workplace and no waste.

But the most important consideration is to be mindful that you are alive for eating the food, and to thank the ingredients themselves as well as the producers and the blessings of nature. This is the basic tenet of traditional Japanese vegetarian cuisine.

~~~~~~

CUTTING
STYLES FOR
VEGETABLES

Hitokuchi-giri: 1¼-inch (3 cm) bite-size pieces

Hanagiri: flower shape ¼ inch (5 mm) thick

Hangetsu-giri: half-moons ¼–½ inch (5–10 mm) thick

Ichogiri: half-moons ¼ inch (5 mm) thick, halved to make rounded triangular shapes similar to ginkgo leaves

Jabara-giri: fine, deep diagonal cuts are made down the length of both sides of a Japanese cucumber to create an accordion—or "bellows"—shape (some people place a chopstick on either side of the cucumber as a guide, so as not to cut clear through the cucumber). The cucumbers are then cut crosswise into pieces ¾–1½ inches (2–4 cm) long and typically dressed with a vinegar treatment.

Mijingiri: Fine dice

Rangiri: ¾- to 1¼-inch (2–3 cm) irregular ("random"), triangular chunks

Saikoro kiri: larger dice (½ inch/1 cm), usually for carrots and daikon

Sasagaki: feather-like cuts made by rotating burdock or carrot in your nondominant hand and shaving off pieces with a knife held in your dominant hand, as if you are hand-sharpening a pencil

Sengiri: fine julienne

Sogigiri: fine to thick diagonal slices, such as for burdock, celery, cucumber and cabbage

Tanzaku-giri: fine rectangular slabs about ¾ inch (2 cm) wide by 1½ inches (4 cm) long

仕込み

Basic Japanese preparation methods, such as extracting dashi, removing acrid elements (*aku nuki*) in nuts or mountain vegetables, or simmering beans are essential building blocks when approaching a Japanese menu. I recommend reading this chapter from start to finish to get an overview of how to approach various treatments that are fundamental to Japanese cuisine. Cutting vegetables or preparing sauces precisely and thoughtfully is also key to successfully executing a dish, so it makes sense to get all of your pieces lined up (*mise en place*) before finalizing a dish.

This chapter is where you will find the foundational dashi recipes used throughout the book. While konbu dashi is probably the one most often called for in recipes, this is not set in stone. Feel free to make *awase dashi* (a combination of konbu dashi plus another dashi such as shiitake dashi) or substitute the konbu dashi with dried gourd or soybean dashi, or whichever dashi takes your fancy.

You will also find miso-based recipes and sauces that can be used in other dishes you make, Western or Japanese. Another essential building block recipe is *kaeshi*,

which serves as the fundamental flavoring base for a trilogy of essential soups and dipping sauces: *mori tsuyu, kaketsuyu, tentsuyu.*

Also included here are various standard preparation methods for removing the bitterness from mountain vegetables or shelling nuts.

There are also a few basic pantry items that can substitute for mainstream ingredients that contain dairy. And, finally, there are a couple of healthy and delicious juices that can be enjoyed as is or spiked with alcohol when the mood is right.

仕込み

SHIKOMI
———
PREP

仕込み

昆布だし　KONBU DASHI

Preparation time: 5 minutes,
plus 4 hours soaking and cooling time
Cooking time: 30 minutes
Makes: 3⅓ cups (26½ fl oz/800 ml)

• 6 × 2-inch (15 × 5 cm) piece
konbu (10 g)

Use the best-quality konbu you can find for the most flavorful result. No need to wipe off the white substance (mannitol) that has formed on the konbu.
-
Break the konbu in half and add to a medium saucepan with 1 quart (32 fl oz/1 liter) of cold water. Let soak for 3 hours. Slowly heat over low heat until steam rises from the water and small bubbles form on the konbu. Allow to cool to room temperature before straining out the konbu and using.

VARIATIONS: If you have time, soak the konbu overnight in the refrigerator and use without heating. Or, if you are in a hurry, skip the soak, but still heat slowly. Cool for at least 30 minutes before using.

~~~~~~

椎茸だし　SHIITAKE DASHI

Preparation time: 5 minutes,
plus 12 hours soaking time
Makes: 3¾ cups (30 fl oz/900 ml)

• 3 dried shiitake

If possible, use Japanese *donko* shiitake to make this dashi. *Donko* are thick-capped with deep fissures in the caps.
-
Soak the shiitake in a generous amount of lukewarm water for 15 minutes to remove any dirt or off smells. Drain, add 1 quart (32 fl oz/1 liter) of cold water, and refrigerate overnight before straining and using.

VARIATION: If you are in a hurry, after the first soak, drain and soak in 1 quart (32 fl oz/1 liter) of hot water with a pinch or two of sugar for 30 minutes before using.

~~~~~~

切り干し大根だし　DRIED DAIKON DASHI

KIRIBOSHI DAIKON DASHI

Preparation time: 5 minutes,
plus 3 hours soaking time
Makes: 3⅓ cups (26½ fl oz/800 ml)

• 1 oz (30 g) dried daikon (kiriboshi daikon), store-bought or homemade (page 308)

In the early winter, the Japan Agriculture farm stands sell *kiriboshi daikon* made by local grandmothers. Alternatively, make your own by slicing daikon into fine strips on a Japanese mandoline (*benriner*, see page 353) and sun-drying them. Or just look for them online. This dashi adds a sweet vegetal note to dishes.
-

Scrub the dried daikon well under cold running water to remove any off smells. Drain and soak for 3 hours in 1 quart (32 fl oz/1 liter) of cold water before straining and using.

かんぴょうだし

DRIED GOURD DASHI

KANPYOU DASHI

Preparation time: 5 minutes,
plus 3 hours soaking time
Makes: 3⅓ cups (26½ fl oz/800 ml)

• ¾ oz (20 g) unbleached dried gourd

If in Japan, purchase the gourd from a reputable dry goods store (*kanbutsu-ya*), otherwise look to the Internet for sourcing.
-
Scrub the gourd under cold running water to remove any off smells. Drain and soak for 3 hours in 1 quart (32 fl oz/1 liter) of cold water before straining and using.

大豆だし

SOYBEAN DASHI

DAIZU DASHI

Preparation time: 5 minutes,
plus 20 minutes soaking time
Cooking time: 5 minutes
Makes: 3½ cups (28 fl oz/850 ml)

• 3½ oz (100 g) dried soybeans
• 1 quart (32 fl oz/1 liter) boiling water

Roasted soybeans add a pleasantly nutty note to this dashi.
-
In a small heavy frying pan, roast the soybeans over low heat until fragrant and lightly browned, about 5 minutes. Place in a bowl and pour the boiling water over. Soak for 20 minutes before straining and using.

野菜の皮だし

VEGETABLE PEEL DASHI

YASAI NO KAWA DASHI

Preparation time: 5 minutes
Cooking time: 10 minutes
Makes: 1 cup (8 fl oz/250 ml)

• 1 handful vegetable peels

Vegetable peels are packed with flavor and minerals, which can be extracted into a delicate dashi, always keeping in mind the balance of flavor from the peels you are using.
-
Drop the vegetable peels into a small saucepan and add 1¼ cups (10 fl oz/300 ml) water. Bring to an almost simmer over low heat, then strain.

KONBU

Konbu (edible kelp) is ubiquitous to Japanese cuisine and arguably the most essential flavor base in Japanese vegetarian dishes. The history of konbu in Japan is so ancient, no reliable records exist to tell us for certain when the use of konbu actually began. Anecdotal evidence has konbu being carried to Japan on board ships coming from the Jiangnan region of China in late Jomon (c. 14,000–300 BCE), the prehistoric period of Japan.

From the seventh and eighth centuries, boats carried konbu from Matsumae in Hokkaido, Japan's northern island, along a westerly route partway down the coast of Honshu, the main island of Japan. But it was not until the middle of the Kamakura period (1185–1333) that kelp-trading boats began actively traveling between Matsumae in Hokkaido and Honshu.

In the Muromachi period (1336–1573), the konbu was transported by ship from Hokkaido to Tsuruga in Echizen Province (currently Fukui prefecture), and then across land to Kyoto and Osaka. Eventually the westerly route extended to Osaka, skirting the southern tip of Honshu and on via the Seto Inland Sea.

In the Edo period (1603–1868), north-bound ships (*kitamaebune*) were used to sail directly from Hokkaido to Osaka, thus increasing the speed and efficiency of shipping the konbu. Kyoto was the undisputed center of haute Japanese cuisine, but Osaka was the merchant center from which all essential food-related goods were disseminated. As a result of the increased shipping, konbu finally became available to the common people of Japan.

This trade route is called the Konbu Road and in the late eighteenth century it was extended to Okinawa and on to China. The Konbu Road might be the most essential reason for the sophistication and breadth of Japanese cuisine across the archipelago.

There are eighteen edible species, though we commonly see four main types: ma-konbu, Rausu konbu, Rishiri konbu, and Hidaka konbu.

Ma-konbu is mainly produced along the Hakodate coast of Hokkaido, with the most prized coming from Kakkumi-hama. These thick, wide strands are generally regarded as the best-quality Japanese konbu. Ma-konbu has an elegant sweetness and makes a clear, yet rich dashi. It also produces excellent *tsukudani* (sweet shoyu–simmered preserve).

Rausu konbu is harvested along the coast adjacent to the town of Rausu at the northern tip of the Shiretoko Peninsula of northeastern Hokkaido. The strands are a soft brown, with a lovely fragrance, producing a yellow-tinged, yet aromatic, rich dashi.

Rishiri konbu is gathered along the coasts of Rishiri Island and Rebun Island off the northwestern coast of Hokkaido, as well as the coastal area of the city of Wakkanai, located at the northernmost tip of Japan. The strands are firm and slightly salty, yielding a clear, gentle-flavored dashi, prized for high-level, elegant cuisine, such as *kaiseki ryori*.

Hidaka konbu is produced along the Hidaka coastal area of southern Hokkaido. The soft strands are a dark blackish green with an appealing viscosity when simmered. Hidaka konbu is perhaps the most readily found konbu in Japanese shops as well as abroad. It makes a good, traditional dashi, but is most suitable for *konbu-maki* (konbu rolls), *tsukudani* (sweet shoyu-simmered preserve), or other dishes in which the konbu is simmered.

Approximately 90 percent of kelp is harvested along coastal areas of Hokkaido, while the rest is harvested along the Sanriku coast in Tohoku (Aomori, Iwate, Miyagi prefectures). The type of konbu that can be harvested depends on the location, and about 90 percent is farmed, rather than wild. Quality varies significantly depending on the region of harvest, whether it is farmed or wild, and its grade.

Konbu is gathered by fishermen who motor out in small boats over vast undersea kelp forests close to shore. Using a glass placed upon the surface of the water to guide him, the fisherman thrusts a long, hooked pole into the roots of the kelp, and wrenches up the heavy strands into a large pile on his boat. Then he motors back to the shore.

The konbu is hauled off the boat to a washing area before being spread on the pebbled beach to dry. It is turned once and then after about a half-day, brought in to be stored while it is still pliant. The drying process is crucial to the care of konbu and involves several steps: drying, softening, rolling, flattening, trimming, weighting, and a final sun-drying before being stored in a large airtight zippered "storage room."

Konbu gathering is tightly controlled and only allowed during a six-week period from around July 21 through August 31. The season starts slowly, with gathering restricted to a short couple of hours three days a week, eventually extending to a five-hour period.

Despite these precautions, due to ocean pollution and global warming, konbu harvests have been steadily declining. In 2019 only 13,000 tons were harvested, compared with 38,000 in 1990; and the price of konbu has doubled in the last five years. Extinction of konbu is a very real possibility, and certainly the highest quality has become quite difficult (and pricey) to obtain. Thankfully for home cooks, gnarled or lower-grade konbu still produces flavorful dashi, so do not despair.

八方だし　HAPPO DASHI

Preparation time: 5 minutes
Cooking time: 5 minutes
Makes: 1 quart (32 fl oz/1 liter)

- 1 quart (32 fl oz/1 liter)
Konbu Dashi (page 22)
- Scant ½ cup (3½ fl oz/100 ml) sake
- Scant ¼ cup (1¾ fl oz/50 ml) hon mirin
- ¼ teaspoon flaky sea salt

Happo dashi is typically made with *katsuobushi* (smoked, fermented, sun-dried skipjack tuna) and konbu, but here only needs the konbu to infuse with a gentle brininess. *Happo dashi* is slightly sweetened by the addition of mirin and sake and is used for flavoring elegant, simmered vegetables.
-
In a medium saucepan, stir the konbu dashi, sake, mirin, and salt together. Bring to a simmer over medium heat, reduce to a low simmer, and cook for 2 minutes to burn off the alcohol. Best the first day but still good for 1 or 2 days after, if refrigerated, covered, in a clean jar.

かえし　KAESHI

Preparation time: 5 minutes, plus 1 week to develop flavor
Cooking time: 10 minutes
Makes: 2½ cups (20 fl oz/600 ml)

- Scant ½ cup (3½ fl oz/100 ml) hon mirin
- 1 cup (3½ oz/100 g) organic granulated sugar or light brown Japanese cane sugar (kibizato, see page 345)
- 2 cups (16 fl oz/500 ml) shoyu

Kaeshi is the flavoring base used in set ratios to create several different essential flavoring broths in Japanese cuisine. Feel free to double or triple the recipe since this base keeps for 6 months or more if stored in a well-sealed jar in the fridge. To make this gluten-free, substitute tamari for the shoyu.
-
In a small saucepan, bring the mirin to a simmer over medium-high heat. Cook until the aroma of alcohol wafts up, about 3 minutes. Stir in the sugar and cook, stirring continuously for another 1 minute or so to melt the sugar. Add the shoyu, stir once, then cook without stirring until the surface is covered with a fine creamy foam, 3–5 minutes. Remove from the heat, cool to room temperature, and store in a clean jar for at least 1 week and up to several months to develop flavor.

盛りつゆ　MORI TSUYU

Preparation time: 5 minutes
Makes: 1⅔ cups (13½ fl oz/400 ml)

- 1¼ cups (10 fl oz/300 ml)
Konbu Dashi (page 22)
- 6 tablespoons (3 fl oz/90 ml) Kaeshi (see above)

Mori tsuyu is the dipping broth that accompanies somen and various udon and soba dishes. Although typically served cold, the broth can also be served warm or hot. The dashi to *kaeshi* ratio is 3.3:1.
-
Stir together the *kaeshi* and dashi. Chill or heat, depending on the dish.

掛けつゆ

KAKETSUYU

Preparation time: 5 minutes
Makes: 2½ cups (20 fl oz/600 ml)

• 2½ cups (20 fl oz/600 ml)
Konbu Dashi (page 22)
• ¼ cup (2 fl oz/60 ml) Kaeshi (page 25)

Kaketsuyu is a warm broth used for serving large bowls of udon or soba noodles with accompanying vegetables, mushrooms, and aromatics. The dashi to *kaeshi* ratio is 10:1.
-

In a small saucepan, stir together the dashi and *kaeshi*. Bring to a simmer over medium heat before using.

天つゆ

TENTSUYU

Preparation time: 5 minutes
Makes: 1⅔ cups (13½ fl oz/400 ml)

• 1¼ cups (10 fl oz/300 ml)
Konbu Dashi (page 22)
• 5 tablespoons (2½ fl oz/75 ml) Kaeshi
(page 25)

Tempura can be served with a variety of condiments: plain or flavored sea salt, or lemon, but classically a small bowl of *tentsuyu* and a mound of finely grated daikon and ginger are served alongside tempura. *Tentsuyu* is warmed before serving. The dashi to *kaeshi* ratio is 4:1.
-

In a small saucepan, stir together the dashi and *kaeshi*. Warm slightly before serving.

ころも

TEMPURA BATTER

KOROMO

Preparation time: 5 minutes
Makes: ½ cup (4 fl oz/125 ml)

• ½ cup (4 fl oz/125 ml) ice water
or cold sparkling water
• ½ cup (2⅔ oz/75 g) unbleached
cake flour
• ¼ teaspoon fine sea salt

Eggless tempura batter is often called "*shojin koromo*" (temple batter). The resulting crispy coating on the vegetables is exquisitely light, so a strong reason not to add the pesky egg (which introduces a slightly spongy note if not careful).
-

In a medium bowl, stir the water into the flour and salt with a pair of cooking chopsticks until amalgamated but not necessarily completely smooth. The batter will still have a few lumps. Use immediately.

ご飯

JAPANESE RICE

GOHAN

Preparation time: 10 minutes,
plus 30 minutes draining and
soaking time
Cooking time: 20 minutes
Makes: 5 cups (1.2 liters/2 lb/900 g)

• 2¼ cups (540 ml/1 lb/450 g)
Japanese short-grain rice (see page 351)

Cooking rice in a heavy pot rather than a rice cooker will yield perfectly cooked rice that will lose heat over time but will not be left for hours to oversteam (as happens with the rice cooker). Cast-iron pots (*tetsu gama*, see page 354) keep the heat for about 1 hour, clay pots (*donabe*, see page 353) for about 30 minutes. In Japan, rice and rice-related ingredients such as sake are measured in *go* (合)—a volume measurement equal to 180 ml. There are many varieties of japonica rice used daily in Japan— these are short-grain cultivars not to be confused with glutinous rice (sold abroad as "sweet" rice). Look for "sushi rice" if you cannot find Japanese rice.
-
Place the rice in a large wire-mesh sieve and set in a medium bowl in a clean kitchen sink. Fill the bowl to the top with water, lift out the sieve of rice,

and dump the water. Scrub the rice between your fingers to remove starch, set the sieve back in the bowl, and run cold water for 2–3 minutes until the water is clear. Lift out the sieve of rice, discard the rinsing water (or use for simmering white root vegetables such as taro or lotus root), and set back on top of the bowl to drain for 10 minutes.

Tip the rice into a small heavy pot with a tightly fitting lid and add 2¼ cups (18¼ fl oz/540 ml) cold filtered water. Cover and let sit for 20 minutes.

Set the pot over high heat, covered. In about 5 minutes you should see bubbling around the edges of the lid. Reduce the heat to low and cook for 12 minutes. Remove from the heat and allow to rest for 5 minutes before fluffing and serving.

~~~~~~

玄米

BROWN RICE

GENMAI

Preparation time: 10 minutes,
plus 4–6 hours soaking time
Cooking time: 40 minutes
Makes: 5 cups (1.2 liters/2 lb/900 g)

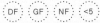

• 2¼ cups (540 ml/1 lb/450 g)
Japanese short-grain brown rice
• ½ teaspoon flaky sea salt

Brown rice absorbs water much more slowly than white rice due to the bran layer enclosing the kernels. The general rule of thumb soaking time for brown rice is 6 hours, but for a chewier texture soak between 3 and 4 hours, and for a softer texture soak for 8 hours. You can cook brown rice in the rice cooker, but I prefer a heavy pot to yield best aroma and plump grains.
-
Place the rice in a large wire-mesh sieve and set inside a large bowl in a clean kitchen sink. Fill the bowl to the top with water, lift out the sieve of rice, and dump the water. Scrub the rice between your fingers, set the sieve back

in the bowl, and run cold water for 2–3 minutes until the water is clear. Lift out the sieve of rice and allow to drain for 10 minutes.

Slide the rice into a heavy cast-iron pot and add 3¼ cups (26 fl oz/ 750 ml) cold filtered water. Cover with a tightly fitting lid and leave to soak for 4–6 hours in a cool spot.

Set the pot over high heat, covered. In about 7 minutes you should see bubbling around the edges of the lid. Reduce the heat to low and cook for 30 minutes. Remove from the heat and allow to rest for 10 minutes before gently fluffing and serving.

雑穀

ZAKKOKU

Preparation time: 5 minutes
Makes: 6 tablespoons

• 2 tablespoons flattened barley (oshi mugi, see page 351)
• 1 tablespoon foxtail millet (awa, see page 351)
• 1 tablespoon barnyard millet (hie, see page 351)
• 1 tablespoon proso millet (kibi, see page 351)
• 1 tablespoon black rice (kuromai, see page 351)

Zakkoku is an ancient grain mix that is added to rice when cooking to contribute texture, fiber, and flavor. It often contains pressed barley, various millets, black rice, red rice, or even dried beans. For the recipes in this book, if you do not hand-mix your own *zakkoku*, source Japanese "grain mixture for rice," but avoid any that contain beans because they will affect the cooking time. In Japan, *zakkoku* is said to improve metabolism, promote regularity, and prevent obesity since it is rich in minerals and high in dietary fiber. Modern Japanese have a much softer diet than before, so adding fiber encourages people to chew more and enjoy the contrasting textures. If the specific varieties of Japanese millet are out of reach, just use the variety (or varieties) of millet available to you locally.
-

In a small bowl, stir the flattened barley, millets, and black rice together. It keeps for several months if stored in an airtight jar in a cool dark place.

Use about 2 tablespoons for every 2¼ cups (540 ml/1 lb/450 g) of white rice. Before adding to the rice, pour boiling water over the *zakkoku* to cover and leave for 20 minutes to soak. Drain and add to soaked rice with 2 extra tablespoons of water before cooking.

RICE ZAKKOKU: For a simple *zakkoku* mixture, use red rice and black rice in a ratio of 1:1 to add color and texture to white rice. Use 1 tablespoon of the combination for every 2¼ cups (540 ml/1 lb/450 g) of rice. Add 1 tablespoon of water to the rice soaking water when you stir in the soaked, strained *zakkoku* before cooking.

~~~~~~

ごま塩

SESAME SALT

GOMA SHIO

Preparation time: 10 minutes
Cooking time: 5 minutes
Makes: About 5 teaspoons

• 1 teaspoon flaky sea salt
• 4 teaspoons (10 g) white, black, or gold sesame seeds

This sesame salt is the key to elevating some of the restrained *okayu* dishes to the sublime and will stay fresh for 1 week if stored in an airtight container.
-
Warm a small frying pan over low heat and add the salt. Keep stirring with a flat wooden spoon until the salt is well dried, 1–2 minutes. Slide into a Japanese grinding bowl (*suribachi*, see page 354) and finely grind. Scrape into a small bowl and reserve the *suribachi*.

Heat the frying pan again over medium heat until you can feel the warmth rising. Remove from the heat and add the sesame seeds. Shake them around the pan, return to low heat, and warm for about 30 seconds or until fragrant. Add the sesame to the *suribachi* and smash until powdery. (Caveat: The seeds should not become paste-like.)

Scrape the sesame into the small bowl of salt and mix until evenly incorporated. Store in an airtight container. Keeps for 1 week.

三杯酢   SANBAIZU

Preparation time: 5 minutes
Cooking time: 1 minute
Makes: ½ cup (4 fl oz/125 ml)

(V) (DF) (NF) (<5) (<30)

- 3 tablespoons hon mirin
- 3 tablespoons rice vinegar
- 3 tablespoons usukuchi shoyu (see page 344) or shoyu

Sanbaizu is a useful dipping vinegar to have around, and it keeps in the fridge almost indefinitely. If you omit the mirin, it becomes *nihaizu*—but the sweetness adds balance, so *sanbaizu* is more versatile.
-

In a very small saucepan, stir the mirin and rice vinegar together. Bring to a bare simmer over medium-high heat and pour into a small bowl or jar. Once cool, stir in the *usukuchi shoyu* or shoyu. Store, covered, in the refrigerator for several weeks or more.

炊き味噌   TAKI MISO

Preparation time: 10 minutes
Cooking time: 5 minutes
Makes: 6 tablespoons

(V) (DF) (GF) (NF) (<5) (<30)

- 6 tablespoons white miso
- 2 teaspoons organic granulated sugar
- 2 tablespoons sake
- 1 teaspoon hon mirin

Taki miso is a sweetened white miso–based sauce used for glazing vegetables. A darker miso such as brown rice or barley can be substituted for the white miso, but delicate miso preparations such as Yuzu Miso (page 29) or *sansho* leaf miso (for the grilled eggplants/aubergines, see page 212) need white miso as the base.
-
In a heavy medium saucepan, stir the miso, sugar, sake, and mirin together. Warm, stirring, over medium heat for about 1 minute, until the bottom portion is bubbling furiously.

Reduce the heat to low and cook, stirring, until the miso is glossy and has returned to its original consistency, about 1 minute. Cool to room temperature, scrape into a glass or plastic (or other nonreactive) container, and store in the fridge for up to 5 days.

AKA TAKI MISO: To make *aka taki miso* (red taki miso), substitute 2 tablespoons soybean miso for 2 tablespoons of the white miso. Use this richer version as a sauce for Steamed Daikon with Miso (page 186) or grilled eggplant (aubergine).

柚子味噌   YUZU MISO

Preparation time: 10 minutes
Makes: 6 tablespoons

(V) (DF) (GF) (NF) (<5) (<30)

- Taki Miso (see above)
- 1 medium yuzu or small Meyer lemon (4½ oz/125 g)

Yuzu miso is a lovely light and citrusy miso used in Carrot and Mountain Yam Rolls (page 156), Shirataki Noodle Squares with Yuzu Miso (page 46), and Pan-Grilled Eggplant with Yuzu Miso (page 210). Feel free to use on other dishes, Japanese or Western, or as a dip for fresh spring or summer crudités, such as radishes, cucumber, celery, or green beans. And depending on the season, you could substitute *sansho* leaves, grated ginger, ground roasted sesame seeds, or Japanese mustard for the yuzu.
-

Scrape the *taki miso* into a small bowl and finely grate the zest of the yuzu over the miso. Juice the yuzu, remove the seeds, and stir the juice into the miso until smoothly incorporated. Keeps for a couple of weeks, if stored in the fridge in an airtight container. Spread a small piece of plastic wrap (cling film) across the surface to avoid discoloration.

田楽味噌   DENGAKU MISO

Preparation time: 10 minutes
Cooking time: 5 minutes
Makes: 6 tablespoons

- 3 tablespoons Hatcho miso or soybean miso
- 2 tablespoons brown rice miso or barley miso
- 1 tablespoon white miso
- ½ tablespoon organic granulated sugar
- 2 tablespoons sake
- 2 tablespoons hon mirin

Dengaku miso is a sweetened sauce made from flavorful miso such as brown rice, barley, or soybean. It is often smeared on vegetables before grilling, or spread on steamed root vegetables such as daikon, mountain yam, or taro. It keeps well, if refrigerated, but should be gently warmed to loosen before using. The balance of the different types of miso can be adjusted, or the white miso can be omitted. *Dengaku miso* also goes well with a sprinkling of 7-spice powder (*shichimi togarashi*, see page 350).
-
In a heavy medium saucepan, stir together all three misos, the sugar, sake, and mirin. Bring to a simmer over medium heat, stirring constantly. Reduce the heat to low and cook, stirring, until the sugar has completely melted and the sauce is thick and shiny, 3–4 minutes.

ごまバター   SESAME-UME PASTE

GOMA BATA-

Preparation time: 5 minutes
Makes: 6 tablespoons

- 2 tablespoons Japanese gold sesame paste
- 2 teaspoons sour "plum" paste (bainiku, see page 350)
- 2 tablespoons mild honey

This "butter" (*bata-*) is rich from the sesame, while the well-rounded sweetness of the honey softens the salty, fruity sour "plum" paste, and it is blissfully butter-free. Dab on the side of a bowl of white rice, or smear on a grilled piece of mochi or wheat toast.
-

Smash the sesame paste, sour "plum" paste, and honey together in a mortar until well blended. Keeps for several weeks, if stored in an airtight container in a cool dark place.

寺納豆ペースト   TERA NATTO–SESAME PASTE

TERA NATTOU PE-SUTO

Preparation time: 15 minutes
Makes: Scant ⅔ cup (5¼ fl oz/150 ml)

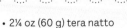

- 2¼ oz (60 g) tera natto (see page 350)
- 2 tablespoons Japanese white sesame paste
- ⅛ teaspoon sansho powder

Tera natto is the original version of what we know as natto (see natto, page 351) today. Steamed soybeans are fermented with koji, then dried and aged for one year. Outside of Japan, look for dried natto. This paste is a haunting combination, and absolutely delicious. Dollop onto a bowl of white rice or into Potato Soup with Tera Natto (page 250) to give an indescribable flavor boost.
-

Purée the *tera natto* with the sesame paste and *sansho* in a mini-prep processor, scraping down the sides a few times, until well incorporated and smooth. (Alternatively, go old-school and smash in a Japanese grinding bowl—*suribachi*, see page 354—much more work, however.)

トマトときのこのソース

TOMATO-MUSHROOM SAUCE

TOMATO TO KINOKO NO SO-SU

Preparation time: 20 minutes
Cooking time: 15 minutes
Makes: 1¼ cups (10 fl oz/300 ml)

- 2 medium tomatoes (14 oz/400 g)
- Boiling water
- 1 medium celery stalk without leaves (2⅔ oz/75 g), thick bottoms trimmed off
- 1¾ oz (50 g) maitake
- 1¾ oz (50 g) shimeji
- 1 tablespoon mild olive oil
- 1 teaspoon ketchup
- ¼ teaspoon flaky sea salt
- ⅛ teaspoon freshly ground black pepper
- 1 teaspoon shoyu
- 1 teaspoon Hatcho miso or soybean miso

This sauce is used in Tofu and Tomato Gratin (page 210), but it is such a versatile sauce, I included the recipe in this section too. Use for dressing noodles or in variations of the gratin recipe.
-
Make a small crosscut in the skin of each tomato and place in a small heatproof bowl. Pour boiling water over to cover and allow to sit for 5 minutes. Drain the tomatoes and dry the bowl. Peel and finely chop the tomatoes and return to the bowl. Finely dice the celery, maitake, and shimeji.

In a medium saucepan, warm the olive oil over medium heat for about 30 seconds. Add the chopped tomatoes, celery, maitake, and shimeji and cook, stirring occasionally, until thickened, 5–7 minutes. Stir in the ketchup, salt, pepper, shoyu, and miso and simmer over low heat for an additional 10 minutes.

大豆のソース

SOYBEAN SAUCE

DAIZU NO SO-SU

Preparation time: 10 minutes
Makes: 1¼ cups (10 fl oz/300 ml)

- 1 cup (6 oz/170 g) Simmered Soybeans (page 32), cooled
- 4 tablespoons Soy Milk Mayonnaise (page 36)
- 1 tablespoon ketchup
- ½ teaspoon flaky sea salt

Mostly soybeans, this unctuous sauce is on the surface rich like hummus, but ultimately light and low in oil. Use as a dipper for fried or rolled dishes or vegetable crudités.
-
In a food processor or blender, pulse the beans with a scant ⅔ cup (5¼ fl oz/150 ml) of their cooking liquid until creamy.

Scrape into a small bowl and fold in the mayonnaise, ketchup, and salt to make a creamy, flavorful sauce.

ゆで大豆

SIMMERED SOYBEANS

YUDE DAIZU

Preparation time: 5 minutes,
plus overnight soaking time
Cooking time: 30 minutes to 1 hour
Makes: 2 cups (12 oz/340 g)

• 1 cup (5½ oz/160 g) dried soybeans

Simmered soybeans are nutty with a slight sweetness and can be eaten as is or added to soups, salads, or dishes such as curry rice (see Vegetarian Japanese-Style Curry, page 234). Puréed with some of their cooking liquid and other ingredients, simmered soybeans form the base for a versatile Soybean Sauce (page 31).
-
Rinse the beans in a wire-mesh sieve under cold running water. Soak the beans overnight. (Refrigerate if soaking in the hot, muggy summer.)

Drain and slide into a medium saucepan. Fill to cover generously with cold water and bring just to a boil over medium-high heat. Reduce to a brisk simmer and cook for about 1 hour, depending on the soybeans and texture you would like (older beans will take longer than freshly dried beans). As the beans cook, skim off the scum that accumulates on the surface of the water. Check for desired doneness (a bit firmer for

salads or dishes that will require further cooking or flavoring, softer for sauce), remove from the heat and let cool to room temperature in the cooking liquid. The beans keep for 2 or 3 days, if stored in the fridge (preferably in the cooking liquid).

SWEET SHOYU-SIMMERED SOYBEANS: In a small saucepan, add 1 cup (170 g) simmered soybeans, scant ½ cup (3½ fl oz/ 100 ml) water, 1 tablespoon shoyu, 2 tablespoons mirin, and 1 tablespoon sake. Bring to a boil over medium-high heat and cook at a lively simmer until the liquids have been completely absorbed by the soybeans (watch carefully so the soybeans do not scorch), about 10 minutes. In the last minute or so, you will need to pick up the pan and swirl it just above the heat to allow the last liquid to evaporate. Store in the fridge. Serve as a snack or a bite before dinner.

ゆで小豆

SIMMERED AZUKI BEANS

YUDE AZUKI

Preparation time: 5 minutes
Cooking time: 45 minutes to 1 hour
Makes: 2 cups (16 oz/500 g)

• 1 cup (7 oz/200 g) azuki beans

Simmered azuki beans have a natural vegetal sweetness and can be used in savory dishes as well as desserts. They pair quite well with simmered kabocha (see page 347) and provide a complementary foil to the rich squash.
-
Rinse the azuki in a wire-mesh sieve under cold running water. Shake off, slide into a medium saucepan, and fill to cover generously with cold water. Bring to a boil over high heat, reduce to a gentle simmer, and cook for about 15 minutes. Throw in

½ cup (4 fl oz/125 ml) of cold water (*bikkuri mizu*) to shock, return to a simmer, and cook until the beans are soft, but not falling apart, 30–45 minutes. If the beans seem a bit pale after simmering, strain the liquid into a small saucepan and cook down over medium-low heat until about one-quarter of the liquid remains. Fold as much as you'd like into the cooked beans for color and shine. Store leftovers with any remaining cooking liquid in the fridge, but if you do not use within 2–3 days, freeze in small batches to use later.

黒豆

SWEET-SIMMERED BLACK BEANS

KUROMAME

Preparation time: 10 minutes,
plus 24 hours soaking time
(and ideally overnight steeping)
Cooking time: 2 hours 30 minutes
Makes: 1⅔ cups (12¾ oz/365 g)

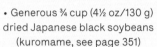

• Generous ¾ cup (4½ oz/130 g)
dried Japanese black soybeans
(kuromame, see page 351)
• ½ teaspoon baking soda
• ½ cup (3½ oz /100 g) organic
granulated sugar or Japanese refined
light brown sugar (sanonto,
see page 339)
• 1 tablespoon shoyu

Sweet-simmered black soybeans are often found on the New Year table in Japan but can appear as a sweet bite on *zensai* plates or bento boxes, or on the table any time of year. It is often said they are difficult to do well, perhaps because the beans should retain their lovely sheen and shape but still be meltingly soft inside. Beans tend to fall apart, so do not despair if some of your bean insides separate from their skins. The black beans used in Japan are a variety of soybean, so South American small black turtle beans cannot be used since they are too small. Rancho Gordo's heirloom Ayocote Negro Beans from California are a great option if you are in the United States.
-
In a medium saucepan, combine the black soybeans and baking soda and fill to cover generously with cold water. Cover and leave in a cool spot for 24 hours.

Drain, rinse, and return to a clean medium saucepan. Add 3 cups (24 fl oz/700 ml) cold water and simmer gently for 1 hour.

Stir in half of the sugar along with a generous ¾ cup (6¾ fl oz/200 ml) water and simmer for another 30 minutes.

Stir in the shoyu, remaining sugar, an additional generous ¾ cup (6¾ fl oz/200 ml) water and cook at a bare simmer for 1 more hour. The beans should always stay submerged in the cooking liquid, so add a little water as you go, if necessary.

Transfer to a covered container and allow to come to room temperature before covering and leaving overnight to deepen the sweetness (if possible). Serve at room temperature. Keeps well, stored in the refrigerator for about 10 days.

わらびのアク抜き

DEALKALIZED FIDDLEHEAD FERNS

WARABI NO AKU-NUKI

Preparation time: 5 minutes,
plus cooling time
Makes: 3½ ounces (100 g)

• 3½ oz (100 g) fiddlehead ferns,
tough bottoms removed
• Scant ½ teaspoon baking soda
• Boiling water

Most fiddlehead ferns need to have their bitterness removed before using, so dealkalizing the fiddleheads makes them easier to consume. If you are pressed for time, you can cut out some of the cooling time and just rinse in cold water and proceed.
-

Place the fiddlehead ferns in a heatproof medium bowl with the baking soda and pour boiling water over to cover. Allow to cool to room temperature before rinsing with cold water.

あく抜き筍　BOILED BAMBOO SHOOT

AKU-NUKI TAKENOKO

Preparation time: 20 minutes,
plus 1 hour cooling time
Cooking time: 1 hour
Makes: 12 oz (340 g)

• 2 or 3 small unpeeled
bamboo shoots (2 lb 10 oz/1.2 kg)
• 1 cup (2¼ oz/65 g) rice bran
• 2 dried red japones chiles

Simmering unpeeled bamboo shoot with rice bran is the method used to remove bitterness and is called *nuka yugaki*. Every minute that elapses after being dug up allows the shoots to develop bitterness, so if the bamboo is dug up and boiled within mere minutes, this step is not necessary. Be sure to perform this operation as soon as you bring the bamboo home. Historically, every house grew and milled their own rice, so rice bran was plentiful and had many culinary and household uses. While we still grow and mill our rice, these days most people purchase rice bran at the supermarket or farmstand.
-
Scrub the bamboo shoots with a natural-fiber brush (*tawashi*) and rinse with cold water. Slice off the end tips diagonally with a sharp heavy kitchen knife. Make a vertical cut ½–¾ inch (1–2 cm) deep into the bamboo shoots, starting at the edge where you just removed the tip—this cut will help the heat penetrate to the center of the shoots.

Place the unpeeled bamboo shoots into a deep, heavy pan big enough to fit them side by side lying down. Add the rice bran and chiles and fill to cover with cold water. Heat over medium-high heat until almost boiling. Be careful because the added rice bran tends to encourage water to boil over. Place a drop lid (or lid from a smaller pot) directly on top of the bamboo shoots, reduce to a gentle simmer, and cook for 1 hour (or 45 minutes if very small; even if quite large, do not cook more than 1 hour).

The bamboo shoots should stay submerged, so check the water every 30 minutes and add more as necessary. After 1 hour has elapsed, check that you can insert a bamboo skewer into the center. Allow to cool in the cooking liquid.

Once cooled, peel the outer tough layer of skin from the vertical cut. Grab the top portion and twist off to reveal the soft inner tips. Rinse the shoots and pare off any remaining hard parts around the circumference of the bottom edge. Store refrigerated, submerged in cold water for up to 5 days, but change the water every day.

ふきの下ごしらえ

PARBOILED FUKI

FUKI NO SHITA-GOSHIRAE

Preparation time: 20 minutes
Cooking time: 5 minutes
Makes: 6 stalks

• 6 stalks fuki (10½ oz/300 g)
• 1 teaspoon flaky sea salt
• 2 tablespoons ash (optional)

Like many mountain vegetables, *fuki* (see page 346) needs to have its bitterness (*aku*) removed before using. Firepit ash is still commonly used as the method to remove bitterness and mild toxins from mountain vegetables.

-

Trim off a small portion of the ends of the *fuki* to refresh, then halve (or cut into thirds) crosswise to fit into a medium saucepan. Lay the *fuki* out on a large cutting board and sprinkle with the salt. Place both palms flat on each stalk and roll back and forth in the salt (*itazuri*) to soften slightly.

Fill a medium saucepan three-quarters full with water, add the ash, if using, and bring to a boil over high heat. Drop the *fuki* into the pan and parboil for 30 seconds. Refresh under cold running water. Remove the strings by peeling back about 1 inch (2.5 cm) of the strings around the thickest end. Gather the strings together and pull all the way down the stalk to remove in one whack. Store for several days submerged in cold water in a covered, nonreactive container in the fridge, but change the water each day.

鬼皮をむいた栗

SHELLED WHOLE CHESTNUTS

ONI KAWA WO MUITA KURI

Preparation time: 45 minutes, plus 1 hour soaking time
Cooking time: 3 minutes
Makes: 1¾ pounds (850 g)

• 2¼ lb (1 kg) whole unshelled chestnuts

Soaking, a quick boil, and a sharp kitchen knife are all you need to peel chestnuts.

-

Place the chestnuts in a large saucepan and fill to cover generously with cold water. Soak for 1 hour.

Bring to a boil over high heat and cook for 3 minutes. Drain and peel by inserting the bottom corner of a sharp knife into the hard portion on the bottom of the chestnut and peeling the thick outer skin back away from the inner nut.

ゆでぎんなん

BOILED GINKGO NUTS

YUDE GINNAN

• Preparation time: 15 minutes
• Cooking time: 10 minutes
• Makes: 12

• 12 ginkgo nuts, cracked slightly

Ginkgo nuts are typically boiled in their shells before cracking open and removing the inner skin covering each nut.

-

Place the ginkgo nuts in a small saucepan and add cold water to cover. Bring to a boil over high heat and cook for 10 minutes.

Drain, refresh under cold running water. Press down on the shells with the wide end of a heavy knife blade. Remove the shells and inner papery skin.

戻した高野豆腐

RECONSTITUTED KOYADOFU

MODOSHITA KOUYADOUFU

Preparation time: 20 minutes
Makes: 4 pieces

• 4 pieces (⅓ oz/9 g each) freeze-dried tofu (koyadofu, see page 352)

Freeze-dried tofu (*koyadofu*) is an ingredient that originated in Japan several hundred years ago as a method for preserving tofu. *Koyadofu* must be reconstituted before using; and by soaking in multiple changes of water, the acrid taste of the baking soda used in processing is also removed.

-

Place the *koyadofu* in one layer in a rectangular pan with sides. Pour hot but not boiling water into the pan to cover the *koyadofu* (taking care not to pour the hot water directly on the *koyadofu*). Once the *koyadofu* has cooled and reinflated, lift the pieces out one by one from the water with a spatula. Discard the water in the pan. Put the *koyadofu* back into the pan and fill with cold water to purge any lingering baking soda used in the freeze-drying process. After 5 minutes, discard the water and fill with clean cold water. Repeat several times. Drain one last time before using.

~~~~~~

豆乳マヨネーズ

SOY MILK MAYONNAISE

TOUNYUU MAYONE-ZU

Preparation time: 15 minutes, plus 15 minutes thickening time
Makes: 1 cup (8½ oz/240 g)

• ¼ cup (2 fl oz/60 ml) soy milk, at room temperature
• 1½ teaspoons Dijon mustard
• ½ teaspoon flaky sea salt
• 1½ teaspoons rice vinegar
• Generous ¾ cup (6¾ fl oz/200 ml) neutral oil, such as canola (rapeseed), peanut, or unroasted sesame

This is a slight variation of a method originally from Food52, via Kyoko Ide, who read it in a booklet that came with a handheld wand blender that she purchased in Japan. (It is possible to use a whisk, but the mayonnaise will not be as light in color or thick in texture.) Having made traditional French-style mayonnaise for decades, I can attest to the tastiness of this egg-free method. It also has the benefit of lightness so might be a better choice for many traditional dishes that include mayonnaise. Source the best soy milk possible. I like the rich and creamy version produced by Hodo Foods of Oakland, California. Be sure to use a large enough mixing bowl because it spatters—and be prepared for your hand and wrist to get tired!

-

In a deep bowl with a narrow bottom, combine the soy milk, mustard, salt, and vinegar. Leave for 15 minutes to thicken. Using a hand blender, process to combine. Continue blending and add the oil in small dollops at a time until all the oil has been added and the mayonnaise is stiff. Keeps for several days (or longer), stored in an airtight container in the fridge.

7-SPICE MAYO: Stir ⅛ teaspoon 7-spice powder (*shichimi togarashi*, see page 350) into 2 tablespoons mayonnaise. MISO MAYO: Stir 1 teaspoon brown rice miso or barley miso into 2 tablespoons mayonnaise. SHOYU MAYO: Stir ½ teaspoon shoyu into 2 tablespoons mayonnaise.

豆腐マヨネーズ

TOFU MAYONNAISE

TOUFU MAYONE-ZU

Preparation time: 15 minutes,
plus 1 hour tofu weighting time
Makes: ½ cup (5¼ oz/150 g)

- 5¼ oz (150 g) cotton tofu
(momendofu, see page 352) or
Japanese-style soft block tofu
- 1 tablespoon rice vinegar
- ½ teaspoon flaky sea salt
- A grind or two of black pepper
- ⅛ teaspoon yellow mustard powder
(karashi, see page 350)
- 2 tablespoons good-tasting
canola (rapeseed) oil

Using tofu as the base for this "mayonnaise" yields a low-oil, slightly vinegary, slightly spicy version that is nonetheless creamy and luscious thanks to the texture of the tofu. For this reason, it is essential to use a good-tasting, soft-textured tofu.
-
Place the tofu on a plate and set another plate on top for 1 hour to press out excess liquid.

Squeeze the tofu by handfuls and drop into a Japanese grinding bowl (suribachi, see page 354). Mash well to a creamy paste.

Smash in the vinegar and fold in the salt, pepper, and mustard until well incorporated. Slowly drizzle in the oil, mixing continuously and vigorously, until completely emulsified. Will keep in the refrigerator for 3–4 days.

ホイップクリーム

LIGHTLY WHIPPED CREAM

HOIPPU KU-RIMU

Preparation time: 5 minutes
Makes: 1¼ cups (10 fl oz/300 ml)

- Generous ¾ cup (6¾ fl oz/200 ml)
heavy (double) cream
- 1 tablespoon organic granulated sugar
- ½ teaspoon vanilla extract

Use this lightly sweetened and lightly whipped cream to top fruit desserts or cakes.
-
In a medium bowl with an electric mixer, whip the cream, sugar, and vanilla on high speed until

thickened and ribbons appear on the surface, about 5 minutes. The cream should drop from a spoon in dollops, but not be stiff.

VEGAN WHIPPED CREAM

ヴィーガンホイップクリーム

VI-GAN HOIPPU KURI-MU

Preparation time: 15 minutes
Makes: 1¼ cups (10 fl oz/300 ml)

• About ¼ cup (2 fl oz/60 ml)
  aquafaba, drained from
  canned chickpeas
• ⅛ teaspoon cream of tartar
• 2 tablespoons organic
  granulated sugar
• ½ teaspoon vanilla extract

Vegan whipped creams are often made from coconut cream, but coconut flavors do not integrate well with Japanese menus. This method, a bit reminiscent of egg white meringue, uses aquafaba, the liquid from canned chickpeas. Here, it makes sense to source the highest quality available. A 15-ounce (425 g) can will yield about ½ cup (4 fl oz/120 ml) aquafaba. Use half for this recipe and freeze the other half for up to 3 months.

-

In a medium bowl, with an electric mixer, combine the aquafaba and cream of tartar and beat on high speed until soft peaks form, about 1 minute. Add the sugar in three additions: Sprinkle each third evenly over the top of the "cream" and beat for 1 minute after each addition. Add the vanilla and beat until dense and fluffy, about 1 minute more, for a total of 5 minutes. Serve immediately because the "cream" will separate, even if stored in the fridge.

~~~~~~

PARMESAN-STYLE VEGAN "CHEESE"

ヴィーガンパルメザン風
チーズ

VI-GAN PARUMENZAN-FUU CHI-ZU

Preparation time: 10 minutes,
plus 2–3 hours chilling time
Makes: about 6 ounces (170 g)

• 5¼ oz (150 g) raw cashews
• 1 tablespoon rice vinegar
• ½ teaspoon flaky sea salt
• Large pinch of yellow mustard
  powder (karashi, see page 350)

This Parmesan-style vegan "cheese" is brighter and more flavorful than the popular cashew/nutritional yeast versions. An added bonus is that you can crumble and use as is, directly after processing, or you can grate it, after chilling, for a softer texture.

-

In a mini-prep food processor, process the cashews until finely ground, but not amalgamated. Add the vinegar, salt, and mustard and pulse until the mixture forms clumps.

You can use it right away (as is) or chill to make it grateable. Turn out onto two large pieces of plastic wrap (cling film) and gather up the ends to cinch each one into a ball. Twist the plastic wrap up tightly and flatten the balls into disks. Secure each with a rubber band and refrigerate until hard enough to grate, 2–3 hours. Keeps for several days, if refrigerated, otherwise pop the plastic-wrapped disks into a 1-quart (950 ml) freezer bag and store in the freezer for a month or two.

すいかジュース

WATERMELON JUICE

SUIKA JYU-SU

Preparation time: 20 minutes,
plus 1–2 hours chilling time
Cooking time: 35 minutes
Makes: about 1 quart (32 fl oz/l liter)

• 1 small watermelon (3 lb 10 oz/1.65 kg)
• ½ teaspoon fine sea salt

Eating watermelon is how we combat the hot, muggy Japanese summer and replenish the body's natural water loss. Sprinkling salt on watermelon before eating draws out the water and enhances its sweetness. Here the salt is added after the juice is concentrated.

-

Halve the watermelon and scrape out the seeds with your fingers, dropping them into a coarse wire-mesh sieve set over a medium bowl. Scoop out the watermelon flesh with an ice cream scoop and drop into the sieve. Press the watermelon through the sieve with the back of a large spoon to remove any small seeds. Slide the flesh and juices into a blender along with any juices lingering in the hollowed-out watermelon halves—you will have about 2¼ pounds (1 kg). Blend until smooth.

Pour into a medium saucepan, bring to an almost boil, adjust to a gentle simmer, and cook for 30 minutes to concentrate. Off the heat, stir in the salt to dissolve. Refrigerate before serving.

~~~~~~

トマトジュース

TOMATO JUICE

TOMATO JYU-SU

Preparation time: 20 minutes,
plus 2½ hours cooling and chilling time
Makes: 3¾ cups (30 fl oz/900 ml)

• 4 large tomatoes (2¼ lb/1 kg)
• Boiling water
• 1 tablespoon flaky sea salt
• 2 teaspoons yuzu, sudachi,
  or Meyer lemon juice
• 2 green shiso leaves, finely chopped
• Original-style hot pepper sauce

Homemade tomato juice is completely refreshing and totally different than the canned versions. And it is the one vegetable juice that does not need a juicing machine, so anyone can whirl this up—provided you have a blender.

-

Place the tomatoes in a large heatproof bowl and pour boiling water over them to cover. When cool enough to handle, remove from the water and peel while holding over a medium bowl to catch the juices. Remove the cores and discard along with the peels. Drop the tomatoes and the juices into a blender with the salt, citrus juice, half of the shiso, and a few shakes of hot sauce. Blend until smooth, then blend 1 more minute to fully liquefy. The juice will be pink and frothy. Chill before serving garnished with the remaining shiso. Keeps for 2–3 days, if stored in an airtight container in the fridge.

Although colloquially translated as "before the meal," the kanji characters for *zensai* (前菜) actually mean "before greens." In other words, greens that you eat before the meal. Strictly speaking, the *zensai* dishes should be made up of the bits and pieces that result from preparing your menu that day and might appear on a plate in the form of little mounds of each. But *zensai* can also refer to a one-dish appetizer served before a meal. As the culture of food evolves, so does the acceptable range that can be applied to a term.

Typically, the *zensai* course is served at formal meals or at restaurants, rather than casual family dinners, but do not let that deter you from preparing these lovely little dishes because the small-bite format might be my favorite way to eat Japanese food. While small bites characterize *kaiseki* cuisine (a stylized high-level Japanese cuisine that is akin to a tasting menu, but much lighter and more restrained), many eateries, from casual izakaya to more upscale *kappo ryori*, serve a small selection of *zensai* bites to accompany the first beer or flask of sake a guest orders. This small course is called *otoshi* and is a bit like an amuse-bouche (a bite to stimulate your appetite). And as a special request, Soba Ro, one of my favorite local restaurants, creates a special-order "double" *zensai* plate for me when I stop by for lunch.

This chapter is just a suggestion of possible *zensai* dishes, so there is no need to restrict yourself to the set I have included here. Dressed dishes (Aemono, see page 68) lend themselves to being served as a small bite as well. Actually, as long as the bite can be eaten cold or at room temperature, many dishes in this book can be served as a *zensai* bite.

In keeping with the original philosophy of *zensai*, however, I have included vegetable peel dishes and geléed squares, as well as some other treatments that seemed like perfect fits for a *zensai* plate.

As always, the main point to keep in mind in building a plate or menu is balance of texture, flavor, color, and style of preparation.

ZENSAI

BEFORE THE MEAL

ふき味噌　FUKI MISO

Preparation time: 20 minutes
Cooking time: 10 minutes
Makes: Scant ½ cup (120 g)

- 2 tablespoons (¾ oz/20 g) pine nuts
- 2 teaspoons fine sea salt
- 9 or 10 butterbur buds
(fuki no to, see page 346)
- ½ tablespoon unroasted sesame oil
- 5¼ oz (150 g) brown rice
miso or barley miso
- 1 tablespoon hon mirin
- 1 tablespoon light brown cane
sugar (kibizato, see page 345)
- 1 tablespoon ground white
sesame seeds

Fuki miso is one of the beloved and greatly anticipated condiments prepared in the spring in Japan. Made from butterbur buds (*fuki no to*), *fuki miso* is salty, earthy, funky, wild . . . and turns a bowl of rice into a soul-fulfilling meal. Especially if there are a few other vegetables dishes on the table. Serve as part of a plate of tiny savory bites before a meal (*zensai*) or dabbed on the side of a bowl of rice.
-
Heat a small, dry frying pan over medium-low heat and add the pine nuts. Toast, stirring continuously, until lightly colored and fragrant, 30–60 seconds. Slide into a small grinding bowl (*suribachi*, see page 354) or mortar and smash to a powder. Set aside.

Fill a medium pot two-thirds with water and the salt and bring to a boil over high heat. Drop in the butterbur buds and cook for 1 minute. Scoop out with a wire-mesh sieve and shake off excess water. Chop finely.

In a heavy medium pot, warm the oil over medium heat. Scrape in the butterbur buds and pine nut powder and cook, stirring continuously, for 1–2 minutes to evaporate any lingering water.

Stir in the miso, mirin, sugar, and sesame seeds and continue cooking over medium heat, stirring continuously, until the sugar has melted completely and the mixture is glossy, 1–2 minutes.

~~~~~~

梅味噌　SOUR PLUM MISO

UME MISO

Preparation time: 15 minutes
Cooking time: about 2 minutes
Makes: 1¼ cups (300 g)

- 4 salted sour "plums"
(umeboshi , see page 350)
- 1 small handful tororo konbu
(see page 349)
- 2 tablespoons sake (or a little
more to adjust consistency)
- 1 cup (8½ oz/240 g) brown rice miso
- 2 tablespoons hon mirin
- 2 tablespoons fine tendrils
of green shiso leaves
- 1 tablespoon gold sesame seeds,
warmed in a dry frying pan until
fragrant and coarsely ground

Miso is an excellent vehicle for adding bright aromatics to enhance this salty, funky condiment. Dab a bit on the side of your bowl of white rice when eating a simple Japanese meal of rice and pickles accompanied by a side dish or two. Sour plum miso is also useful as a condiment for a homey bowl of plain simmered rice (*okayu*) or wheat noodles such as udon or somen. The balance in this subtly flavored miso is exceptional and pairs well with fresh crudité vegetables as a dip in the summer or stirred into a small bowl of natto instead of the typical shoyu and mustard.
-
Remove the pits (stones) from the *umeboshi* and chop the flesh well.

Heat a dry frying pan over low heat. When the heat rises from the surface, parch the *tororo konbu* carefully in the pan, turning constantly with wooden cooking chopsticks for about 1 minute, to crisp without burning. Crumble into a small bowl and set aside.

In a small saucepan, bring the sake to a simmer over high heat to just burn off the alcohol. Immediately remove from the heat.

In a small bowl, stir together the miso, mirin, and most of the sake and fold in the *umeboshi*, shiso, *tororo konbu*, and sesame seeds. The mixture should not be overly stiff, nor loose and gloopy. Add a few more drops of alcohol-burned-off sake if needed to thin the miso, but easy does it.

野菜味噌

VEGETABLE MISO

YASAI MISO

Preparation time: 15 minutes
Cooking time: 10 minutes
Makes: 1¼ cups (300 g)

• 4 inches (10 cm) small lotus root (2⅔ oz/75 g), peeled
• 4 inches (10 cm) medium carrot (1¾ oz/50 g), peeled or scrubbed
• 4 inches (10 cm) medium burdock (1 oz/25 g), scrubbed
• 1 tablespoon lightly roasted gold sesame oil (or ½ tablespoon each dark roasted and unroasted sesame oil)
• 1 cup (8½ oz/240 g) brown rice miso or barley miso

There are various "misos" in Japan that involve stir-frying an ingredient *with* miso. In this unique method, no mirin is added to counteract the saltiness of the miso; instead the root vegetables provide a naturally sweet back taste for a delicious result. Use this deeply flavored miso as a condiment for tofu *nabe* or smear it on blanched *konnyaku*, parched in a dry frying pan, then grill until caramelized. The lotus root and burdock will discolor, so chop and stir-fry immediately after peeling and scrubbing. This is a useful method for using up small bits and pieces of root vegetables. The rule of thumb is:

Cut into a fine dice, use a small amount of sesame oil for stir-frying to soften, add miso in a ratio of 1:1 to the vegetables, and stir-fry slowly over low heat to finish.
-
Chop the lotus root, carrot, and burdock into a fine dice.

In a medium frying pan, heat the oil over medium heat and add the lotus root, carrot, and burdock. Stir-fry until softened, about 5 minutes. Spoon in the miso and continue stir-frying over very low heat until fragrant and slightly dried, another 5–6 minutes. It keeps, stored in the fridge, for about 2 weeks.

~~~~~~

柚味噌の釜

YUZU MISO POTS

YUZU MISO NO KAMA

Preparation time: 45 minutes
Cooking time: 10 minutes
Makes: 4

• 5 small yuzu or round Meyer lemons
• 4 tablespoons white miso
• 5 small tender edible chrysanthemum greens (shungiku, see page 347), 1 oz (25 g)
• 12 enoki mushrooms, quartered crosswise

In our area of Japan, yuzu miso is usually a simple affair in which a full-flavored miso, such as brown rice or barley, is slightly sweetened with mirin and or sake, stir-fried gently over low heat to soften the alcohol, and infused with freshly slivered yuzu peel. Here, in this interesting, completely compelling version, the mild miso is brightly citrusy and the edible chrysanthemum greens (*shungiku*) lend a lovely crunch and hauntingly bitter flavor. Very good.
-
Pare off the yellow zest of one of the yuzu, avoiding the bitter white pith. Finely sliver the zest.

Slice a fine bit off the bottom (blossom end) of the remaining 4 yuzu so they sit flat (if using lemon, you will need to cut a bit more off). Cut the tops (stem ends) off about one-quarter of the way down from the stem dimple and reserve the tops. Hollow out

the yuzu. Squeeze the juice out of the scooped out pulp and the remaining whole yuzu and strain out the seeds. Mash 1 tablespoon of the yuzu juice and the slivered zest into the miso. (Use any remaining juice for another dish.)

Remove the *shungiku* leaves from the stalks, keeping any fine stems, and cut crosswise into ½-inch (1 cm) pieces. (If you have washed the leaves, make sure they are quite dry.) Fold the enoki and *shungiku* into the yuzu-miso and pack into the 4 hollowed-out yuzu. Fit the tops back on the yuzu.

Set a bamboo steamer over a large wok filled one-third of the way with water and bring to a boil. Set the yuzu in the steamer basket, cover, and steam over high heat for about 8 minutes. Serve these luscious little bites warm, as a revitalizing palate awakener.

梅豆腐

CHILLED UME-TOFU SQUARES IN DASHI

UMEDOUFU

Preparation time: 30 minutes,
plus 2–3 hours pressing and chilling
Cooking time: 10–15 minutes
Makes: 4 squares

- 10½ oz (300 g) cotton tofu
(momendofu, see page 352)
or Japanese-style soft block tofu
- 1 tablespoon hon kuzu
(see page 352)
- 2 medium umeboshi
(see page 350)
- Canola (rapeseed) oil,
for greasing the pan
- Generous ¾ cup (6¾ fl oz/200 ml)
Konbu Dashi (page 22)
- ½ tablespoon shoyu
- A pinch of flaky sea salt
- Scant ½ cup (3½ fl oz/100 ml)
baby water lily buds
(junsai, see page 349)
- Boiling water

Junsai, harvested from ponds from May to September, are baby water lily buds called "water shield" in English. They have a natural gelatinous covering so add a cool, slippery element to summer dishes. They might be available at Japanese markets, otherwise just omit or substitute with blanched julienned green beans or cooked edamame. Salted sour "plums" (*umeboshi*, see page 350) have been prepared in Japan for a millennium, since the Heian period (794–1185) and are purported to have many health-improving qualities, including aiding digestion and combatting summer fatigue during the rainy season. The combination here makes a subtle, but lovely little bite.
-
Place the tofu on a dinner plate and weight with a small cutting board for 1 hour.

Smash the *kuzu* to a fine powder in a Japanese grinding bowl (*suribachi*, see page 354). Squeeze the tofu by handfuls to express excess moisture and drop into the *suribachi*. Mash into the *kuzu* until well incorporated.

Cut out the *umeboshi* pits (stones) and discard. Finely chop the *umeboshi* and fold into the smashed tofu.

Dampen a folded-up piece of paper towel with the oil and grease the bottom and sides of a 5½ × 4½ × 2-inch (14 × 11 × 4.5 cm)

nagashikan mold (see page 353) or a 4⅜ × 8½-inch (11.5 × 21 cm) loaf pan (bottom lined with parchment paper). Scrape the *ume*-tofu mixture into the pan and rap smartly on the counter to eliminate air pockets and make sure the tofu is evenly distributed into the pan.

Set a bamboo steamer over a large wok filled one-third of the way with water and bring to a boil. Place the pan in the steamer, cover, and steam over high heat for about 10 minutes until set. Remove from the steamer, blot off accumulated moisture, and lay a piece of plastic wrap (cling film) on the surface. Refrigerate for at least 2 hours to chill.

In a small saucepan, stir the dashi, shoyu, and salt together over medium heat to dissolve the salt. Transfer to a small bowl and refrigerate for 1 hour to chill.

Place the *junsai* in a wire-mesh sieve and pour boiling water over for 10 seconds. Refresh by running the sieve under cold water. Shake off excess water and set the sieve over a bowl to drain. Store in the fridge for 1 hour to chill.

Unmold the *umedofu*, cut into 4 squares, and place each on a small shallow individual dish. Stir the *junsai* into the cold dashi and spoon around the *umedofu*. Serve immediately as a light, palate-cleansing bite.

CHILLED UME-TOFU SQUARES IN DASHI

しらたきの玉すだれ

SHIRATAKI NOODLE SQUARES WITH YUZU MISO

SHIRATAKI NO TAMA-SUDARE

Preparation time: 35 minutes,
plus 2 hours chilling time
Cooking time: 5 minutes
Makes: twelve 1¾ × 1½-inch
(4.5 × 3.75 cm) squares

• 1 thick strand (¼ oz/7 g) agar
  (kanten, see page 352)
• 7 oz (200 g) shirataki noodles
  (see page 353)
• Boiling water
• 2 cups (16 fl oz/500 ml)
  Konbu Dashi (page 22)
• 3 tablespoons Yuzu Miso (page 29)

Setting rubbery, slippery *shirataki* noodles in a dashi gelée hardened with agar yields refreshing little squares that respond well to any sort of seasonal miso treatment as a condiment. Here, the cold squares are eaten with yuzu miso, but are equally compelling served with *sansho* miso, sesame miso, or miso mustard sauce. Use the best quality *shirataki* possible, since they are the main ingredient.
-
Tear the *kanten* into small pieces, drop into a medium bowl, and add cold water to cover. Drain after 10 minutes.

Cut the *shirataki* crosswise into 1½-inch (4 cm) lengths, slide into a wire-mesh sieve, and pour boiling water over them for 10 seconds. Shake off well. Distribute the *shirataki* across the bottom of a 6 × 5½ × 2-inch (15 × 14 × 4.5 cm) *nagashikan* mold (see page 353) or two 4⅜ × 8½-inch (11½ × 21 cm)

loaf pans (lined with parchment paper), covering as evenly as possible.

In a small saucepan, bring the dashi and drained *kanten* to a simmer over medium heat. Adjust the heat and cook, stirring, at a gentle simmer, until the *kanten* has completely melted, 3–5 minutes. Pour over the *shirataki* noodles in the mold. Cool to room temperature, then refrigerate for at least 2 hours.

Unmold the geléed dashi and *shirataki* and cut into 12 squares. Serve one or two squares per person and spoon the yuzu miso on top of each square. Keeps for several days in the fridge, if well sealed with plastic wrap (cling film); do not cover with foil since the foil will leach out onto the surface of the squares.

~~~~~~

大根の葉の佃煮

DAIKON LEAF TSUKUDANI

DAIKON NO HA NO TSUKUDANI

Preparation time: 10 minutes
Cooking time: 5 minutes
Makes: ½ cup (4 fl oz/125 ml)

• 1 tablespoon dark roasted sesame oil
• 1 bunch (7 oz/200 g) tender daikon
  greens, finely chopped
• 1 tablespoon shoyu
• ½ teaspoon 7-spice powder (shichimi
  togarashi see page 350)

Tsukudani is typically a sticky-sweet condiment often made from small fishes and is traditionally cooked down for several hours in a combination of sugar, shoyu, and dashi. This bright version uses no sugar, and the greens are mostly dry-roasted, so comparatively quick to execute. Good as an accompaniment to simple rice dishes or as a *zensai* bite, the condiment will keep for several days, if refrigerated.
-

In a large frying pan, warm the sesame oil over medium-low heat. Add the daikon greens and stir-fry until wilted, about 3 minutes. Take care not to brown—adjust the heat, if needed. Add the shoyu and toss to distribute. Once the shoyu has been absorbed and the daikon leaf has become dry and crumbly, about 3 minutes more, remove from the heat and stir in the *shichimi togarashi*. Scrape into a small bowl to cool.

SHIRATAKI NOODLE SQUARES WITH YUZU MISO

POTATO SALAD

ポテトサラダ

POTETO SARADA

Preparation time: 30 minutes
Cooking time: 35 minutes
Makes: 4 cups (1 kg)

- 1½ lb (700 g) medium potatoes, unpeeled
- ½ large carrot (3½ oz/100 g), scrubbed and cut into ½-inch (1 cm) dice
- ½ large onion (3½ oz/100 g), cut into ½-inch (1 cm) dice
- 1½ teaspoons flaky sea salt
- 10 slender green beans (1¾ oz/50 g)
- ¾ cup (6 oz/175 g) Soy Milk Mayonnaise (page 36)
- ½ teaspoon freshly ground black pepper
- 1 medium bunch (7 oz/200 g) green or purple mizuna

For French and German potato salads, just-cooked potatoes are sliced and dressed with a vinaigrette while still hot. American potato salads feature cooled and cubed cooked potatoes cloaked with mayonnaise. Japanese potato salad is unusual in that the potato is mashed before being mixed with mayonnaise and almost always includes carrot, onion, and some sort of green vegetable such as cucumber or peas. Make Mini Potato Croquettes (page 130) with the leftovers.

Place the unpeeled potatoes in a steamer basket set over a large wok filled three-quarters with boiling water and steam until the centers are soft, about 30 minutes. Peel while hot by rubbing in paper towels and place in a medium bowl. Smash while still hot with a potato masher.

Lay a sheet of parchment paper in the steamer basket and strew the carrot and onion on the paper. Sprinkle with ¼ teaspoon of the salt. Cover and cook over rapidly boiling water for 3–5 minutes, until soft. Remove the steamer basket from the wok, set on a large dinner plate, and let the vegetables cool to room temperature.

Bring a medium saucepan of water to a boil over high heat. Add the green beans and blanch for 1–3 minutes, depending on thickness. Drain, refresh under cold running water, and pat dry in a clean tea towel. Slice off the stem ends and cut the beans crosswise into ¾-inch (2 cm) pieces.

Add the cooled carrot, onion, green beans, mayonnaise, remaining 1¼ teaspoons salt, and the black pepper to the smashed potato and fold together until the ingredients are evenly incorporated.

Cut the top 2 inches (5 cm) of the mizuna leaves off and use the bottom portion for another dish. Scoop a generous portion of potato salad into a pretty serving bowl and mound a handful of the mizuna leaves next to the salad. Serve family-style for lunch or as a vegetable side dish. (Alternatively, serve individually on four salad plates.)

アスパラガス二種のソース

ASPARAGUS WITH AVOCADO AND RED PEPPER SAUCES

ASUPARAGASU NI-SHU NO SO-SU

Preparation time: 45 minutes
Cooking time: 10 minutes
Serves: 4

- 6 thick spears asparagus (7 oz/200 g)
- 1 tablespoon fine sea salt
- 1 large red bell pepper (6 oz/175 g)
- 2 tablespoons plus 2 teaspoons olive oil
- ¾ teaspoon flaky sea salt
- 2 small tomatoes (8 oz/225 g)
- 8 French green olives, such as Picholine, pitted
- 1 small avocado (6 oz/180 g)
- Scant ⅓ cup (2½ fl oz/75 ml) soy milk

Blanched asparagus served with two flavorful yet contrasting dipping sauces makes an irresistible healthy bite to serve before dinner. The avocado sauce will discolor, so use immediately, while the red pepper sauce keeps well, if stored in an airtight container in the fridge.
-
Trim off a bit of the ends of the asparagus to refresh and peel the bottom one-third of each asparagus. Set up a large bowl of ice and water. Bring a medium pot filled three-quarters with water and the fine salt to a boil over high heat. Blanch the asparagus until heated through, about 30 seconds. Scoop out and immediately plunge into the ice bath to refresh. Pat dry and cut crosswise into thirds. Arrange on a small serving platter.

Core and seed the pepper and cut into irregular triangular pieces (*rangiri*, see page 17). In a medium frying pan, heat

2 tablespoons of the olive oil over medium-low heat and add the pepper. Gently stir-fry until softened and completely cooked through, 5–7 minutes. Scrape into a blender with the oil and add ¼ teaspoon of the flaky salt.

Core and cut the tomatoes into rough triangular pieces and drop into the blender with the bell pepper. Add the pitted olives and remaining 2 teaspoons olive oil and whirl until smooth. Scrape out into a small bowl.

Peel and pit (destone) the avocado. Pare off any discolored spots and drop into a clean blender. Add the soy milk and remaining ½ teaspoon flaky salt and blend until smooth. Scrape into a small bowl.

Give each person two small saucers in which to spoon a little of each dipping sauce and serve with the asparagus.

うどのアボカド和え

UDO WITH SMASHED AVOCADO

UDO NO ABOKADO-AE

Preparation time: 30 minutes
Serves: 4

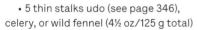

- 5 thin stalks udo (see page 346), celery, or wild fennel (4½ oz/125 g total)
- 2 tablespoons rice vinegar
- Boiling water
- 1 small avocado (6¼ oz/175 g)
- ¼ teaspoon flaky sea salt
- 4 small sprigs sansho leaves, for garnish

It is possible to substitute celery or fennel for the *udo*, though the almost licorice-like profile of this mountain vegetable is as hard to describe as it is to duplicate. If you can find *udo* you will not regret the effort, but be sure to use fine stalks. Use the peels to make Udo Peel Kinpira (page 50).
-
Peel the *udo*. Fill a medium bowl halfway with cold water and add the vinegar. Cut the *udo* into ¼-inch (5 mm) dice and slide into the bowl for 5 minutes (or until you are ready to proceed).

Drain the *udo* in a wire-mesh sieve and douse with boiling water for 10 seconds. Refresh under cold running water until cool to the touch and pat dry with a clean tea towel.

Halve, pit (destone), and peel the avocado. In a medium bowl, smash the salt into the avocado with a fork. Toss the *udo* with the avocado to coat and spoon into 4 small pretty dishes. Garnish with the *sansho* leaf sprigs and serve as a bright bite before dinner.

湯葉とアボカドのタルタル

AVOCADO AND YUBA TARTARE

YUBA TO ABOKADO NO TARUTARU

Preparation time: 15 minutes
Serves: 4

- ¼ teaspoon flaky sea salt
- 1 teaspoon grated fresh wasabi
- Juice of 1 small lime
- 1 medium avocado (7½ oz/210 g)
- 3 oz (85 g) fresh yuba
  (see page 352)
- ½ teaspoon usukuchi shoyu
  (see page 344)

The juxtaposition of creamy textures of the delicate *yuba* and firm avocado make a beguiling small bite before dinner—though be sure to avoid overly ripe or mushy avocado. The combination of citrus notes from the lime and gentle heat from the wasabi add a welcome spark of brightness.
-
In a small bowl, stir the salt into ½ teaspoon of the wasabi. Add the lime juice slowly, stirring to emulsify.

Halve the avocado, remove the pit (stone), and peel. Cut the avocado into ½-inch (1 cm) cubes and toss in the lime juice/wasabi mixture to coat. Cut the *yuba* crosswise into ¾-inch (2 cm) pieces and fold gently into the avocado. Spoon into small individual bowls, dribble a little *usukuchi shoyu* over the top of each, and dab on the remaining wasabi. Serve immediately.

うどの皮のきんぴら

UDO PEEL KINPIRA

UDO NO KAWA NO KINPIRA

Preparation time: 20 minutes
Cooking time: 5 minutes
Serves: 4

- 3 oz (85 g) udo peels (see page 346)
- ½ tablespoon dark
  roasted gold sesame oil
- ½ tablespoon shoyu
- ½ tablespoon hon mirin
- ⅛ teaspoon 7-spice powder
  (shichimi togarashi, see page 350)

Kinpira is a classic shoyu-flavored stir-fried vegetable dish prepared all over Japan, but with myriad variations. Here only the peel is used, as a method to respect the whole vegetable and not waste, a philosophy that is one of the basic tenets of Japanese vegetarian food. Make this when you are preparing another udo dish, such as Cherry Blossom Rice with Udo (page 270) or Udo with Smashed Avocado (page 49).
-
Soak the peels in a bowl of ice water and leave for at least 10 minutes to remove bitterness. Check the peels for any strings and pull off. When ready to serve, dry the peels well in a clean tea towel and cut crosswise into 2-inch (5 cm) pieces.

In a medium frying pan, heat the sesame oil over medium heat and slide in the peels. Stir-fry until shiny and slightly softened,

about 1 minute. Add the shoyu and mirin and continue stir-frying over high heat until the liquids have been absorbed, 30 seconds or so. Sprinkle in the *shichimi togarashi* and scrape into a small serving bowl. Serve warm or at room temperature.

EGGPLANT PEEL KINPIRA: Soak 1¾ oz (50 g) Japanese eggplant (aubergine) peels in plenty of cold water for 5 minutes to remove bitterness. Drain, pat dry, and julienne. In a small frying pan, heat 1 teaspoon dark roasted sesame oil over high heat. Slide in the peels and stir-fry for 1 minute to soften. Add 2 teaspoons shoyu and 1 teaspoon *hon mirin*, stir once to evaporate, then pinch into small mounds on four saucers and serve as a hot bite with drinks before dinner.

AVOCADO AND YUBA TARTARE

ねぎぬた

NEGI NUTA

Preparation time: 15 minutes
Cooking time: 5 minutes
Serves: 4, with leftovers

• 4 medium negi or 12 fat scallions (spring onions), 10½ oz (300 g), ends and tips cut off
• 1 tablespoon yellow mustard powder (karashi, see page 350) mixed with 1 tablespoon hot water
• 2 teaspoons rice vinegar
• 4 teaspoons Happo Dashi (page 25) or 3 teaspoons Konbu Dashi (page 22) plus 1 teaspoon mirin
• ⅛ teaspoon shoyu
• 3½ oz (100 g) Taki Miso (page 29)

This classic preparation of Japanese leek-like green onions (*negi*) typically includes clams of some kind. But here, quickly blanching softens the natural pungency of the *negi*, and the clams are not missed.
-
Bring a medium pot of water to a boil over high heat. Cut the *negi* crosswise into 1¼-inch (3 cm) pieces. Separate the white lower portions and drop into the boiling water. After 60 seconds, add the top cross section that juts up to the green tops. Cook for 20 seconds before dropping the green top pieces into the boiling water. Cook for 10 more seconds (a total of 90 seconds for the harder bottom portions, 30 seconds for the cross section pieces, and 10 seconds for the green tops). Scoop out with a wire-mesh sieve and allow to cool to room temperature.

Pat dry in a clean dish (tea) towel and slide into a medium bowl.

In a small bowl, slowly mix the mustard, rice vinegar, *happo dashi*, and shoyu together with the *taki miso*. Scrape into the bowl of *negi*, toss well until all the pieces are cloaked with the sauce, and mound into four small bowls. (Alternatively, stack the *negi* attractively in small bowls and drizzle with the mustard miso sauce.) The pieces hold up well until the next day, though the vegetables and sauce are best stored separately.

いちじくの胡麻出汁

DASHI-STEEPED FIGS WITH SESAME SAUCE

ICHIJIKU NO GOMA-DASHI

Preparation time: 25 minutes
Cooking time: 1–2 minutes
Makes: 4

• 4 medium figs (2½ oz/70 g each)
• Boiling water
• Generous 1⅔ cups (13½ fl oz/400 ml) plus 2 tablespoons Konbu Dashi (page 22)
• 3 tablespoons plus ¼ teaspoon hon mirin
• ⅛ teaspoon flaky sea salt
• ¼ teaspoon shoyu
• 4 tablespoons Japanese white sesame paste

Steeping figs in sweetened dashi infuses them with a delicate juiciness that juxtaposes well with the rich sesame sauce. Serve this as a sweet-savory course with salt-forward dishes to complement.
-
Cut a shallow, lengthwise slit through the skins of each fig (but don't cut into the flesh) and place them in a heatproof medium bowl. Pour boiling water over to cover, leave for 1–2 minutes to soak, then discard the water and dry the bowl. Peel the figs, returning them to the empty bowl and set aside.

In a small saucepan, stir together 1⅔ cups (13½ fl oz/400 ml) of the dashi, 3 tablespoons of the mirin, and the salt. Bring to a simmer to dissolve the salt and burn off a little alcohol. Pour the hot dashi over the figs and allow to come to room temperature.

In a small bowl, stir the remaining 2 tablespoons dashi, ¼ teaspoon mirin, and the shoyu into the sesame paste. Remove the figs from the dashi and set each one on an attractive plate. Dollop the sesame sauce on top of each fig so it runs down the side a bit and serve. The figs are also good chilled, but the sesame sauce should be served at room temperature.

NEGI NUTA

JAPANESE TOFU

Japanese tofu is like ethereal custard. Most often eaten cold (*hiyayakko*), it is also enjoyed poached in konbu dashi (*yudofu*) in the winter. Either way, the tofu is served drizzled with soy sauce and perhaps garnished with chopped *negi* (Japanese "leeks") or scallions (spring onions), and a little finely grated ginger.

Smashed tofu-dressed dishes (*shira-ae*) seasoned with sesame, miso, mirin, etc. are also common ways to eat tofu. Tofu stir-fries are much rarer because Japanese tofu is soft. Deep-fried tofu pouches (*usuage*) appear more commonly in simmered or dressed dishes but can also be used in stir-fried dishes. Thick deep-fried tofu (*atsuage*) is used in hearty simmered dishes.

For the recipes in this book, I recommend seeking out the softest tofu available—hopefully one made by a local tofu-maker. Ultimately just do the best you can, but avoid any tofu harder than medium. Medium tofu is suitable for *shira-ae* or possibly simmered dishes, but not really for dishes that call for a soft, fresh tofu. The benefit of medium tofu is that you can skip the pressing step. You will also need to smash in a food processor since the Japanese grinding bowl (*suribachi*) will not be adequate for breaking down the stiffer curds characteristic of medium tofu. Beyond texture, flavor is also important, so keep that in mind as well when selecting tofu. You are looking for a soft, round, beany taste in the mouth, with no lingering acrid elements from the coagulant.

If you have access to top-quality fresh soy milk, then by all means make your own soft tofu. Stir a generous ½ teaspoon (3 ml) nigari into ½ cup (4 fl oz/125 ml) soy milk in a handle-less teacup or *chawan mushi* cup. Cover and steam over medium-high heat for 15 minutes, then allow to rest in the steamer, covered, for 5 minutes before serving.

Yuba is the delicate skin that is harvested off the soy milk as it heats in the tofu-making process. In Japan it is rolled into compact logs and sold in small packages by some tofu-makers. In Oakland, California, Hodo Foods has a dedicated *yuba* producing-area so they are able to package larger amounts, though their *yuba* is no less dear. *Yuba* is highly perishable and is a hands-on operation, so pricey. Nonetheless, if you can source fresh *yuba*, I highly recommend making the splurge. Think of it as burrata—but without the richness of heavy cream.

There are two primary types of soft tofu in Japan: *momen* (cotton) and *kinugoshi* (silken). *Momen dofu* is made by briefly stirring a coagulant such as *nigari* (the by-product liquid that remains after removing all the salt solids from concentrated sea water) into soy milk that has been heated to 175°F (80°C). The curds that form are ladled into muslin-lined wooden or stainless steel forms with holes on the sides for drainage, weighted, and left to solidify as they cool. *Momen dofu* is so named because of the cotton cloth used in the production, and the characteristic faint imprint of the textured cloth that results on the surface of the tofu. In the case of fresh, artisanal *kinugoshi dofu*, the *nigari* is carefully added to the heated soy milk in one shot (*ippatsu yose*) and then allowed to coagulate. To yield an exquisite texture requires great skill, so it is only made by the top tofu-makers in Japan. Both types of fresh tofu are sold packed in water and have a shelf life of about one week.

Besides fresh tofu, there are three kinds of deep-fried tofu: *usuage* (deep-fried tofu pouches), *atsuage* (thick deep-fried tofu), and *ganmodoki* (tofu patties). To make *usuage*, the tofu blocks are cut into thin slabs, lightly pressed, and then deep-fried twice to encourage the thin pieces of pressed tofu to puff up for lightness and to create a pocket for stuffing. *Atsuage* are made from blocks of tofu, pressed as is, then deep-fried. *Ganmodoki* are produced by first pressing out excess moisture from the tofu, then smashing it to a creamy consistency, and adding a combination of root vegetables, mushrooms, or seaweed, cut into small pieces, and a binder such as finely grated mountain yam. The patties are deep-fried and typically used in simmered dishes. *Yaki-dofu* (grilled pressed tofu) can be used in sukiyaki or other one-pot dishes (*nabe*), though we prefer fresh, uncooked tofu for these dishes.

Believed to have been invented in China over 2,000 years ago, tofu is said to have been brought to Japan by monks during the Nara period (710–794), though there are several other theories floating around (such as tofu entering Japan via Korean prisoners of war). In any case, the first known written mention of tofu was recorded in the 1183 diary of a priest at the Kasuga-taisha Shrine in what is now the city of Nara, in Nara prefecture. And by the Heian period (794–1185), the peak of the imperial court of classical Japan, tofu was widely enjoyed by the higher ranks of Japanese society (nobles, samurai, and monks). As vegetarian temple cuisine (*shojin ryori*) spread throughout Japan during the Kamakura (1182–1333) and Muromachi (1336–1573) periods, so did tofu consumption and production. But it was not until the Edo period (1603–1868) that tofu became a food for the common people, which resulted in original Japanese tofu preparations such as dried frozen tofu (*koyadofu*), deep-fried tofu patties (*ganmodoki*), deep-fried tofu pouches (*usuage*), grilled tofu (*yaki-dofu*), and silken tofu (*kinugoshi dofu*). In 1782, the first dedicated cookbook on tofu was published. *Tofu Hyakuchin* introduced one hundred different tofu dishes, forty-four of which featured shoyu as the main seasoning, followed by eighteen that used miso. Still today, shoyu is widely regarded as the seasoning of choice for tofu (whether served hot or cold).

Previously firm in texture like its Chinese predecessor, with the popularization of tofu in the Edo period and the rise in artisanal craftsmen, Japanese tofu gradually evolved into the softer, whiter, more delicately flavored product that it is today. The most significant change in Japanese tofu, however, occurred during World War II and the postwar years of shortages that lasted through the 1950s. During the war, tofu-makers were prohibited from using *nigari* because it became a crucial source of magnesium in the construction of lightweight aircrafts. Obliged to use calcium sulfate, the taste and texture of tofu suffered considerably. The upside was increased calcium intake to supplement the poor wartime diet, greater production yields that helped feed the country, as well as increased profits. New methods were developed to boost overall food production, including a whole-bean silken tofu coagulated with calcium sulfate. Although production of this particular tofu was suspended after the end of the war, modernization of the Japanese tofu industry had begun in earnest.

In the name of progress and profitability, drastic changes in Japanese tofu-making took place between 1950 and 1960. The use of naturally occurring *nigari* shifted almost completely to calcium sulfate, and Japanese soybeans were virtually replaced by American ones, despite the intrinsic loss in flavor. At one point, defatted soybean grits (*dasshi kako daizu*) instead of whole beans came into popularity, though that practice has not continued (except in the production of soy sauce). Another huge change was the shift from well water to municipal water due to

industrial ground water pollution. Deep well and spring water are said to be the most crucial elements in tofu production (as well as many other traditional Japanese foods and seasonings such as sake, mirin, rice vinegar, and shoyu). The loss of clarity in the delicate tofu and the introduction of inherent unpleasant chemical tastes from the municipal water resulted in a significant decrease in quality of the tofu.

Modern machinery eventually replaced traditional equipment and stainless steel was favored over wooden boxes and barrels. The shift from the artisanal family tofu shop to the mechanized tofu factory had taken hold.

I have witnessed the marked attrition of local tofu-makers in these last three decades since arriving in Japan in 1988, but the decline actually began in the early 1960s. From 1960 to 1980, the number of small tofu shops in Japan almost halved. Unable to compete with large-scale tofu producers, small tofu-makers steadily lost lucrative contracts such as hospitals or schools. Also, sons were less interested in taking over the family's business, so shops shuttered. Today, most urban Japanese purchase their tofu at supermarkets and there is less and less artisanal tofu readily available.

Basic tofu has been made in Japan for a very long time: Soy milk is produced from soaked, simmered soybeans from which the solids are separated. The soybean pulp (*okara*) is a thrifty, nutritious by-product of tofu-making, and is a common ingredient in traditional Japanese vegetarian cuisine.

However, there were those in Japan who dubbed *okara* "industrial waste" and set about eliminating *okara* from the tofu-making process. After ten years in development, in 1999 a Japanese tofu machine company debuted equipment to produce an

ultrafine whole-bean soy powder that could be used to make whole-bean tofu (*marugoto-tofu*).

This is only the most recent of a long string of so-called innovations that have been introduced to the tofu-making industry over the course of the last hundred years, but it might be the most far-reaching. Still not well known in Japan, or widely available, artisanal tofu producers are alarmed at the potential negative effects this new machinery and production method will bring to Japanese tofu. Only time will tell, but I share these deep misgivings, because labeling can be so misleading and confusing.

As with all foods, it makes sense to read the labels and contents when purchasing tofu. Some things to look for: Japan-grown and/or organic soybeans; the use of naturally occurring *nigari* over the chemical compound calcium sulfate; and no added ingredients such as defoamers (glycerin fatty acid ester, lecithin, magnesium carbonate). Japanese soybeans have been used in food production (primarily tofu-making) for over a millennium, so these good-tasting, high-protein beans are perfectly suited for Japanese soy-based foods and seasonings. Other beans grown around the world (such as in the United States, Canada, or China) are a variety with high oil content and grown for optimum oil output. Using *nigari* yields a softer tofu and is preferred for Japanese tofu, while calcium sulfate produces a harder result, so is prevalent in Korean- and Chinese-style tofu production. As for the use of defoamers, this basically comes down to cutting corners in the production process and their addition would seem to detract from the healthy aspect of tofu. Ultimately, the choice of product is a personal and cultural decision.

冷奴とオクラ

COLD TOFU AND OKRA

HIYAYAKKO TO OKURA

Preparation time: 15 minutes
Serves: 4

• 2 medium okra, tops removed
• 1 small myoga (see page 348),
halved lengthwise
• 10½ oz (300 g) cotton tofu
(momendofu, see page 352) or
Japanese-style soft block tofu
• 1 tablespoon shoyu

In Japan, the tofu is always soft: whether cotton tofu (*momendofu*) or silken tofu (*kinugoshi dofu*)—akin to a set custard—and lends itself to being served cold with a drizzle of shoyu and some flavorful condiments to complement. Cold tofu (*hiyayakko*) is as delicious as it is easy, so is one of the most beloved summer Japanese dishes.

-

Finely chop the okra into a homogenous mass. Place the *myoga*, cut side down, on a cutting board and slice thinly lengthwise. Separate the threads.

Quarter the tofu and place on four individual saucers. Spoon a small mound of the okra in the center of each piece of tofu and add a healthy pinch of the *myoga* threads. Drizzle with the shoyu and serve cold to accompany any Japanese summer meal: breakfast, lunch, or dinner.

~~~~~~

オクラと味噌マヨネーズ

OKRA WITH MISO MAYONNAISE

OKURA TO MISO MAYONE-ZU

Preparation time: 5 minutes
Cooking time: 30 seconds
Serves: 4

• ½ tablespoon brown rice miso
or barley miso
• 2 tablespoons Soy Milk Mayonnaise
(page 36)
• 8 medium okra (2½ oz/75 g),
brown portions of tops pared off

Parboiled okra is wonderful dipped into homemade mayonnaise or miso. But combining the two to make a miso mayonnaise is brilliant and even better. Serve as a small bite with tea or drinks before dinner.

-

Stir the miso into the mayonnaise and set aside.

Bring a small saucepan of water to a boil over high heat. Drop in the okra and cook for 30 seconds. Drain, pat dry, and halve lengthwise. Once cool, serve 4 halves per person with a heaping teaspoon of the miso mayonnaise.

OKRA WITH MISO MAYONNAISE

大根の豆腐マヨネーズ和え

DAIKON WITH TOFU MAYONNAISE

DAIKON NO TOUFU MAYONE-ZU-AE

Preparation time: 15 minutes
Cooking time: 2 minutes
Serves: 4, as a small bite

• 2¼-inch (6 cm) piece daikon
• ½ teaspoon sea salt, plus
  a couple pinches
• ¼ cup (2⅔ oz/75 g) Tofu Mayonnaise
  (page 37)
• ½ oz (15 g) daikon sprouts
  (kaiware daikon, see page 349),
bottom thirds cut off and discarded
• ¼ teaspoon red shiso powder
  (aka shiso, see page 351)

The key point here is to just barely cook the daikon, so the pieces retain some crunch but are not raw. Paired with the creamy, low-oil mayonnaise, this dish is as fresh and refreshing as it is lovely.
-
Cut the daikon crosswise into 1¼-inch (3 cm) pieces and peel. Slice the pieces finely lengthwise and then cut those slabs lengthwise into ½-inch (1 cm) wide pieces (*tanzaku-giri*, see page 17). Separate the pieces with your fingers so they are not sticking together.

Bring a medium saucepan of water to a boil with the salt over high heat. Drop the daikon into a wire-mesh sieve and dip in and out of the boiling water. Refresh under cold running water until cool to the touch. Shake off and blot dry in a clean tea towel.

Right before serving, in a medium bowl, fold the tofu mayonnaise into the daikon with half the daikon sprouts until well-distributed. Mound on four small dishes, sprinkle with red shiso powder, lean the remaining daikon sprouts attractively against each mound, and serve.

大根の皮の梅肉和え

DAIKON PEEL WITH UME

DAIKON NO KAWA NO BAINIKU-AE

Preparation time: 15 minutes,
plus 20 minutes salting and flavoring
Serves: 4, as a small bite

• 2¼ oz (60 g) thick peels of one
  small unblemished daikon
• A couple pinches flaky sea salt
• ¾ teaspoon sour "plum" paste
  (bainiku, see page 350)

Japanese sour "plums" (*ume*) are, for the most part, brined, then sun-dried for preserving. Good-quality *ume* paste without additives or artificial colorings is readily available outside of Japan from macrobiotic sources. This small bite is outstanding and not to be overlooked.
-
Cut the peels in halves or thirds crosswise into about 2¼-inch (6 cm) pieces. Stack into manageable piles and julienne. In a small bowl, gently massage the salt into the

daikon peel. After 10 minutes, lift the peel from the bowl, leaving any lingering salt crystals. Rinse under cold running water, shake off, and pat dry in a clean tea towel.

Drop into a medium bowl and, using chopsticks, toss with the sour "plum" paste to distribute well. Let sit for 10 minutes to develop flavor, then mound on small plates for a refreshing palate cleanser.

DAIKON PEEL WITH UME

そら豆の寒天寄せ

FAVA BEAN GELÉE

SORAMAME NO KANTEN-YOSE

Preparation time: 30 minutes,
plus 2 hours chilling time
Cooking time: 15 minutes
Serves: 4

- 12 large fava bean (broad bean) pods (1 lb/450 g)
- 8 thin center slices (4 inches/ 10 cm long) of Japanese cucumber, cut with a vegetable peeler or mandoline
- 1¼ cups (10 fl oz/300 ml) Konbu Dashi (page 22)
- 2 teaspoons usukuchi shoyu (see page 344)
- ⅛ teaspoon fine sea salt
- 2 tablespoons sake
- 1 tablespoon (4 g) agar flakes
- 2 green shiso leaves, cut into a chiffonade

Fava beans (broad beans) are the first sign of spring all over the world, and Japan is no exception. The season is short here, so there are a variety of ways to prepare. Here the pods are roasted to bring out the flavor of the beans inside. Also, in the spirit of no waste, you can roast the inside skin portions and eat them as well. Serve this delicately vegetal gelée as a first course.

Cut a small lengthwise slit in the seam of each fava bean (broad bean) to allow the steam to escape. Heat an iron grill pan over high heat and grill the fava bean pods until black spots appear on both sides, about 3 minutes per side. Remove the pods to a work surface. Once cool enough to handle, cut one end off with a pair of kitchen scissors and carefully cut up the length of the pod. Gently pop the beans out and peel them.

Lay out 4 large pieces of plastic wrap (cling film) on a rectangular pan with sides and set a 2¼-inch (6 cm) round stainless steel cookie

cutter on each piece. Bring the ends of the plastic wrap up around the sides of the cutter and secure tightly around the outside of the cutter with a rubber band (this will help the soft gelée from oozing out of the form). Enclose the outside of the forms tightly with a piece of heavy-duty foil for good measure. Curl two pieces of cucumber inside each of the forms to line evenly. Divide the peeled fava beans among the cookie cutters.

In a small saucepan, combine the dashi, usukuchi shoyu, salt, and sake. Sprinkle the agar over the liquids in the pan and bring almost to a boil over high heat, without stirring. Adjust to a bare simmer and cook, stirring occasionally, until the flakes have completely dissolved and the mixture has thickened, 5–7 minutes. Cool for about 5 minutes, then pour evenly over the fava beans in each cutter. Refrigerate for at least 2 hours before carefully unmolding and serving immediately as a small bite, garnished with the shiso.

こんにゃくの梅和え

KONNYAKU WITH UME AND SESAME

KONNYAKU NO UME-AE

Preparation time: 15 minutes
Serves: 4

- 7 oz (200 g) white konnyaku, cut into ¾-inch (2 cm) cubes
- Boiling water
- ½ tablespoon white sesame seeds, warmed in a small dry pan until fragrant
- 1½ tablespoons sour "plum" paste (bainiku, see page 350)
- ½ tablespoon hon mirin

Rubbery, slippery konnyaku makes a perfect foil for the restrained, yet clearly present sour "plum" paste. Sour "plum" (ume) makes any dish vibrant and here is no exception. Finding white konnyaku (rather than brownish gray) is essential, and if possible, the bainiku should be infused with red shiso for a more stunning contrast to the white konnyaku.

Place the konnyaku in a wire-mesh sieve and douse with

boiling water for 10 seconds. Blot dry in a clean tea towel.

Smash the sesame seeds in a Japanese grinding bowl (suribachi, see page 354) or spice grinder. Mash the sour "plum" paste and mirin into the sesame until well emulsified. Add the konnyaku and toss well to distribute. Mound in a small serving bowl or on individual saucers and serve as a refreshing bite to accompany a Japanese meal. Keeps well for several days, if stored in the fridge.

FAVA BEAN GELÉE

こんにゃくのくるみ味噌和え

KONNYAKU WITH MISO AND WALNUTS

KONNYAKU NO KURUMI MISO-AE

Preparation time: 15 minutes
Serves: 4

• 10½ oz (300 g) konnyaku, cut into ¾-inch (2 cm) cubes
• Boiling water
• 1 tablespoon white sesame seeds, warmed in a small dry frying pan until fragrant
• 3 tablespoons coarsely chopped walnuts
• 3 tablespoons brown rice miso
• 2 tablespoons hon mirin

The resilient texture of the *konnyaku* juxtaposes nicely with the sweet and salty miso and crunchy walnuts, making this dish a tasty bite with beer before dinner.
-
Drop the *konnyaku* into a wire-mesh sieve and pour boiling water over for 10 seconds. Shake off and set aside.

Smash the sesame seeds coarsely in a Japanese grinding bowl (*suribachi*, see page 354). Add the walnuts, miso, and mirin and mash a little more to break down the walnuts. Fold in the *konnyaku* until all the pieces are evenly coated. Spoon onto small plates and serve.

~~~~~~

こんにゃくサラダ

KONNYAKU SALAD

KONNYAKU SARADA

Preparation time: 40 minutes
Serves: 4

• 7 oz (200 g) konnyaku noodles (ito konnyaku, see page 353)
• Boiling water
• ⅛ small daikon (4½ oz/125 g), peeled or scrubbed
• ½ medium carrot (2¾ oz/80 g), peeled or scrubbed
• ½ teaspoon flaky sea salt
• 1 teaspoon shoyu
• Generous ¾ cup (6¾ fl oz/200 ml) Soy Milk Mayonnaise (page 36)
• 1 small handful daikon sprouts (kaiware daikon, see page 349), bottom thirds cut off and discarded

The rubbery, yet delightfully slippery quality of the *konnyaku* noodles lends an unexpected texture to this root vegetable salad. In Japan, the *konnyaku* noodles are sold in large balls so they need to be cut. Outside of Japan the noodles might already be cut to serving size—just use your best judgment on deciding if the noodles need to be cut further or not.
-
If the *konnyaku* noodles are a tight ball, cut crosswise, then place in a wire-mesh sieve and douse with boiling water for 10 seconds. Cool to refresh in cold running water, then blot dry in a clean tea towel. If needed, cut the noodles crosswise into 3¼-inch (8 cm) lengths and set aside.

Slice the daikon and carrot into julienne 1½ inches (4 cm) long, place in a medium bowl, and massage lightly with the salt. Let sit 10 minutes, then squeeze gently, blotting with paper towel, and drop into a clean medium serving bowl with the *konnyaku* noodles.

Stir the shoyu into the mayonnaise until well emulsified and fold into the *konnyaku*, daikon, and carrot. Garnish with the daikon sprouts and serve as a cold side dish to accompany a Japanese meal.

KONNYAKU SALAD

なすの叩き混ぜ

CHOPPED EGGPLANT WITH MISO

NASU NO TATAKI-MAZE

Preparation time: 30 minutes
Cooking time: 10 minutes
Serves: 4, as a small bite

• 4 medium Japanese eggplants
(aubergines), 10½ oz (300 g)
• 1 tablespoon brown rice miso
or barley miso
• 1 teaspoon grated fresh ginger
• 1 tablespoon finely chopped
green shiso leaves
• 1 tablespoon pine nuts, warmed
slightly in a dry frying pan
• 1 tablespoon white sesame seeds,
warmed slightly in a dry frying pan
• 1 teaspoon finely slivered green
shiso leaves, for garnish

Eggplant (aubergine) replaces raw sardine or horse mackerel fillets in this classic preparation. White sesame seeds are often included in *tataki*-style dishes, but here the addition of pine nuts give a lovely richness to this slightly unusual (but completely delicious) treatment. Serve as a condiment to white rice or to smear on baguette toasts.
–
Grill the eggplants (aubergines) in a fish griller, toaster oven (mini oven), or 4 inches (1.75 cm) from the top of a preheated broiler (oven grill), until blackened on all sides, about 10 minutes.

Peel the eggplants and slice off the calyx ends. Finely chop the eggplant on a large cutting board with the miso and ginger, until creamy and well amalgamated. Scrape into a medium bowl and fold in the chopped shiso, pine nuts, and sesame seeds. Garnish with a pinch of slivered shiso leaves.

柚子のかぶ包み

ROLLED TURNIP WITH YUZU

YUZU NO KABU-ZUTSUMI

Preparation time: 30 minutes
Serves: 4

• 1 medium turnip (3½ oz/100 g), peeled
• ⅛ teaspoon flaky sea salt
• 1 small yuzu or Meyer lemon
• 8 stalks mitsuba (see page 346)
• Boiling water

Salted turnips with yuzu are a classic combination, but if you take the time to roll each piece of turnip around the yuzu zest and tie it with a stalk of aromatic *mitsuba* leaves, the presentation will be stunning, and each bite will be a freshly bright explosion in your mouth. You will have some odds and ends from the turnips that could be used up by finely grating and adding to miso soup if you like. Use the juice from the citrus in a salad or similar treatment.
–
Cut out 8 thin crosswise center slices from the turnip with a razor-sharp knife or Japanese mandoline (*benriner*, see page 353). In a medium bowl, massage the slices with the salt and let sit for 10 minutes.

Meanwhile, curl the *mitsuba* in a wire-mesh sieve and douse with boiling water for 10 seconds. Shake off and cool to room temperature.

Peel the zest of the yuzu with a sharp knife. Stack a few at a time and slice into fine threads.

Remove the turnip slices from the bowl, picking up one slice at a time, and lay out side by side on a cutting board. Divide the yuzu zest among the sliced turnip rounds, placing the zest in the center of each slice. Roll up carefully, wrap a piece of *mitsuba* several times around the middle portion of each one, and tie. Serve two per person as a palate-cleansing bite.

ROLLED TURNIP WITH YUZU

生野菜とレモン味噌の
ディップ

CRUDITÉS WITH LEMON MISO DIP

NAMA YASAI TO REMON MISO NO DIPPU

Preparation time: 45 minutes,
plus about 10 minutes cooling time
Cooking time: 40 minutes
Makes: Generous ¾ cup (200 ml) dip

• ½ small organic lemon (2¼ oz/60 g),
scrubbed and halved crosswise
• 2 cups (16 fl oz/500 ml)
Konbu Dashi (page 22)
• 6½ tablespoons white miso
• 2 small carrots (3½ oz/100 g),
scrubbed and halved lengthwise
• 4 small Japanese green peppers
(piman, see page 347) or red and yellow
sweet peppers (3½ oz/100 g), halved
lengthwise, cored, and seeded
• 4 medium radishes with
leaves (2¼ oz/60 g), scrubbed
and halved lengthwise
• 3 small stalks celery (2¼ oz/60 g),
cut into batonnets 3 inches (1¼ cm)
long and ½ inch (1 cm) thick

Dipping raw vegetables into
a heady miso such as brown rice
or barley is a brilliant instant dish
to serve with a cold drink before
dinner in the summer. But adding
lemon to mild white miso yields
a fresh and brightly elegant dip
that might be suitable with a flute
of champagne or a small cup of
sake. Substitute freely with any
seasonal crudités.
-
Pry the seeds out of the lemon
halves and discard. Bring a medium
saucepan three-quarters full
of water to a boil over high heat.
Drop in the lemon and simmer
briskly for 20 minutes.

Drain, add the dashi to the pan,
bring to a simmer over medium-
high heat, and simmer briskly for
20 more minutes.

Scoop out the lemon but do not
discard the simmering dashi.
Slice a bit off the ends and cut
the lemon into a rough dice. Drop
into a blender with a scant ⅔ cup
(5¼ fl oz/150 ml) of the cooking
liquid. Process until smooth.

Scrape the lemon paste into
a small bowl and, once cooled
to room temperature, stir in the
miso until well incorporated.
Arrange the vegetables artfully
on a platter or individual plates
and serve with the lemon miso.

一口冷奴の緑酢がけ

COLD TOFU WITH CUCUMBER VINEGAR

HITOKUCHI HIYAYAKKO NO MIDORIZU-GAKE

Preparation time: 10 minutes
Serves: 4

• 2 small Japanese cucumbers
(5¼ oz/150 g), unpeeled
• 4 tablespoons Konbu Dashi
(page 22)
• 2 teaspoons shoyu
• 2 teaspoons rice vinegar
• 10½ oz (300 g) silken tofu
(kinugoshi dofu, see page 352),
cut into 4 squares

Serving cold tofu in the summertime is one method for combatting
the hot, humid weather in Japan.
Here the cucumber vinegar is
an especially refreshing and tasty
dressing for the tofu, but also could
be combined with lightly roasted
sesame oil or fruity olive oil as
a dressing for summer tomatoes.
-

Finely grate the cucumber and
scrape into a small bowl. Stir
in the dashi, shoyu, and vinegar.

Place each square of cold tofu
on a small saucer and spoon
the dressing onto the center
of each. Serve as a light side dish
for a summer meal.

COLD TOFU WITH CUCUMBER VINEGAR

和え物

The heartbeat of Japanese vegetarian food are the small dishes of vegetables that are served on the side, complementing the fried or soupy dishes, while adorning the menu by contributing variety and refreshing flavor notes. And as these dishes have myriad combinations and garnishes, they allow an ideal opportunity for creativity. It is in these cold side dishes that seasonality can truly shine. While there are many variations to a traditional dish, it is important to keep in mind the essence of the dish, and the basic parameters.

For instance, *shira-ae*, a dressed dish with a tofu-based sauce starts with tofu . . . or *yuba* (the skin harvested while heating soy milk during the tofu-making process). From there, some people might add salt, shoyu, or miso— or a combination of the three. Sweeteners could be sugar or mirin. Ground sesame seeds or sesame paste are optional, as is a touch of rice vinegar. And it is possible to add yuzu peel or *hoshigaki* (dried persimmon), but ginger or dried chile are never included. Beyond that, the amount of sweet or sesame or "salt" varies greatly depending on the cook. But *shira-ae* always starts with tofu (. . . or *yuba*).

Goma-ae, a classic *aemono* treatment often used on spinach (*horenso no goma-ae*) in Japanese restaurants around the world, also has myriad variations. *Goma* is "sesame" in Japanese, so obviously all *goma-ae* dishes contain sesame. The sesame could be in the form of a paste or ground seeds but could also include some whole roasted seeds as well. *Goma-ae* dishes are most often made with blanched, refreshed vegetables as the base but can also be made from salt-massaged fresh vegetables such as cucumber. Sugar or mirin are the sweeteners, the amount of which depends on the cook. Miso is often paired with the sesame to give a creamier cloaking for the vegetables, sometimes with a pinch of salt or dribble of shoyu for balance. Shoyu can be used instead of miso and a splash of rice vinegar can provide a welcome note of acid. Slivered yuzu or ginger, ginger juice, or shiso chiffonade might be used as aromatics. However, in general, it's best not to go too far off track when starting out. Perhaps sticking within the boundaries of the recipes presented in this book would be the way to gain understanding before experimenting or exploring.

和え物

AEMONO

DRESSED

和え物

バター筍木の芽味噌和え

BUTTERED BAMBOO SHOOT WITH SANSHO LEAF MISO

BATA– TAKENOKO KINOME MISO-AE

Preparation time: 15 minutes
Cooking time: 5 minutes
Serves: 4

- 7 oz (200 g) Boiled Bamboo Shoot (page 34)
- 2 tablespoons (1 oz/30 g) unsalted butter
- ½ teaspoon shoyu
- 1 handful (3 g) sansho leaves
- 2 tablespoons white miso
- 1 tablespoon sake
- 1 tablespoon hon mirin
- 1 sprig sansho leaves, for serving

Sansho leaves are harbingers of spring and lose their delicate flavor if ground too soon, so be sure to do this step just before cooking the bamboo shoot. The richness of the butter and the generous amount of aromatic *sansho* leaves makes this an exceptionally exquisite dish.
-
Cut the bamboo shoot into ½-inch (1 cm) quartered rounds or wedges (depending on the shape of the bamboo).

Heat a medium frying pan over medium-high heat. Add the butter and once melted, slide in the bamboo shoot. Sprinkle in the shoyu for a little color and aroma and stir-fry gently until the bamboo pieces are fragrant and warmed to their centers, 2–3 minutes.

In a medium grinding bowl (*suribachi*, see page 354) or mini-prep processor, grind the *sansho* leaves until broken down. Mix in the white miso, sake, and mirin until well emulsified. Toss the slightly cooled bamboo into the *suribachi* (or a medium bowl) with the *sansho* miso and toss until evenly coated. Mound into four small dishes or a pretty serving bowl, garnish with the *sansho* sprig, and serve immediately.

筍木の芽和え

BAMBOO SMOTHERED IN SANSHO LEAVES

TAKENOKO KINOME-AE

Preparation time: 30 minutes
Cooking time: 10 minutes
Serves: 4

- 4½ oz (125 g) Boiled Bamboo Shoot (page 34)
- 1¼ cups (10 fl oz/300 ml) Happo Dashi (page 25)
- 2¼ oz (60 g) udo (see page 346)
- 1 tablespoon rice vinegar
- ⅓ oz (10 g) sansho leaves
- 3 oz (80 g) Taki Miso (page 29)

Sansho leaves have a compelling almost menthol-like flavor that marries particularly well with bamboo shoot. Most often used in moderation as a garnish, here the leaves are smashed to a paste and envelop the mild bamboo as an intriguing foil. If you are unable to source *udo*, omit.
-
Quarter the bamboo shoot lengthwise and cut crosswise into ¼-inch (5 mm) thin quarter-moons (*ichogiri*, see page 17). Slide into a small saucepan with the *happo dashi* and bring to a simmer over medium-high heat. Adjust to a low simmer and cook for 10 minutes. Remove from the heat and allow the bamboo to cool in the dashi.

Peel the *udo* and cut into ½-inch (1 cm) irregular rounded-triangular pieces (*rangiri*, see page 17). Drop into a small bowl, fill with ½ cup (4 fl oz/125 ml) cold water to cover, and add the rice vinegar.

Smash the *sansho* leaves in a Japanese grinding bowl (*suribachi*, see page 354) until completely broken down. Mash in the *taki miso*, little by little, to make a smooth homogenous paste. Drain the *udo*, pat dry, and fold into the *sansho* miso. Scoop the bamboo out of the dashi with a slotted spoon or wire skimmer. Shake off and slide into the *sansho* miso with the *udo*. Gently fold in with a rubber spatula, sprinkling in a splash of the bamboo cooking liquid if the *sansho* miso is too thick. Mound into four small bowls and serve as a bright accompaniment to a Japanese meal.

BUTTERED BAMBOO SHOOT WITH SANSHO LEAF MISO

そら豆白和え

FAVA SHIRA-AE

SORA-MAME SHIRA-AE

Preparation time: 30 minutes,
plus overnight pressing
Cooking time: 2 minutes
Serves: 4

• 7 oz (200 g) cotton tofu
(momendofu, see page 352) or
Japanese-style soft block tofu
• 2 teaspoons organic sugar
• 1 teaspoon usukuchi shoyu
(see page 344)
• ¼ teaspoon flaky sea salt
• ½ teaspoon Japanese white
sesame paste
• 7 oz (200 g) shelled fava (broad) beans
• 1 tablespoon fine sea salt

Smashed tofu treatments (shira-ae) lend lusciousness to delicate vegetables or creaminess to bitter ones. Here the shira-ae is intentionally understated to allow the favas (broad beans) to be the focal point.
-
Set the tofu in a small rectangular pan and place a salad plate on top. Store in the fridge overnight to slowly press out excess water.

Remove from the refrigerator and smash with the sugar, usukuchi shoyu, flaky salt, and sesame paste in a Japanese grinding bowl (suribachi, see page 354)

until fluffy. Set aside to take a bit of the overnight chill off.

Carefully pinch off the dark portion at the inner side dimple of each fava bean (broad bean). In a medium saucepan, bring 2½ cups (600 ml) water and the fine salt to a boil. Drop in the favas and cook for 2 minutes. Drain and cool to room temperature.

Remove and discard the thin skins without breaking the favas apart and fold the beans into the tofu mixture. Mound in four small bowls and serve.

ほうれん草白和

SPINACH SHIRA-AE

HOURENSOU SHIRA-AE

Preparation time: 30 minutes, plus
at least 3 hours tofu weighting time
Cooking time: 1 minute
Serves: 4, generously

• 10½ oz (300 g) cotton tofu
(momendofu, see page 352) or
Japanese-style soft block tofu
• 1 bunch (7 oz/200 g) spinach,
preferably with bottoms intact
• ½ dried persimmon
(hoshigaki, see page 350) or
3 unsulfured dried apricots
• 2 tablespoons Japanese white
sesame paste
• ½ tablespoon hon mirin
• 1 tablespoon shoyu
• ¼ teaspoon flaky sea salt

The creamy smashed tofu and rich sesame paste balance with the slightly bitter spinach. In Japan the pinky-white roots are also used, thus adding crunch.
-
Set the tofu on a plate and place a cutting board on top for 3 hours in a cool place (or overnight in the refrigerator) to extract moisture.

Soak the spinach in a large bowl of cold water in the sink. Swish gently to remove dirt, grasp handfuls out and drain in a colander. Refill the bowl with clean water and swish again. Allow the dirt to settle and drain the spinach as before. Align the spinach by the connected bottoms.

Bring a large pot of water to a boil over high heat. Grasp the spinach by the tops and dunk the ends into the boiling water for a count of 45 seconds. Let go and push the spinach into the boiling water to submerge completely. Scoop out with a wire-mesh sieve into

the colander (set over the rinsing bowl). Refresh with cold running water to cool. Drain and squeeze by handfuls. Align on the cutting board and finely chop the pinky-white ends. Cut the stems and leaves into 1¼-inch (3 cm) lengths and squeeze all the spinach by handfuls again.

Slice off the calyx, remove the seeds, and halve the dried persimmon crosswise. Finely julienne. (If using dried apricots, julienne as is.) Scissor the spinach and persimmon together in a bowl with your fingers to separate the dried fruit slivers.

Squeeze the tofu by handfuls and drop into a Japanese grinding bowl (suribachi, see page 354). Smash until completely smooth. Mash in the sesame paste, mirin, shoyu, and salt until well incorporated. Fold in the spinach and persimmon and mound in a serving bowl.

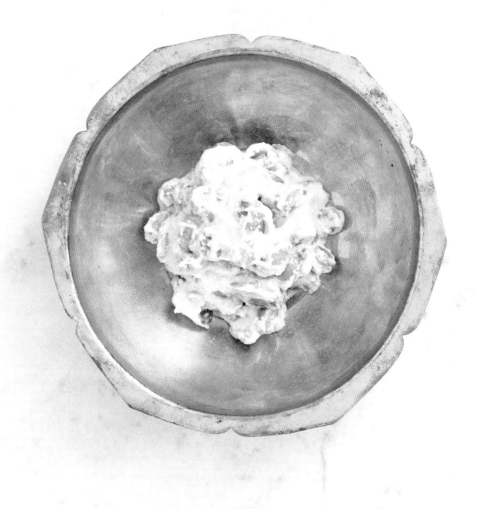

FAVA SHIRA-AE

えんどう豆の葛とじ

SILKY GREEN PEAS WITH SANSHO

ENDOU-MAME NO KUZUTOJI

Preparation time: 20 minutes,
plus cooling time
Cooking time: 10 minutes
Serves: 4

• 14 oz (400 g) unshelled fresh
green peas (or 6 oz/170 g, if shelled)
• ¼ teaspoon flaky sea salt
• A large pinch organic
granulated sugar
• Generous ¾ cup (6¾ fl oz/200 ml)
Happo Dashi (page 25)
• 1 tablespoon hon kuzu
(see page 352) mixed with
3 tablespoons water until smooth
• ¾ teaspoon finely chopped
sansho leaves

Green peas are so delicate they deserve equally understated treatment to allow them to stand on their own. *Kuzu* is the most prized starch in Japan and is reserved for elegant dishes that rely on *kuzu*'s naturally silky viscosity. Serve as a light refresher before or during a meal.

–

Shell the peas.

Bring a small saucepan three-quarters full of water to a boil with the salt and sugar. Drop in the peas and boil for 2–3 minutes, depending on size. Drain in a wire-mesh sieve.

Add the *happo dashi* to the empty saucepan with the peas. Bring to a boil over high heat and remove the pan from the heat. Allow to cool to room temperature in the cooking liquid to absorb flavor.

Scoop the peas out and set aside. Reserve the cooking liquid. Stir the *hon kuzu* slurry into the reserved pan of liquid and bring to a simmer over medium heat. Cook at a gentle simmer, stirring continuously until the liquid is clear and starting to thicken, 1–2 minutes.

Stir in the peas and continue gently cooking and stirring continuously until thickened and glossy, about 3 minutes longer. Fold in ½ teaspoon of the *sansho* leaves and spoon the peas with the silky sauce into four small saucers. Pinch the remaining *sansho* leaves over the peas and serve as an exquisite first course in the spring. Best warm but also good chilled.

SILKY GREEN PEAS WITH SANSHO

菜の花の筍ソースがけ

FLOWERING BLOSSOMS WITH BAMBOO SHOOT SAUCE

NANOHANA NO TAKENOKO SO-SU GAKE

Preparation time: 30 minutes
Cooking time: 20 minutes
Serves: 4

- 7 oz (200 g) Boiled Bamboo Shoot (page 34)
- 2 quarts (2 liters) Konbu Dashi (page 22)
- 1 teaspoon flaky sea salt
- 2 teaspoons hon mirin
- 1 bunch (5¼ oz/150 g) flowering brassica greens (nanohana, see page 347) or broccoli rabe (rapini), tough ends cut off

Serving flowering brassica greens (*nanohana*) dressed with a subtly sweet and creamy bamboo sauce tames and complements their natural bitter profile. The contrast between the slightly salty sauce and completely unsalted *nanohana* is intentional.
-
Place the bamboo shoot in a medium pot with the dashi and bring to a simmer over medium-high heat. Cook at a brisk simmer for 20 minutes. Scoop out the bamboo but leave the dashi.

When cool enough to handle, dice the bamboo shoot and drop into a blender with a generous ¾ cup (6¾ fl oz/200 ml) of the cooking liquid, the salt, and the mirin. Blend until smooth.

Bring a medium pot of water to a boil over high heat. Drop in the flowering greens and boil for 20 seconds. Scoop out with a fine-mesh sieve, shake off excess water, and roll in a clean tea towel to blot dry.

Align the greens on a cutting board and cut crosswise into 1¼–1½ inch (3–4 cm) pieces. Stack in cascading mounds on four saucer-like plates, spoon the bamboo sauce over, and serve as part of a spring collation.

~~~~~~

菜の花のからし和え

NANOHANA WITH MUSTARD DRESSING

NANOHANA NO KARASHI-AE

Preparation time: 30 minutes
Cooking time: 5 minutes
Serves: 4

- 1 small bunch (5¼ oz/150 g) flowering brassica greens (nanohana, see page 347) or broccoli rabe (rapini), tough ends cut off
- 2 teaspoons fine sea salt
- 1¼ cups (10 fl oz/300 ml) Happo Dashi (page 25)
- 4 teaspoons usukuchi shoyu (see page 344)
- 1 deep-fried tofu pouch (usuage, see page 352)
- 2 teaspoons shoyu
- 1 tablespoon yellow mustard powder (karashi, see page 350) mixed with 1 tablespoon hot water

Flowering brassica greens (*nanohana*) are appealingly bitter and thus pair well with creamy or rich treatments. But a spicy mustard dressing can also enliven the greens and make a bold addition to the table.
-
Cut the greens crosswise into 1½-inch (4 cm) pieces. Set up a large bowl of ice and water. Bring a medium pot of water to a boil over high heat with the salt and drop in the greens. Boil until the stems are just softened, 2–3 minutes, depending on thickness. Scoop out with a wire-mesh sieve and plunge immediately into the ice bath. Once cold to the touch, pull out of the ice water, shake off, and pat dry in a clean tea towel.

Drop the greens into a bowl and toss with the dashi to distribute well. Toss with 2 teaspoons of the *usukuchi shoyu* and set aside.

Heat a medium frying pan or grill pan over high heat and, once hot, sear both sides of the *usuage* until light brown spots appear, 1–2 minutes per side. Halve lengthwise, then cut crosswise into ¼-inch (5 mm) strips.

Drain the greens in a wire-mesh sieve and discard the soaking liquid. Squeeze by handfuls and drop into a medium bowl.

In a small bowl, slowly mix the remaining 2 teaspoons *usukuchi shoyu*, the shoyu, and mustard powder into a paste. Scrape into the bowl of greens and toss well to distribute evenly. Fold in the *usuage* and serve immediately, mounded into four small bowls.

NANOHANA WITH MUSTARD DRESSING

なすのわさび和え

EGGPLANT WITH WASABI

NASU NO WASABI-AE

Preparation time: 25 minutes
Serves: 4

- ¼ teaspoon flaky sea salt
- 2 medium Japanese eggplants (aubergines), 5¼ oz (150 g), sliced crosswise into fine rounds
- 1 large myoga (1 oz/25 g), halved lengthwise
- 2 green shiso leaves, cut into fine threads
- 1 teaspoon white sesame seeds, warmed in a dry frying pan until fragrant
- 1 teaspoon grated fresh wasabi
- Shoyu, for serving

Salt-massaging is a method used in Japanese cuisine to "cook" vegetables without heat. While not typically eaten raw, salt-massaged eggplant (aubergine) has an appealingly spongy consistency that is especially welcome in the summer. Here the bright piquancy of the shiso and wasabi balance well against the flavorful *myoga* and sesame.
-
In a medium bowl, massage the salt gently into the eggplant (aubergine). Let sit for 10 minutes. Gather the eggplant into your hands (leaving behind any salt crystals), enclose in paper towels, and squeeze to express excess moisture. Wipe out the bowl and return the eggplant to the bowl.

Place the *myoga* on a cutting board, cut side down, and slice finely lengthwise. Separate the threads with your fingers and add to the bowl of eggplant with the shiso. Toss well.

Mound attractively into four individual small bowls. Sprinkle with the sesame seeds and dab with a little wasabi. Drizzle with a few drops of shoyu, and serve as a refreshing bite with sake. Best freshly prepared.

EGGPLANT WITH WASABI

梅ときゅうりのあえ物

CUCUMBER WITH UME AND SHISO

UME TO KYUURI NO AEMONO

Preparation time: 30 minutes
Serves: 4

• 4 small Japanese cucumbers
(10½ oz/300 g), unpeeled
• 2¼ × 3¼-inch (6 × 8 cm)
piece soaked konbu left over from
making unheated konbu dashi
• 2 salted sour "plums"
(umeboshi, see page 350)
• 4 green shiso leaves, cut into
fine threads

If you want to take this bright summer dressed dish to another level, include the inner nut (tenjinsan, 天神さん) of the umeboshi to add texture and an almond-like note to the salad.
-
Finely julienne the cucumbers into thin threads 1½ inches (4 cm) long. Finely julienne the konbu from the short side.

Pit (destone) the umeboshi by scraping away the flesh with the back of a knife. If using the tenjinsan, rap the umeboshi pit to break open and pry out the inner nut. Finely chop the inner nut. Finely chop the flesh of the umeboshi to a smooth paste.

In a bowl, toss together the cucumber, konbu, umeboshi, and tenjinsan (if using) until the ingredients are evenly distributed. Fold in the shiso and serve as a light summer salad. Best soon after being tossed since the salty umeboshi will cause the cucumber to weep.

キャベツサラダ

CABBAGE SALAD

KYABETSU SARADA

Preparation time: 20 minutes
Serves: 4

• ¼ head cabbage (9 oz/250 g), cored
• ¾ teaspoon flaky sea salt
• 1 tablespoon freshly squeezed
sudachi, yuzu, or Meyer lemon juice
• 1 tablespoon lightly roasted
gold sesame oil
• ½ teaspoon 7-spice powder
(shichimi togarashi, see page 350)

Spring cabbage is sweet and tender and pairs well with a lively citrus-based dressing. Sudachi is a small round Japanese citrus that yields a lovely tart and fragrant juice, but yuzu or Meyer lemon can be substituted. If prepared with olive oil instead of sesame oil, this salad integrates well into Western menus. And if you cannot source lightly roasted gold sesame oil, substitute unroasted and dark roasted sesame oil in a ratio of 1:1.
-
Finely shred the cabbage with a razor-sharp knife and slide into a medium bowl. Sprinkle with ¼ teaspoon of the salt and massage in gently. Leave for 10 minutes.

Scoop out with your fingers, leaving any lingering salt particles at the bottom of the bowl, and spread across a large piece of paper towel. Blot dry.

Rinse and dry the bowl. Drop the cabbage back into the bowl and toss with the citrus juice, oil, remaining ½ teaspoon salt, and ¼ teaspoon of the shichimi togarashi. Serve in a pretty bowl or on small plates, sprinkled with the remaining ¼ teaspoon shichimi togarashi.

CUCUMBER WITH UME AND SHISO

TOFU-STUFFED TOMATOES

トマトの豆腐詰め

TOMATO NO TOUFU-ZUME

Preparation time: 1 hour,
plus 15 minutes chilling time
Serves: 4

- 4 small tomatoes (2¾ oz/80 g each)
- 3 teaspoons olive oil
- 1 teaspoon flaky sea salt
- ⅛ teaspoon green yuzu kosho (see page 350)
- 7 oz (200 g) thick deep-fried tofu (atsuage, see page 351) or medium tofu
- 2 tablespoons (5 g) dried daikon (kiriboshi daikon, see page 350), soaked in cold water to cover for 20 minutes
- 4 green shiso leaves, finely chopped

The *kiriboshi daikon* and *yuzu kosho* add a pleasant acidity to balance out the sweetness of the tomatoes. The textures in this dish are compelling: juicy tomato, crunchy *kiriboshi daikon*, and creamy smashed tofu. If you are unable to source *atsuage*, use medium tofu (outside of Japan). Serve as a refreshing course for lunch or dinner in the summer.

-

Core the tomatoes and slice off about ¼ inch (5 mm) of the tops. Keep the bottoms and tops as sets and slice a fine layer off the bottoms to aid in sitting flat. Place inside a rectangular container just large enough to hold them. Scoop out the insides of the tomatoes with a spoon (taking care not to pierce the bottoms or sides), chop finely, and scrape into a medium bowl, taking care not to lose the juices.

In a small bowl, stir together 2 teaspoons of the olive oil, ½ teaspoon of the salt, and the *yuzu kosho*. Fold into the chopped tomatoes.

Cut the fried skin off the *atsuage* and chop finely. Mash the white portion roughly and drop into a small bowl with the chopped skin.

Scoop the *kiriboshi daikon* out of the water, pat dry in a clean tea towel, and finely chop. Fold into the *atsuage* with the shiso.

Drizzle the remaining 1 teaspoon olive oil into the hollowed-out tomatoes and sprinkle in the remaining ½ teaspoon salt. Divide the tofu mixture among the tomatoes. Spoon the chopped tomato mixture little by little into the tomatoes on top of the tofu mixture by using a bamboo skewer to encourage even distribution into the tofu mixture. This will take about 15 minutes total to get the tomato mixture added.

Replace the tops and refrigerate for 15 minutes before serving. Serve on four small individual plates along with a fork and knife.

TOFU-STUFFED TOMATOES

柿の白和え   # PERSIMMON AND APPLE SHIRA-AE

KAKI NO SHIRA-AE

Preparation time: 30 minutes,
plus 1–2 hours tofu weighting time
Cooking time: 5 minutes
Serves: 4

• 10½ oz (300 g) cotton tofu
(momendofu, see page 352)
or Japanese-style soft block tofu
• 4 tablespoons (1 oz/30 g) white
sesame seeds
• 1 tablespoon hon mirin
• ½ teaspoon usukuchi shoyu
(see page 344)
• ½ teaspoon flaky sea salt
• 1 firm Fuyu persimmon (8¼ oz/235 g),
peeled and cored
• ½ medium sweet apple (125 g),
unpeeled, quartered, and cored
• ½ teaspoon fine sea salt
• ½ bunch (2¼ oz/60 g) edible
chrysanthemum greens (shungiku,
see page 347), hard ends cut off

Persimmon *shira-ae* is one of the first dishes that my Japanese farmer husband made for me when we were newly married. Here, the addition of apple and chrysanthemum greens is stunning. *Shira-ae* has many variations, and this version features a dominant amount of sesame, which gives a rich depth to the dish.

-

Place the tofu on a plate and place a small cutting board on top to press out excess water for 1–2 hours in a cool spot.

Heat a small dry frying pan over medium heat and add the sesame seeds. Warm until fragrant, stirring continuously and lifting the pan up regularly to avoid scorching, 1–2 minutes. Slide the sesame into a Japanese grinding bowl (*suribachi*, see page 354) and smash until mostly broken down, but still a little flaky.

Add the drained tofu, mirin, *usukuchi shoyu*, and flaky salt to the bowl and mash until fluffy. Taste for balance of sweet and saltiness: The mixture should be pleasantly sweet with a back taste of salt. Adjust if needed.

Cut the persimmon into a thick julienne and the apple quarters crosswise into thin slices (*ichogiri*, see page 17). Soak in 1 cup (8 fl oz/ 250 ml) cold water with the fine sea salt for 10 minutes.

Bring a medium pot of water to a boil. Hold the stem ends of the *shungiku* in the boiling water for 10 seconds. Let go of the greens and poke them down into the boiling water with a wooden spoon. Scoop them out immediately with a wire-mesh sieve and refresh under cold running water. Squeeze out the excess liquid and cut the greens crosswise into ½-inch (1 cm) lengths. Scissor with your fingers to separate.

Drain the persimmons and apples and pat dry in a clean tea towel. Toss in the smashed tofu mixture with the *shungiku* and serve. Best the first day but holds up to the next.

PERSIMMON AND APPLE SHIRA-AE

春菊ごま和え

CHRYSANTHEMUM GREENS GOMA-AE

SHUNGIKU GOMA-AE

Preparation time: 30 minutes
Cooking time: 1 minute
Serves: 4

• 6 tablespoons Happo Dashi (page 25) or Konbu Dashi (page 22)
• 4 teaspoons shoyu
• 1 teaspoon flaky sea salt
• 1 small bunch (4½ oz/125 g) edible chrysanthemum greens (shungiku, see page 347)
• 2 tablespoons Japanese white sesame paste
• 1½ tablespoons ground white sesame seeds
• ½ tablespoon white sesame seeds, warmed in a dry frying pan until fragrant
• 1 tablespoon hon mirin
• ¼ teaspoon rice vinegar
• 1 small lavender or yellow edible chrysanthemum flower

Chrysanthemum greens (shungiku) have a haunting bitterness that goes particularly well with sesame. Here the dressing benefits from the addition of ground sesame seeds to the sesame paste—giving it both added texture and depth of flavor.
-
In a small bowl, stir together 4 tablespoons of the dashi and 2 teaspoons of the shoyu and set aside.

Bring a medium pot of water to a boil over high heat with the salt. Add the shungiku, pushing down to submerge, and scoop out with a wire-mesh sieve. Shake off and squeeze well to express any lingering water. Spread in a rectangular pan and pour the shoyu-dashi mixture over the greens. Toss to distribute. Allow to cool to room temperature.

In a small bowl, mash the sesame paste, ground seeds, whole seeds, mirin, and rice vinegar with the remaining 2 tablespoons dashi and 2 teaspoons shoyu until smooth.

Squeeze the greens and cut into 1½-inch (4 cm) lengths. Stack on four small saucers and drizzle attractively with the sesame sauce in a cascading fashion over the center of each stack of greens. Gently remove the petals from the flower centers and strew lightly over the greens and sesame sauce to add a bit of contrasting color to the dish.

~~~~~~

柿ときゅうりの胡麻和え

PERSIMMON AND CUCUMBER GOMA-AE

KAKI TO KYUURI NO GOMA-AE

Preparation time: 45 minutes
Serves: 4

• 1 firm Fuyu persimmon (8¼ oz/235 g)
• 1 teaspoon flaky sea salt
• 2 medium Japanese cucumbers (7 oz/200 g)
• 3 tablespoons Japanese white sesame paste
• 1 teaspoon usukuchi shoyu (see page 344)
• 1 teaspoon shoyu
• 2 teaspoons hon mirin
• 2 teaspoons Happo Dashi (page 25)

If cucumbers are no longer in season in your area, you can substitute blanched green beans, though the cucumber does add a wonderful contrast in texture.
-
Cut the calyx off the persimmon, peel, and halve lengthwise. Remove the seeds and discard. Pare off any hard areas. Quarter each half lengthwise into wedges and cut the wedges crosswise into ¼-inch (5 mm) slices. Toss with ¼ teaspoon of the salt and leave for 10 minutes.

Meanwhile, cut the cucumber diagonally into ¼-inch (5 mm) slices. Massage gently with ¼ teaspoon of the salt and set aside for 10 minutes.

Remove the persimmon slices from the salt and blot dry in a tea towel. Squeeze the cucumber slices to express excess liquid and allow them to break down a little.

Mash the sesame paste, usukuchi shoyu, shoyu, and mirin together in a Japanese grinding bowl (suribachi, see page 354).

Squeeze the cucumbers once more and add to a bowl. Toss in the sesame dressing until evenly coated, then fold in the persimmon and happo dashi.

CHRYSANTHEMUM GREENS GOMA-AE

もやしの辛子和え

MUSTARD-FLAVORED BEAN SPROUTS AND DAIKON

MOYASHI TO DAIKON NO KARASHI-AE

Preparation time: 25 minutes
Serves: 4

- 2 teaspoons yellow mustard powder (karashi, see page 350)
- ¼ teaspoon flaky sea salt
- 3¼-inch (8 cm) length of thin daikon (5¼ oz/150 g), peeled and julienned
- 7 oz (200 g) mung bean sprouts (moyashi, see page 349), small beard root pinched off the ends
- A handful of daikon leaves, finely chopped
- Boiling water
- 1 teaspoon dried wakame, soaked in cold water for 10 minutes
- 1½ tablespoons shoyu

Bean sprouts have an irresistible crunchy texture but are a bit bland, so seasoning them with something piquant such as mustard powder makes sense. Prepare this in the winter or spring when daikon is in season and is sold with the leaves intact. Pinching off the small yellow "beard roots" of the sprouts is optional but will improve the overall texture of the dish.

-

In a small bowl, whisk 1 teaspoon warm water into the mustard powder to form a smooth paste. Leave it for at least 10 minutes to "mature" as you proceed with the rest of the dish.

In a medium bowl, lightly massage the salt into the daikon and leave for 10 minutes. Squeeze gently, leaving any salt crystals in the bottom of the bowl and drop into a clean serving bowl.

Place the bean sprouts and daikon leaves in a wire-mesh sieve and pour boiling water over for 10 seconds. Shake off and blot dry in a clean tea towel. Drain the wakame.

Add the bean sprouts, daikon leaves, and wakame to the bowl with the daikon. Stir the shoyu into the mustard paste and pour over the ingredients in the bowl. Toss and serve immediately.

きゅうりの精進 スパゲッティー

SPAGHETTI WITH CUCUMBER, OLIVES, AND CAPERS

KYUURI NO SHOUJIN SUPAGETTI-

Preparation time: 30 minutes
Cooking time: 15 minutes
Serves: 4

- 4 tablespoons fine sea salt (2% by volume or weight of the water amount)
- 4 medium Japanese cucumbers (14 oz/400 g)
- 3 tablespoons olive oil
- 1 tablespoon finely chopped fresh ginger
- 2 dried red japones chiles, cut crosswise into fine rings
- 12 oz (350 g) spaghetti, broken in half
- 16 small Japanese or French green olives such as Picholine, pitted and roughly chopped
- 1 tablespoon salt-packed capers, soaked, drained, and roughly chopped

This slightly salty, slightly oily spaghetti dish combines classic Italian ingredients with Japanese, coming together into a deliciously enticing dish for a light summer meal.

-

In a large pot, bring 4 quarts (4 liters) of water to a boil with the salt. Cut the cucumber into a ¼-inch (5 mm) dice.

In a large frying pan, warm the olive oil over low heat. Scrape in the ginger and chiles and stir until fragrant, about 1 minute.

Drop the spaghetti into the salted boiling water, stir well, and cover. After 30 seconds, uncover and stir to make sure the noodles are not sticking together. Cover again and stir again after

30 seconds more have elapsed. Once the water comes back to a boil, you can remove the lid. Cook for 2 minutes less than the package directions.

While the pasta is cooking, add the cucumber, olives, capers, and a generous ¾ cup (6¾ fl oz/200 ml) of the pasta water to the frying pan and bring to a simmer. Measure out another generous ¾ cup (6¾ fl oz/200 ml) of pasta water and set aside.

Once the spaghetti has cooked for 2 minutes less than required on the package, drain and slide into the frying pan. Toss over high heat with the reserved pasta water for 2 minutes to finish cooking. Serve hot or at room temperature.

MUSTARD-FLAVORED BEAN SPROUTS AND DAIKON

トマト生姜ソース
スパゲッティー

TOMATO-GINGER SAUCE SPAGHETTI

TOMATO SHOUGA SO-SU SUPAGETTI-

Preparation time: 30 minutes
Cooking time: 25 minutes
Serves: 4

- 2 tablespoons fine sea salt
- 2 medium tomatoes
  (14 oz/400 g)
- 3 tablespoons olive oil
- 2 tablespoons finely diced young ginger (shin shoga, see page 348)
- ½ dried red japones chile, cut into fine rings
- 1 medium stalk celery
  (2½ oz/75 g), finely diced
- 2-inch (5 cm) square piece konbu, left over from making konbu dashi, finely diced
- 1 teaspoon flaky sea salt
- 12 oz (350 g) spaghetti, broken in half
- 2 teaspoons black sesame seeds, warmed in a dry frying pan until fragrant

Japanese-style spaghetti has almost as many fans abroad as it does in Japan. Here the tomato sauce includes young ginger, thus giving it an unusual twist, and the black sesame seeds contrast stunningly against the light red sauce. If you do not have konbu leftover from making dashi, then just soften a small piece of konbu or omit.

-

Fill a large pot three-quarters with water, add the fine salt, and bring to a boil over high heat

Boil a kettle of water. Place the tomatoes in a heatproof bowl and pour the boiling water over to cover. Leave for about 10 minutes. Drain and wipe out the bowl. Working over the bowl, core and peel the tomatoes. Cut into ½-inch (1 cm) pieces and scrape into the bowl with any juices.

In a medium saucepan, heat 1 tablespoon of oil over medium-high heat. Add the tomatoes and juices, bring to an almost boil, adjust to an active simmer, and

cook until the tomatoes have broken down a bit and the sauce is glossy, about 5 minutes.

In a large frying pan, heat the remaining 2 tablespoons oil over low heat. Add the ginger and chile and stir until fragrant, about 1 minute. Stir in the tomato sauce, celery, konbu, and flaky salt and cook over medium heat until the celery has softened and the sauce has thickened, about 5 minutes.

Add the spaghetti to the boiling pot of water and cook to al dente according to the package directions. Drain.

While the spaghetti is cooking, add a soup ladleful of the boiling pasta water to the tomato sauce. Continue simmering for 3 more minutes over medium heat to reduce slightly.

Slide in the spaghetti and toss for about 1 more minute over high heat. Swirl into attractive mounds on four medium plates and sprinkle with the sesame seeds.

~~~~~~

おろし納豆

NATTO WITH GRATED DAIKON

OROSHI NATTOU

Preparation time: 20 minutes
Cooking time: 1–2 minutes
Serves: 4

- 2 tablespoons Konbu Dashi (page 22)
- 2 teaspoons sake
- 2 teaspoons hon mirin
- 1 teaspoon usukuchi shoyu (see page 344)
- 2 packs (3 oz/85 g each) small-bean natto, unaerated (page 351)
- 3½ oz (100 g) finely grated daikon

Natto has diehard fans, but some people cannot get around the thick whipped-up threads surrounding the beans. Here, the natto is not aerated, and the spicy wetness of grated daikon helps mitigate natto's funkiness, thus rendering it much more widely appealing. Try to source natto made locally rather than in Japan, since imported natto has been frozen for shipping so loses some of its unusual delicacy.

-

In a small saucepan, bring the konbu dashi, sake, and mirin to a simmer over medium heat. Stir in the *usukuchi shoyu* and pour into a small glass measuring cup to cool for about 10 minutes.

Divide the natto among four miso soup bowls and spoon the grated daikon over one half of the natto in each bowl. Add the cooled dashi and serve as a tasty, healthy bite to start the day.

NATTO WITH GRATED DAIKON

NATTO

Often compared to funky washed cheeses or stinky socks, natto has a bad rep in the smell department, but is packed with probiotics and protein, thus a perfect breakfast food to get you started on your day. Natto aficionados (including me) would take exception to the maligning descriptions of natto's aroma, or its sticky characteristic once whipped up to a wonderful slimy mass. We embrace the fermented nose on natto and are addicted to the nutty, yet sharply complex flavors that jump around in our mouths. However, the feat of guiding a tenuous clump of these lovely fermented beans clinging to a pair of chopsticks from our bowls to our mouths can be daunting for the uninitiated, especially since the gossamer natto "threads" created seem to take on a life of their own.

Also, freshly fermented organic small-batch natto has a completely different profile from your run-of-the-mill mass-produced natto from large food companies. A couple of decades ago, we could still procure organic green, brown, and black natto at a local upscale supermarket. No longer. Yamaki Jozo, an organic soy sauce, miso, tofu, and pickle company in our town was our main source of organic natto for many years but their natto-maker retired a few years ago. It took about two years to develop a relationship with another local maker to produce the high standard necessary for the Yamaki organic proprietary natto. During those two years we didn't eat natto.

Shimonita is a town in Gunma prefecture, nearby where we live, well known for three things: natto, *negi* (Japanese "leeks"), and *konnyaku* (devil's tongue). My nephew, who is interested in fermentation, came to Japan for a visit, so I thought a trip to see how natto was made would be fitting. We had introduced him to natto on a previous visit many

years earlier and, as a vegetarian, protein-rich natto became one of his staple foods.

Shimonita Natto, Yamaki Jozo's new supplier, is located off the Shimonita exit of the Joetsu Expressway. By good fortune, the morning we visited was the first day of work for Miyu Arai, and the ebullient owner Takamichi Nanto enthusiastically walked the three of us newbies through the process of making natto. It was clear he loved his métier and that he was a natural-born teacher. According to Nanto, "*Washoku* (Japanese cuisine) is the food culture of eating soybeans with rice," and there is a long history of growing soybeans around the edges of the rice fields because the crops are symbiotic.

Donning paper masks, coats, and hairnets, we trooped into the anaerobic production rooms. At Shimonita Natto, 463 pounds (210 kg) of soybeans are steamed and fermented each day and all steps in the production process are done by hand. In the main room, a half-dozen workers, suited head to toe in white hooded coveralls, moved in synchronization as they scooped the fermented beans into pine paper (*kyogi*), folded into cone-like shapes that would be next folded into triangular-shaped packages after weighing. Getting the natto folded in the *kyogi*, packed in cellophane wrappers, and stored in the walk-in refrigerator as swiftly as possible is a main priority. Once in a cool environment, the fermented beans will become dormant, thus slowing (though never fully halting) fermentation to increase shelf life.

Each day, eight varieties of soybeans are first soaked overnight, then steamed at 212°F (100°C) for 90 minutes until soft, before being inoculated with natto spores. The beans are spread out on wooden trays and left to ferment in the fermenting room (*muro*) for 23 hours at 106°F (41°C), thus encouraging

the prized *neba-neba* (sticky) texture that characterizes natto. Workers take turns sleeping at the factory to check on the delicate baby natto beans throughout the night, ensuring that the temperature stays constant for optimal growth of the spores.

The last step of our tour was a presentation performed by Nanto's wife. She held up placards and entertained us with the story of Mametan. Another born teacher like her husband, the storyboards were created for educating local children about the wonder of natto. As a teacher and cook for Japanese children myself, I incorporate natto into any number of dishes: a particular favorite is fried rice strewn with natto and a squiggle of mayonnaise (we like organic Matsuda Mayonnaise). The classic way to eat natto is whipped up to a creamy mass with seasonings such as Japanese mustard and soy sauce and maybe some chopped scallion (spring onion), spooned over a small bowl of rice. But it is also a perfect vehicle in which to drop freshly pounded gooey *mochi* (pounded glutinous rice) at the New Year. A light scattering of nonagitated natto beans enlivens and enhances a vegetarian pizza before serving, and natto can also be blended into mayonnaise for a rich, yet complex dressing for salads. When first trying natto, it's best to start with a measured amount, eaten in a familiar way (such as on a pizza), using the freshest small-batch natto available.

Always concerned with traditions being carried into the future, at the end of our tour I asked Nanto if he had someone to take over. His eyes lit up and he told me he has a son working with him, but then laughed and turned to his new worker and said, "But maybe it will be Arai! Whoever loves natto will be the next president!"

アスパラガスとブロッコリー のナムル

ASPARAGUS AND BROCCOLI NAMUL

ASUPARAGASU TO BUROKKORI- NO NAMURU

Preparation time: 20 minutes
Cooking time: 10 minutes
Serves: 4

• 6 medium spears asparagus
(7 oz/200 g), bottom thirds peeled
(or broken off if tough)
• 1 medium head broccoli
(14 oz/400 g)
• 1 tablespoon fine sea salt
• 4 teaspoons hon mirin
• 1 teaspoon flaky sea salt
• 1 teaspoon organic granulated sugar
• 2 tablespoons dark roasted
sesame oil
• 1 tablespoon white sesame seeds

Namul is a Korean dish in which blanched vegetables or greens are dressed with a salt- or shoyu-based sesame oil dressing. Here, the added step of pan-roasting brings out depth of flavor. Korean preparations such as kimchi and *namul* have reached into mainstream Japanese cooking and integrate well with a Japanese menu. The broccoli stems can be used for Miso-Pickled Broccoli Stems (page 320) or Creamy Broccoli Stem Soup (page 250).
-
Cut the asparagus crosswise into 1½-inch (4 cm) pieces and the broccoli into small bite-size florets (7 oz/200 g). Save the stems for another recipe.

Bring a small pot three-quarters full of water to a boil. Add the broccoli and fine salt and cook for 1 minute. Scoop out with a wire-mesh sieve, shake off, and pat dry in a clean tea towel.

In a small saucepan, bring the mirin to a boil over high heat. Remove from the heat immediately and pour into a small bowl. Immediately stir in the flaky salt and sugar to dissolve the crystals while the mirin is still hot. Add the sesame oil and sesame seeds, and stir well to emulsify.

Heat a large frying pan over medium-high heat. Slide in the asparagus and broccoli and pan-roast, stirring, to soften and char slightly, until fragrant, 3–5 minutes. Toss together with the dressing in a medium bowl and serve warm or at room temperature.

アスパラガズの白和え

ASPARAGUS SHIRA-AE

ASUPARAGASU NO SHIRA-AE

Preparation time: 15 minutes,
plus 2 hours tofu weighting time
Cooking time: 5 minutes
Serves: 4

• 10½ oz (300 g) cotton tofu
(momendofu, see page 352)
or Japanese-style soft block tofu
• 1 large dried shiitake, soaked
in boiling water for 30 minutes
• 2 teaspoons fine sea salt
• 8 medium spears asparagus
(10½ oz/300 g), bottom third peeled
(or broken off if tough)
• 1 tablespoon white sesame seeds
• 1 tablespoon Soybean Dashi (page 23)
or Konbu Dashi (page 22)
• 1 tablespoon usukuchi shoyu
(see page 344)
• 2 teaspoons hon mirin
• 1 teaspoon flaky sea salt

Smashed tofu dishes vary in sweetness and seasoning balance: miso vs salt or shoyu, sugar vs mirin, and added sesame or not. But the result is always the same: luscious, creamy tofu enveloping lightly blanched vegetables. The elegance of this style of dish is unmistakable, yet there is an inherent humbleness of the preparation because tofu is such a basic ingredient in Japan.
-
Place the tofu in a rectangular pan to catch the drips and set a small cutting board on top for 2 hours to press out water. Keep in a cool place or the fridge.

Drain the shiitake and discard the soaking liquid. Discard the stem and finely sliver the cap.

Bring a pot of water to a boil over high heat with the fine salt and drop in the asparagus. Blanch for 30 seconds. Scoop out, shake off, and pat dry in a clean tea towel. Cut crosswise, at a diagonal, into 1¼-inch (3 cm) lengths.

Heat a small frying pan over medium-low heat and add the sesame seeds. Shake the pan to control the heat, warming the sesame for a several seconds until fragrant. Slide into a Japanese grinding bowl (*suribachi*; see page 354) or mortar and smash to a powder. Add the pressed tofu and mash to a creamy consistency. Smash in the dashi, *usukuchi shoyu*, mirin, and flaky salt. Fold in the shiitake and mound into four small bowls.

Japanese vinegared dishes are not like Western vinegar-based pickles. They are meant to be consumed within a day or two and have prescribed ratios of vinegar to sweetener. Sugar and nonfermented syrup-like mirin swept Japan post World War II, but slowly there seems to be a shift back toward using artisanal *hon mirin* in the Japanese kitchen. I am partial to Mikawa Mirin, available abroad rebottled under various labels (such as Mitoku—Natural Imports, see page 355). Since *hon mirin* (see page 346) appears in many guises (in Japan and abroad), look to a reputable organic bottled seasoning line instead of the Asian grocery store for a good-quality mirin.

If authentically made mirin is not within your reach (though to avoid running around town, the Internet can be your best friend for sourcing), then I would use a good-tasting organic granulated sugar as a substitute. I would not recommend the more popular mirin varieties that pop up on searches that are made from glucose syrup, water, alcohol, rice, corn syrup, and salt (in that order). When evaluating products, it is very important to read the details carefully. Although the description of such products may say they are made from sake and other select ingredients, this can be deceiving. Traditional mirin is not made from sake per se, it is fermented from short-grain

Japanese rice and glutinous rice and sometimes combined with fermented and distilled rice *shochu*, before being aged for several months to over a year. Also, sake is not "rice wine" nor mirin "sweet rice wine" because the fermentation process to produce these alcohols bears no resemblance to vinification.

Anecdotal evidence shows that most American kitchen pantries have a bottle of rice vinegar that often is nothing akin to authentic, traditionally brewed rice vinegars (see page 345), such as the all-organic Fujisu vinegars, produced by Iio Jozo in the deep countryside a few hours outside of Kyoto, or the Oochi line of organic vinegars produced by Sennari in the hills above Hiroshima, or the 100 percent organic Ohyama vinegars produced in the Miyazaki countryside. Sake is carefully brewed in-house from organic rice and then slowly fermented into rice vinegar. The result is a well-balanced, beautifully round, flavorful line of vinegars that will serve all your vinegar needs, both Japanese and Western. Iio Jozo, Sennari, and Ohyama vinegars are available outside of Japan. Look in the organic section of your market for a reputable organic bottled seasoning line.

Pure rice vinegar (*junmai su*, see page 345) should be fermented from white rice sake and is the standard vinegar used in this book.

(Other versions contain little rice and are fermented from ethyl alcohol, not sake.)

Feel free to substitute an excellent black vinegar, also called brown rice vinegar (*kurosu*, see page 345). *Kurosu* is most commonly made by fermenting brown rice and brown rice koji in black earthenware pots, but it can also be made by fermenting brown rice sake. Iio Jozo, Sennari, and Ohyama all make top-quality *kurosu*, but if you are looking for an amazing aged *kurosu*, Kakuida is the pioneer in this genre. In the United States, their five-year-aged black vinegar is available through The Japanese Pantry (see Resources, page 355), and Nihon Ichiban (page 355) offers quite a few Kakuida vinegars as well.

Japanese vinegar treatments (*sunomono*) use the ratio of 2:1 or 1:1 for rice vinegar to mirin (or sugar), plus a slight bit of salt (either in the solution or as a ten-minute presalt step).

If you are unable to source top-shelf mirin and rice vinegar, you should probably heat them briefly, to burn off alcohol and soften the acid in the vinegar. Bring to a quick boil and immediately remove from the heat. The heating will also help dissolve the salt. But be sure to cool before using. The heating step is not always included in the recipes in this book because I use Mikawa Mirin and Iio Jozo vinegars.

酢の物

SUNOMONO

VINEGARED

酢の物

春キャベツ胡麻酢和え

SPRING CABBAGE WITH SESAME VINEGAR

HARU KYABETSU GOMASU-AE

Preparation time: 25 minutes
Cooking time: 8 minutes
Serves: 4

• 3 dried shiitake, soaked in cold water to cover for 1 hour
• 5 tablespoons hon mirin
• 4 tablespoons shoyu
• 4 large cabbage leaves (9 oz/250 g)
• Flaky sea salt
• ½ medium carrot (2⅔ oz/75 g)
• 1 usuage (see page 352)
• 3 tablespoons white sesame seeds, warmed in a dry frying pan until fragrant
• 4 tablespoons rice vinegar
• 1 sheet nori, snipped into fine threads

This vibrant dish is colorful and healthful since cabbage contains essential vitamins such as C to ward off colds, K for enhancing bones and blood, and the so-called vitamin U (a derivative of the amino acid methionine) for improving the gastric tract. The sweetness of the cabbage also juxtaposes well against the tart vinegar dressing.

-

Reserving the soaking liquid, pluck the shiitake out of the water. Slice the shiitake into fine slivers and add to a small saucepan with the soaking liquid and 3 tablespoons each of the mirin and shoyu. Bring to a simmer and gently cook over low heat for 5 minutes. Cool in the cooking liquid.

Slice the cabbage into fine shreds, drop into a bowl, and massage in ¼ teaspoon flaky sea salt. Leave for 10 minutes. Cut the carrot into fine threads 1¼ inches (3 cm) long and massage with a pinch of flaky sea salt in a small bowl. Leave for 10 minutes.

Squeeze the cabbage by handfuls (leaving any lingering salt crystals behind) and drop into a clean medium bowl. Squeeze the carrot and add to the cabbage. Toss well to distribute evenly.

Heat a medium frying pan over medium-high heat without oil and crisp the *usuage* up for about 30 seconds on each side. Halve lengthwise and cut finely crosswise. Drain the shiitake and discard the cooking liquid.

Slide the sesame seeds into a Japanese grinding bowl (*suribachi*, see page 354) and smash coarsely. Mash in the rice vinegar, remaining 2 table-spoons mirin, 1 tablespoon shoyu, and a pinch of flaky sea salt. Pour over the cabbage and carrots, scraping out all adhering sesame, and toss with the *usuage* and shiitake.

Mound attractively in a shallow bowl or small pretty serving platter and strew the nori threads around the circumference.

~~~~~~

ウドの梅酢

UDO IN UMESU

UDO NO UMESU

Preparation time: 15 minutes, plus 1 hour soaking time
Pickling time: 1 day
Serves: 4

• 1 long thin stalk (4½ oz/120 g) udo (see page 346)
• 4 tablespoons sour plum "vinegar" (umesu, see page 345)
• 2 tablespoons hon mirin
• 2 tablespoons Konbu Dashi (page 22)

Umesu (sold as plum "vinegar") is the brine that comes up when salting and pressing *ume* (sour "plums") for air-drying. The brine is salty, sour-y, and fruity all at once and goes well with crunchy white or green vegetables such as daikon, turnips, *udo*, or cucumbers. Substitute celery if you cannot find *udo*, but skip the one-hour soak.

-

Peel the *udo* and cut crosswise into 1½-inch (4 cm) pieces.

Halve the thicker bottom pieces lengthwise, but leave any fine tops as is. Place in a medium bowl and fill to cover generously with cold water. Soak for 1 hour.

In a medium container with a lid, mix the *umesu*, mirin, and dashi together. Drain and blot the *udo* dry. Add the *udo* to the container and leave for 1 day in a cool spot.

Serve as a pickle with soup and rice on the side.

SPRING CABBAGE WITH SESAME VINEGAR

キュウリの生姜酢

CUCUMBER IN GINGER VINEGAR

KYUURI NO SHOUGA-SU

Preparation time: 30 minutes
Serves: 4

- 2 medium Japanese cucumbers
  (7 oz/200 g)
- 1 tablespoon flaky sea salt
- 1 small myoga (½ oz/15 g), for garnish
- Scant ½ cup (3½ fl oz/100 ml)
  Konbu Dashi (page 22)
- 1½ tablespoons usukuchi shoyu
  (see page 344)
- ½ tablespoon shoyu
- 1 tablespoon rice vinegar
- 1 tablespoon freshly squeezed
  yuzu or Meyer lemon juice
- 1 teaspoon freshly squeezed
  ginger juice

Ginger juice lends a refreshing note to this vinegar treatment and heightens the mild vegetal quality of the cucumber. Finely grate the ginger and squeeze in your palm to get the vibrant juice. This dish is a bright palate-cleansing bite that is a welcome addition to any summer menu.
-
Make fine diagonal cuts about one-third of the way through the cucumbers, on each side, taking care not to cut all the way through (*jabara-giri*, see page 17). Lop off the ends and cut the cucumbers crosswise into about ¾-inch (2 cm) pieces. In a medium bowl, stir the salt into 2 cups (16 fl oz/500 ml) water, until

mostly dissolved. Add the cucumber and soak for at least 10 minutes. Remove from the soaking brine and pat dry.

Halve the *myoga* lengthwise, then place it cut side down on the cutting board and slice finely lengthwise. Fluff and separate the pieces.

In a medium bowl, stir the dashi, *usukuchi shoyu*, shoyu, rice vinegar, and yuzu juice together and toss the cucumber pieces in the dashi/vinegar solution. Spoon out into four small bowls or saucers and sprinkle with the ginger juice. Pinch a small mound of *myoga* on top and serve.

みょうがの甘酢

SWEET-VINEGARED MYOGA

MYOUGA NO AMAZU

Preparation time: 10 minutes
Pickling time: 1 hour
Serves: 4

- 4 tablespoons rice vinegar
- 3 tablespoons hon mirin
- ½ teaspoon fine sea salt
- ¼ teaspoon shoyu
- 8 medium myoga (2½ oz/70 g)
- Boiling water

Myoga is a quintessential summer pickle or garnish for various cold dishes. Perhaps because *myoga* shares the same genus (*Zingiber*) as ginger, it is often dubbed "Japanese ginger" in English. But calling *myoga* a type of ginger is misleading since, other than the outward appearance of the leaves and stems, *myoga* shares no intrinsic qualities with ginger "roots," which are cultivated in open fields under direct sunlight. *Myoga* is a bud of the *Zingiber mioga* plant that grows under heavy shade and has a bright, indescribable pungency that is decidedly unlike ginger.
-

In a small bowl, stir together the rice vinegar, mirin, salt, and shoyu to make sweet vinegar (*amazu*).

Place the *myoga* in a wire-mesh sieve and pour boiling water over for 10 seconds. Shake off, pat dry, and place in a heavy-duty 1-quart (950 ml) resealable bag. Add the *amazu* while the *myoga* is still warm and leave to cool and pickle at room temperature for 1 hour before serving. Store in the refrigerator for up to 2 weeks.

MYOGA IN UMESU: Use 6 table-spoons sour plum "vinegar" (*umesu*, see page 345) instead of the sweet vinegar (*amazu*) for a puckery, salty pickle with fruity overtones.

CUCUMBER IN GINGER VINEGAR

RICE VINEGAR

Vinegar is said to be the oldest seasoning in the world, mentioned around 5000 BCE in writings from the southern part of Mesopotamia (later called Babylonia). Records show that people made alcohol during this period: Stored dates and raisins developed into alcohol, and over time, that alcohol converted naturally into acetic acid (vinegar) with the help of ambient bacteria.

Vinegar-making in Japan can be traced back to the fourth and fifth centuries when sake and vinegar brewing knowledge was first brought to Japan from China. These rudimentary methods were gradually refined and in the eighth century, during the Nara period (710–794), the current method of using koji spores (*Aspergillus oryzae*) to produce sake became established. At the time, consumption of sake was reserved for the aristocracy and religious ceremonies and not available to the common people. To this day, sake is an integral part of Shinto ceremonies (such as weddings) and is a standard offering for the gods—from home altars to famous shrines.

Along with sake consumption spreading to the general Japanese populace, vinegar use as a seasoning became mainstream in the Edo period (1603–1868) and vinegar-making burgeoned. At the end of Edo, modern versions of sushi, such as *inari-zushi* (sweet shoyu–simmered tofu skins stuffed with vinegared rice) and *nigiri-zushi* (raw fish on mounds of hand-pressed vinegared rice) were introduced, and widely enjoyed by the common people.

In the Taisho period (1912–1926), cheap synthetic vinegar, consisting of glacial acetic acid (made from petroleum and limestone) or acetic acid mixed with water, along with chemical seasonings and artificial sweeteners, began being mass-produced. Due to dire food shortages during World War II and the postwar era (1937–1953), it was prohibited to make vinegar from rice, so eventually synthetic vinegar occupied most of the market. Beginning in 1970, however, makers were required to label these vinegars as "synthetic," and today synthetic vinegar is almost nonexistent (and mostly confined to Okinawa). That said, "brewed vinegars" have a huge range in quality: From artisanal vinegars fermented from in-house brewed organic sake to large-scale inexpensive vinegars "brewed" from ethyl alcohol and *amazake* (a fermented rice drink).

Put simply, brewed vinegar is made from raw materials such as grains (i.e., rice, wheat, corn), vegetables, or fruits, along with sugar (naturally occurring or added) that ferment into alcohol and then convert into vinegar through the action of acetic acid bacteria (naturally occurring or added). Since rice is the staple food in Japan, rice vinegar is the vinegar of choice for Japanese cuisine.

Artisanal rice vinegar, characterized by the sweetness and mellowness of rice, begins with top-quality organic rice. There are few vinegar-makers in Japan going to these kinds of lengths to produce such a vinegar, but of note are Iio Jozo (Fuji Su) outside of Kyoto, Sennari (Oochi Vinegar) in Hiroshima, and Ohyama (Yamadai Vinegar) in Miyazaki prefecture.

Traditional vinegar develops slowly over time. Gently fermenting from the surface film of acetic acid bacteria floating on the top of the liquid in the container (be it a stainless tank, wooden barrel, or stoneware jars), the alcohol gradually converts to vinegar. The craftsman's task is merely to monitor the environment and ensure optimal conditions for healthy vinegar to grow. That is the incredible magic and awe-inspiring simplicity of vinegar-making.

Post World War II brought acute food shortages in Japan. These shortages were accompanied by a desperate need for Japan to build up her manufacturing infrastructure to allow the economy to recover from the devastating and debilitating effects of war. With the exodus to urban areas, Japan urgently had to feed her people, so methods were developed to speed up production on many of the key ingredients used in Japanese cuisine, such as rice vinegar, miso, shoyu, and mirin. Large scale-production of these key ingredients also allowed for them eventually to be brought to the West. Consequently, rice vinegar became a common ingredient in Western recipes and a bottle of Marukan or Mizkan rice vinegar could be found in many home kitchens. Even though these industrially produced vinegars were extremely acrid and lacked the intrinsic flavor of rice, they unfortunately became the standard for rice vinegar around the world (including in Japan). However, large-scale production cannot exist without enhanced methods to speed up fermentation, such as artificially pumping air into the vinegar to finish the fermentation process in only one day, thus only a handful of artisanal vinegar companies still exist in Japan.

Without the rice farmer, we would not have rice, so the best vinegar-makers foster a close and supportive relationship with their contract farmers. Since vinegar is made from alcohol, producing a top-quality, delicious sake in-house is the first step.

Rice is harvested in the late autumn and sake is made in the winter. Rice is husked, then polished partially to remove a certain amount of bran, washed, soaked overnight, and then steamed in a large vessel. After dumping the rice out onto a large shallow-sided wooden "table," the rice is spread flat and cooled to about 104°F (40°C). Koji spores (*Aspergillus oryzae*) are wafted over the top, then, moving at a brisk clip so as not to allow the rice to cool too much, the rice is turned by hand by the workers. More koji is wafted over the steamed grains, then the flat container is picked up or wheeled at a breakneck pace through the brewery to a warm, humid, anaerobic room called a *koji muro*. The koji-inoculated rice is tended carefully over the following 48 hours as the spores propagate and eventually coat the rice grains with a white, slightly fuzzy covering.

From this point, a yeast starter (*shubo*) is made by combining inoculated rice, deep well or spring water, and sake brewing yeast in small tanks to ferment for about two weeks. The next step is to transfer the *shubo* to large stainless steel or enamel vats where water, koji rice, and steamed rice are added in three stages (*sandan-shikomi*). After about thirty days of maturation, the vinegar-making mash (*sumoto-moromi*) has developed a rich, sweet taste full of amino acids that will eventually become a complex, nuanced vinegar.

Seed vinegar and deep well or spring water is added to large tanks along with the *sumoto-moromi*. A film of acetic acid bacteria is laid on the surface of the liquid and the contents of the tank are warmed to 104°F (40°C). After a few days, the entire surface of the liquid becomes filmed with acetic acid bacteria. It will take anywhere from 80 to 120 days for the alcohol in the tank to fully convert to vinegar. After fermentation is complete, the vinegar is transferred to a maturing tank where it is further aged. Iio Jozo (widely regarded as the top vinegar house in Japan) ages their vinegar for about 300 days. And during the aging process, they transfer the vinegar several times to another tank to aerate—a crucial step for softening the acidity that results in their signature mild, yet flavorful vinegar.

Junmai su (pure rice vinegar) is the first vinegar to seek out for preparing the recipes in this book, but *kurosu* (brown rice vinegar) is also an excellent choice and perhaps more easily found.

Kurosu (literally, "black vinegar") is confusingly translated as "brown rice vinegar" in English—perhaps so as not to mix it up with the inky Chinese black vinegar. *Kurosu* is produced in stoneware jars in southern Japan. Of note are Kakuida's three-, five-, and fifteen-year-old vinegars and Ohyama's Yamadai brown rice vinegar.

Kurosu is mild in the mouth and characterized by a rich, deep color and flavor. It is fermented in black earthenware jars that dot the hillsides in various areas of southern Japan. Steamed brown rice, deep well or spring water, and brown rice koji are added to the earthenware jars (which naturally contain the acetic acid bacteria from previous batches) and are left to ferment in the hot sun during the day, while cooling down at night as the breeze drifts off the nearby sea and the early morning fog creeps in before the day warms up.

It takes about one year for the contents in the jars to ferment into alcohol and then convert into vinegar. Typically, the vinegar is further aged for one year in the jars before bottling. Recently Kakuida and a few other vinegar companies are aging for longer to encourage increased complexity in their vinegars. These vinegars have a unique characteristic and should be used thoughtfully, so as not to overwhelm delicate flavors.

Rice vinegar in its artisanal form can literally replace all vinegars in your kitchen if you wished to simplify— and in truth that is the case in my own kitchen. After making my own red wine vinegar for over a decade from a "mother" carefully hand-carried back from a farmwife friend in the Dordogne in France, I found myself reaching more and more for those nuanced and deep-flavored Japanese pure rice vinegars from Iio Jozo or the caramely aged brown rice vinegars from Kakuida. They pair equally well with delicate canola (rapeseed) oil, lightly roasted high-grade sesame oils, or extra virgin olive oil, and the result is soft, round, and beautifully balanced.

切り干し大根とにんじんの
胡麻酢和え

KIRIBOSHI DAIKON AND CARROT WITH SESAME VINEGAR

KIRIBOSHI DAIKON TO NINJIN NO GOMASU-AE

Preparation time: 45 minutes
Cooking time: 5 minutes
Serves: 4, with leftovers

- ½ medium carrot (2⅔ oz/75 g), peeled or scrubbed
- 1½ oz (40 g) dried daikon (kiriboshi daikon, see page 350), soaked in boiling water for 30 minutes
- 2 dried shiitake, soaked in ½ cup (4 fl oz/125 ml) boiling water for 30 minutes
- Scant 5 tablespoons (2¼ fl oz/70 ml) hon mirin
- 2 tablespoons plus 1 teaspoon shoyu
- 3½ oz (100 g) mung bean sprouts
- Boiling water
- ½ teaspoon flaky sea salt
- 3 tablespoons white sesame seeds
- Scant ¼ cup (1¾ fl oz/50 ml) rice vinegar
- ½ usuage (see page 352)
- 1 teaspoon dark roasted sesame oil

A medley of dried and fresh ingredients come together with a light yet flavorful dressing rich in sesame. The *usuage* (deep-fried tofu pouch) adds spongy juiciness and the bean sprouts lend a satisfying crunch. What might, on the surface, seem like a humble side dish, is as delicious as it is healthy.
-
Julienne the carrot into threads 1¼ inches (3 cm) long.

Drain the *kiriboshi daikon*, blot dry, and if the pieces are long, cut into manageable lengths, about 1¼ inches (3 cm). Scoop the shiitake out of the soaking water and give them a gentle squeeze in your fist to express excess water back into the bowl. Measure out 2 tablespoons of the soaking liquid and set aside. (Save any remaining to use as dashi in another dish, if you like.)

Pare off the shiitake stems, discard, and finely slice the caps. Drop into a small saucepan with the reserved soaking liquid and 2 tablespoons each mirin and shoyu. Bring to a simmer over medium heat and cook gently for 2 minutes. Cool to room temperature in the cooking liquid, then drain.

Place the bean sprouts in a wire-mesh sieve and pour boiling water over them for 10 seconds. Shake off, pat dry, and toss in a bowl with ¼ teaspoon of the salt. Set aside.

In a small dry frying pan, warm the sesame seeds over medium-high heat, stirring continuously, until aromatic. Slide into a Japanese grinding bowl (*suribachi*, see page 354) and crush coarsely. (Reserve the frying pan to sear the *usuage*.) Add the vinegar, remaining scant 3 tablespoons (40 ml) mirin, ¼ teaspoon salt, and 1 teaspoon shoyu into the sesame and mash together.

Heat the frying pan again over medium-high heat and sear the *usuage* for about 1 minute on each side to recrisp and brown ever so slightly. Halve lengthwise and cut crosswise into strips ¼ inch (5 mm) wide. Do not wash the pan.

In the same frying pan, heat the oil over medium-low heat. Add the carrot and stir-fry until slightly glossy and a tad wilted, about 30 seconds. Scrape into a small bowl to cool.

Once all the ingredients have cooled to room temperature, toss the *kiriboshi daikon*, shiitake, bean sprouts, *usuage*, and carrot in the sesame vinegar and serve in one communal bowl or individual small plates. Best the first day but will hold up well for a day or two, stored in the fridge.

KIRIBOSHI DAIKON AND CARROT WITH SESAME VINEGAR

わかめともやしの梅酢和え

WAKAME AND BEAN SPROUTS IN UMESU

WAKAME TO MOYASHI NO UMESU-AE

Preparation time: 25 minutes
Serves: 4, generously

- 1 teaspoon dried wakame
- 7 oz (200 g) mung bean sprouts (moyashi, see page 349)
- Boiling water
- ½ tablespoon finely slivered fresh ginger
- 2 tablespoons sour plum "vinegar" (umesu, see page 345)

Serve this extremely refreshing condiment-like salad as a palate cleanser or as a foil for other richer dishes on the menu. Pinching off the "beard roots" of the sprouts will improve the texture but is optional.

-

Soak the wakame in plenty of cold water for 10 minutes to reconstitute. Drain and shake off excess water.

Pinch off the small yellow "beard roots" clinging to the ends of the moyashi and place in a wire-mesh sieve. Pour boiling water over for 10 seconds. Cool under cold running water and shake off.

Blot the wakame and moyashi dry in a clean tea towel and toss in a medium bowl with the ginger and umesu. Serve in small individual bowls. Keeps well for a couple of days in the fridge.

モロヘイヤ梅酢和え

MOROHEIYA IN UMESU

MOROHEIYA UMESU-AE

Preparation time: 15 minutes
Cooking time: 1 minute
Serves: 4

- 1 bunch (5¼ oz/150 g) moroheiya (see page 347), hard end portions of stem cut off
- ½ teaspoon fine sea salt
- 1 tablespoon sour plum "vinegar" (umesu, see page 345)

Boiled moroheiya (jute mallow) dressed in sour plum "vinegar" (umesu) can be eaten as is, as a condiment to white rice, or stirred into cellophane noodles with julienned cucumbers for a bright summer salad. Substitute water spinach if you cannot find moroheiya.

-

Cut the leaves off the stems of the moroheiya, and cut the stems crosswise into 1¼-inch (3 cm) pieces.

Bring a medium saucepan full of water to a boil with the salt.

Drop the stems into the water and cook for 40 seconds. Add the leaves and push them into the hot water with a pair of chopsticks. Cook for an additional 20 seconds. Scoop out with a wire-mesh sieve and refresh under cold running water. Shake off and squeeze by handfuls.

Halve the handfuls crosswise and toss with the umesu. Serve on small saucers as a "pickle," accompanied with a bowl of rice and a bowl of soup. It will keep for a few days, if refrigerated, though it might discolor.

WAKAME AND BEAN SPROUTS IN UMESU

山芋なます

SWEET VINEGARED MOUNTAIN YAM

YAMA-IMO NAMASU

Preparation time: 45 minutes
Cooking time: 5 minutes
Pickling time: 1 hour
Serves: 4

• 1 thin mountain yam
(7 oz/200 g), scrubbed
• 6 tablespoons rice vinegar
• 4 tablespoons hon mirin
• 1 teaspoon flaky sea salt
• 2 dried shiitake, soaked in
¼ cup (2 fl oz/60 ml) hot water
for 20 minutes
• 1 tablespoon shoyu
• 1 small Japanese cucumber
(2½ oz/75 g), cut crosswise
into thin rounds
• 1 small carrot (2½ oz/75 g),
scrubbed and finely julienned

There are several varieties of mountain yam, but notably two distinct shapes are widely available: *Yamato imo* looks a bit like a clubbed foot, whereas *naga imo* (long yam) resembles a daikon in shape. Typically, *yamato imo* is used for grating up to a deliciously slimy mass, while the long yam is best cut into pieces and pickled or cooked. Use the long-shaped mountain yam for this recipe. And be sure to wash your hands and forearms with warm, soapy water immediately after handling this itchy root vegetable.
-
Peel the mountain yam, quarter it lengthwise, and slice crosswise into quarter-rounds 1¾ inches (2 cm) thick. Drop the pieces into a medium bowl and fill with cold water to cover.

In a small saucepan, bring the vinegar, 3 tablespoons of the mirin, and ½ teaspoon of the flaky salt almost to a boil over medium-high heat. Remove from the heat and stir to dissolve the salt. Cool to room temperature.

Drain the mountain yam, place in a medium bowl, and toss with the cooled vinegar/mirin solution. Weight with a plate and another object on top to keep the mountain yam submerged

for 1 hour. (Alternatively pack in a heavy-duty resealable plastic bag and roll up to squeeze out all the air.)

Reserving the soaking water, remove the shiitake, cut off the stems, and thinly slice the caps. Slide the slices into a small saucepan and add the soaking water and the shoyu and remaining 1 tablespoon mirin. Bring to a simmer over medium heat and cook for 5 minutes to soften.

In separate bowls, massage ¼ teaspoon of the salt into the cucumber and the remaining ¼ teaspoon into the carrot. Let each sit for 10 minutes before rinsing quickly with cold water and patting dry on a clean tea towel. Drain the shiitake.

Remove the weight from the mountain yam and stack the yam in the bottom of four small bowls. Spoon the cucumber into the bowl on one side of the yam and the shiitake on the other side. Arrange a pinch of the carrot across the top of the yam and serve as a cold composed salad. (Alternatively, toss all of the ingredients together in a medium serving bowl and serve family-style or in small bowls.)

SWEET VINEGARED MOUNTAIN YAM

長いもの酢の物

MOUNTAIN YAM WITH VINEGARED SESAME SAUCE

NAGA-IMO NO SUNOMONO

Preparation time: 20 minutes
Serves: 4

• 4¾-inch (12 cm) piece medium mountain yam (10½ oz/300 g), scrubbed
• 2 tablespoons Japanese white sesame paste
• 1 tablespoon Konbu Dashi (page 22)
• 2 teaspoons shoyu
• 1 teaspoon organic granulated sugar
• 1 tablespoon rice vinegar
• ½ teaspoon black sesame seeds

When cutting the mountain yam, you can place a clean cloth on top of the cutting board, so the slippery pieces won't slide around when you are julienning. Afficionados of mountain yam love its viscosity when finely grated, but for the uninitiated, fresh julienned pieces or pickled crunchy rounds are an excellent way to enjoy the crisp texture of mountain yam. And here the rich sesame sauce provides a lovely balance against the delicately flavored mountain yam.

-

Peel the mountain yam and halve crosswise. Slice lengthwise into thin slabs and arrange into manageable stacks. Cut the slabs lengthwise into pieces ½ inch (1 cm) wide (*tanzaku-giri*, see page 17) and place in attractive log-shaped piles on four small saucers. (Wash your hands and forearms well with warm sudsy water to counteract the itchy properties of the mountain yam.)

In a small bowl, mix the sesame paste, dashi, shoyu, sugar, and vinegar together. Spoon on top of the mountain yam, sprinkle lightly with the sesame seeds, and serve as a cold side dish.

菜の花の甘酢漬け

SWEET-VINEGARED NANOHANA

NANOHANA NO AMAZU-ZUKE

Preparation time: 10 minutes
Pickling time: 1 day
Serves: 4

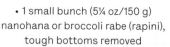

• 1 small bunch (5¼ oz/150 g) nanohana or broccoli rabe (rapini), tough bottoms removed
• Boiling water
• 4 tablespoons rice vinegar
• 2 tablespoons hon mirin
• ¼ teaspoon fine sea salt
• ¼ teaspoon shoyu

Nanohana are the budding greens that bolt from crucifers in the spring. Broccoli rabe (rapini) or broccolini can easily be substituted. A sweet vinegar treatment softens and balances the natural bitterness of *nanohana*, but also shortens the window for eating, since the vinegar will cause the greens to lose vibrancy.

-

Set the *nanohana* in a wire-mesh sieve and pour boiling water over for 10 seconds. Shake off excess water and arrange side by side on a clean tea towel. Roll up and pat gently to allow the towel to absorb moisture. Align the pieces in a rectangular refrigerator container.

In a small bowl, stir together the vinegar, mirin, salt, and shoyu to dissolve the salt. Pour over the *nanohana*, tipping the container to make sure all the greens are wet. Cover, refrigerate, and allow to pickle for 1 day.

Cut into 2-inch (5 cm) pieces before serving. The vinegar solution will cause discoloration, so best to eat this up at once.

MOUNTAIN YAM WITH VINEGARED SESAME SAUCE

かぶと干し柿のなます

TURNIP AND DRIED PERSIMMON IN SWEET VINEGAR

KABU TO HOSHIGAKI NO NAMASU

Preparation time: 25 minutes,
plus 30 minutes soaking time
Cooking time: 1–2 minutes
Serves: 4

- 4 tablespoons rice vinegar
- 2 tablespoons organic granulated sugar
- 2 teaspoons plus a pinch of fine sea salt
- 4 small turnips (7 oz/200 g), scrubbed, with ½ inch (1 cm) of the stems left intact
- 1 small carrot (1¾ oz/50 g), peeled
- 1 dried persimmon (hoshigaki, see page 350) or 7 unsulfured dried apricots (2¼ oz/60 g)
- ¼ teaspoon finely slivered yuzu zest

Namasu is a sweet-vinegared vegetable treatment typically made with daikon and carrot. In this lovely, gentle version, slightly bitter turnips replace the daikon, giving balance to the sweetness of the dried persimmon.
-
In a small saucepan, combine a scant ½ cup (3½ fl oz/100 ml) water, the vinegar, sugar, and a pinch of salt. Bring to a boil over high heat to dissolve the sugar and salt. Pour into a heatproof medium bowl and cool to room temperature.

Add a scant 1¼ cups (10 fl oz/ 300 ml) water to a separate bowl and stir in the 2 teaspoons salt.

Peel the turnips if the skin is tough and halve lengthwise. Set the cut sides down on the cutting board and cut lengthwise again into slices ¼ inch (5 mm) thick. Slip into the bowl of salt water.

Cut the carrot crosswise into 1¼-inch (3 cm) lengths and then lengthwise into pieces ½ inch (1 cm) wide. Stack the pieces and slice into very fine slabs (*tanzaku-giri*, see page 17). Slide into the bowl with the turnips. Soak the vegetables for 30 minutes.

Cut the calyx off the *hoshigaki* and remove the seeds if there are any. Slice the flesh into fine strips and soak in the cooled vinegar solution, separating the sticky pieces with your fingers.

After 30 minutes, skim the turnip and carrot from the bowl of salt water, and drop onto a clean tea towel. Blot dry.

Toss with the *hoshigaki* in the sweet vinegar along with the yuzu zest. Keeps for a day or two, if refrigerated, but best the first day since the turnip will weep out liquid.

TURNIP AND DRIED PERSIMMON IN SWEET VINEGAR

かぶのもみ漬け

MASSAGED TURNIPS IN SWEET VINEGAR

KABU NO MOMIZUKE

Preparation time: 30 minutes
Cooking time: 1 minute
Serves: 4, with leftovers

• 4 small turnips with greens
(12¼ oz/350 g)
• ¾ teaspoon flaky sea salt
• 1 tablespoon dried wakame, soaked
in cold water for 10 minutes
• 4 tablespoons rice vinegar
• 2 tablespoons mirin
• ½ tablespoon finely slivered yuzu zest

Salt-massaged turnips are the most ubiquitous quick pickles in Japan. Here, adding wakame and rice vinegar contributes spark to the traditional method and thus makes a surprisingly fresh and brightly irresistible bite.
-
Cut the tops off the turnips, leaving ½ inch (1 cm) of the tender stems protruding from the turnips, and reserve the greens. Slice off the roots as well. Halve the turnips lengthwise, place cut side down on the cutting board, and cut lengthwise into ¼-inch (5 mm) slices. Slide into a medium bowl and massage with ¼ teaspoon of the salt. Leave for 10 minutes.

Bring a large saucepan of water to a boil over high heat. Drop in the turnip greens and blanch for 1 minute. Scoop out, refresh under cold running water, and squeeze down the length of the greens to express the excess water. Squeeze into a tight ball and cut crosswise into shreds ½ inch (1 cm) wide. In a small bowl, scissor to separate the leaves, and massage with ¼ teaspoon of the salt.

Drain the wakame and shake off. In a medium serving bowl, toss the wakame with the vinegar, mirin, and remaining ¼ teaspoon salt. Lift the turnip pieces out of the salt, give them a light squeeze, and drop into the bowl of wakame. Do the same with the turnip greens. Toss to distribute the ingredients evenly, sprinkle with the yuzu zest, and serve.

~~~~~~

りんごの落花生酢和え

APPLE WITH PEANUT VINEGAR

RINGO NO RAKKASEI SU-AE

Preparation time: 55 minutes
Cooking time: 5 minutes
Serves: 4

• 1 sweet apple (7 oz/200 g), unpeeled
• 1 small onion (3½ oz/100 g), halved
lengthwise and peeled
• ⅓ teaspoon flaky sea salt
• 1 tablespoon dried hijiki
(see page 349), soaked in
cold water for 20 minutes
• ½ tablespoon fine sea salt
• 1 small bunch (3½ oz/100 g) edible
chrysanthemum greens (shungiku,
see page 347), tough ends cut off
• 3 tablespoons finely chopped
roasted peanuts
• 3 tablespoons rice vinegar
• 3 tablespoons hon mirin

Apples in Japan are by and large sweet, rather than tart. Use Jonagold or Red Delicious for this recipe. Fresh and lovely, this crunchy "salad" would make a beautiful lunch dish. Substitute a peppery green if you cannot find shungiku.
-
Quarter the apple and cut out the core and stem sections. Cut the apple pieces and onion halves lengthwise into fine slices. Gently massage ¼ teaspoon of the flaky salt into the onion slices, rinse under cold water, and pat dry on a clean tea towel. Toss the apple with the remaining ¼ teaspoon flaky salt and leave to macerate for 10 minutes. Squeeze the apple pieces gently to express liquid and set aside.

Drain the hijiki in a wire-mesh sieve, blot well with paper towel and set aside.

Bring a medium saucepan of water to a boil with the fine salt. Hold the shungiku by the leafy tops and dunk the stems into the boiling water. Count to 10, then drop the greens into the water and poke them down with chopsticks to submerge. Cook for 20 seconds more. Refresh under cold running water, squeeze, and cut into 1¼-inch (3 cm) lengths.

In a small bowl, mix together the peanuts, vinegar, and mirin. In a medium serving bowl, toss the apple, onion, hijiki, and shungiku with the dressing and serve as a bright salad. Best the first day but also good the second.

APPLE WITH PEANUT VINEGAR

五色菜の落花生酢和え

FIVE-COLORED VEGETABLES WITH PEANUT VINEGAR

GOSHOKU-NA NO RAKKASEI SU-AE

Preparation time: 45 minutes
Cooking time: 5 minutes
Serves: 4, generously

- 1 medium carrot (5¼ oz/150 g), scrubbed
- Boiling water
- 3½ oz (100 g) enoki mushrooms, spongy bottom cut off, halved crosswise
- ½ bunch (2⅔ oz/75 g) edible chrysanthemum greens (shungiku, see page 347), thick ends cut off
- 5¼ oz (150 g) shirataki noodles
- ½ cup (2¼ oz/60 g) roasted peanuts
- 3 tablespoons rice vinegar
- 3 tablespoons shoyu
- 3 tablespoons hon mirin
- 1 deep-fried tofu pouch (usuage, see page 352)

Peanuts provide an unexpected depth of flavor and add crunch to this noodle and vegetable salad. Perfect for a cold lunch on a summer day. If you cannot find edible chrysanthemum greens (*shungiku*, see page 347), use another peppery green such as mizuna or cress, but pour hot water over for 10 seconds rather than blanch. The brilliant colors on this salad make the presentation stunning.

-
Slice the carrot into finely julienned threads, scrape into a wire-mesh sieve, and pour boiling water over them for 10 seconds to slightly cook. Place the enoki in another wire-mesh sieve and pour boiling water over them for 10 seconds. Set both sieves in the kitchen sink to drain. Gently blot the enoki with a paper towel to remove excess water. Pat the carrots in another towel to dry well.

Bring a medium saucepan of water to a boil over high heat. Hold the *shungiku* stems in the boiling water for 10 seconds, then push the greens down into the water to cook for 20 seconds more. Scoop out with a wire-mesh sieve and cool down under cold running water. Skim the boiling water carefully to make sure there are no lingering pieces of *shungiku* and slide the *shirataki* into the water to cook for 3 minutes. Scoop out and let drain in the sink. Squeeze the *shungiku* and cut crosswise into 1¾-inch (4 cm) pieces. Blot off lingering water from the *shirataki* and cut crosswise into 1¾-inch (4 cm) lengths.

Smash the peanuts in a Japanese grinding bowl (*suribachi*, see page 354) or nut grinder until the oils have released. Mash in the vinegar, shoyu, and mirin to make a smooth paste.

In a dry frying pan, sear the *usuage* over medium heat for 1 minute on both sides to re-crisp. Halve lengthwise and cut crosswise into strips ¼ inch (5 mm) wide.

Toss the cooled *usuage*, enoki, carrot, *shungiku*, and *shirataki* in the peanut mixture.

Serve in the *suribachi* or an attractive serving bowl. Leftovers hold up until the following day though the texture and flavors will lose some bounce.

FIVE-COLORED VEGETABLES WITH PEANUT VINEGAR

こごみの胡麻酢だれ

FIDDLEHEAD FERNS IN SESAME VINEGAR

KOGOMI NO GOMASU-DARE

Preparation time: 20 minutes
Cooking time: 10 minutes
Serves: 4

- 12 furry fiddlehead ferns (kogomi, see page 346), 5¼ oz (150 g)
- 1¼ cups (10 fl oz/300 ml) Happo Dashi (page 25)
- 3 teaspoons usukuchi shoyu (see page 344)
- 1 teaspoon hon mirin
- 2 tablespoons Japanese white sesame paste
- 1 teaspoon organic granulated sugar
- ½ teaspoon shoyu
- 1 teaspoon rice vinegar

Fiddlehead ferns are the one Japanese mountain vegetable that is easily found outside of Japan. The creamy sesame-vinegar dressing softens the pronounced forest taste of the ferns and makes a strikingly appealing combination.
-
Cut the tough bottoms off the fiddleheads and discard. Halve the fiddleheads crosswise into 3–4-inch (1.25–1.5 cm) pieces.

Set up a large bowl of ice and water and set a stainless steel bowl in it. In a small saucepan, bring the *happo dashi* to a simmer over medium heat. Stir in 2 teaspoons of the *usukuchi shoyu* and the mirin. Add the fiddleheads and simmer until the bottom portions can be easily pierced with a bamboo skewer, 2–3 minutes. Transfer the fiddleheads and cooking liquid to the bowl set in the ice bath to shock-cool (this keeps their bright green color).

In a medium bowl, stir together the sesame paste, sugar, shoyu, rice vinegar, and remaining 1 teaspoon *usukuchi shoyu*. You will need to beat vigorously to a smooth paste. Adding it 1 teaspoon at a time, add a total of 2 teaspoons of the fiddlehead's cooking liquid, beating well. Taste and add a drop or two more of shoyu, if desired.

Stack the fiddleheads attractively on a salad plate or shallow bowl, spoon the sesame-vinegar sauce across the middle of the fiddleheads allowing it to drip down either side of the stack, and serve as part of a light meal.

~~~~~~

柚釜紅白なます

NAMASU-STUFFED YUZU POTS

YUZU-KAMA KOUHAKU NAMASU

Preparation time: 40 minutes
Serves: 4

- 4 medium yuzu or rounded lemons (4½ oz/130 g each)
- 2 tablespoons rice vinegar
- 2 tablespoons Japanese light brown cane sugar (kibizato, see page 345) or organic granulated sugar
- 1⅛ teaspoons fine sea salt
- 9 oz (250 g) daikon, peeled
- 3 oz (85 g) carrot, peeled

Gorgeously simple, hollowed-out yuzu shells make a stunning presentation for *namasu*—the traditional dish of julienned daikon and carrot in sweet vinegar. These can be made ahead of time and stored in the fridge before serving.
-
Cut off about 10 percent of the yuzu at the stem end and scoop out the insides with a grapefruit spoon. Squeeze to extract the juice, strain, and set aside. Scrape the pith off the cut-off top portions and finely julienne the yellow zest. Set aside.

In a medium bowl, mix the vinegar, 1 tablespoon of the yuzu juice, the sugar, and 1 teaspoon of the salt to dissolve.

Cut the daikon and carrot into fine julienne 2 inches (5 cm) long. Massage with the remaining ⅛ teaspoon salt, then rinse off the salt in plenty of cold water. Drain in a wire-mesh sieve and pat dry in a clean tea towel.

Fold the daikon and carrot into the vinegar mixture and mix well until evenly distributed. Spoon the mixture into the yuzu pots and garnish with the yuzu zest.

NAMASU-STUFFED YUZU POTS

大根と干し柿のなます

DAIKON AND DRIED PERSIMMON WITH MITSUBA

DAIKON TO HOSHIGAKI NO NAMASU

Preparation time: 20 minutes, plus 30 minutes maceration time
Cooking time: 5 minutes
Serves: 6

• ¼ small daikon (9 oz/250 g), peeled and julienned
• ½ teaspoon flaky sea salt
• 1 medium shiitake, stem removed
• 2 tablespoons sake
• 1 tablespoon usukuchi shoyu (see page 344)
• 1 dried persimmon (hoshigaki, see page 350) or 7 unsulfured dried apricots
• 1 tablespoon finely slivered yuzu or Meyer lemon zest
• 1 tablespoon freshly squeezed yuzu or Meyer lemon juice
• 1 small bunch mitsuba (see page 346), cut crosswise into ¾-inch (2 cm) pieces

Daikon is the star of this dish, so be sure to use winter daikon at its peak. Although the other ingredients are added with restraint, the *hoshigaki* (dried persimmon) almost melts into the daikon, making this a very enticing cold salad-like dish.
-
Place the daikon in a medium bowl and massage lightly with the salt. Allow to sit for 10 minutes. Scoop the daikon out of the bowl in handfuls, leaving any salt crystals, and squeeze the daikon gently to remove excess moisture. Drop into a clean medium bowl as you go and set aside.

In a small dry frying pan, sear the shiitake cap lightly over medium heat (or on a grate set directly over a low flame) for 2 or 3 minutes and cut into fine slices. Drop into the bowl with the daikon.

In a small saucepan, stir together the sake and *usukuchi shoyu* and heat briefly. Transfer to a small bowl to cool.

Remove the calyx from the *hoshigaki*, pry out the seeds with your fingers, and cut the flesh lengthwise into thin strips.

Once the sake and *usukuchi shoyu* have cooled, add the *hoshigaki* and scissor apart the sticky pieces with your fingers. Stir in the yuzu zest and juice.

Add the *hoshigaki*/yuzu mixture to the daikon and shiitake and toss. Leave for 30 minutes to develop flavor.

Fold in the *mitsuba* and serve in a pretty ceramic bowl. This dish holds up well for a day or two, if stored in the fridge.

~~~~~~

柿なます

PERSIMMON NAMASU

KAKI NAMASU

Preparation time: 30 minutes
Cooking time: 3 minutes
Serves: 4, generously

• 1 firm Fuyu persimmon (8¼ oz /235 g), peeled and cored
• 4 tablespoons (60 ml) rice vinegar
• 3 tablespoons (45 ml) hon mirin
• Pinch of fine sea salt
• 4-inch (10 cm) piece medium daikon, peeled
• 2-inch (5 cm) piece medium carrot, peeled
• A couple pinches of flaky sea salt
• 1 usuage (see page 352)

Finely grated fresh persimmon adds a refreshingly unexpected twist, elevating this traditional dish of julienned daikon and carrot in sweet vinegar to the sublime. And deep-fried tofu pouches (*usuage*) contribute texture but can be omitted if you are unable to source.
-
Grate the persimmon on a circular grater (*oroshiki*, see page 354) or metal grating plate (*oroshigane*, see page 354) into a medium bowl. Stir in the vinegar, mirin, and fine salt and set aside.

Cut the daikon and carrot into fine julienne 2 inches (5 cm) long

and massage with the flaky salt in a medium bowl. Leave for 10 minutes.

Heat a dry frying pan over medium heat and sear the *usuage* for 1–1½ minutes on both sides to crisp up. Halve lengthwise and cut crosswise into strips ¼ inch (5 mm) wide.

Scoop the daikon and carrot out of the bowl and squeeze by handfuls to express the liquid. Drop into the bowl of sweet vinegar–seasoned grated persimmon. Toss with the *usuage* and serve on individual small saucers.

DAIKON AND DRIED PERSIMMON WITH MITSUBA

揚げ物

When you are looking for something rich and oily, like meat, but not, *agemono* contributes that element to a meal. Typically, Japanese fried foods are eaten in moderation and they tend toward the light side (except the heavier meat preparations such as *katsu*, a breaded fried pork cutlet that seems to be popular in Western countries these days). That said, an entire meal of tempura can be an eye-opening experience. Tempura restaurants tend to be quite pricey, and while they lean toward vegetables, there are fish bites interspersed as well (although fried tofu and *yuba* renditions can be used to replace the fish if the restaurant has a flexible mindset). As you reach the close of an entire menu based on tempura, you should feel sated but not overwhelmed. Tempura (as well as sushi) was a favorite stand-up meal in the outside eateries during the Edo period (1603–1868), but has since moved indoors and, like sushi, when served at a dedicated restaurant is regarded as haute cuisine.

Classically, any number of vegetables (or fruits) are dipped in eggless batter (*shojin koromo*) and fried to a light and crispy result. This tempura batter is made up of white flour mixed with still or sparkling water. But sometimes a combination of flour and potato starch is used. Recently my son Andrew (who assists me with recipe testing) and I have been using organic brown rice flour—which is readily available outside of Japan . . . and gluten-free.

Fritters are also popular and are less reliant on being served piping hot from the oil. Often presented with just a pinch of salt, fritters can just as easily be accompanied by a dish of tempura dipping sauce (*tentsuyu*, see recipe page 26) on the side or lightly simmered in the *tentsuyu* to add succulence.

In this book I use the Kondo method of deep-frying in a high-sided sauté pan with only 1¼ inches (3 cm) of oil. Deep-frying at home in a large pot leaves you with a lot of oil to dispose of, so frying in just enough

oil to keep the foods submerged perhaps makes more sense. Fumio Kondo is the chef owner of Tempura Kondo in Tokyo and the author of several illuminating books on the best, precise method for cooking different fish and vegetables as tempura. He advises against cast iron since it is hard to control temperature fluctuations, and I have two dedicated modern nonstick coated pans I use for deep-frying— one large and one medium.

I cannot stress how crucial the oil itself is to successfully prepare Japanese tempura. I use a clarified organic Japanese rapeseed oil made by Yonezawa Shoten in Saitama. Outside of Japan, I had good results using unroasted sesame oil to produce lightly ethereal Japanese fried foods. The oil cost may be the main cost when preparing vegetarian tempura.

AGEMONO

DEEP-FRIED

筍ボール

BAMBOO SHOOT BALLS

TAKENOKO BO-RU

Preparation time: 15 minutes
Cooking time: 5 minutes
Makes: 20 small balls

- ¼ cup (1½ oz/40 g) unbleached all-purpose (plain) flour
- A few pinches of flaky sea salt
- 1 cup (8 fl oz/250 ml) finely grated Boiled Bamboo Shoot (page 34)
- Neutral oil, such as canola (rapeseed), peanut, or safflower, for deep-frying
- ½ teaspoon black sesame seeds

While the custom of digging bamboo shoots in the spring is common in Japan and other parts of Asia, Western countries also grow bamboo. Should you have access to a home or forest bamboo grove in the spring, try to dig your own shoots. Once they are boiled, the bamboo shoots keep several days if stored in a refrigerated container with plenty of cold water, but change the water each day to maintain freshness. Substitute vacuum-packed bamboo if you cannot find fresh and use a fine-toothed ceramic or metal grater to grate the bamboo. These tasty little balls are crispy on the outside and ooey-gooey on the inside.
-
In a medium bowl, slowly stir the flour and a pinch of salt into the grated bamboo with your fingers until the flour is completely incorporated and the mixture is cohesive. Roll into twenty 1¼-inch (3 cm) balls.

In a large high-sided sauté pan, heat 1¼ inches (3 cm) oil over medium heat until about 340°F (170°C). To check the oil temperature, sprinkle a few pinches of flour into the oil. The flour should sink to the bottom of the pan, then immediately float back up to the surface, and there will be a few medium-sized bubbles.

Gently slip the bamboo shoot balls into the oil and fry for about 3 minutes, turning every 45 seconds, until lightly colored and buoyant and the bubbling has subsided. Skim out and drain briefly on a rack set over a pan to catch the drips. Divide among four small plates, sprinkle lightly with the sesame seeds and a couple of pinches of salt and serve as a hot bite before dinner or as part of a full meal.

BAMBOO SHOOT BALLS

新ごぼうとアスパラガスの
かき揚げ

YOUNG BURDOCK AND ASPARAGUS KAKIAGE

SHIN GOBOU TO ASUPARAGASU NO KAKIAGE

Preparation time: 20 minutes
Cooking time: 10 minutes
Makes: 8 small or 4 large fritters

- ⅔ cup (3½ oz/100 g) unbleached
pastry flour
- 1 teaspoon baking powder
- ½ medium burdock (2⅔ oz/75 g),
preferably spring crop, scrubbed
- 4 medium spears asparagus
(5¼ oz/150 g), bottom one-third peeled
(or broken off if tough)
- 10 small green shiso leaves,
cut into fine threads
- Neutral oil, such as canola (rapeseed),
peanut, or safflower, for deep-frying
- Flaky sea salt, for serving

Kakiage made from drier ingredients such as burdock and asparagus hold up well even when consumed at room temperature because the strands are slightly separated and not fried in a fritter-like clump. There is no spongy center to this kind of *kakiage* so it incorporates well into a *teishoku* meal of many dishes served on a large tray. (Each person receives their own tray and, given the variety of dishes, most of them are served at room temperature.) The spring ingredients in this *kakiage* make it exceptionally aromatic and fresh feeling.
-
In a medium bowl, whisk the flour and baking powder together.

Hold the burdock in your nondominant hand and cut off shavings with a sharp knife, while rotating the root in your hand like you are hand-sharpening a pencil (*sasagaki*, see page 17)—drop as you go into a bowl of cold water to avoid discoloration.

Cut the asparagus in the same manner, dropping it into the bowl of flour and baking powder. Drain the burdock and toss with chopsticks in the flour mixture with the asparagus and shiso until the vegetables are evenly coated. Stir in ⅔ cup (5½ fl oz/160 ml) ice water, mixing as little as possible.

In a large high-sided sauté pan, heat 1¼ inches (3 cm) oil over medium heat until about 355°F (180°C). To check the oil temperature, flick a few drops of batter into the oil. The batter should sink about halfway to the bottom of the pan, then immediately bounce back up to the surface, and there will quite a few lively medium-sized bubbles.

Give the mixture one last stir and scoop up a pile of the vegetables with a slotted serving spoon. Shake off excess batter and quietly slip into the oil at the edge of the pan. Repeat with more piles of battered vegetables but watch for excessive bubbling. You do not want the oil to overflow! If need be, fry in batches. Cook until golden on both sides, about 90 seconds per side. Drain briefly on a wire rack set over a pan to catch the drips. Sprinkle with a little salt and serve.

YOUNG BURDOCK AND ASPARAGUS KAKIAGE

POTATO CHIP SALAD

ポテトチップスサラダ

POTETO CHIPPUSU SARADA

Preparation time: 45 minutes,
plus 30 minutes soaking time
Cooking time: 10 minutes
Serves: 4, generously

• 1 lb (450 g) medium potatoes,
peeled and cut into very thin rounds
• Neutral oil, such as canola
(rapeseed), peanut, or safflower,
for deep-frying
• ½ tablespoon curry powder
• 1 teaspoon flaky sea salt
• 2 tablespoons rice vinegar
• 4 tablespoons canola (rapeseed) oil
• 1 small head red lettuce
(3½ oz/100 g), torn into large
bite-size pieces
• 2 medium Japanese cucumbers
(5¼ oz/150 g), cut crosswise
into 1¼-inch (3 cm) pieces and
lengthwise into fine slabs
(tanzaku-giri, see page 17)
• 2 medium tomatoes (7 oz/200 g),
cut into ¾-inch (2 cm) dice
• 1 large stalk celery (3½ oz/100 g),
cut crosswise at a diagonal
into thin pieces 1¼ inches (3 cm)
long and ¼ inch (5 mm) wide (sogigiri,
see page 17)

The homemade fried potato
chips add irresistible crunch to
this surprising and completely
delicious summer salad. And the
curry vinaigrette adds a depth
of flavor that sparks up this
distinctive dish, making it an
excellent candidate for a main
meal lunch.

-

Soak the potatoes in cold water
for 30 minutes. Drain and pat
dry in a clean tea towel, taking
care to remove as much moisture
as possible.

In a large high-sided sauté pan,
heat 1¼ inches (3 cm) neutral oil
over medium heat until about
340°F (170°C). To check the oil
temperature, drop a potato slice
into the oil. The potato should
sink to the bottom of the pan,
then immediately bounce back
up to the surface, and there will
be a few medium-sized bubbles.

Fry the potato slices in batches,
turning, until golden and the
bubbles have subsided, about
3 minutes. Drain on a rack set
over a pan to catch the drips.
(Note: If the potatoes you are
using have too much moisture,
you might need to fry them twice
to crisp them up properly.)

In a small bowl, mix together the
curry powder, salt, and vinegar.
Slowly whisk in the canola
(rapeseed) oil to emulsify.

Line four salad plates with
the lettuce and strew with the
cucumber and tomatoes. Mound
the potato chips in the middle,
then scatter the celery over
the top. Drizzle with the curry
vinaigrette and serve immediately
as a light lunch course.

POTATO CHIP SALAD

MOUNTAIN VEGETABLES

As the snows melt and spring approaches, mountain vegetables (*sansai*) start to flourish. Appealingly unusual in a range of flavors, these mountain vegetables are the true harbingers of Japanese spring. While the typical Western spring vegetables, such as peas and asparagus, have a mild vegetality, Japanese mountain vegetables are refreshingly bitter.

With the exception of fiddlehead ferns, *fuki*, *udo*, and *mitsuba*, most mountain vegetables are foraged exclusively in the wild and are not cultivated. And as such they are only available at this time of year—though the seasonal lines are blurring. But without exception, when you ask someone when is the best time to enjoy their regional cuisine, spring is the answer and mountain vegetables the reason. *Sansai* are prized by people all over Japan and a great source of pride for local areas. Much anticipated, and typically eaten as tempura, pickled, or in dressed dishes, *sansai* appear on menus from early spring into early summer. Unfortunately, these unique mountain vegetables are not grown outside of Japan, except the ubiquitous fiddlehead ferns. The only caveat would be not to go out foraging on your own as a novice. It is best to buy mountain vegetables harvested by knowledgeable foragers, since there are many lookalike plants that are toxic.

Known as long-stamen chives in English, *nobiru* (*Allium macrostemon*) is a wild onion found all over East Asia near water sources such as garden faucets, streams, or rice fields. With thin, chive-like "leaves" and white, sometimes pinkish, bulbed bottoms, *nobiru* starts to appear toward the end of winter and lasts well into the spring. Best eaten raw, swiped into a mound of miso, *nobiru* also adds a piquant note to soups and egg dishes and can be used as a substitute for chives or scallions (spring onions). Similar wild onions are native to North America, the United Kingdom, and Europe.

Butterbur buds (*fuki no to*) the size of golf balls emerge from the ground after the thaw, peeking out through the snow or desiccated leaf cover in the forests or fields. *Fuki no to* are perhaps the most representative, yet unique mountain vegetables in Japan, though the roots should be avoided because they contain mild toxins. These wide-open buds with a faintly pungent, menthol-like flavor are most often deep-fried as tempura and eaten dipped in sea salt. But they can also be coarsely chopped and gently simmered with miso, sake, and mirin to make *fuki no to miso*—a compelling condiment to dab on the side of a bowl of freshly cooked white rice.

In the Araliaceae family, the Japanese angelica tree (*Aralia elata*) produces thick-stemmed shoots with frilly purple-tinged leaves (*tara no me*) on the end of branches in the late winter and early spring. *Tara no me* is known colloquially as the king of mountain vegetables, perhaps for its versatility and universality. Also in the Araliaceae family, *koshi abura* is dubbed the queen of mountain vegetables: thin-stemmed buds with soft green leaves found on a native Japanese tree (*Chengiopanax sciadophylloides*). Both *tara no me* and *koshi abura* are mildly bitter, with naturally restorative properties. Sometimes called mountain asparagus, *yama udo* (*Aralia cordata*), is yet another mountain vegetable in the Araliaceae family that produces slightly furry buds with soft spiky tops in the spring. Unlike the fragrant *koshi abura* and *tara no me*, *yama udo* has a distinctly resin-like flavor that aids digestion. All these buds and shoots are snapped off judiciously (leaving enough for the tree to thrive) and are batter-fried as tempura, but can be simmered, then dressed with shoyu-flavored dashi (*ohitashi*) or a smashed tofu and sesame treatment (*shira-ae*).

Japanese wild parsley (*seri*) is foraged in early spring and, depending on the variety, appears as a tangled mass of crunchy, pink-tinged stalks with tiny peppery leaves, or as upright fine stalks with almost celery-like leaves. Not to be confused with *seri* is *mitsuba*, another aromatic green often translated as "trefoil" but, confusingly, can also be called "Japanese wild parsley." *Mitsuba* is grown hydroponically year-round, and is ubiquitous in miso soup with clams, both in Japan and abroad. But spring-foraged mountain *mitsuba* has an unparalleled depth of flavor and is at once peppery and pungent in an oddly appealing way. Both *seri* and *mitsuba* are lovely with eggs, in soups, and as tempura.

Fiddlehead ferns are the one mountain vegetable readily found in forests all over the world. In Japan, there are two main species, *warabi* (eagle ferns: long and thin with finely curled tops) and *kogomi* (ostrich ferns: fuzzy, tight-headed with thick stems). *Warabi* need to be rubbed with ash from the firepit or baking soda, and soaked in cold water before cooking, though *kogomi* can be consumed as is. After blanching, they are most often eaten simply, dressed with shoyu-dashi.

While seasonality is becoming less well-defined in Japan, spring remains a time of great collective joy at the blooming and falling of the cherry blossoms—emblematic of our own ephemeral lives. But also, mountain vegetables remind us of how the natural world mirrors and delivers what we need at any given moment. In spring, we need bitter foods to wake up our appetites and stimulate our senses after the bleak winter. And the healthful qualities of these foods ready our bodies for the hot summer months approaching. This is the beauty of seasonality.

じゃが芋餅のあんかけ

POTATO MOCHI WITH SILKY SAUCE

JYAGAIMO MOCHI NO ANKAKE

Preparation time: 25 minutes
Cooking time: 35 minutes
Makes: 8 small pieces

- 2 medium potatoes
(5¼ oz/150 g each), scrubbed
and unpeeled
- 2 tablespoons whole milk
- 4 teaspoons shoyu
- 1 tablespoon plus 2 teaspoons mirin
- 2 tablespoons potato starch
- 2 tablespoons shiratamako
(see page 353)
- Neutral oil, such as canola
(rapeseed), peanut, or safflower,
for deep-frying
- 8 tablespoons Konbu Dashi
(page 22)
- 2 teaspoons hon kuzu
(see page 352) mixed with
2 tablespoons water until smooth

Shiratamako is a flour made from glutinous rice (*mochigome*) and is used to prepare soft "mochi" confections. Here it is mixed into cooked mashed potato to add body for these mochi-like deep-fried morsels. Substitute soy milk for dairy-free.

-

In a medium saucepan of cold water, bring the potatoes to a boil over high heat. Cook until easily pierced with a bamboo skewer, about 20 minutes. Peel while hot.

In a medium bowl, smash the potatoes with a fork or potato masher. Stir in the milk, 2 teaspoons of the shoyu, 1 tablespoon of the mirin, the potato starch, and *shiratamako* until the ingredients are well incorporated. Divide into 8 pieces and pat well into rounded ovals (similar to the Edo period *koban* coin), making sure all air pockets are eliminated.

In a high-sided medium sauté pan, heat 1¼ inches (3 cm) oil over medium-low heat until about 340°F (170°C). To check the oil temperature, sprinkle a few pinches of potato starch into the oil. The starch should sink to the bottom of the pan, then immediately float back up to the surface, and there will be a few medium-sized bubbles.

Carefully slip the potato mochi into the oil, taking care it does not overflow, and cook until crispy and golden on both sides, about 3 minutes per side. Be careful, for popping (due to air pockets).

In a small saucepan, stir together the dashi and remaining 2 teaspoons each shoyu and mirin. Bring to a simmer over medium heat. Reduce the heat to low, scrape in the *kuzu* slurry, and cook gently while stirring continuously until the dashi mixture is glossy, about 5 minutes.

Serve one or two hot mochi per person, drizzled with the silky sauce.

一口コロッケ

MINI POTATO CROQUETTES

HITOKUCHI KOROKKE

Preparation time: 30 minutes
Cooking time: 2 minutes
Makes: 12 small balls

- ¼ recipe (8½ oz/240 g)
Potato Salad (page 48)
- 1 heaping tablespoon unbleached
all-purpose (plain) flour
- 3 tablespoons finely grated
mountain yam
- 4 tablespoons organic panko
- Neutral oil such as canola
(rapeseed), peanut, or safflower,
for deep-frying

These meltingly soft little crisp-fried bites are made from leftover potato salad. Here, instead of dipping in beaten eggs, mountain yam is used to wet the balls before rolling in panko and frying. These balls are perfect as is, but also delicious dipped into Red Pepper Sauce (page 49).

-

Roll the potato salad into twelve heaping 1-teaspoon rounded balls. Dust with the flour, shake off excess, and set on a large dinner plate.

Scrape the mountain yam into a shallow bowl and wash your hands and forearms with hot soapy water to alleviate the mountain yam's natural (temporary) itchy properties.

Place the potato balls to the far left of your workspace and the bowl of grated mountain yam to the right of the balls. Pour some of the panko onto a large plate and set to the right of the mountain yam. Place another large plate to the right of the panko.

Smooth the mountain yam around each ball and set on top of the panko. Wash and dry your hands. Roll each ball to coat with panko and place on the clean dinner plate, adding a little more panko if needed.

In a high-sided medium sauté pan, heat 1¼ inches (3 cm) oil over medium-high heat until about 355°F (180°C). To check the oil temperature, sprinkle a few pinches of panko into the oil. The panko should sink about halfway down in the oil, then immediately float back up to the surface, creating a flurry of medium-sized bubbles.

Slip the croquettes, one by one, into the oil, introducing them at the side of the pan. Take care the oil does not bubble over and if necessary, fry in batches. Cook, turning, until crispy and deeply golden, 60–90 seconds. Drain briefly on a rack set over a pan to catch the drips. Serve as a hot bite before dinner.

飛龍頭

TOFU CROQUETTES

HIRYUZU

Preparation time: 45 minutes,
plus 2–3 hours tofu weighting time
Cooking time: 10 minutes
Makes: 8 small croquettes

• 10½ oz (300 g) cotton tofu
(momendofu, see page 352)
or Japanese-style soft block tofu
• 3½ oz (100 g) Boiled Bamboo
Shoot (page 34)
• 4 inches (10 cm) medium mountain
yam (7 oz/200 g), scrubbed and peeled
• 2 dried shiitake, soaked in
boiling water for 30 minutes
• 1¾ oz (50 g) maitake
• ½ medium carrot (2⅔ oz/75 g)
• ¼ teaspoon flaky sea salt
• 2 teaspoons shoyu
• 4 tablespoons shiratamako
(see page 353)
• 4 tablespoons potato starch
• 6 tablespoons all-purpose
(plain) flour
• Neutral oil, such as canola
(rapeseed), peanut, or safflower, for
deep-frying and shaping the patties

You can add any bits and pieces
of vegetables or peels from other
dishes, if you have them; just
keep the balance so the tofu and
flours still serve as binders for
the croquettes. These croquettes
are also good simmered in shoyu-
flavored dashi or add richness to
a *nabe*, such as "Three Birds, One
Stone" Nabe (page 260). Grating
the bamboo shoot the way it
grows (from the bottom to the
top) will help avoid fiber buildup
on the grater.
-
Place the tofu on a plate and set
another plate on top for 2–3 hours
to press out excess water. Scrape
into a medium bowl and mash
by hand.

Finely grate the bamboo shoot
and mountain yam on a ceramic
grating plate (*oroshiki*, see page
354) or metal grating plate
(*oroshigane*, see page 354) and
slide into the bowl with the
tofu. (Immediately wash your
hands and forearms to alleviate
the temporary itchiness of the
mountain yam.)

Drain the shiitake. Remove the
stems from the shiitake and
reserve for another dish. Finely
chop the shiitake caps, maitake,
and carrot and fold into the tofu
mixture until evenly distributed.
Sprinkle in the salt and shoyu
and mix until well incorporated.
In a small bowl, whisk together
the *shiratamako*, potato starch,
and flour. Beat into the other
ingredients with a wooden spoon
until smooth.

Oil your hands and pat the mixture
into 8 small round patties.

In a large high-sided sauté
pan, heat 1¼ inches (3 cm) oil
over medium heat until about
340°F (170°C). To check the oil
temperature, sprinkle a few
pinches of flour into the oil. The
flour should sink to the bottom
of the pan, then immediately
bounce back up to the surface,
and there will be a few medium-
sized bubbles.

Gently add the croquettes and
deep-fry until golden on both
sides, about 5 minutes per side.
Drain briefly on a wire rack
set over a pan to catch drips.
Serve hot.

さつま芋コロッケ

SWEET POTATO CROQUETTES

SATSUMA-IMO KOROKKE

Preparation time: 45 minutes
Cooking time: 40 minutes
Makes: 8 croquettes

- 2 medium sweet potatoes
 (1 lb/475 g), peeled
- 1 small ear corn (3½ oz/100 g)
- ½ tablespoon unroasted sesame oil
- 1 medium onion (3½ oz/100 g), diced
- 1 small carrot (1¾ oz/50 g), diced
- 4 tablespoons coarsely chopped
 cooked edamame or green peas
- 1 teaspoon flaky sea salt
- ½ teaspoon freshly ground
 black pepper
- 2 tablespoons all-purpose
 (plain) flour
- 2 eggs, at room temperature (for a
 vegan version, see recipe introduction)
- ¾ cup (60 g) organic panko
- Neutral oil, such as canola
 (rapeseed), peanut, or safflower,
 for deep-frying
- 1 lemon, cut into small wedges,

Kabocha croquettes might be more popular than sweet potato ones, but I find the sweet potato provides a lighter vehicle for these crunchy patties. The unusual additional ingredients in these croquettes make them extra special and extra tasty. For parties, double or triple the recipe and form the mixture into small balls, to serve as a healthy (albeit fried) bite with drinks. Substitute the eggs with finely grated mountain yam for a vegan version.

-

Place the peeled sweet potatoes in a bamboo or metal steamer and cook over a pot of rapidly boiling water until completely soft in the center, about 25 minutes. Mash while hot with a potato masher or heavy-duty fork.

Fill a small pot with water and bring to a boil. Remove from the heat and dunk in the corn for 30 seconds. Allow the corn to cool to room temperature before cutting the kernels off the cob with a razor-sharp knife. (If you do not precook the corn slightly, any kernels that escape will explode in the oil.)

In a large frying pan, warm the sesame oil over medium heat. Add the diced onion and carrot and cook, stirring, until softened but not colored, 3–5 minutes. Scrape the sautéed onion and

carrot into the bowl with the mashed sweet potato and fold in with the corn kernels, edamame, salt, and pepper. Form eight small but fat, rounded, bale-shaped cylinders (tawara-gata) and roll them in the flour, making sure that all surfaces have been dusted. Shake off excess flour.

In a shallow soup bowl, whisk the eggs until homogenous. Make a mound of panko on one side of a clean baking sheet. Working one by one, dip each croquette into the egg, allowing excess to drip off, and roll in the panko to coat evenly. Line up on the opposite side of the baking sheet from the panko side. Add panko as needed.

In a large high-sided sauté pan, heat 1¼ inches (3 cm) oil over medium heat until about 340°F (170°C). To check the oil temperature, sprinkle a few pinches of panko into the oil. The panko should sink to the bottom of the pan, then immediately float back up to the surface, and there will be a few medium-sized bubbles.

Slip the croquettes into the oil, taking care it does not overflow, and fry until golden on all sides, 3–5 minutes. Drain briefly on a rack set over a pan to catch the drips. Serve hot with a lemon wedge.

SWEET POTATO CROQUETTES

なすのはさみ焼きカツ

EGGPLANT CUTLETS

NASU NO HASAMI-YAKI KATSU

Preparation time: 55 minutes
Cooking time: 10 minutes
Makes: 8 cutlets

- 2¼ inches (6 cm) medium lotus root (6¼ oz/175 g)
- 6¼ oz (175 g) okara (see page 352)
- 1 teaspoon flaky sea salt
- ½ teaspoon freshly ground black pepper
- 4 small (2¼ oz/60 g each) Japanese eggplants (aubergines)
- 1 cup (2⅔ oz/75 g) panko
- 4 tablespoons all-purpose (plain) flour
- 2 tablespoons potato starch, mixed with 6 tablespoons water
- 8 tablespoons canola (rapeseed) or unroasted sesame oil
- 2 tablespoons Dengaku Miso (page 30)

These vegetarian *katsu* have several steps, but the crispy breaded eggplant (aubergine) and creamy *okara* filling yields a tasty result. A potato starch slurry substitutes for eggs here when making vegan breaded foods. If you don't want waste, stir-fry the lotus peels, eggplant side cuttings, and flesh from around the eggplant tops in a small amount of sesame oil and season with a few splashes of shoyu for *kinpira*.

-

Peel the lotus root. Finely grate on a ceramic grater (*oroshiki*, see page 354) or metal grating plate (*oroshigane*, see page 354) and drain for about 10 minutes in a fine wire-mesh sieve set over a bowl to catch the drips. Scrape into a medium bowl and mix in the *okara*, salt, and pepper, until well-incorporated.

Lop off the calyxes and slice the curved sides off each eggplant (aubergine) lengthwise. Halve the eggplants lengthwise into slices about ½ inch (1 cm) wide. Place 4 pairs of eggplant on the cutting board, making sure they are roughly the same size and shape. Press one-quarter of the lotus-*okara* mixture in your palm to form a flat mass the size of the eggplant slices. Lay the flattened mixture in between two of the eggplant pairs, as if

you are filling a sandwich. Repeat with the rest of the mixture to fill all 4 pairs of eggplant slices. Wash and dry your hands to remove any lingering filling. Pick up each eggplant sandwich, one by one, and press the "cutlets" together to smooth the edges and eliminate air pockets.

Mound the panko on one side of a baking sheet. Sprinkle a dinner plate with the flour and carefully dredge the eggplant sandwiches in the flour to cover. Shake off. Dip in the potato starch slurry, then roll in the panko. Align the "cutlets" on the side of the baking sheet opposite the mound of panko.

In a large frying pan, heat the oil over medium heat. Add the eggplant cutlets to the pan and cook, flipping carefully after about 1 minute to cook the top and then the two sides, until the eggplant is completely soft, the *okara* filling is cooked through, and the panko is crispy and golden, about 5 minutes.

Remove to a cutting board and smear the top of each cutlet with the *dengaku miso*. Halve crosswise with a very sharp knife and serve blistering hot as a vegetable main dish or crunchy snack before dinner.

じゃが芋ボール

CURRY-FLAVORED GRATED POTATO FRITTERS

JYAGAIMO BO-RU

Preparation time: 30 minutes
Cooking time: 3 minutes
Serves: 4

• 2 medium potatoes
(10½ oz/300 g), peeled
• ¼ teaspoon curry powder
• ½ teaspoon flaky sea salt
• ½ teaspoon gold sesame seeds
• Neutral oil, such as canola
(rapeseed), peanut, or safflower,
for deep-frying

Patting finely grated raw potato into small balls yields appealingly light, fried morsels. They are great to snack on before dinner or to serve as a hot bite with a room-temperature spread.
-
Set a fine-mesh sieve over a medium bowl. Grate the potatoes on a ceramic grater (*oroshiki*, see page 354) or metal grating plate (*oroshigane*, see page 354) and scrape into the sieve to drain for 10 minutes. Remove the sieve to a small plate and pour off the potato water from the draining bowl, taking care to keep the white starch that has pooled up on the bottom of the bowl. Mix the grated potato into the starch and stir in the curry powder, salt, and sesame seeds.

In a large high-sided sauté pan, heat 1¼ inches (3 cm) oil over medium heat until about 340°F (170°C). To check the oil temperature, pinch off a tiny portion of the potato mixture and drop into the oil; it should sink to the bottom of the pan, then immediately bounce back up to the surface, and there will be a few bubbles.

Use two soup spoons to form small oval fritters and slip them into the oil, at the edge of the pan. Watch that the oil does not bubble over, and fry in batches if need be. Cook until golden and the bubbling has quieted, about 1½ minutes. Skim out and drain briefly on a rack set over a pan. Serve hot on four plates.

~~~~~~

ピーマンのおから詰め揚げ

OKARA-FRIED PEPPERS

PI-MAN NO OKARA-ZUME AGE

Preparation time: 45 minutes
Cooking time: 6 minutes
Serves: 4

• 7 oz (200 g) okara (see page 352)
• 2 tablespoons Japanese white
sesame paste
• 1 tablespoon usukuchi shoyu
(see page 344)
• 1 teaspoon flaky sea salt
• 2 small Japanese green and red
peppers (piman, see page 347) or
3 sweet red and yellow
peppers (7 oz/200 g)
• 4 tablespoons potato starch
• Neutral oil, such as canola
(rapeseed), peanut, or safflower,
for deep-frying
• ½ cup (2⅔ oz/75 g) unbleached
all-purpose (plain) flour

Soybean pulp (*okara*), a by-product of making soy milk, is the ultimate low-budget, healthy ingredient, often used for texture and to add bulk (and flavor) to vegetable dishes in Japanese country or temple cooking.
-
In a medium bowl, mix the *okara*, sesame paste, *usukuchi shoyu*, and salt together well.

Halve the peppers lengthwise, cut off the core section, and pull out the seeds and veins. Finely chop any useable parts and add to the *okara* mixture. Squish the mixture together with your hands until it forms a cohesive mass.

Stuff the mixture into each of the pepper halves and coat well with the potato starch, making sure

all surfaces are covered. Lightly shake off any excess.

In a large high-sided sauté pan, heat 1¼ inches (3 cm) oil over medium heat until about 340°F (170°C). To check the oil temperature, flick a few drops of the below batter into the oil. The batter should sink to the bottom of the pan, then immediately bounce back up to the surface, and there will be a few bubbles.

In a shallow bowl, whisk ¾ cup (6 fl oz/180 ml) cold water into the flour. Dip the peppers into the batter until well coated and slip into the oil. Fry until crispy and golden, about 3 minutes per side. Drain briefly on a rack set over a pan. Serve hot as a light main course with vegetable sides.

AGEDASHI TOFU ON SILKY ENOKI

えのきと揚げ出し豆腐

ENOKI TO AGEDASHI-DOUFU

Preparation time: 30 minutes, plus 1 hour tofu weighting time
Cooking time: 4 minutes
Serves: 4

- 10½ oz (300 g) cotton tofu (momendofu, see page 352) or Japanese-style soft block tofu
- 1¼ teaspoons flaky sea salt
- 10 thin green beans (1 oz/25 g)
- Neutral oil, such as canola (rapeseed), peanut, or safflower, for deep-frying
- 2 tablespoons potato starch
- 2 tablespoons brown rice flour (see komeko, page 353)
- 1⅔ cups (13½ fl oz/400 ml) Konbu Dashi (page 22)
- 2 tablespoons sake
- 2 teaspoons usukuchi shoyu (see page 344)
- 5 oz (140 g) enoki, spongy bottoms cut off, halved crosswise

Enoki mushrooms lend a slippery contrast to the fried tofu and the green bean garnish finishes the dish with a splash of color and a bright crunch. Although served warm, this light dish is a welcome addition to any summer menu.

-

Place the tofu on a salad plate. Set another plate on top to press out excess water for 1 hour, taking care that the plate is not so heavy that it breaks the tofu. Cut the tofu in quarters.

Bring a medium saucepan three-quarters full of water to a boil with 1 teaspoon of the salt. Drop in the green beans and cook for 30 seconds. Scoop out with a wire-mesh sieve and leave in the sink to cool. Cut off the stem ends and slice diagonally into ¾-inch (2 cm) pieces.

In a high-sided medium sauté pan, heat 1¼ inches (3 cm) oil over medium heat until rippling, about 355°F (180°C). To check the oil temperature, sprinkle a few pinches of rice flour into the oil. The flour should sink about halfway to the bottom, then immediately float back up to the surface, and there will be quite a few lively medium-sized bubbles.

In a shallow bowl, whisk the potato starch and rice flour together. Gently roll each quarter piece of tofu in the starch/rice flour mixture to coat generously. Shake off the excess and slide into the oil. Cook for about 2 minutes, turn, and cook until golden all over, about 1 minute longer. Remove the tofu pieces one by one with a skimmer and drain on a rack set over a pan to catch the drips.

In a medium saucepan, stir the dashi, sake, *usukuchi shoyu*, remaining ¼ teaspoon salt, and enoki together. Bring to an almost simmer over medium-high heat.

Spoon the enoki and broth into four shallow bowls. Add a quarter piece of fried tofu and mound the green beans evenly on top of each piece of tofu. Serve hot.

AGEDASHI TOFU ON SILKY ENOKI

揚げワンタン

DEEP-FRIED TEMPLE TRIANGLES

AGE WANTAN

Preparation time: 45 minutes,
plus 1 hour tofu weighting time
Cooking time: 5 minutes
Makes: 16 triangles

• 2⅔ oz (75g) cotton tofu
(momendofu, see page 352) or
Japanese-style soft block tofu
• ⅛ teaspoon flaky sea salt
• 1 large leaf napa cabbage
(Chinese leaf), finely chopped (60 g)
• 1 dried shiitake, soaked in
warm water to cover for 30 minutes
• 1 salted sour "plum" (umeboshi,
see page 350), chopped to a paste
• 2 large green shiso leaves,
finely chopped
• 16 wonton wrappers
• Neutral oil, such as canola
(rapeseed), peanut, or safflower,
for deep-frying
• A few pinches of flour, for testing
the oil temperature

The umeboshi and shiso in these tantalizing fried bites give the creamy filling a delightful zing. Serve blistering hot before dinner or as part of a full meal.
-
Place the tofu on a salad plate and set another plate on top to press out excess water for 1 hour. Squeeze by handfuls over the sink and drop into a medium bowl.

Massage the salt into the cabbage in a bowl and let sit for 10 minutes. Firmly squeeze out as much liquid as possible and add to the bowl with the tofu.

Remove the shiitake from the soaking liquid. Finely chop and add to the bowl. Scrape in the umeboshi and shiso and mix well with your fingers. Roll into 16 balls and place on a piece of parchment paper.

Set the stack of wrappers and a small bowl of water next to your workspace. Working one by one, cup a wrapper in your nondominant hand, with a point facing you, like a diamond. Place a ball on the wrapper, just above the center line of the diamond and dip your finger in the water. Dampen the two sides of the diamond where the filling is located. Fold the wrapper over the filling and match the sides together to make a triangle. Seal well.

In a large high-sided sauté pan, heat 1¼ inches (3 cm) oil until about 340°F (170°C). To check the oil temperature, sprinkle flour into the oil; it should sink to the bottom, then immediately float back up to the surface, and there will be a few bubbles.

Working in two batches, fry the triangles until lightly golden all over, about 30 seconds on each side. Drain briefly on a rack set over a pan to catch the drips.

青しそのチーズ巻き

"CHEESE"-STUFFED GREEN SHISO ROLLS

AOSHISO NO CHI-ZU MAKI

Preparation time: 30 minutes
Cooking time: 1 minute
Makes: 12 small bites

• 12 gyoza wrappers
• 12 green shiso leaves, stems removed
• 3½ oz (100 g) vegan meltable
"cheese" (similar to mozzarella)
• Neutral oil, such as canola (rapeseed),
peanut, or safflower, for deep-frying
• A few pinches of flour, for testing
the oil temperature

Eating cheese is a relatively recent custom in Japan, so here the vegan option substitutes nicely, especially if it is soy milk–based. The result is a crispy, creamy bite to serve as a small fried course or with pre-dinner drinks.
-
Lay the gyoza wrappers on your workspace or a baking sheet. Line each one with a shiso leaf (the outside of the leaf should be against the wrapper). Cut the "cheese" into ¼-inch (5 mm) batonnets. Place about 2 batonnets in the middle of each shiso leaf. Roll up tightly.

In a large high-sided sauté pan, heat 1¼ inches (3 cm) oil over medium heat until about 340°F (170°C). To check the oil temperature, sprinkle flour into the oil; it should sink to the bottom, then immediately float back up to the surface, and there will be a few bubbles.

Slip the rolls into the oil and fry for 1 minute. Skim out and drain briefly on a rack set over a pan to catch the drips. Serve hot on four small plates lined with a folded piece of tempura blotting paper.

DEEP-FRIED TEMPLE TRIANGLES; "CHEESE"-STUFFED GREEN SHISO ROLLS; FRIED YUBA-WRAPPED BEAN SPROUTS (PAGE 140)

もやしのゆば包み

FRIED YUBA-WRAPPED BEAN SPROUTS

MOYASHI NO YUBA-ZUTSUMI

Preparation time: 25 minutes
Cooking time: 5 minutes
Makes: 8 rolls

- 4 sheets dried yuba (1 oz/25 g)
- Pinch of baking soda
- 2 teaspoons unroasted sesame oil
- 3 cups (7 oz/200 g) mung bean sprouts (moyashi, see page 349), small yellow "beard roots" pinched off the ends
- 1 teaspoon yellow mustard powder (karashi, see page 350), mixed with ½ teaspoon warm water
- 4 tablespoons white miso
- Neutral oil, such as canola (rapeseed), peanut, or safflower, for deep-frying
- A few pinches of flour, for testing the oil temperature

At its best, *yuba* is a creamy mass of skimmed-off skin from the top of soy milk as it heats up to make tofu. While fresh *yuba* may be a bit of a challenge to find abroad, dried *yuba* is attainable. Look at Japanese or Asian grocery stores or online. These come out burning hot, so it's best to give them a minute or two to cool. They are great served as a savory bite with drinks before dinner. Pinching off the "beard roots" will improve texture but is optional.
-
In a medium bowl, combine the *yuba* and baking soda and add hot tap water to generously cover. Soak for 5 minutes, drain, and pat dry in a clean tea towel. Halve each piece crosswise. Arrange the rectangular pieces on a large baking sheet, with a short side facing you.

In a large frying pan, heat the sesame oil over medium-high heat. Add the bean sprouts and stir-fry for about 1 minute, to cook slightly. Scrape into a small bowl.

Muddle the mustard paste into the miso and scrape into the bowl with the bean sprouts. Toss gently until well distributed.

Place a thick line of bean sprouts horizontally across the bottom of each piece of *yuba* and roll up tightly like spring rolls (no need to fold in the sides, it's a straight roll up). Once rolled, fry as soon as you can.

In a large high-sided sauté pan, heat 1¼ inches (3 cm) oil over medium-low heat until about 340°F (170°C). To check the oil temperature, sprinkle the flour into the oil. The flour should sink to the bottom of the pan, then immediately float back up to the surface, and there will be a few medium-sized bubbles.

Slip the rolls into the oil and cook, turning frequently, until golden and crispy, about 2 minutes. Drain for 1–2 minutes on a rack set over a pan to catch the drips.

納豆の包み揚げ

NATTO AND SHISO TRIANGLES

NATTOU NO TSUTSUMI-AGE

Preparation time: 20 minutes
Cooking time: 1 minute
Makes: 8 triangles

- 3 oz (85 g) small-bean natto
- 4 small green shiso leaves,
  finely chopped
- 2 teaspoons shoyu
- 8 wonton wrappers
- ¼ teaspoon yellow mustard
  powder (karashi, see page 350)
- 1 teaspoon shoyu
- Neutral oil, such as canola
  (rapeseed), peanut, or safflower,
  for deep-frying

I made a similar recipe from *The Heart of Zen Cuisine* when I was first in Japan—natto wrapped in shiso and nori and deep-fried— and those rolls converted me to liking natto. This particular method comes from Harumi Kawaguchi, a Zen nun friend.
-
Finely chop the natto with a sharp knife. Scrape into a small bowl and mix in the chopped shiso and 1 teaspoon of the shoyu with a spoon. Portion out eight small mounds of natto onto a plate to ensure even distribution of the filling.

Set a stack of wrappers and a small bowl of water next to your workspace. Working one by one, cup a wrapper in your nondominant hand, with a point facing you, like a diamond. Dollop the natto on the wrapper, just above the center line of the diamond and dip your finger in the water. Dampen the two sides of the "diamond" where the filling is located. Fold the wrapper over the filling and match the sides together to make a triangle. Seal the edges well, taking care that no natto is caught in the seal.

Make *karashijoyu* (mustard shoyu): In a small bowl, stir ⅛ teaspoon warm water into the mustard and leave for 10 minutes to allow the flavor to develop. Stir the shoyu into the mustard and set aside. (Alternatively, if the natto comes with little packets of good-quality shoyu and mustard, you could use those.)

In a large high-sided sauté pan, heat 1¼ inches (3 cm) of oil over medium heat—the oil should not be too hot because the wonton skins brown quickly. The oil should be just barely starting to shimmer. Fry the natto triangles for 30 seconds, flip and cook until lightly golden all over, about 30 seconds longer. Skim out and drain briefly on a rack set over a pan to catch the drips.

Serve hot with a tiny saucer per person of *karashijoyu*. Dip a corner in the *karashijoyu* before taking a bite. Good with a cold beer.

みょうが天

MYOGA TEMPURA

MYOUGA TEN

Preparation time: 10 minutes
Cooking time: 2 minutes
Serves: 4, as a small bite

• Neutral oil, such as canola
(rapeseed), peanut, or safflower,
for deep-frying
• 6 medium myoga (3 oz/85 g),
halved lengthwise
• ¼ recipe Tempura Batter (page 26)
• A pinch of fine sea salt

Myoga is often translated erro-neously as "Japanese ginger." While the plant itself resembles a ginger plant, *myoga* is a perennial that grows in a shady section of the garden. Ginger plants, on the other hand, are annual (since the whole root is harvested) and they need full sun, so are grown in the fields. *Myoga* peek out from the ground around the base of the plant starting from the early summer. They are pinky-tan buds with an appealing earthy, slightly hot flavor with nice crunch. Deep-fried as tempura, *myoga* is succulent and refreshing.

-

In a deep-sided medium sauté pan, heat 1¼ inches (3 cm) oil over medium heat until about 340°F (170°C). To check the oil temperature, flick a few drops of the tempura batter into the oil. The batter should sink to the bottom of the pan, then immediately bounce back up to the surface, and there will be a few medium-sized bubbles.

Dip the *myoga* halves into the tempura batter, shake off, and slip into the oil. Deep-fry, turning, until lightly golden in spots, 60–90 seconds. Do not overdo it—the pieces should not be dark golden. Skim out of the oil, shake off excess, and drain briefly on a rack set over a pan to catch the drips.

Sprinkle with a little salt and serve three halves per person on individual saucers lined with a folded piece of tempura blotting paper.

~~~~~~

梅干しの薄衣揚げ

LIGHTLY FRIED UMEBOSHI

UMEBOSHI NO USUGOROMO-AGE

Preparation time: 15 minutes,
plus 2–3 hours soaking time
Cooking time: 1 minute
Serves: 4, as a small bite

• 4 salted "sour" plums
(umeboshi, see page 350)
• 2 tablespoons cold sparkling water
• 2 tablespoons unbleached
pastry flour
• Neutral oil, such as canola
(rapeseed), peanut, or safflower,
for deep-frying

Umeboshi dipped in a light batter and deep-fried make tasty little hot puckery bites to serve as a palate cleanser during a full meal. Avoid *umeboshi* with MSG.

-

Open a small hole in the stem end of each *umeboshi* and soak in a medium bowl for 2–3 hours to leach off salt. Remove from the water and pat dry.

In a small bowl, whisk the sparkling water into the flour.

In a small high-sided sauté pan, heat 1¼ inches (3 cm) of the oil over medium heat until

340°F (170°C). To check the oil temperature, flick a few drops of the tempura batter into the oil. The batter should sink to the bottom of the pan, then immediately bounce back up to the surface, and there will be a few medium-sized bubbles.

Give the batter in the bowl a stir, then drop in the *umeboshi*. Pick up each *umeboshi*, one by one, shake off excess batter, and slip into the oil. Fry until golden and crisp, about 20 seconds on each side. Drain briefly on a rack set over a pan to catch the drips, then serve immediately.

うどの穂の天ぷら

UDO TOPS TEMPURA

UDO NO HO NO TENPURA

Preparation time: 10 minutes
Cooking time: 8 minutes
Serves: 4

• Neutral oil such as canola
(rapeseed), safflower, or peanut,
for deep-frying
• 2 handfuls udo tops (4 oz/115 g)
• ¼ recipe Tempura Batter (page 26)
• ¼ teaspoon flaky sea salt

Udo stalks are often cut into fine slabs, battered, and deep-fried for spring tempura. But the stalks can be a bit challenging to eat unless you approach the tempura pieces sideways, since their grain goes lengthwise. Using *udo* tops is the perfect solution to this issue, plus the tops have a lovely frilliness and fry up beautifully.

–

In a large high-sided sauté pan, heat 1¼ inches (3 cm) oil over medium heat until about 340°F (170°C). To check the oil temperature, flick a few tiny drops of tempura batter into the oil. The batter should sink to the bottom of the pan, then immediately bounce up to the surface, creating a few medium-sized bubbles.

Cut a cross into the bottom of any thick pieces and drop the *udo* tops into the tempura batter. Toss to coat, shake off excess batter, and slip into the hot oil. Cook until the batter is lightly colored and crispy and the bubbles have mostly quieted, 6–8 minutes. Skim out and drain on a rack set over a pan to catch the drips. Sprinkle with the salt.

Serve hot as a bite before dinner with a cold thimbleful of sake.

~~~~~~

紅生姜天

PICKLED RED GINGER TEMPURA

BENISHOGA TEN

Preparation time: 15 minutes
Cooking time: 10 minutes
Serves: 4

• 1 small piece mountain yam,
scrubbed and peeled
• 1 cup (5¼ oz/150 g) unbleached
pastry flour
• ½ teaspoon fine sea salt
• 3½ oz (100 g) pickled red ginger
(benishoga, see page 350), drained
• 7 parts canola (rapeseed) oil
• 3 parts tablespoons dark roasted
sesame oil

Pickled red ginger (*benishoga*) often contains red dye, so take care to find a natural version (I use Ohsawa brand packages of julienned threads). These hot little fried morsels make addictive bites before dinner, especially when served with a frothy beer. *Benishoga* is packaged in *umesu* (see page 345), so save the *umesu* and use it in other dishes.

–

On a metal grating plate (*oroshigane*, see page 354), finely grate the mountain yam to a viscous consistency to make 2 tablespoons.

Place the flour in a medium bowl. Add ½ cup (4 fl oz/125 ml) water, the grated mountain yam, and the salt and stir to make a smooth batter. Fold in the drained *benishoga*.

In a large high-sided sauté pan, heat 1¼ inches (3 cm) oil until about 355°F (180°C). To check the oil temperature, flick a few drops of batter into the oil. The batter should sink about halfway to the bottom of the pan, then immediately bounce back up to the surface, and there will be quite a few lively medium-sized bubbles.

Quietly introduce serving-spoon-size small ovals of batter into the oil and fry, turning, until golden and cooked through, about 7 minutes. Drain briefly on a rack set over a pan to catch drips. Serve hot.

揚げオクラとトマトのマリネ **FRIED OKRA WITH TOMATO SAUCE**

AGE-OKURA TO TOMATO NO MARINE

Preparation time: 45 minutes,
plus cooling and chilling time
Cooking time: 5 minutes
Serves: 4, generously

- 5 medium tomatoes
  (5¼ oz/150 g each)
- 2 tablespoons apple cider vinegar
- 1 tablespoon olive oil
- 5 large capers, finely chopped
- 2 small Japanese green olives or
  Picholine, pitted and finely chopped
- 1 tablespoon olive brine
  (from the jar of olives)
- 1 green shiso leaf, finely chopped
- 1 teaspoon flaky sea salt
- Neutral oil, such as canola
  (rapeseed), peanut, or safflower,
  for deep-frying
- 7 oz (200 g) okra, brown portions
  of tops pared off
- 1 tablespoon potato starch

The fields produce plenty of okra and tomatoes in the summertime and they go together well. Here the fresh tomato sauce is intentionally light to balance the fried element of the okra.
-
Finely dice 2 of the tomatoes and scrape into a small bowl. Stir in the vinegar, olive oil, capers, olives, olive brine, and shiso. Refrigerate to chill.

Slice the remaining 3 tomatoes into rounds ½ inch (1 cm) thick and sprinkle with ¼ teaspoon of the salt. Heat a large well-seasoned cast-iron skillet or nonstick frying pan over medium-high heat. Place the tomatoes in the pan in one layer and sear for about 2 minutes on each side to caramelize. Line a dinner plate with overlapping layers of the tomatoes. Once cooled, refrigerate to chill.

In a large high-sided sauté pan, heat 1¼ inches (3 cm) oil over medium-low heat until you can feel some heat rise from the pan. The oil temperature should be lower than normal frying temperature, about 320°F (160°C).

Arrange the okra horizontally to you on a cutting board and sprinkle with ½ teaspoon of the salt. Roll the okra in the salt with your flattened palms to break down the fibers a little (*itazuri*). Wipe off the salt and any moisture with a paper towel, remove the tops, and halve the okra lengthwise. Dust lightly with the potato starch, shake off, and slip into the oil. Fry, turning, for about 1 minute. Drain briefly on a rack set over a pan to catch the drips. Once cool, refrigerate to chill.

Once chilled divide the tomato slices among four salad plates to one side so they are overlapping slightly. Arrange the okra halves in an attractive, yet haphazard fashion in the middle of the plates or stack them in the center of the plate so the okra tops are laying across the bottom of the tomato slices. Sprinkle evenly with the remaining ¼ teaspoon salt. Spoon the tomato sauce over the haphazardly arranged okra, allowing the okra to peek through from the sauce. Alternatively, mound the tomato sauce over some of the bottoms of the stacked okra at the opposite side of the plate from the tomato slices.

Serve as a light side course on a hot summer night.

FRIED OKRA WITH TOMATO SAUCE

TARO, SOBA GAKI, AND CELERY LEAF TEMPURA

里いも、そばがきとセロリの
葉天

SATO IMO, SOBA GAKI TO SERORI NO HA TEN

Preparation time: 30 minutes
Cooking time: 15 minutes
Serves: 4, generously

- Rice washing liquid or cold water
- 8 very small taro roots
  (2 oz/25 g each), peeled
- 1 cup (4¼ oz/120 g) Japanese
  buckwheat flour (sobako,
  see page 353) or French "light"
  buckwheat flour
- Generous ¾ cup
  (6¼ fl oz/185 ml) boiling water
- 2 tablespoons shiratamako
  (see page 353)
- ⅔ cup (2¾ oz/80 g) sifted unbleached
  all-purpose (plain) flour
- Neutral oil, such as canola
  (rapeseed), peanut, or safflower,
  for deep frying
- 4 large pieces celery tops
  (thin stalks with plenty of leaves),
  3½ inches (9 cm) long
- ½ teaspoon flaky sea salt,
  for serving

When approaching tempura, it is always important to think about textures and flavor profiles of what you will be frying and adding to the plate. And of course, seasonality comes into play. The combination here is particularly well balanced with the slightly viscous, yet resilient texture of the taro to the "mochi-mochi" soft soba gaki and finally the bitter yet bright celery leaves. The light kiss of batter gives each piece an ethereal crispness that somehow enhances their distinct textures. Simmering taro (or daikon) in rice washing liquid will help them lose any natural bitterness and will preserve their white flesh. If you do not have any rice washing liquid handy, just use cold water.
-
Fill a medium saucepan with rice washing water or cold water and add the taro. Bring to a boil over medium-high heat, adjust to a gentle simmer, and cook until a bamboo skewer can be easily inserted into the centers, 3–5 minutes. Drain and set aside to air dry.

Fill the bottom of a double boiler halfway with water and bring to a boil over high heat. Add the buckwheat flour to the top of the double boiler (preferably one with a rounded bottom) and stir the soba flour continuously with a wooden spoon until "cooked" and hot to the touch, about 5 minutes.

Remove the top of the double boiler onto your work surface and add the boiling water all at once. Stir vigorously with the wooden spoon, smashing and beating

the mixture until well combined and completely smooth. Roll immediately into 12 small balls (soba gaki).

In a medium bowl, whisk 1⅓ cups (10½ fl oz/325 ml) cold water into the shiratamako until smooth. Quickly whisk in the flour until incorporated but avoid overmixing.

In a large high-sided sauté pan, heat 1¼ inches (3 cm) of the oil over medium-high heat until about 340°F (170°C). To check the oil temperature, flick a few drops of batter into the oil. The batter should sink to the bottom of the pan, then immediately bounce back up to the surface, and there will be a few medium-sized bubbles.

Dip the celery tops in the batter, shake off, and slide into the oil. Fry, turning, until lightly golden on all sides, about 60 seconds. Drain on a rack set over a pan to catch the drips. Roll the taro in the batter, shake off, and fry for about 90 seconds, turning for even coloring. Drain on the rack next to the celery. Drop the soba gaki into the batter, roll around to coat evenly, then slip into the oil. Fry until lightly colored, about 60 seconds. Drain briefly.

Line a plate with a folded-up piece of tempura blotting paper and arrange the taro, soba gaki, and celery tops in an attractive fashion. Spoon the salt in a small mound on a corner of the plate and serve hot.

TARO, SOBA GAKI, AND CELERY LEAF TEMPURA

舞茸天

MAITAKE TEMPURA

MAITAKE TEN

Preparation time: 15 minutes
Cooking time: 10 minutes
Serves: 4

- Unroasted sesame oil,
  for deep-frying
- 2 tablespoons dark
  roasted sesame oil
- Generous ¾ cup
  (6¾ fl oz/200 ml) sake
- 2 teaspoons fine sea salt
- ⅔ cup (3½ oz/100 g) unbleached
  cake or udon flour
- 1 large cluster maitake
  mushrooms (5¼ oz/150 g),
  torn into 4 pieces
- ½ teaspoon flaky sea salt

Maitake mushrooms are the perfect vehicle for temple-style eggless tempura. They are fragrant and soft, so the crunchy light coating of crispy batter envelops the mushroom pieces beautifully. While a light sprinkling of sea salt might be the best seasoning for maitake tempura, dipping in Tentsuyu (page 26) might offer a slightly lighter feel to the rich mushroom.
-
In a large high-sided sauté pan, heat 1¼ inches (3 cm) unroasted sesame oil with the dark roasted sesame oil over low heat, keeping a close eye on it.

In a medium bowl, whisk the sake and ½ teaspoon of fine salt into the flour, but do not overbeat.

In another medium bowl, stir the remaining 1½ teaspoons fine salt into 1 cup (8 fl oz/250 ml) cold water. Swish each maitake piece through the salty water, shake off, and drop into the batter.

Increase the heat under the oil to medium-low and heat to about 340°F (170°C). To check the oil temperature, flick a few drops of batter into the oil; they should sink to the bottom of the pan, then immediately bounce back up to the surface, and there will be a few bubbles.

Roll each piece of maitake in batter to coat, shake off the excess, and slip into the oil. Fry, turning, until the oil starts to quiet and the maitake is crispy and shows slight coloring, 2–3 minutes. Drain briefly on a rack set over a pan to catch drips. Serve hot sprinkled with the flaky salt.

柿の天ぷら

PERSIMMON TEMPURA

KAKI NO TENPURA

Preparation time: 15 minutes
Cooking time: 3 minutes
Serves: 4

- 1 firm Fuyu persimmon
  (8¼ oz/235 g), peeled
- 2 tablespoons sake
- 3 tablespoons unbleached
  cake flour
- Neutral oil, such as canola
  (rapeseed), safflower, or peanut,
  for deep-frying

Fuyu persimmons, which are nonastringent, can be eaten raw, when still hard, so the point here is to deep-fry at a high enough temperature that the batter crisps up quickly but the persimmon does not get mushy. Serve as a welcome hot bite midway through a Japanese meal featuring several room-temperature side dishes.
-
Cut the persimmon in 8 wedges. Core and bevel the edges. In a medium bowl, stir the sake and 2 tablespoons water into the flour. Drop in the persimmon pieces and toss to coat.

In a large high-sided sauté pan, heat 1¼ inches (3 cm) oil over medium-high heat, until about 355°F (180°C). To check the oil temperature, flick a few drops of batter into the oil; they should sink about halfway to the bottom of the pan, then immediately bounce back to the surface, and there will be quite a few bubbles.

Pick up one persimmon piece at a time with a pair of chopsticks (or your fingers), shake off excess batter, and slide into the oil, introducing at the edge of the pan. Take care that the oil does not overflow. Fry until golden on all sides, 1–2 minutes. Drain briefly on a rack set over a pan to catch the drips.

Serve 2 pieces per person on individual saucers as a small bite.

PERSIMMON TEMPURA; MAITAKE TEMPURA

小松菜の信田巻き

KOMATSUNA SHINODA-MAKI

KOMATSUNA NO SHINODA-MAKI

Preparation time: 25 minutes
Cooking time: 6 minutes
Serves: 4, as a small bite

• ½ bunch (3½ oz/100 g) komatsuna
(see page 346) or bok choy
• 4 teaspoons shoyu
• 2 deep-fried tofu pouches
(usuage, see page 352)
• 2 tablespoons potato starch
• 2 tablespoons canola (rapeseed)
or unroasted sesame oil

Deep-fried tofu pouches (usuage) re-crisp nicely when heated in a frying pan with a little oil, and the Japanese mustard greens (komatsuna) provide a juicy center to these rolls. Serve these hot, if possible, as a bite with tea or drinks, but they hold up well at room temperature.
-
Fill a medium saucepan with water and bring to a boil over high heat. Hold the komatsuna (or bok choy) stems in the boiling water for 30 seconds, let go, push the greens in to submerge, and cook for another 30 seconds. Scoop out with a wire-mesh sieve and refresh under cold running water until cool to the touch. Squeeze well, then lay out crosswise on a cutting board, stem ends aligned. Sprinkle with the shoyu, making sure it adheres to the komatsuna and does not pool up on the board.

Cut the usuage in half crosswise with a sharp knife. Use the knife to slice open the short sides so you can open the pieces into rectangles. Lay out on a second cutting board, skin side down, and sprinkle both sides with the potato starch and shake off excess. Position the usuage with a long side facing you.

Cut the komatsuna pieces crosswise into the same lengths as the usuage and lay a thin log of komatsuna ½ inch (1 cm) up from the bottom edge of each piece of usuage. Roll tightly into a long cigar-like shape, with no gaps.

In a frying pan, heat the oil over low heat. Once you can feel the heat rising from the pan, lay the rolls in the pan and cook, gently turning, to crisp up, until golden, about 5 minutes. Halve each roll diagonally for serving.

~~~~~~~~~~~~~~~~~~~~~~~~~~~~~~~~

れんこんと長いもの
柚子ごしょう揚げ

DEEP-FRIED LOTUS ROOT AND MOUNTAIN YAM WITH YUZU KOSHO

RENKON TO NAGA-IMO NO YUZU GOSHOU-AGE

Preparation time: 35 minutes
Cooking time: 5 minutes
Serves: 4

• 2¼ inches (6 cm) lotus root
(5¼ oz/150 g)
• 4 inches (10 cm) medium
mountain yam
(7 oz/200 g), scrubbed
• 2 teaspoons green or
red yuzu kosho (see page 350)
• All-purpose (plain) flour, for dusting
• Neutral oil, such as canola
(rapeseed), peanut, or safflower,
for deep-frying
• Flaky sea salt, for serving

Lightly flavored with salty, spicy, citrusy yuzu kosho, these squishy, crispy bites are beguiling. They can be fried so each piece is distinct, or in clumps of two or three, depending on their size.
-
Peel the lotus and mountain yam. Cut into bite-size triangular chunks (rangiri, see page 17) and scrape into a medium bowl. Dab in the yuzu kosho and toss to distribute. Leave for 10 minutes.

Use paper towels to blot off liquid that has pooled around the vegetable pieces in the bowl. In a clean bowl, lightly dust the pieces with flour and shake off.

In a large high-sided sauté pan, heat 1¼ inches (3 cm) oil over medium heat until 340°F (170°C). To check the oil temperature, sprinkle a little flour into the oil; it should sink to the bottom of the pan, then immediately float back to the surface, and there will be a few bubbles.

Quietly slip spoonfuls of the floured pieces into the oil at the edge of the pan to avoid disturbing the oil. Fry for about 4 minutes, breaking up any big clumps and turning, until crispy and golden. Drain briefly on a rack set over a pan, sprinkle lightly with salt and serve.

KOMATSUNA SHINODA-MAKI

ポテトしんじょの豆乳碗

POTATO SHINJO IN SOY MILK DASHI

POTETO SHINJO NO TOUNYUU-WAN

Preparation time: 45 minutes,
plus 1 hour tofu weighting time
Cooking time: 25 minutes
Serves: 4

- 5¼ oz (150 g) cotton tofu (momendofu, see page 352) or Japanese-style soft block tofu
- 1 medium potato (5¼ oz/150 g)
- Flaky sea salt
- 4 rounds (¼ inch/5 mm thick) zucchini (courgette)
- 4 medium shiso leaves, finely chopped
- 2-inch (5 cm) square piece of konbu (left over from making the dashi, below), finely diced
- 3 tablespoons potato starch
- Neutral oil, such as canola (rapeseed), peanut, or safflower, for deep-frying
- Generous ¾ cup (6¾ fl oz/200 ml) Konbu Dashi (page 22)
- Scant ½ cup (3½ fl oz/100 ml) soy milk
- 4 teaspoons usukuchi shoyu (see page 344)
- 4 tablespoons sake
- 1 teaspoon grated fresh wasabi

The presentation of this dish, with the wasabi on top of the zucchini (courgette) coin, is gorgeous and the soy milk adds a bit of richness to the konbu dashi, making a beautifully light foil for the deep-fried *shinjo*. Ultimately there are a few fiddly steps, yet still well worth the time spent. Prepare and serve on a special occasion.

-

Place the tofu in a small container with sides and set a weight on top to press out excess water for 1 hour.

Peel the potato, add to a medium saucepan of well-salted water, and bring to a boil. Cook until tender, about 20 minutes. Drain and smash well in a Japanese grinding bowl (*suribachi*, see page 354). Let cool. Bring a small saucepan of water and a large pinch of salt to a boil and drop in the zucchini rounds. Scoop out after 30 seconds and allow to cool to room temperature.

Add the tofu, shiso, konbu, 1 tablespoon of the potato starch, and ¼ teaspoon salt to the cooled potato and mash together until well blended. Form into 4 balls (*shinjo*). Dust with the remaining 2 tablespoons potato starch.

In a high-sided medium sauté pan, heat 1¼ inches (3 cm) oil over medium heat until hot, about 355°F (180°C). To check the oil temperature, sprinkle a few pinches of potato starch into the oil. The starch should sink about halfway to the bottom of the pan, then immediately float back up to the surface, and there will be quite a few lively medium-sized bubbles.

Shake off excess potato starch from each *shinjo* and introduce gently into the oil. Fry, turning, until golden on all sides, about 8 minutes. Drain briefly on a rack set over a pan to catch the drips.

In a medium saucepan, bring the dashi, soy milk, *usukuchi shoyu*, sake, and ¼ teaspoon salt just to an almost boil over medium-high heat (be careful not to boil the soy milk because it will separate).

Divide the broth among four lacquer bowls. Add one *shinjo* to each bowl, set a piece of zucchini on top and a dab of wasabi. Serve immediately as an elegant first course.

POTATO SHINJO IN SOY MILK DASHI

根菜かき揚げ

ROOT VEGETABLE FRITTERS

KONSAI KAKIAGE

Preparation time: 45 minutes
Cooking time: 10 minutes
Serves: 4

- ¼ medium burdock root (1¾ oz/50 g), scrubbed
- ¼ medium carrot (1¾ oz/50 g), peeled or scrubbed
- 1 piece (6 × 3¼ inches/15 × 8 cm) of konbu, left over from making dashi
- ½ recipe Tempura Batter (page 26)
- 3 tablespoons julienned pickled red ginger (benishoga, see page 350)
- Neutral oil, such as canola (rapeseed), peanut, or safflower, for deep-frying
- Flaky sea salt, for serving

Julienned root vegetables enlivened with bright threads of pickled ginger make these fritters irresistible. Serve as an appetizer with drinks before dinner or as a hot bite with dinner.
-
Julienne the burdock, carrot, and konbu and add to the tempura batter along with the *benishoga*, stirring until the ingredients are well distributed.

In a large high-sided sauté pan, heat 1¼ inches (3 cm) oil until 355°F (180°C). To check the oil temperature, flick a few drops of batter into the oil; they should sink about halfway to the bottom of the pan, then immediately bounce back to the surface, and there will be quite a few bubbles.

Dollop small ladles of the battered vegetables into the oil and fry for 4 minutes. Flip and cook 2 minutes on the other side. Flip again and cook on the first side until crispy and golden on the outside and no longer spongy in the center, about 2 minutes longer. Keep pushing the fritters down into the oil as you fry and watch for the bubbles to subside a bit. Drain briefly on a rack set over a pan, and serve hot with a pinch or two of salt.

根菜の皮のかき揚げ

ROOT VEGETABLE PEEL FRITTERS

KONSAI NO KAWA NO KAKIAGE

Preparation time: 45 minutes
Cooking time: 5 minutes
Serves: 4

- 4 inches (10 cm) medium burdock (1¾ oz/50 g), scrubbed
- 2 handfuls nonjuicy root vegetable peels (carrot, udo, sweet potato), removed with a vegetable peeler
- 5 tablespoons unbleached udon flour or pastry flour
- 2 tablespoons shiratamako (see page 353)
- Neutral oil, such as canola (rapeseed), peanut, or safflower, for deep-frying
- 4 small wedges green yuzu or lemon, for serving
- ¼ teaspoon flaky sea salt, for serving

Using up root vegetable peels by turning them into fritters is genius, and almost requires no recipe. Make these when you are preparing root vegetable soup or simmered dishes. Be sure to soak the udo peel until you are ready to proceed, since it discolors if left out in the air.
-
Cut off shavings of the burdock, as if you were hand-sharpening a pencil (*sasagaki*, see page 17). Soak in cold water. Cut the vegetable peels crosswise into ¾-inch (2 cm) pieces. Drain and blot dry the burdock. Toss with the peels in a medium bowl.

In a small bowl, whisk the udon flour and *shiratamako* together and sprinkle over the vegetables. Toss to distribute with a pair of cooking chopsticks. Sprinkle in a scant ½ cup (3½ fl oz/100 ml) cold water and toss gently to wet the flour.

In a large high-sided sauté pan, heat 1¼ inches (3 cm) oil over medium heat until 340°F (170°C). To check the oil temperature, sprinkle a few pinches of the flour mixture into the oil; they should sink to the bottom of the pan, then immediately float back to the surface, and there will be a few bubbles.

With a round serving spoon, scoop out 4 heaping spoonfuls of the ingredients and add them to the oil one at a time, slipping them into the oil at the edge of the pan. Fry for 1 minute, flip, then 1 more minute, before flipping and cooking until crispy and golden on both sides, 1½ minutes longer. Drain briefly on a rack set over a pan to catch the drips.

Arrange the *kakiage* on saucers lined with a folded piece of tempura blotting paper. Serve hot with a yuzu or lemon wedge and a small mound of salt.

ROOT VEGETABLE PEEL FRITTERS

長芋とにんじんの信田巻き

CARROT AND MOUNTAIN YAM ROLLS

NAGA-IMO TO NINJIN NO SHINODA-MAKI

Preparation time: 30 minutes
Cooking time: 10 minutes
Makes: 6–8 small bites

- 6–8 thick stalks mitsuba
  (see page 346)
- Boiling water
- 1¾ oz (50 g) scrubbed and peeled
  mountain yam, halved lengthwise
- 1¾ oz (50 g) peeled carrot
- ½ teaspoon flaky sea salt
- 2 deep-fried tofu pouches
  (usuage, see page 352)
- 2 tablespoons potato starch
- 4–6 tablespoons Yuzu Miso (page 29)
- 2 tablespoons unroasted
  sesame or canola (rapeseed) oil

The creamy, citrusy yuzu miso brings the crunchy mountain yam and soft, sweet carrot together beautifully in these crispy little fried rolls, while the aromatic *mitsuba* adds a brightly refreshing note to the whole. Serve as a bite before dinner or as part of a multidish meal. Make more if you have a crowd, but keep it manageable. Depending on the size of your *usuage*, this recipe will make 6 to 8 bites.
-
Place the *mitsuba* in a wire-mesh sieve and pour boiling water over for 10 seconds. Refresh under cold running water and pat dry.

Cut the mountain yam and carrot into batonnets ½ inch (1 cm) thick. Massage the carrot with the salt. Bring a medium saucepan of water to a boil over high heat. Drop in the carrot, cook for 5 minutes, scoop out in a wire-mesh sieve, and cool under cold running water to refresh.

Slice open the two short sides and one of the long sides of the

usuage with a razor-sharp knife and open out to make one flat rectangle. Dust the inside of both *usuage* with the potato starch and shake off excess.

Place each *usuage* on a cutting board with a long side facing you, and smear yuzu miso across the middle third. Place a line of carrot and mountain yam batonnets across the middle one-third of the yuzu miso, alternating colors (if you are able!). Roll up tightly into a long cigar-like shape, making sure no gaps remain.

In a frying pan, warm the oil over medium-low heat. Place each roll, seam side down, in the pan and fry, carefully turning with a pair of cooking chopsticks (*saibashi*, see page 354) or tongs, until golden on all sides, about 5 minutes.

Remove to a cutting board and allow to cool before cutting crosswise into 3 or 4 fat rounds, depending on the size of your *usuage*. Tie each roll with a knot of *mitsuba* and serve.

ごぼうのスティック揚げ

DEEP-FRIED BURDOCK STICKS

GOBOU NO SUTIKKU-AGE

Preparation time: 20 minutes
Cooking time: 15 minutes
Serves: 4

- ½ small burdock root
  (scant 3 oz/75 g)
- Neutral oil, such as canola
  (rapeseed), peanut,
  or safflower, for deep-frying
- 1 tablespoon black sesame seeds
- ¼ recipe Tempura Batter (page 26)
- Flaky sea salt, for serving

Adding black sesame to the batter contrasts nicely with the brownness of the burdock root in this fiber-rich snack.
-
Scrub the burdock with a natural fiber vegetable brush (*tawashi*). Pat dry and cut into fine batonnets 3 inches (7.5 cm) long and ¼ inch (5 mm) thick.

In a large high-sided sauté pan, heat 1¼ inches (3 cm) oil over medium heat until 340°F (170°C). To check the oil temperature, flick a few drops of batter into the oil;

they should sink to the bottom of the pan, then immediately bounce back up to the surface, and there will be a few bubbles.

In a medium bowl, stir the sesame seeds into the batter. Slide in the burdock and toss to coat, then slip into the oil one by one. Fry, turning slowly, until the bubbling has subsided, and the pieces are golden, about 3 minutes for al dente or 5 minutes to cook through. Drain briefly on a rack set over a pan. Sprinkle lightly with the salt and serve hot.

CARROT AND MOUNTAIN YAM ROLLS

大根揚げびたし

DEEP-FRIED DAIKON IN BROTH

DAIKON AGE-BITASHI

Preparation time: 20 minutes
Cooking time: 20 minutes
Serves: 4

- 1⅔ cups (13½ fl oz/400 ml)
  Konbu Dashi (page 22)
- 3 tablespoons sake
- 2 teaspoons usukuchi shoyu
  (see page 344)
- ½ teaspoon fine sea salt
- Neutral oil, such as canola (rapeseed),
  safflower, or peanut, for deep-frying
- ½ small daikon (1 lb/500 g)
- 2 tablespoons brown rice flour
  (see page 353), for dusting
- 1 teaspoon finely julienned yuzu
  or Meyer lemon zest
- 2 stalks mizuna, cut crosswise into
  2-inch (5 cm) pieces, for serving
- 2 tablespoons grated daikon,
  for serving

Deep-frying seals the surface of vegetables and allows the insides to steam to a meltingly soft consistency. Simmering in broth after frying removes some of the oils but also infuses the fried ingredient with gentle flavors and added juiciness.

-

In a medium saucepan, bring the dashi, sake, *usukuchi shoyu*, and salt to a simmer over medium heat. Remove from the heat, cover, and set aside.

In a large, high-sided sauté pan, heat 1¼ inches (3 cm) oil over medium-low heat to 320°F (160°C).

Cut the daikon crosswise into rounds ½ inch (1 cm) thick. Peel and bevel the edges of the rounds. Dust with flour, shake off, and

slip into the oil in batches, taking care that the oil does not overflow. Fry until golden on both sides, about 2 minutes per side. Drain on a rack set over a pan to catch the drips. Blot off excess oil with a paper towel.

Add the fried daikon to the dashi, return to a simmer over medium heat, adjust to medium-low heat, and cook gently for 10 minutes.

Arrange 2 overlapping rounds of daikon on each of 4 plates with a spoonful of the cooking liquid. Make a stack of mizuna and place next to the daikon. Spoon a mound of grated daikon onto the uppermost round of daikon, pinch some yuzu zest on the grated daikon, and serve warm or at room temperature as a first course.

柚子のフリッター

YUZU FRITTERS

YUZU NO FURITTA-

Preparation time: 30 minutes
Cooking time: 10 minutes
Serves: 4

- 2-inch (5 cm) piece daikon
  (2⅔ oz/75 g), peeled
- 2 medium yuzu or small Meyer lemons
- 5 tablespoons sake
- ½ cup (2⅔ oz/75 g) unbleached cake
  or pastry flour
- 1 tablespoon black sesame seeds
- Neutral oil, such as canola
  (rapeseed), peanut, or safflower,
  for deep-frying
- ½ tablespoon shoyu, for serving

Make these black-flecked fried yuzu rounds during the height of winter when the insides of the yuzu are still juicy. The grated daikon has a natural hotness that juxtaposes nicely with the fried yuzu, yielding a bold bite before dinner or in the middle of a meal.

-

Grate the daikon into a sieve lined with cheesecloth (muslin) to drain. Pare off the ends of the yuzu and squeeze any juice out into a small bowl. Slice the yuzu crosswise into rounds ¼ inch (5 mm) thick. Poke out the seeds with a chopstick or bamboo skewer.

In a medium bowl, whisk the sake and 3 tablespoons cold water into the flour. Stir in the sesame seeds to make a smooth batter.

In a large high-sided sauté pan, heat 1¼ inches (3 cm) oil over medium heat until 340°F (170°C). To check the oil temperature, flick a few drops of batter into the oil; they should sink to the bottom of the pan, then immediately bounce back to the surface, and there will be a few bubbles.

Dredge the yuzu slices in the batter to cover all surfaces. Working in batches to avoid crowding, cook the fritters until lightly golden, 2–3 minutes. Drain briefly on a rack set over a pan.

Line four plates with a folded-up piece of tempura blotting paper and place a few slices on each. Squeeze the grated daikon gently and mound next to the yuzu. Drizzle the daikon with the yuzu juice and shoyu and serve hot.

DEEP-FRIED DAIKON IN BROTH

揚げ餅椀

DEEP-FRIED MOCHI IN BROTH

AGE MOCHI WAN

Preparation time: 15 minutes
Cooking time: 10 minutes
Serves: 4

- 3 tablespoons finely grated peeled daikon
- 2 green shiso leaves, finely chopped
- 1⅔ cups (13½ fl oz/400 ml) Konbu Dashi (page 22)
- 2 tablespoons sake
- 2 teaspoons usukuchi shoyu (see page 344)
- ¼ teaspoon flaky sea salt
- 4 thin rounds of medium turnip
- Neutral oil, such as canola (rapeseed), safflower, or peanut, for deep-frying
- 4 pieces dried brown or white rice mochi

If possible, serve in a lidded lacquer bowl (o-wan, see page 354) for the full effect. This elegant course should appear midway through a meal as a dish to satisfy hunger and soothe the soul. The medley of textures and flavors with the gentle dashi, crisp, gooey mochi, and peppery grated daikon with aromatic shiso is remarkable. The turnip rounds serve as a handy, and pretty, vehicle for keeping the grated daikon from slipping down into the dashi before serving.
-
In a small bowl, stir the daikon and shiso together. Set aside.

In a small saucepan, bring the dashi, sake, usukuchi shoyu, and salt just to a boil over high heat. Remove from the heat, slide in the turnip rounds, and allow them to "cook" for 2 minutes. Scoop out the turnip with a slotted spoon and drain in a small wire-mesh sieve set over a small bowl to catch the drips. Return the dashi to the stove over very low heat to keep warm.

In a high-sided medium sauté pan, heat 1¼ inches (3 cm) oil until you can just start to feel the heat rising, about 320°F (160°C)—lower than usual for deep-frying.

Slip in the mochi and as it puffs, take care to dislodge from the bottom of the pan, otherwise the pieces will become misshapen. Cook for 3 minutes on one side, flip, cook 1 minute on the other, flip again and cook 1 more minute on the first side. Remove from the oil and drain on a rack set over a pan to catch the drips.

Place one mochi in each of four lidded lacquer bowls (o-wan, see page 354). Lay a turnip round on each mochi and pinch a mound of the grated daikon/shiso mixture into the center of each turnip round. Pour the broth around the circumference of the mochi, place the lids on the bowls, and serve.

DEEP-FRIED MOCHI IN BROTH

青のり揚げ

DEEP-FRIED KOYADOFU WITH GREEN NORI

AONORI-AGE

Preparation time: 30 minutes
Cooking time: 15 minutes
Makes: 12 small balls

- 1 cup (8 fl oz/250 ml) Konbu Dashi (page 22)
- 1 tablespoon shoyu
- ½ tablespoon hon mirin
- ¼ teaspoon fine sea salt
- 4 Reconstituted Koyadofu (page 36), quartered
- ½ cup (4 fl oz/125 ml) finely grated mountain yam
- 1 cup (75 g) panko
- 4 tablespoons green nori powder (aonori, see page 349)
- Neutral oil, such as canola (rapeseed), peanut, or safflower for deep-frying
- Flaky sea salt, for serving

The first time I ate green nori it was pounded into fresh mochi. I loved the way the nori perfumed the soft rice. It was served with grated daikon and soy sauce and was probably the best thing I had tasted thus far in Japan.
-
In a medium saucepan, bring the dashi, shoyu, mirin, and fine salt just to a boil over medium-high heat. Slip in the *koyadofu*, adjust the heat, and simmer gently for 5 minutes. Scoop the *koyadofu* out from the dashi with a slotted spoon and drain in a wire-mesh sieve. Once the *koyadofu* is cool enough to handle, squeeze each piece lightly in your fist to express the simmering liquid. Tear into pieces, dropping as you go into a medium bowl with the grated mountain yam. Fold in the panko and green nori and form into 12 balls the size of golf balls.

In a large high-sided sauté pan, heat 1¼ inches (3 cm) oil over medium heat until about 340°F (170°C). To check the oil temperature, sprinkle a few pinches of panko into the oil; they should sink to the bottom of the pan, then immediately float back to the surface, and there will be a few bubbles.

Deep-fry the balls for about 6 minutes until golden all over. Drain briefly on a rack set over a pan to catch the drips. Sprinkle with a little flaky salt and serve hot with drinks before dinner or as a part of a full meal.

~~~~~~~~~~~~~~~~~~~~~~~

ふきの薄衣揚げ

DEEP-FRIED BUTTERBUR

FUKI NO USUGOROMO-AGE

Preparation time: 15 minutes
Cooking time: 5 minutes
Serves: 4

- 4½ oz (125 g) thin stalks fuki (see page 346)
- Boiling water
- Neutral oil such as canola (rapeseed), safflower, or peanut, for deep-frying
- 4 tablespoons sake
- 2 tablespoons unbleached pastry flour
- ½ teaspoon fine sea salt

The batter here is purposely light to allow the unusual flavor of butterbur (*fuki*) to shine through and be the star. Serve these blistering hot as a bite before dinner with a cold beer.
-
Set up a bowl of ice and water. Cut the *fuki* in thirds crosswise and place in a wire-mesh sieve. Pour boiling water over for 10 seconds, then drop into the ice bath. Peel back about 2 inches (5 cm) of the outside strings of one piece. Gather the strings together and pull down to remove. Repeat with the other pieces.

Dry well in a clean tea towel and cut crosswise into 1¾–2-inch (4–5 cm) lengths.

In a large high-sided sauté pan, heat 1¼ inches (3 cm) oil over medium heat until 340°F (170°C). To check the oil temperature, sprinkle a little flour into the oil; it should sink to the bottom of the pan, then immediately float back to the surface, and there will be a few bubbles.

In a medium bowl, whisk the sake into the flour and salt and drop in the *fuki* pieces. Stir with a pair of chopsticks to coat lightly and introduce one by one into the hot oil. Deep-fry until the batter is lightly colored and the bubbles have largely subsided, 2–4 minutes, depending on thickness. Be careful not to overcook because the *fuki* becomes floppy. Drain briefly on a rack set over a pan and serve immediately.

じゃが芋と高野豆腐の
すり揚げ

DEEP-FRIED POTATO AND KOYADOFU PATTIES

JYAGAIMO TO KOUYADOUFU NO SURI-AGE

Preparation time: 1 hour
Cooking time: 30 minutes
Makes: 8 small pieces

- 2 medium potatoes
(10½ oz/300 g),
peeled and quartered
- 2 tablespoons canola (rapeseed) oil
- 1 small onion (3½ oz/100 g),
finely diced
- 1 medium carrot (5¼ oz/150 g),
scrubbed and finely diced
- 1 teaspoon flaky sea salt
- ½ teaspoon freshly ground
black pepper
- 1 tablespoon dried hijiki
(see page 349), soaked in
cold water for 20 minutes
- 6 tablespoons (1¾ oz/50 g) chopped
walnuts
- 4 tablespoons unbleached
all-purpose (plain) flour
- 4 freeze-dried tofu (koyadofu,
see page 352), coarsely grated
on a box grater
- 1 egg, at room temperature (for a
vegan version, see recipe introduction)
- Neutral oil, such as canola
(rapeseed), peanut, or safflower
for deep-frying
- 4 tablespoons dark roasted
sesame oil

There are quite a few ingredients here, but don't be intimidated; they do not take as long to prepare as you might think. These little patties are best the first day but also good the next, reheated in a covered dry frying pan over low heat. For a vegan version, substitute the egg with finely grated mountain yam.
-
Place the potato quarters in a small saucepan, cover generously with cold water, and bring to a boil over high heat. Cook until soft in the centers, 10–12 minutes. Drain and smash with a potato masher or heavy-duty fork.

In a medium frying pan, heat the canola (rapeseed) oil over medium-low heat and scrape in the onion and carrot. Stir-fry gently for about 5 minutes to soften. Add ½ teaspoon of the salt and ¼ teaspoon of the pepper and scrape into a small bowl to cool.

Drain the hijiki and pat dry. Add the hijiki, carrot/onion mixture, walnuts, remaining ½ teaspoon salt and ¼ teaspoon pepper to the smashed potatoes. Pat out about 8 small oval-shaped patties (similar to the Edo period koban coin) and place on a baking sheet. Sprinkle with the flour and roll around on all sides to coat. Shake off excess and place at one end of a second baking sheet. Mound the grated koyadofu onto the opposite end of the baking sheet, leaving the middle clear. Crack the egg into a shallow soup

bowl and beat with a fork. Dip each patty into the beaten egg, one by one, allow excess egg to drip back into the bowl, and roll in the koyadofu to coat evenly. Place in the empty spot in the middle of the baking sheet.

In a large high-sided sauté pan, heat 1¼ inches (3 cm) of the neutral oil with the sesame oil over medium heat until shimmering, about 355°F (180°C). To check the oil temperature, sprinkle a few pinches of grated koyadofu into the oil. The koyadofu should sink about halfway to the bottom of the pan, then immediately float back up to the surface, and there will be quite a few lively medium-sized bubbles.

Carefully slip in the patties, making sure that the oil is not in danger of boiling over. Cook until golden all over, about 3 minutes per side. Drain briefly on a rack set over a pan to catch the drips. Serve hot.

チーズのはさみ揚げ

DEEP-FRIED CHEESE-STUFFED KOYADOFU

CHI-ZU NO HASAMI-AGE

Preparation time: 20 minutes,
plus 30 minutes maceration time
Cooking time: 5 minutes
Serves: 6

- ½ cup (4 fl oz/125 ml)
Konbu Dashi (page 22)
- 4 Reconstituted Koyadofu (page 36)
- 4 large green shiso leaves,
torn in half lengthwise
- 1¼ oz (35 g) mozzarella cheese,
cut into 8 slices ¼ inch (5 mm) thick
- 4 tablespoons unbleached
all-purpose (plain) flour
- ½ cup (4 fl oz/125 ml/150 g)
finely grated mountain yam
- 1 cup (2⅔ oz/75 g) organic panko
- Neutral oil, such as canola
(rapeseed), peanut, or safflower,
for deep-frying
- Flaky sea salt, for serving

Cheese appears occasionally in Japanese dishes, though it is not a traditional ingredient. Processed cheese and canned grated Parmesan were perhaps the most common cheeses a few decades ago. Nowadays, however, a wide range of cheeses are available at most Japanese supermarkets and mozzarella is a clear favorite.
-
In a medium saucepan, heat the dashi over medium heat. Halve the reconstituted koyadofu crosswise and carefully lower into the hot dashi. Adjust to a gentle simmer and cook for 5 minutes. Drain and squeeze out the excess broth when cool enough to handle.

Cut a pocket into each koyadofu. Wrap a shiso leaf half around each slice of cheese and slide into the koyadofu pockets. Add the flour to a shallow bowl and, one at a time, roll each piece of koyadofu in the flour. Shake off the excess and place on a large dinner plate. Scrape the mountain yam over the koyadofu, smoothing around all surfaces of each piece.

Spread half of the panko onto one half of a baking sheet. Pick up each half piece of koyadofu, allowing excess yam to drip off, and place each one on top of the panko. Sprinkle the remaining half of the panko over the koyadofu and roll carefully to coat evenly.

In a large high-sided sauté pan, heat 1¼ inches (3 cm) oil over medium heat until about 340°F (170°C). To check the oil temperature, sprinkle a few pinches of panko into the oil. The panko should sink to the bottom of the pan, then immediately float back up to the surface, and there will be a few medium-sized bubbles.

Slip the koyadofu into the oil and fry until crispy and golden, about 2 minutes per side. Drain briefly on a rack set over a pan to catch the drips.

Serve immediately, sprinkled with a pinch or two of salt, as a snack before dinner with carbonated beverages—these are best hot since the cheese will harden when left to sit.

DEEP-FRIED CHEESE-STUFFED KOYADOFU

蒸し物 & 煮物

Steaming is a gentle, hands-free method of cooking vegetables (and other foods), and the resulting vegetables make good candidates for rich sesame- or miso-based sauces. Unlike with boiling, when you steam the vegetables on a plate, you can catch any juices that run out and add them to the finished dish. Root vegetables such as kabocha, potatoes, sweet potatoes, turnips, or daikon are particularly good steamed, rather than simmered because they retain their shape and do not become water-logged. Steaming is also an excellent method for rendering vegetables such as eggplant (aubergine) silky soft, much in the way that frying does, but without the oil. In fact, legendary tempura chef Fumio Kondo, owner of Tempura Kondo in Tokyo and author of several excellent books on tempura, maintains that when cooking ingredients dipped in batter as for tempura, you are actually steaming the vegetables, and only deep-frying the batter.

You will need a steamer setup consisting of a wok plus a bamboo steamer for steamed dishes or a dedicated stainless steel steamer. In restaurants, you could use a perforated rectangular pan set inside a hotel pan (Gastronorm), plus foil and a lid (if possible).

As a rule of thumb, simmered dishes (*nimono*) are mostly simmered until just cooked through, then cooled to room temperature to slowly absorb the cooking liquid, before being heated up again for serving. A typical countrywoman, my mother-in-law conscientiously simmered each vegetable separately and then put them all together in one pot to season: simmering in dashi prominently flavored with shoyu and sugar. In a busy household, most likely the simmered foods are cooked and served right away.

Nimono are often comforting dishes that remind someone of their grandmother. However, with a slightly more modern approach, *nimono* can become attractive and contemporary, with the added benefit of being warming, if served hot. And *nimono* dishes hold up well over the course of a couple days, if refrigerated. Just reheat and serve at any meal. Some Japanese swear that *nimono* dishes get better over time (though I prefer them the first day).

蒸し物 ＆ 煮物

MUSHIMONO & NIMONO

STEAMED & SIMMERED

ふきと厚揚げの煮物

SIMMERED ATSUAGE AND FUKI

FUKI TO ATSUAGE NO NIMONO

Preparation time: 15 minutes,
plus 30 minutes cooling time
Cooking time: 10 minutes
Serves: 4

• 7 oz (200g) thick deep-fried tofu
(atsuage, see page 350)
• 2½ cups (20 fl oz/600 ml)
Happo Dashi (page 25)
• 1 tablespoon organic
granulated sugar
• 1½ tablespoons usukuchi shoyu
(see page 344)
• ½ tablespoon shoyu
• 2 tablespoons hon mirin
• 4 thin stalks Parboiled Fuki (page 35)
or de-stringed celery (5¼ oz/150 g)

Simmered foods are an important part of Japanese vegetarian fare because their juiciness is both comforting and nourishing. Also, they have the benefit of being versatile and can be served at any meal: morning, noon, or night. Although I prefer simmered foods when they are freshly made, they keep for several days if stored in the fridge. Substitute celery if you cannot find *fuki*.

-

Place the *atsuage* in a wire-mesh sieve and pour water over for 10 seconds to remove oil. Pat dry. Halve through the middle to create two equal-size thinner rectangular pieces of tofu. Cut each of those into 6 pieces to create square-shaped chunks.

Nestle the *atsuage* into a medium saucepan and add the *happo dashi*, sugar, *usukuchi shoyu*, shoyu, and mirin. Bring to a simmer over medium-high heat. Remove from the heat and allow to cool to room temperature in the cooking liquid to absorb flavor.

Add the *fuki*, bring to a boil over high heat, and immediately remove the pan from the heat. Spoon the *atsuage* onto one side of a shallow serving bowl with some of the cooking liquid. Stack the *fuki* attractively alongside, and serve.

ゆばとえんどうの煮物

SIMMERED SNOW PEAS WITH YUBA

YUBA TO ENDOU NO NIMONO

Preparation time: 35 minutes
Cooking time: 5 minutes
Serves: 4

• 1 large dried wood ear
mushroom, soaked in cold water
cover for 20 minutes
• 1 tablespoon shoyu
• 1⅔ cups (13½ fl oz/400 ml) plus
1 tablespoon Konbu Dashi (page 22)
• 1 tablespoon plus 2 teaspoons
hon mirin
• 1 teaspoon usukuchi shoyu
(see page 344)
• 1 teaspoon flaky sea salt
• 20 snow peas (mangetout), 3½ oz
(100 g), stems and strings removed
• 2½ oz (70 g) fresh yuba
(see page 352), cut crosswise into
½-inch (1 cm) pieces

The delicate texture and flavor of *yuba* (skin skimmed off slowly heating soy milk during the tofu-making process) calls for a similarly mild vegetable such as snow peas (mangetout) to complement and enhance the exquisite creamy *yuba*. And the garnish of highly seasoned chewy wood ear mushroom adds an unexpected flavor accent.

-

Drain the mushroom, cut off any hard portions, and julienne. Slide into a very small saucepan with the shoyu and 1 tablespoon each dashi and mirin. Bring to a simmer over medium heat. Remove from the heat and leave in the cooking liquid.

In a medium saucepan, combine the remaining 1⅔ cups (13½ fl oz/ 400 ml) dashi, 2 teaspoons mirin, *usukuchi shoyu*, and salt and bring to a simmer over

medium heat. Drop in the snow peas (mangetout) and cook for 1 minute. Remove from the heat immediately and scoop the peas out of the cooking liquid but do not discard the liquid.

To serve hot, arrange the peas on one side of a shallow serving bowl and the *yuba* on the other side. Pour some of the warm snow pea cooking liquid over the *yuba* to flavor. Pinch the mushroom slices up with a pair of chopsticks. Shake off and drop in a mound in the middle of the bowl—straddling the *yuba* and snow peas.

To serve cold, refrigerate the snow peas and mushroom separately in their respective cooking liquids and the *yuba* with a little of the snow pea cooking liquid (to season it).

SIMMERED SNOW PEAS WITH YUBA

なすとじゅんさいのお椀

EGGPLANT AND JUNSAI IN DASHI

NASU TO JUNSAI NO OWAN

Preparation time: 20 minutes
Cooking time: 25 minutes
Serves: 4

• 3 medium Japanese eggplants
(aubergines), 8 oz (225 g)
• ¼ teaspoon flaky sea salt
• 5¼ oz (150 g) baby water lily buds
(junsai, see page 349)
• Boiling water
• 3 cups (24 fl oz/700 ml)
Konbu Dashi (page 22)
• 1 tablespoon usukuchi shoyu
(see page 344)
• 1 teaspoon hon kuzu
(see page 352) mixed with
1 tablespoon water until smooth
• ¾ teaspoon sour "plum" paste
(bainiku, see page 350)
• ¾ teaspoon finely slivered
yuzu zest
• ¾ teaspoon finely slivered
fresh ginger

Wanmono are beautifully re-strained, yet nuanced simmered dishes served in lacquer bowls with lids. As you lift off the lid, a billow of fragrant steam envelops your senses. This is Japanese cuisine at its very best. Do not fret if you cannot find the elusive *junsai* (baby water lily buds, also called water shield); the vinegar solution they are packed in adds a bit of acid along with their signature gelatinous texture, but they can be omitted.
-
Peel the eggplants (aubergines) and align on a medium plate. Rub with ⅛ teaspoon of the salt.

Set a bamboo steamer over a large wok filled one-third of the way with water and bring to a boil. Place the plate of eggplant in the steamer, cover, and steam until soft, about 20 minutes. Remove from the steamer, slice off the calyx ends and cut each eggplant crosswise into ¾-inch

(2 cm) lengths. Leave on the plate with the juices to cool.

Place *the junsai* in a small heatproof bowl and cover with boiling water. Swish around once or twice, drain in a wire-mesh sieve, and refresh under cold running water.

In a medium saucepan, bring the dashi, *usukuchi shoyu*, and remaining ⅛ teaspoon salt to a simmer over medium heat. Scrape the *kuzu* slurry into the saucepan and cook gently over low heat, stirring constantly, for 3 minutes to thicken slightly.

Arrange 2 or 3 pieces of eggplant in each of four lidded lacquer bowls (*o-wan*, see page 354) and divide the *junsai* among the bowls. Ladle over the dashi, dab a small bit of the *bainiku* on one of the eggplants, and sprinkle with the yuzu zest and ginger. Cover and serve immediately as a light first course.

~~~~~~

そら豆の含め煮

SIMMERED FAVA BEANS

SORA-MAME NO FUKUME-NI

Preparation time: 20 minutes,
plus 4 hours chilling time
Cooking time: 5 minutes
Serves: 4

• 9 oz (250 g) shelled fava (broad)
beans, from 1¾ lb (800 g) unshelled
• 1⅔ cups (13½ fl oz/400 ml)
Happo Dashi (page 25)
• 1 tablespoon organic sugar
• 2 teaspoons usukuchi shoyu
(see page 344)
• ¼ teaspoon fine sea salt
• 1 heaping tablespoon sansho
leaves, finely chopped

The season for fava beans (broad beans) is extremely short in Japan—maybe only two or three weeks—so enjoying them in a variety of ways is essential to take advantage of their fleeting appearance.
-
Pinch off the hard part on the back of the favas (broad beans) and carefully pop out the inner beans, without splitting them apart.

Set up a large bowl of ice and nestle a smaller metal bowl into the ice. In a small saucepan, bring the *happo dashi* to a simmer over medium-high heat. Stir in the

sugar, *usukuchi shoyu*, and salt. Reduce to medium heat and add the fava beans. Cook for 1½ minutes, then pour the favas and the dashi into the bowl set in the ice bath to cold-shock. (This will help keep their bright green color.) Once chilled, refrigerate the bowl of fava beans and dashi for at least 4 hours to absorb the flavors.

Drain, discard the dashi, and fold the *sansho* into the beans. Spoon out into four small complementary bowls and serve as a cooling course with a light meal.

EGGPLANT AND JUNSAI IN DASHI

トマトの煮物

DASHI-SIMMERED TOMATOES

TOMATO NO NIMONO

Preparation time: 30 minutes,
plus 4 hours chilling time
Cooking time: 10 minutes
Serves: 4

- 4 medium tomatoes (1¾ lb/800 g)
- Boiling water
- 1⅔ cups (13½ fl oz/400 ml) Konbu Dashi (page 22)
- ⅛ teaspoon flaky sea salt
- 2 tablespoons shoyu
- 1 tablespoon hon mirin
- 4 sprigs sansho leaves, for garnish

The key to the success of this understated, yet elegant, dish is preparing it at the height of summer when tomatoes are at their best—and making sure not to waste any of the precious juices of the tomatoes. And as a point, avoid using overripe tomatoes in Japanese cuisine. If you cannot find *sansho* leaves, *mitsuba* can be substituted, or green shiso leaves, cut into a fine chiffonade. The mild tomatoes contrast beautifully with the shoyu-forward dashi, making an exquisitely balanced dish.

-

Place the tomatoes in a heatproof medium bowl and pour boiling water over to cover. After 1 or 2 minutes, gently scoop out with a slotted spoon and place in a medium stainless steel bowl. Core and peel the tomatoes carefully over the bowl, so as not to lose any juices, placing each tomato back in the bowl, core side down, as it is peeled. Discard the peels.

In a small saucepan, bring the dashi, salt, shoyu, and mirin just to a simmer over medium heat. Remove from the heat and pour over the tomatoes. Place the bowl over (but not in) a pan of simmering water and cook uncovered for 10 minutes. Meanwhile, set up a large bowl of ice and water. When the tomatoes have finished cooking, remove the bowl from the pan and set the bowl in in the ice bath to cool.

Once cooled, place the tomatoes, core side down, in a square or rectangular pan that will just hold them. Add the pooled-up juices and refrigerate for 4 hours.

Place one tomato, core side down, on each of four pretty saucers with a spoonful of the juices. Garnish with a small sprig of *sansho* and serve as a refreshing course for lunch or dinner.

かぼちゃの煮物

KABOCHA SIMMERED IN DASHI

KABOCHA NO NIMONO

Preparation time: 15 minutes,
plus cooling time
Cooking time: 15 minutes
Serves: 4, with leftovers

- ½ small (10½ oz/300 g) kabocha (see page 347), seeded
- 1¼ cups (10 fl oz/300 ml) Konbu Dashi (page 22)
- Scant ½ cup (3½ fl oz/100 ml) Shiitake Dashi (page 22)
- 1 tablespoon usukuchi shoyu (see page 344)
- 1 tablespoon sake
- ¼ teaspoon flaky sea salt

Simmered kabocha is ubiquitous in many Japanese cookbooks, but do not overlook this simple preparation. The beauty is in the restrained simmering liquids and the flavorful summer kabocha.

-

Place the kabocha cut side down on a cutting board and use a small knife to remove some of the skin by slicing it off decoratively at random intervals. Cut the kabocha into ¾ × 1¼-inch (2 × 3 cm) chunks and bevel the sharp edges. Place the kabocha pieces, skin side down, in a medium saucepan and add the konbu dashi, shiitake dashi, *usukuchi shoyu*, sake, and salt.

Bring to a boil over high heat. Place a drop lid (*otoshibuta*, see page 354) or parchment paper on top of the kabocha, reduce the heat to low and simmer gently until the liquids have reduced and the kabocha is tender, about 15 minutes. (You want the kabocha pieces to keep their shape, so you don't want them banging about in the pan as they simmer.) Transfer to a medium bowl and allow to cool in the cooking liquid.

Serve at room temperature as a vegetable side dish.

DASHI-SIMMERED TOMATOES

かぼちゃとあずきのいとこ煮

SIMMERED KABOCHA WITH AZUKI

KABOCHA TO AZUKI NO ITOKO-NI

Preparation time: 20 minutes
Cooking time: 15 minutes
Serves: 4, generously

• 10½ oz (300 g) seeded kabocha
(see page 347), unpeeled
• 7 oz (200 g) Simmered
Azuki Beans (page 32)
• 1⅔ cups (13½ fl oz/400 ml)
Konbu Dashi (page 22)
• 1 teaspoon flaky sea salt
• 4 tablespoons sake

Itoko-ni is a classic Japanese simmered dish with myriad variations. Here, the dashi is flavored with salt and sake, rather than shoyu and mirin, thus allowing the natural sweetness of the kabocha to shine through clearly, and the azuki are added after removing the kabocha so they retain their taste and color.
-
Cut the kabocha into 1¼ × 2-inch (3 × 5 cm) pieces and bevel the sharp edges so there is an attractive ¼-inch (5 mm) exposed edge around the skin portion. Slide the kabocha into a medium saucepan, add the dashi, salt, and sake and bring to a simmer over medium heat. Place a drop lid (*otoshibuta*, see page 354) or piece of parchment paper on top and cook at a gentle simmer until a bamboo skewer can slip easily into the center of the kabocha but the pieces remain intact, 8–10 minutes.

Scoop the kabocha out with a slotted spoon (do not discard the cooking liquid) and mound on a pretty serving dish. Add the azuki to the liquid in the pan and simmer briskly over medium heat for 5 minutes to develop flavor and reduce the liquid. Spoon out into an attractive pile next to the kabocha and serve warm or at room temperature as part of a larger meal.

里芋の梅炊き

UME-SIMMERED TARO

SATO IMO NO UME-DAKI

Preparation time: 45 minutes,
plus 2 hours chilling time
Cooking time: 20 minutes
Serves: 4

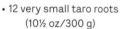

• 12 very small taro roots
(10½ oz/300 g)
• 1 tablespoon rice bran
• 1⅔ cups (13½ fl oz/400 ml)
Happo Dashi (page 25)
• 4 salted sour "plums" (umeboshi,
see page 350), pitted and finely
chopped to a paste
• 2 tablespoons sake
• 2 tablespoons hon mirin
• A pinch or two of flaky
sea salt (optional)
• 2 large stalks komatsuna
(see page 346), 1¾ oz (50 g)
• 1 teaspoon white sesame seeds,
warmed in a dry frying
pan until fragrant

This is a beautifully subtle dish with sophistication and nuance from the interplay between the soft taro, tart, fruity *ume*, fresh vegetality of the *komatsuna*, and the accent of rich sesame.
-
Cut the ends off and peel each taro. Place in a medium saucepan and fill with cold water to just cover. Add the rice bran and bring to a boil over high heat. Cook the taro until a bamboo skewer can just pierce to the center, about 10 minutes. Drain and rinse under cold running water until cold.

Rinse out the saucepan and add the taro, *happo dashi*, and *umeboshi*. Bring to a boil over high heat, reduce to a simmer, and cook for about 5 minutes to allow the *umeboshi* to flavor the simmering liquid. Stir in the sake and mirin and simmer for 1–2 minutes more, then taste the saltiness. It should be mildly salty, so add the pinch or two of salt, if needed. Remove from the heat, transfer to a medium bowl, and cool to room temperature. Refrigerate for 2 hours to chill.

Meanwhile, bring a small saucepan of water to a boil and hold the *komatsuna* stems in the boiling water for 30 seconds. Let go of the *komatsuna*, pushing the leaves into the water, and boil for an additional 30 seconds. Drain in a wire-mesh sieve and refresh under cold running water until cool to the touch. Drain and squeeze well. Align on a cutting board and cut into 1¾-inch (4 cm) lengths. Stack the *komatsuna* in a small bowl or plate and refrigerate for 1 hour to chill.

Spoon the taro with some of its cooking liquid into four small bowls, mound a stack of *komatsuna* on top, sprinkle with sesame seeds, and serve.

The definitive collection of 250 Japanese vegetarian recipes for home cooking, and a companion to the bestselling *Japan: The Cookbook*

Japan: The Vegetarian Cookbook showcases the elegant simplicity of Japanese vegetarian cuisine, with recipes divided by cooking style and created using the freshest seasonal ingredients. Japanese vegetarian food is prepared with mindfulness; the natural produce is treated with respect and appreciation, and this is reflected in the stunning food imagery throughout. Alongside the recipes, Nancy Singleton Hachisu shares her expert knowledge, with fascinating insights into the ingredients, culture, and the years of ritual and tradition that shaped this unique cuisine.

UME-SIMMERED TARO

小いものゆばあんかけ

SIMMERED BABY TARO WITH CREAMY YUBA

KO-IMO NO YUBA ANKAKE

Preparation time: 30 minutes,
plus 2 hours chilling time
Cooking time: 15 minutes
Serves: 4

- 12 very small taro roots
  (10½ oz/300 g), peeled
- Rice washing water or cold water
- 1⅔ cups (13½ fl oz/400 ml)
  Konbu Dashi (page 22)
- 2 tablespoons shoyu
- 1 tablespoon hon mirin
- 2 tablespoons finely grated
  peeled mountain yam
- 3½ oz (100 g) fresh yuba
  (see page 352)
- 2 teaspoons soy milk
- ⅛ teaspoon flaky sea salt
- Green nori powder (aonori, see page
  349), for serving

Simmering the taro in rice washing water keeps the flesh white, but if you have not saved any rice water, you could sprinkle in a little rice bran or rice grains for cooking. Just be sure to rinse after draining the taro. The contrast between the soft, yet resilient taro and the creamy, slightly viscous *yuba* sauce is extremely appealing, and the green nori adds a salty note that ties the dish together, so should not be skipped.
-
Place the taro in a medium saucepan and add cold rice washing water or cold tap water to cover. Bring to a boil over medium heat and simmer briskly until a bamboo skewer can slip easily into the centers of the taro, about 8 minutes.

Drain the taro, rinse out the saucepan, and return the taro to the pan. Add the dashi, shoyu, and mirin and simmer over medium heat. Reduce to a gentle simmer and cook for 5 minutes. Transfer to a bowl to cool to room temperature. Refrigerate for at least 2 hours to chill.

Scrape the mountain yam into a Japanese grinding bowl (*suribachi*, see page 354) and smash in the *yuba*, soy milk, and salt until the milk is amalgamated into the mountain yam and *yuba*. Store in the refrigerator if not using right away.

Remove the taro from the fridge, discard the cooking liquid, and mound the taro in a ceramic serving bowl or individual saucers. Dollop the *yuba* sauce into the center of the taro pieces, sprinkle with a little green nori for accent, and serve as a cold course during the summer.

ふきの伽羅煮

DASHI-SIMMERED FUKI WITH TORORO KONBU

FUKI NO KYARA-NI

Preparation time: 30 minutes
Cooking time: 5 minutes
Serves: 4

- 4½ oz (125 g) Parboiled Fuki (page 35)
- 1¼ cups (10 fl oz/300 ml)
  Konbu Dashi (page 22)
- 1½ tablespoons sake
- 1 tablespoon shoyu
- ¾ teaspoon hon mirin
- ½ dried red japones chile
- 2 tablespoons shredded
  tororo konbu (see page 349)
- A couple pinches of sansho powder

Butterbur (*fuki*) resembles celery in appearance but not in flavor. *Fuki* has a wild, almost licorice taste, unlike celery's vegetal profile. Nonetheless, celery can be used as a substitute for the hard-to-obtain-outside-Japan *fuki*. Handling raw *fuki* tends to leave blackened fingers, so the strings are removed after boiling.
-
Cut the *fuki* crosswise into pieces 1¼–1½ inches (3–4 cm) long. In a medium saucepan, bring the dashi, sake, shoyu, mirin, and chile to a boil over medium heat. Drop in the *fuki*, reduce to a gentle simmer, and cook until fully flavored, 3–5 minutes. Transfer to a bowl, cool to room temperature, then refrigerate.

Heat a cast-iron skillet over low heat until heated through. Lay the *tororo konbu* across the bottom of the pan and parch briefly, tossing until crispy. Finely shred by hand and drop into a bowl.

Scoop the *fuki* out into a shallow bowl with a slotted spoon. Top with the *tororo konbu* and a tiny sprinkling of *sansho* powder and serve.

SIMMERED BABY TARO WITH CREAMY YUBA

SOY MILK CHAWAN MUSHI

豆乳茶碗蒸し

TOUNYUU CHAWAN-MUSHI

Preparation time: 25 minutes
Cooking time: 25 minutes
Serves: 4

• 3½ oz (100 g) edamame pods
• ½ teaspoon flaky sea salt
• ½ medium carrot (2⅔ oz/75 g),
scrubbed
• Scant ⅔ cup (5¼ fl oz/150 ml)
Konbu Dashi (page 22)
• ¼ teaspoon usukuchi shoyu
(see page 344)
• 1 teaspoon mirin
• 1 teaspoon black sesame seeds,
warmed in a dry frying pan
until fragrant
• 2 cups (16 fl oz/500 ml) soy milk
• 2½ teaspoons liquid nigari

Adding *nigari* to the dashi-flavored soy milk in this eggless *chawan mushi* will allow the custard to set. This dish is a bit like a gilded soft tofu (*yosedofu*), but the simmered ingredients give a depth of flavor to an otherwise unadorned preparation. In spring, substitute green peas for the edamame.

—

Bring a medium saucepan of water to a boil and drop in the edamame. Cook over high heat for 3 minutes. Drain and refresh under cold running water to cool. Pop the beans out of the pods and toss with ¼ teaspoon of the salt. Let sit for 10 minutes, then divide among four generous ¾ cup (6¾ fl oz/200 ml) handle-less teacups (*chawan*, see page 354).

Cut the carrot crosswise into rounds ¼ inch (5 mm) thick. Stamp out leaf or flower shapes with a vegetable cutter (save the scraps for another use). In a small saucepan, bring the dashi, *usukuchi shoyu*, mirin, remaining ¼ teaspoon salt, and the carrot shapes to a simmer over medium heat. Simmer briskly for 5 minutes and skim out the carrot to drain in a small wire-mesh sieve set over a bowl. Set the cooking liquid aside. Divide the carrot among the *chawan mushi* cups and add ¼ teaspoon black sesame seeds to each cup.

In a 2-cup (500 ml) liquid measuring cup, stir together the soy milk, *nigari*, and 4 teaspoons of the cooled cooking liquid, making sure the ingredients are well combined but not frothy. Divide the mixture among the four teacups and cover each one with a ceramic top or a piece of plastic wrap (cling film).

Set a bamboo steamer over a large wok filled one-third of the way with water and bring to a boil. Place the cups in the steamer, cover, and cook over high heat for 5 minutes. Reduce the heat to low and steam for 10 more minutes until set. Serve hot.

~~~~~~

KONBU-SIMMERED BAMBOO

筍の煮物

TAKENOKO NO NIMONO

Preparation time: 15 minutes,
plus 1 hour cooling time
Cooking time: 10 minutes
Serves: 4

• 1 lb 5 oz (600 g) Boiled Bamboo
Shoot (page 34)
• 1¼-inch (3 cm) square piece konbu
• 3⅓ cups (26½ fl oz/800 ml)
Happo Dashi (page 25)
• 1 tablespoon organic sugar
• 2 tablespoons hon mirin
• 2 tablespoons usukuchi shoyu
(see page 344)
• ¼ teaspoon flaky sea salt
• 4 sprigs sansho leaves, for garnish

Bamboo shoots are harvested in the spring when the *sansho* leaves are just starting to appear, so they naturally go well together in a dish. Here the bamboo is gently seasoned to maintain its essential integrity and beautifully subtle flavor.

—

Cut the thick bottom portion of the bamboo shoot crosswise into 1-inch (2.5 cm) half-rounds. Halve the tip portion lengthwise.

Place the konbu in the bottom of a medium saucepan. Add the *happo dashi* and bring to boil over high heat. Stir in the sugar, mirin, *usukuchi shoyu*, and salt. Reduce to a simmer, and cook over medium-low heat for 7–8 minutes to absorb flavors. Remove the pan from the heat and allow the bamboo to cool to room temperature in the liquid.

Bring the bamboo back to a simmer over medium-high heat to rewarm before spooning into a medium serving bowl with a little of the cooking liquid. Garnish with the sprigs of *sansho*.

SOY MILK CHAWAN MUSHI

STEAMED TURNIP CLOUDS

かぶら蒸し

KABURA MUSHI

Preparation time: 1 hour,
plus 20 minutes draining time
Cooking time: 45 minutes
Serves: 4

• 3 small turnips
(8¼ oz/235 g), peeled
• ⅓ small mountain yam (3½ oz/100 g),
scrubbed and peeled
• ½ teaspoon flaky sea salt
• 1¾ oz (50 g), enoki, spongy ends
cut off, halved crosswise
• 2 cups (16 fl oz/500 ml)
Konbu Dashi (page 22)
• 1 small potato (3½ oz/100 g)
• Neutral oil, such as canola
(rapeseed), peanut, or safflower,
for deep-frying
• 1¼ inches (3 cm) medium carrot,
peeled
• ½ small lily bulb (2¼ oz/60 g),
scales separated
• 2 dried wood ear mushrooms,
soaked in cold water for 20 minutes
• 1 tablespoon plus ¾ teaspoon shoyu
• 1 tablespoon hon mirin
• 2 tablespoons hon kuzu
(see page 352) mixed with
6 tablespoons water until smooth
• 12 Boiled Ginkgo Nuts (page 35)
• 1 teaspoon grated fresh wasabi

Use a circular ceramic grater (*oroshiki*, see page 354) or fine-toothed metal grating plate (*oroshigane*, see page 354) to grate the turnip and mountain yam into an ethereal texture for this iconic dish. Serve when autumn suddenly turns cool and you want a warming bowl of vegetable clouds to mitigate the brisk evening. There are many steps to this recipe, but you will not be disappointed by the stunning result.

-

Finely grate the turnip (see above) and scrape into a fine-mesh sieve set over a bowl for 15 minutes to drain. Finely grate the mountain yam on the Japanese grater as well, and scrape into a Japanese grinding bowl (*suribachi*, see page 354). Smash well with a grinding pestle (*surikogi*) until completely smooth and homogenous. Mash in the drained turnip with ¼ teaspoon of the salt until well combined.

In a small saucepan, bring the enoki and a generous ⅓ cup (3 fl oz/90 ml) of the dashi to a simmer over medium-high heat. Cool to room temperature in the dashi before draining. Set aside.

Place a fine-mesh sieve over a medium bowl. Peel and finely grate the potato into the sieve and allow to drain for 20 minutes. Pour off the clear liquid that has accumulated in the bowl but keep the white starch. Mix the drained potato into the starch with ⅛ teaspoon of the salt and roll into 4 balls.

In a small high-sided sauté pan, heat 1¼ inches (3 cm) oil over medium heat until you can feel the heat rising.

Slip in the potato balls and fry, turning, until golden on all sides, about 3 minutes. Drain on a rack set over a pan to catch the drips.

Slice the carrot crosswise into 4 rounds ¼ inch (5 mm) thick. Cut those into flower shapes with a small vegetable cutter. Bring a small saucepan of water to a boil over high heat. Drop in the carrot flowers and cook until tender, 3–5 minutes. Scoop out with a wire-mesh sieve and set aside. Drop the lily bulb scales into the boiling water and cook for 1 minute. Drain and set aside.

Drain the wood ear mushrooms and drop into a small saucepan with 1 tablespoon each shoyu, mirin, and dashi. Bring just to a simmer over medium-high heat and allow to cool in the cooking liquid before draining.

In a small saucepan, bring the remaining scant 1⅔ cups (13½ fl oz/400 ml) dashi, ⅛ teaspoon salt, and ¾ teaspoon shoyu to a simmer over medium-low heat. Scrape the *kuzu* slurry into the saucepan and stir continuously over low heat until thickened and glossy, 5–7 minutes.

Divide the potato balls, enoki, and lily bulb scales evenly among four heat-resistant, rounded tea bowls (*chawan*, see page 354) that can hold about 1 cup (8 fl oz/250 ml). Pour the grated turnip and mountain yam mixture over the top, poke the drained wood ear mushrooms and ginkgo nuts into the viscous mixture so they are still a bit visible, lay a carrot flower artfully on top, and add the thickened dashi.

Set a bamboo steamer over a large wok filled one-third full of water and bring to a boil. Arrange the bowls in the steamer, cover with a double thickness of cheesecloth (muslin), then place the steamer cover on top. Steam over high heat until set, 20–25 minutes. Serve hot with a dab of wasabi.

STEAMED TURNIP CLOUDS

かぶの飾り炊き合わせ

SIMMERED TURNIPS WITH NEGI

KABU NO KAZARI TAKIAWASE

Preparation time: 15 minutes,
plus 30 minutes cooling time
Cooking time: 15 minutes
Serves: 4

• 6 small turnips (14 oz/400 g),
with ½ inch (1 cm) of the stems intact
• ¼ teaspoon uncooked Japanese rice
• 2¼ oz (60 g) negi or fat scallions
(spring onions), white part only
• 4-inch (10 cm) square piece konbu
• 3 cups (24 fl oz/700 ml) Happo Dashi
(page 25)
• 2 tablespoons hon mirin
• 1 tablespoon usukuchi shoyu
(see page 344)
• ½ teaspoon fine sea salt
• 2 teaspoons hon kuzu (see page 352)
• 1 teaspoon finely julienned yuzu or
Meyer lemon zest

Turnips are a quintessential winter vegetable, and here are simmered until translucent and juicy. The luscious, gentle broth and soft *negi* are enlivened by the bright spark of yuzu zest, making this a surprisingly flavorful, yet comforting dish.

-

Scrub the turnips well to refresh the skin and dislodge any dirt particles around the stems (peel if the skin is tough). Quarter the turnips, through the stem ends, into wedges. Bevel the sharp edges. Drop into a medium saucepan with the rice and fill to cover generously with cold water. Bring to a simmer over high heat, reduce the heat to medium-low, and simmer until a bamboo skewer can be inserted into their centers, about 3 minutes. Skim out with a wire-mesh sieve and refresh under cold running water until cool to the touch.

Place the *negi* on a cutting board and make a vertical cut through the top few layers of each. Remove the hard green core and cut the white parts into fine threads about 1¾ inches (4 cm) long (*shiraga negi*). Set aside.

Place the konbu on the bottom of a medium saucepan. Add the *happo dashi*, mirin, *usukuchi shoyu*, and salt to the pan, and then the turnip pieces. Bring to a boil over high heat, reduce the heat to low, and simmer gently for 5 minutes. Remove from the heat and allow to cool in the cooking liquid.

In a small bowl, add a spoonful of the cooled cooking liquid to the *kuzu* and stir until smooth.

When ready to serve, scoop out the konbu and turnips (discard the konbu). Scrape the *kuzu* slurry into the dashi and bring almost to a boil over medium heat. Adjust to a gentle simmer, and cook, stirring constantly, until slightly thickened and silky, 5–7 minutes. Stir in the turnip to warm briefly for about 1 minute and remove from the heat.

Spoon the turnip pieces with some of the silky broth into shallow lacquer or ceramic bowls. Mound the *negi* alongside and pinch the yuzu zest between the *negi* and the turnips, as garnish. Serve warm or at room temperature. Best the first day but keeps for a few days, if refrigerated.

SIMMERED TURNIPS WITH NEGI

かぶのシチュー

TURNIP STEW

KABU NO SHICHŪ

Preparation time: 20 minutes
Cooking time: 10 minutes
Serves: 4

• 4 small turnips, with their greens
(10½ oz/300 g)
• 2 tablespoons canola (rapeseed) oil
• 3 tablespoons unbleached
all-purpose (plain) flour
• 2 cups (16 fl oz/500 ml) soy milk
• Generous ¾ cup (6¾ fl oz/200 ml)
Konbu Dashi (page 22)
• 2 teaspoons gold sesame seeds,
warmed in a dry frying pan until fragrant
• 1 teaspoon flaky sea salt

Turnips quickly turn to mush if overcooked, so the key to this dish is gauging the perfect moment when the turnips are no longer raw but still retain a slight crunch. This is a lovely, creamy bowl of white stew that benefits from its very simplicity so should not be overlooked as too homely. Adding salt during the cooking process causes the soy milk to separate, so it is best to sprinkle in just before serving.

-

Lop off the turnip tops, leaving about ½ inch (1 cm) of the stems. Scrub the turnips well and cut lengthwise into 6 wedges. Pick through the greens and discard any yellow, brown, or wilted sections. Cut the greens and stems crosswise into 1¼-inch (3 cm) pieces.

In a small heavy saucepot, warm the oil over medium heat. Add the flour and cook by spreading the flour across the bottom of the pan with a flat wooden spoon, stirring constantly, until the flour has cooked but not browned, about 3 minutes. Remove from the heat and whisk in the soy milk off heat until smooth, then whisk in the dashi. Return to low heat, add the turnip pieces, and cook without simmering (the soy milk will separate), stirring continuously, for about 5 minutes. Stir in the leaves and stems and cook until the leaves have wilted, and the turnips can be just pierced with a bamboo skewer, about 2 minutes longer.

Stir in the sesame seeds, ladle into four bowls, and sprinkle with the salt. Serve immediately.

海老芋の煮物

SIMMERED "SHRIMP POTATOES"

EBI-IMO NO NIMONO

Preparation time: 15 minutes
Cooking time: 20 minutes
Serves: 4

• 4 "shrimp potatoes" or
small taro roots (5¼ oz/150 g)
• ½ tablespoon rice bran
• 4-inch (10 cm) square piece konbu
• 2 cups (16 fl oz/500 ml)
Happo Dashi (page 25)
• 1 tablespoon hon mirin
• ¼ teaspoon fine sea salt
• 2 tablespoons usukuchi shoyu
(see page 344)
• 1 teaspoon finely julienned yuzu or
Meyer lemon zest

"Shrimp potatoes" (ebi-imo) are a variety of elongated taro root shaped like a shrimp, which are famous in Kyoto but also found in the southern areas of Japan. The variety is prized for its sweetness and creamy texture and is particularly good for simmered dishes since it holds its shape well. The flavorful dashi used to simmer the taro elevates this simple dish to the sublime.

-

Peel the "shrimp potatoes" with a sharp knife, paring off the pointed end tip. Rinse clean. Place the "shrimp potatoes" in a medium saucepan, fill with cold water just to cover, and add the rice bran. Bring to a boil over high heat, reduce the heat to a brisk simmer, and cook until a bamboo skewer slips easily into the

centers, about 10 minutes. Drain, rinse off any lingering bran, and rinse the pan.

Lay the konbu on the bottom of the rinsed pan and add the happo dashi, mirin, salt, and usukuchi shoyu. Halve the "shrimp potatoes" lengthwise, and place in the pan with the dashi. Bring to a boil over medium-high heat, adjust to a simmer, and cook until the "shrimp potatoes" have absorbed the seasoned broth, 5–7 minutes.

Ladle into four individual bowls with the broth and pinch the yuzu on top. Best hot but also good at room temperature. Keeps for several days, if refrigerated, but rewarm before serving.

TURNIP STEW

ふきの葉の煮物

SIMMERED BUTTERBUR LEAVES

FUKI NO HA NO NIMONO

Preparation time: 10 minutes
Cooking time: 8 minutes
Makes: About ½ cup (4 oz/115 g)

• 2⅔ oz (75 g) butterbur leaves,
from 2–3 stalks of butterbur
(fuki, see page 346)
• 1½ tablespoons dark roasted
gold sesame oil
• 2 tablespoons shoyu
• 2 tablespoons hon mirin
• 2 tablespoons Konbu Dashi
(page 22)
• 1 tablespoon gold sesame seeds

Butterbur buds (*fuki no to*) are a prized spring delicacy and are often deep-fried. Butterbur stalks are mostly simmered in a mirin- and shoyu-flavored dashi, but the leaves are not typically eaten—here they are boiled in a few changes of water to remove bitterness. The result is a surprisingly tasty condiment to eat on a bowl of rice.

-

Bring a medium saucepan three-quarters full of water to a boil over high heat. Drop in the butterbur leaves and boil for 1 minute. Drain, then refresh under cold running water. Repeat the process two more times with fresh water each time for a total of 3 minutes of cooking. Squeeze out excess water and finely chop.

In a medium frying pan, heat the sesame oil over medium-low heat. Squeeze the chopped leaves one more time and drop into the frying pan. Stir with a flat wooden spoon for about 1 minute to distribute the oil into the leaves. Add the shoyu, mirin, and dashi and stir over medium-high heat until the liquids have been absorbed, about 2 minutes. Stir in the sesame seeds.

Serve at room temperature as a condiment. Keeps 2 or 3 days if stored, covered, in the fridge.

風呂吹き大根

STEAMED DAIKON WITH MISO

FUROFUKI DAIKON

Preparation time: 20 minutes,
plus 20 minutes cooling time
Cooking time: 35 minutes
Serves: 4

• 4¾-inch (12 cm) piece medium daikon
(10½ oz/300 g)
• 4-inch (10 cm) square piece konbu
• 1⅔ cups (13½ fl oz/400 ml)
Happo Dashi (page 25)
• 4 tablespoons Aka Taki Miso
(page 29)
• 1 teaspoon freshly squeezed
ginger juice

While classically a simmered dish, here the daikon is steamed and thus retains its shape during the cooking process (simmering can sometimes result in dinged edges). There are myriad variations on the miso sauce prep—all subject to one's personal preference. It can be a mélange of misos, sweet from sugar or mirin, or spicy from the addition of 7-spice powder (*shichimi togarashi*, see page 350). To make ginger juice, grate ginger finely and squeeze in your fist.

-

Cut the daikon crosswise into 4 rounds about 1¼ inches (3 cm) thick. Peel the circumference and bevel the edges. Make a crosscut through the top surface of each piece, cutting one-third of the way down into the daikon. This will allow the daikon to cook evenly and absorb more of the gentle dashi steaming liquid.

Set a bamboo steamer over a large wok filled one-third full with water and bring to a boil.

Place the konbu in a small metal pan and add the daikon, crosscut sides down. Add to the steamer, cover, and steam until a bamboo skewer can easily slip into the centers of the daikon, about 20 minutes. Swirl in the *happo dashi* and steam for another 8 minutes. Remove the pan from the steamer basket and cool the daikon in the pan with the dashi.

Spoon the *aka taki miso* into a small bowl with the ginger juice and slowly stir in 1 tablespoon of the daikon cooking liquid, until the miso is loose and shiny.

Once cooled, set each piece of daikon in a shallow bowl and drizzle over the cooking liquid. Spoon on a generous dollop of the loosened *taki miso* and serve.

STEAMED DAIKON WITH MISO

大根の山椒炊き

SANSHO-SIMMERED DAIKON

DAIKON NO SANSHOU-DAKI

Preparation time: 15 minutes
Cooking time: 45 minutes
Serves: 4, generously

• 1 lb 5 oz (600 g) daikon, peeled
• Rice washing water or cold water
• 1⅔ cups (13½ fl oz/400 ml)
  Konbu Dashi (page 22)
• Generous ¾ cup (6¾ fl oz/200 ml)
  Shiitake Dashi (page 22)
• 2 teaspoons green sansho powder
• 2 teaspoons usukuchi shoyu
  (see page 344)
• 1 teaspoon flaky sea salt
• 4 sprigs sansho leaves,
  for garnish (optional)

Sansho is the tongue-numbing native Japanese pepper that grows on the hillsides of Wakayama prefecture—often said to be the birthplace of Japanese cuisine. The best *sansho* powder is green and has notes of citrus. Inferior *sansho* powder is brown and to be avoided. *Sansho* is a natural flavoring for simmered daikon dishes since cooking daikon renders it mild with a neutral profile.

-

Cut the daikon into 1¼-inch (3 cm) irregular triangular pieces (*rangiri*, see page 17) and bevel the edges. Place the daikon in a medium saucepan and add the rice washing water to just cover. Bring to a boil over medium-high heat, reduce the heat to low and cook until a bamboo skewer can be easily inserted into the daikon, about 30 minutes. Drain in a wire-mesh sieve and run cold water over to refresh until the daikon is cool to the touch and translucent.

Rinse the saucepan and gently place the daikon in the pan. Add the konbu dashi, shiitake dashi, *sansho* powder, *usukuchi shoyu*, and salt and cook over medium-low heat for about 10 minutes to flavor and reduce the liquids by one-third. Remove from the heat and cool in the pan to room temperature to absorb the cooking liquid.

When ready to serve, bring back to a simmer, then scoop out into a serving bowl. Garnish with the *sansho* leaves, if desired. Keeps well for a couple of days, stored in the refrigerator in its cooking liquid.

さつまいものレモン煮

LEMON-SIMMERED SWEET POTATO

SATSUMA IMO NO REMON-NI

Preparation time: 10 minutes, plus
3 hours cooling and chilling time
Cooking time: 15 minutes
Serves: 4

• 2 small sweet potatoes
  (5¼ oz/150 g each)
• 4 tablespoons freshly squeezed
  lemon juice
• 2 tablespoons organic
  granulated sugar
• 1 dried gardenia fruit pod
  (kuchinashi, see page 350),
  optional

The gardenia fruit pod (*kuchinashi*) lends color, so try to find it. It should be available online since it is used as a Chinese herbal medicine called *shan zhi zi* (山梔子). The natural sweetness of the sweet potatoes is enhanced by the brightly tart, slightly sweetened cooking liquid, yielding a wonderfully tasty dish that deserves not to be overlooked for its ostensible simplicity.

-

Scrub the sweet potatoes, do not peel, and slice into rounds ½ inch (1 cm) thick. Place in a medium saucepan, add the lemon juice, sugar, and 1⅔ cups (13½ fl oz/ 400 ml) water. Break open the *kuchinashi* (if using) and drop in as well. Bring to a simmer over medium-high heat and cook until the flesh can be easily pierced with a bamboo skewer, 12–15 minutes. Remove the *kuchinashi* and let the sweet potatoes cool to room temperature in the cooking liquid. Refrigerate for 2 hours to chill.

Serve as a sweetly tart side dish or small bite.

LEMON-SIMMERED SWEET POTATO

餅の白菜巻きトロみがけ

NAPA CABBAGE-ROLLED MOCHI WITH SILKY SAUCE

MOCHI NO HAKUSAI-MAKI TOROMI-GAKE

Preparation time: 30 minutes
Cooking time: 25 minutes
Serves: 4

- 4 large leaves (9 oz/250 g) napa cabbage (Chinese leaf)
- 2 deep-fried tofu pouches (usuage, see page 352)
- Boiling water
- 2 pieces (1½ oz/40 g each) dried brown rice mochi
- 3⅓ cups (26½ fl oz/800 ml) Konbu Dashi (page 22)
- 6 tablespoons sake
- 1 tablespoon usukuchi shoyu (see page 344)
- 1 teaspoon flaky sea salt
- 1 tablespoon hon kuzu (see page 352) mixed with 3 tablespoons water until smooth

The layered combination of softly blanched napa cabbage (Chinese leaf) and crisp, squishy fried tofu wrapped around gooey mochi is irresistible as a soft and juicy bite. The rolls are unsalted, contrasting beautifully with the lightly salty dashi, allowing you to enjoy the natural textures and flavors of the roll itself. This is quintessential Japanese vegetarian food.
-
Remove the hard, white middle section of the cabbage leaves and reserve for another dish. Bring a medium saucepot of water to a boil over high heat. Drop the leaves in the water and cook for 30 seconds. Scoop out and refresh under cold running water.

Place the usuage in a wire-mesh sieve and pour boiling water over for 10 seconds. Slice open all the sides of each "pouch" and separate the usuage into a total of four rectangular pieces

In a small covered frying pan, warm the mochi over low heat, turning, until just soft enough to cut with a sturdy knife, 5–6 minutes. Quarter each piece of mochi and set aside.

Lay the 4 best-looking pieces of cabbage leaves about the same size as the usuage halves on a baking sheet in a vertical orientation. Layer the remaining 4 cabbage leaf pieces evenly on top of those leaves (always keeping the size about the size of the usuage). Place one usuage half, skin side down, on top of each stack of leaves. Set 2 pieces of mochi side by side across the short side of each usuage, about ¾ inch (2 cm) in from the bottom edge. Trim off excess cabbage extending from the top or bottom of the usuage and discard. Roll up tightly and secure each roll with two toothpicks: Poke each toothpick through the mochi pieces, inserting the toothpick into the loose end of cabbage and allowing the point to poke through to the other side of the roll like a skewer.

In a small saucepan, combine the dashi, sake, usukuchi shoyu, and salt and bring just to a boil over medium heat. Snugly place the rolls in the pan, side by side, and immediately reduce the heat to low. Simmer gently for 10 minutes. Measure out 1⅔ cups (13½ fl oz/400 ml) of the dashi and transfer to another small saucepan. Cover the rolled cabbage and leave in the remaining dashi to keep warm.

Scrape the kuzu slurry into the small saucepan of dashi and cook over low heat stirring continually, until slightly thickened, about 3 minutes.

Place the cabbage-rolled mochi in small shallow bowls, whole or halved, depending on the size of the usuage. Pour the silky sauce over the rolls and serve hot as a gorgeous first course.

NAPA CABBAGE−ROLLED MOCHI WITH SILKY SAUCE

薄葛仕立ての高野豆腐清し

KOYADOFU AND SPINACH WITH KUDZU DASHI

USUKUZU-JITATE NO KOUYADOUFU-SUMASHI

Preparation time: 30 minutes
Cooking time: 10 minutes
Serves: 4

- 1 small bunch (7 oz/200 g) spinach
- 2 cups (16 fl oz/500 ml) Konbu Dashi (page 22)
- 2 tablespoons usukuchi shoyu (see page 344)
- ½ teaspoon fine sea salt
- 4 pieces Reconstituted Koyadofu (page 36)
- 1 medium carrot (5¼ oz/150 g), peeled and sliced into rounds ¼ inch (5 mm) thick (if the carrot is fat, halve lengthwise and then cut into half-moons)
- 1 tablespoon hon kuzu (see page 352) mixed with 3 tablespoons water until smooth

Freeze-dried tofu (*koyadofu*, see page 352) has been a standard ingredient in Japanese vegetarian cooking since its accidental discovery by monks hundreds of years ago. Of course, the modern method of making *koyadofu* no longer involves freezing the tofu in the snow and drying in the sun. Nonetheless, *koyadofu* dishes are good to have in your repertoire since the main ingredient is dried, so always on hand. Here the silky textures and pretty colors are reminiscent of classic temple food.

-

Bring a medium saucepan of water to a boil. Blanch the spinach for 10 seconds. Scoop out and immediately refresh under cold running water to cool. Drain, shake off, and squeeze. Cut crosswise into 2¼-inch (6 cm) pieces and stack attractively, off center, in four shallow soup bowls.

In a medium saucepan, bring the konbu dashi, *usukuchi shoyu*, and salt to a simmer over medium-high heat. Slip in the *koyadofu* and carrot, reduce the heat to a simmer, and cook gently for 5 minutes to soften the carrot and allow the ingredients to absorb flavor.

Swirl the *kuzu* slurry into the simmering *koyadofu* and carrot. Simmer, stirring constantly, until the liquid has become a silky sauce, about 5 minutes longer.

Drape a piece of *koyadofu* artfully over half of the spinach and spoon the carrots evenly over the bottom end of the *koyadofu* in each bowl. Ladle the silky *kuzu* dashi over the ingredients and serve immediately.

KOYADOFU AND SPINACH WITH KUDZU DASHI

KOYASAN

~~~~~~

As we threaded our way through the grounds of the main historic temples in the heart of Koyasan, I could almost feel the snow crunching beneath my feet. In fact, it was an unusually temperate fall. An occasional breeze ruffled the carpet of orange, yellow, and red leaves. Here and there the sun peeked through the canopy of trees. The thoughts of snow were fanciful at best, but I did wonder if the dead of winter might be the best time to visit Koyasan.

Koyasan is a more than 1,000-year-old settlement of Buddhist temples located in the Koya-Ryujin Quasi-National Park in a remote corner of Wakayama prefecture in southwestern Japan. A sacred site, Koyasan is the starting point for the Kohechi mountain route on the Kumano Kodo pilgrimage. It is also the site of the Tokugawa Family Tomb, where first shogun of Japan, Ieyasu Tokugawa, is enshrined (along with second shogun, Hidetada, and third shogun, Iemitsu). Koyasan was designated a UNESCO World Heritage Site in 2004.

I met Jijyun Inaba several years ago at a fermentation gathering in Kyoto. A Buddhist priest, Inaba is the oldest son of the family who have been historically connected with Kongobuji—the head temple and monastery of Shingon Buddhism, a significant Buddhist sect introduced to Japan in 805, early Heian period, by the priest Kukai (posthumously, Kobo Daishi). The temple itself is renowned for its powerful architecture and the striking collection of centuries-old magnificent sliding doors (*fusuma*) that serve as moving walls throughout the temple.

Upon request, Inaba graciously agreed to introduce me to various behind-the-scenes elements of Koyasan. After spending time in the kitchen with Tomiyo Nakatani, an octogenarian grandmother,

we partook of the resulting *shojin ryori* (temple food) meal in a sacred room reserved only for priests' formal gatherings. The food was cooked from the heart, and each dish showed a detailed attention to color. In that way, it was soul-soothing and personal.

Later that day we sat down with Koukan Nakamura, a priest whose hobby was cooking *shojin ryori*. He showed me hundreds of photos of dishes he had prepared over the years—many with a Western or modern bent. Clearly temple food spans a wide range of parameters, provided one keeps in mind the main precepts.

Nakamura had also cooked traditional monks' devotional food (simple, plain fare during training) for three years at Okunoin—a temple where priests have been preparing a morning meal offering for sect founder, Kobo Daishi, at 6 a.m. and 10 a.m. each day for over 800 years. Observing the orange-garbed monks heft the poles to carry the large wooden box fitted with insert holes for the food vessels (so they will not slip around), and then carry it across the stone bridge to the adjacent mausoleum, is powerful and not to be missed.

The gardens surrounding Kongobuji, designed in the Edo period (1603–1868), are of great import and can be enjoyed through the changing seasons. There is also a magnificent garden of sand and stone that encourages quiet contemplation as well as the Banryutei Rock Garden, the largest rock garden in Japan. One hundred and forty granite rocks, carried from Shikoku, birthplace of Kukai, were used for the composition depicting two dragons rising from a sea of clouds to protect the sanctuary.

Of particular interest for me, however, was the central kitchen with its enormous *irori* (charcoal

ember-cooking and room-heating hearth) and numerous *kamado* (wood-fueled cooking hearths), which in the day could cook 617 pounds (280 kg) of rice feeding up to 2,000 monks. *Irori* and *kamado* were standard cooking hearths in the traditional Japanese kitchen and up until we renovated our family farmhouse in 2000, the kitchen still had a *kamado* for boiling rice and noodles over a wood-burning fire. In the Kongobuji kitchen there was also a large wooden contraption hung from the rafters called a *nezumi otoshi* (mouse "drop"). The *nezumi otoshi* is a suspended shelf for storing grain adjacent to the kitchen—the elevated location was to protect the food from the inevitable rodents scurrying about. Naturally, the creatures would also be able to scuttle down the rafters to access the food, so this ingenious contraption was fitted with a wooden hood a good bit larger than the storage shelf, and draped around the perimeter with Japanese paper (*washi*). The *washi* could not bear the weight of the rodents, so they dropped to the floor. While other "rat guards" have existed in Japan, this particular design of *nezumi otoshi* is unique to Kongobuji (and the envy of anyone who lives in an old farmhouse).

At the height of the Edo period, Koyasan was home to more than 2,000 other temples besides Kongobuji. Given Koyasan's auspicious surroundings (located in a basin, punctuated by eight mountain peaks, thus resembling a sacred lotus flower), this remote area has served as a retreat for countless generations of pilgrims seeking contemplative meditation. These people needed a place to stay, and thus began the tradition of temples taking in paying guests. Today there are about fifty-two temple lodgings (*shukubo*) where you can stay at the temple, eat vegetarian monks' cuisine (*shojin ryori*), and attend morning prayers.

~~~~~~

白菜のクリーム煮

CREAMY NAPA CABBAGE

HAKUSAI NO KURI-MU NI

Preparation time: 25 minutes
Cooking time: 10 minutes
Serves: 4

- 3 large leaves (7 oz/200 g)
napa cabbage (Chinese leaf)
- ¼ bunch (1¾ oz/50 g) spinach
- 1½ oz (40 g) fresh yuba (see page 352)
- 2 tablespoons unroasted sesame oil
- 3 tablespoons unbleached all-purpose (plain) flour
- Scant ⅔ cup (5¼ fl oz/150 ml) Konbu Dashi (page 22)
- 3 fresh medium shiitake (1¾ oz/50 g), stems removed, caps finely sliced
- Generous ¾ cup (6¾ fl oz/200 ml) soy milk
- ½ teaspoon flaky sea salt
- 1½ teaspoons white sesame seeds, warmed in a dry frying pan until fragrant

Napa cabbage (Chinese leaf) becomes meltingly tender when steamed or simmered. Here the creaminess comes from a nondairy velouté made with soy milk and the addition of fresh yuba at the end. The sesame and shiitake give depth and the spinach lends balance to this deceptively nuanced dish. Substitute organic brown rice flour (see page 353) for a gluten-free version.

-

Quarter the cabbage leaves lengthwise. Cut the stem portions crosswise into strips ½ inch (1 cm) wide and the soft leaf portions into 1¼-inch (3 cm) pieces. Keep the two piles separate.

Bring a small saucepan of water to a boil over high heat. Hold the spinach stems into the boiling water for 10 seconds, then push the leaves into the water and scoop out with a wire-mesh sieve. Refresh under cold running water and shake off. Squeeze and cut crosswise into ¾-inch (2 cm) pieces.

Halve the yuba lengthwise, then crosswise into ½-inch (1 cm) pieces. Scrape into a small bowl and set aside.

In a medium saucepan, warm the oil over low heat. Stir in the flour and keep stirring and scraping across the bottom of the pan with a flat wooden spoon until bubbling, but not colored, about 2 minutes. Slowly add the dashi, whisking rapidly to create a smooth sauce. Stir in the stem portions of the cabbage and simmer gently for 2 minutes. Add the rest of the cabbage and the shiitake and cook for 1 more minute. Add the soy milk and heat, stirring for 1 minute. Add the spinach, yuba, salt, and 1 teaspoon of the sesame seeds. Cook for 30 seconds more.

Spoon into shallow bowls and sprinkle with the remaining ½ teaspoon sesame seeds. Serve, alongside a bowl of rice if you like.

炒め物 ＆ 焼物

Whether hot charcoal-grilling, straw-searing, or low-ember charcoal-smoking, cooking by fire is a millennia-long Japanese method of cooking that is still pervasive in modern-day Japan.

The Japanese method of cooking by fire is conveniently quick, thus lending itself to tabletop cooking on a diatomaceous earth brazier (*shichirin*, see page 354)—inside, if the area is well ventilated—or outside. Diatomaceous earth is naturally porous because of the fossilized remains of diatoms that make it up, so as a brazier material it promotes even air exchange for cooking slowly over charcoal. Traditional mountain homes might also still have a metal-lined sunken hearth (*irori*, see page 194) where low fire embers are spread in a large sand-filled fire pit to cook food and heat the room. Pounded rice is formed into a tight cylinder around skewers (*kiritampo*), and the skewers are stuck in the sand over the embers in a teepee formation, to cook slowly, while rotating occasionally. Or a pot of

brothy soup of root vegetables (*kenjinchiru*) can be hung from a large hook (*jizaikagi*) descending from the ceiling, to simmer gently over the embers.

Similar cooking styles can be duplicated successfully with tabletop gas burners, portable electrical units, or on the stove.

Grilling food brings out the intrinsic flavor of ingredients and adds a welcome intense note when building a plant-based menu. While *tare* (a shoyu- or miso-based sauce) is mostly associated with grilled meat or fish, it is also used for brushing vegetables or even fruit, such as persimmons (see Grilled Persimmon with Sansho, page 222), since the *tare* enhances the depth that comes from cooking over charcoal. The caveat here is that shoyu (and miso- or koji-based sauces) will caramelize and burn quickly, so much care should be taken when using for grilling.

Miso *dengaku* is another classic sauce used in grilling—but in this case the *dengaku* is spread over the

grilled vegetable *after* grilling—and then put under a top grill to bubble and caramelize.

The two main Japanese vegetable stir-fry methods are *kinpira* and *abura miso*. Julienned vegetables (or sometimes thin rounds of vegetables) are stir-fried in sesame or canola (rapeseed) oil with dried red chile until half cooked, then finished with a splash of shoyu or miso thinned with sake. *Abura miso* benefits from an addition of a few pinches of fine ginger threads once the vegetable has started frying. Armed with these two basic preparations, you can throw together Japanese stir-fries *à la minute* from whatever vegetables you have on hand. On the farm, these dishes typically contain only one type of vegetable. In town or at the temples, you are more likely to see a medley. And, since Japanese tofu is soft like custard, it would not normally be added to these kinds of vegetable stir-fries. Deep-fried tofu pouches (*abura age*), however, can be tossed into stir-fried greens to contribute a rich note.

炒め物　&　焼物

ITAMEMONO & YAKIMONO

STIR-FRIED & GRILLED

筍南蛮炒め　　BAMBOO SHOOT WITH SPICY MISO

TAKENOKO NANBAN-ITAME

Preparation time: 15 minutes
Cooking time: 5 minutes
Serves: 4

• 4-inch (10 cm) piece of Boiled
Bamboo Shoot (page 34),
about 9 oz (250 g)
• 1 tablespoon barley miso
• 1 tablespoon white miso
• 1 tablespoon dark roasted sesame oil
• 1 small dried red japones chile,
seeded and finely chopped

Bamboo shoot is classically simmered in a subtle dashi and served with a few sprigs of tongue-numbing *sansho* leaves, but I love the gutsiness of this barley miso treatment. Dishes that include *nanban* ("southern barbarian") in their name, usually refer to the inclusion of chile.
-
Quarter the bamboo shoot lengthwise and cut crosswise into ¼-inch (5 mm) quarter-rounds (*ichogiri*, see page 17).

In a small bowl, mash the barley miso and white miso together. Set aside.

In a large frying pan, heat the sesame oil over medium-high heat. Add the bamboo shoot and stir-fry until slightly caramelized around the edges, about 2 minutes. Remove from the heat and fold in the miso until the bamboo pieces are completely enrobed. Toss in the chile and stir once or twice to distribute well.

Serve hot or at room temperature as a strong note to punctuate a spring menu.

新生姜のきんぴら　　YOUNG GINGER KINPIRA

SHIN-SHOUGA NO KINPIRA

Preparation time: 20 minutes
Cooking time: 5 minutes
Serves: 4

• 20 snow peas (mangetout),
3½ oz (100 g), stem ends and
strings removed
• 2 teaspoons fine sea salt
• 1 tablespoon unroasted sesame oil
• 4¼ oz (120 g) young ginger,
scrubbed and cut crosswise into
⅛-inch (3 mm) slices
• 6 tablespoons sake
• 2 teaspoons usukuchi shoyu
(see page 344)
• 2 teaspoons light brown cane sugar
(kibizato, see page 345)
• 1 teaspoon finely slivered lemon zest

When young ginger hits the farm stands, the pale yellow, pink-tinged roots are grabbed up for eating raw with miso or for garnishing soups and salads. But young ginger also adds zing to stir-fried vegetables such as snow peas (mangetout). Here the natural hotness of the ginger plays off nicely with the added sweetness and bright lemon zest. Surely this is spring on a plate.
-
Bring a medium saucepan of water to a boil over high heat. Add the snow peas (mangetout) and salt and cook for 30 seconds. Scoop out the peas with a wire-mesh sieve, shake off, and pat dry in a clean tea towel. Halve crosswise at a diagonal.

In a medium frying pan, heat the sesame oil over high heat. Add the ginger and stir-fry until softened and lightly browned in spots, 1½–2 minutes. Reduce the heat to medium-high and swirl in the sake, *usukuchi shoyu*, and sugar. Cook, stirring, for about 30 seconds more to reduce the liquids and caramelize.

Add the snow peas, toss once or twice to distribute the ingredients, and immediately spoon out onto four individual saucers. Garnish with the lemon zest and serve hot or at room temperature.

YOUNG GINGER KINPIRA

セロリの塩きんぴら

CELERY KINPIRA WITH SALT

SERORI NO SHIO KINPIRA

Preparation time: 20 minutes
Cooking time: 5 minutes
Serves: 4, generously

• 4 medium stalks celery
without leaves (10½ oz/300 g)
• 2 small carrots (5¼ oz/150 g), peeled
• 2 tablespoons lightly roasted
gold sesame oil
• 2 tablespoons sake
• ¼ teaspoon flaky sea salt
• 7-spice powder (shichimi togarashi,
see page 350), for serving

Celery is similar in texture (though not flavor) to *udo* and thus lends itself well to *kinpira* (vegetables stir-fried in sesame oil and finished with shoyu). In this variation, using salt and sake instead of shoyu preserves the vibrant colors of the celery and carrot. Use the celery leaves to make a beautifully light vegetable broth or for Taro, Soba Gaki, and Celery Leaf Tempura (page 146).
-
Cut the celery and carrots into julienne 1½ inches (4 cm) long.

In a large frying pan, heat the oil over medium-high heat until you can feel the heat rising slightly. Drop in the celery and carrot and stir-fry quickly until just starting to soften, 2–3 minutes. Sprinkle in the sake and salt and continue stir-frying for another 1 minute to evaporate the liquid.

Mound into a pretty serving bowl or individual bowls and sprinkle lightly with *shichimi togarashi*. Good hot or at room temperature or even cold from the fridge the following day.

豆乳ポテトグラタン

SPICY SOY MILK POTATO GRATIN

TOUNYUU POTETO GURATAN

Preparation time: 10 minutes
Cooking time: 15 minutes
Makes: 8 small or 1 medium gratin

• 1 lb 5 oz (600 g) boiled or steamed
potatoes, cut into ½-inch (5 mm) slices
• 2 teaspoons flaky sea salt
• 2 teaspoons finely chopped
green shiso leaves
• 1 teaspoon 7-spice powder
(shichimi togarashi, see page 350)
• 8 heaping tablespoons (2¾ oz/80 g)
grated or crumbled Parmesan-Style
Vegan "Cheese" (see page 38)
• 1⅔ cups (13½ fl oz/400 ml) soy milk

This is a recipe that came to me in the middle of a sleepless night, with dreams of recipe-testing dancing in my head. Make this when you have leftover boiled or steamed potatoes.
-
Position a rack in the upper third of the oven and preheat the oven to 425°F (220°C).

In a medium bowl, toss the potatoes with the salt, shiso, and *shichimi togarashi* and distribute evenly among

8 shallow ceramic gratin ramekins or a 7 × 10 ½-inch (18 × 26 cm) oval gratin dish. Strew with the "cheese." Pour a scant ¼ cup (1¾ fl oz/50 ml) soy milk into each ramekin or all the soy milk over the medium gratin.

Bake until the soy milk is bubbling and the "cheese" is lightly browned, about 12 minutes. Serve hot from the oven.

CELERY KINPIRA WITH SALT

夏野菜の梅味噌炒め

UME MISO–SAUTÉED SUMMER VEGETABLES

NATSU YASAI NO UME MISO ITAME

Preparation time: 30 minutes
Cooking time: 10 minutes
Serves: 4, generously

- 3 small Japanese eggplants (aubergines), 9 oz (250 g)
- ½ medium (4½ oz/125 g) zucchini (courgette)
- 1 large red bell pepper (6 oz/175 g)
- 1 teaspoon flaky sea salt
- 10 slender green beans (1 oz/25 g)
- 1½ tablespoons lightly roasted gold sesame oil
- ½ tablespoon fine slivers fresh ginger
- 5 tablespoons sake
- 4 tablespoons Ume Miso (page 42)
- 1 finely chopped miso-pickled ume (from making Ume Miso above), optional
- 1 tablespoon gold sesame seeds, warmed in a dry frying pan until fragrant

If you do not have *ume* miso, just use the full-flavored miso of your choice (not white miso). And in that case, perhaps lean more heavily on the sesame. Miso is a natural match for eggplant (aubergine) and peppers and these miso stir-fries, colloquially "*abura miso*," are served often in the Japanese countryside during the summer. Zucchini (courgette), while not a traditional Japanese vegetable, is now grown commonly across the archipelago. When stir-fried, zucchini tends to weep, so best to keep the proportion small compared to the more dominant eggplant.
-
Slice off the ends of the eggplants (aubergines) and zucchini (courgette) and discard. Halve the eggplants and zucchini lengthwise, then cut crosswise into ½-inch (1 cm) pieces. Soak the eggplant in cold water to keep it from discoloring.

Core and seed the pepper and cut into ¾-inch (2 cm) irregular pieces (*rangiri*, see page 17).

Bring a medium saucepan three-quarters full of water and the salt to a boil over high heat. Add the green beans and cook until their green color just brightens, 1–3 minutes, depending on thickness. Trim off the stem ends and cut the beans crosswise into ¾-inch (2 cm) pieces. Set aside.

Drain the eggplant and blot dry. In a large frying pan, warm 1 tablespoon of the oil over low heat Add the ginger, stir once to coat with oil, then add the eggplant, zucchini, and bell pepper. Increase the heat to high, cover, and cook, stirring occasionally, until lightly browned in spots, 2–3 minutes.

Stir in the remaining ½ tablespoon oil and the sake and toss well. Add the *ume* miso and miso-pickled *ume* (if using) and stir-fry to coat evenly. Reduce the heat to low, cover, and cook until the vegetables are fully softened, 2–3 minutes longer. Fold in the green beans and sesame seeds and serve hot or at room temperature. Keeps well for 2 or 3 days, if refrigerated.

UME MISO–SAUTÉED SUMMER VEGETABLES

ピーマンの炒め物

STIR-FRIED GREEN PEPPERS WITH PINE NUTS

PI-MAN NO ITAME-MONO

Preparation time: 15 minutes
Cooking time: 2 minutes
Serves: 4

- 8 small Japanese green peppers (piman, see page 347), 7 oz (200 g)
- 1 tablespoon dark roasted sesame oil
- 1 tablespoon white sesame seeds, warmed in a dry frying pan until fragrant
- 1 tablespoon shoyu
- 1 tablespoon hon mirin
- 1 tablespoon pine nuts, warmed in a dry frying pan until fragrant

The pine nuts and sesame seeds contribute a rich note to the vegetal green peppers and thus allows the dish to integrate well into a wide range of menus. Make this in the summer when peppers are plentiful. If possible, seek out thin-walled green peppers similar to those found in Japan. Otherwise, substitute bell peppers for the *piman*, but you will need to cook longer since they are much thicker.
-
Halve the peppers lengthwise, cut off their tops, and remove the seeds. Thinly slice the peppers lengthwise.

In a medium frying pan, heat the sesame oil over medium heat. Once hot, toss in the green peppers. Stir-fry for about 1 minute, add the sesame seeds, stir for 15 seconds, then swirl in the shoyu and mirin. Keep stir-frying for 15 seconds over high heat to evaporate the liquid. The peppers should be no longer raw, yet still retain a slight crunch. Stir in the pine nuts and scrape into a pretty medium serving bowl. Serve hot or at room temperature.

キャベツの蒸し煮

PAN-ROASTED SPRING CABBAGE

KYABETSU NO MUSHI-NI

Preparation time: 10 minutes
Cooking time: 10–15 minutes
Serves: 4

- ¼ head cabbage (9 oz/250 g)
- ½ tablespoon unroasted sesame oil
- ½ teaspoon flaky sea salt
- ½ teaspoon 7-spice powder (shichimi togarashi, see page 350)
- 2 tablespoons Soy Milk Mayonnaise (page 36), for serving

Simply roasting cabbage in a dry pan allows the cabbage to steam in its own juices and renders it meltingly soft with a deep intensity. Cooled to room temperature and then eaten with soy milk mayonnaise flavored with fragrant, spicy *shichimi togarashi* makes an unforgettable side dish accompanied by a cold ginger ale or beer.
-
Cut the cabbage (including the core) into 1½–2-inch (4–5 cm) squares.

In a large frying pan, heat the oil over low heat. Once the pan and oil are well heated, add the cabbage and sprinkle with the salt. Cover tightly and cook on the lowest heat possible for 10 minutes. Turn, so the bottom pieces are on top and the top pieces are on the bottom, cover again, and cook until meltingly soft and completely cooked through, about 5 minutes longer. Transfer to a medium bowl and cool to room temperature.

In a small bowl, stir the *shichimi togarashi* into the mayonnaise. Serve the cabbage on individual plates with a dab of the mayonnaise.

STIR-FRIED GREEN PEPPERS WITH PINE NUTS

ピーマンのオーブン焼き

OVEN-GRILLED PEPPERS WITH YUBA

PI-MAN NO O-BUN YAKI

Preparation time: 15 minutes
Cooking time: 2 minutes
Serves: 4

• 4 small Japanese green and red peppers (piman, see page 347) or red and yellow sweet peppers (4¼ oz/120 g)
• 2½ oz (70 g) fresh yuba (see page 352)
• 2 tablespoons shoyu
• 1 tablespoon Konbu Dashi (page 22)

The Japanese green pepper is called *piman* and is oval and thin-walled. Outside of Japan, small red and yellow sweet peppers are a good substitute. While typically eaten green, toward the end of the summer we start to see red *piman*—green ones that have been left to mature on the plants. Here their bitterness is softened with the addition of the creamy *yuba*. *Piman* are loaded with vitamin C, so also help combat summer fatigue.
-
Halve the peppers lengthwise. Discard the core and seeds. Broil (grill) in a toaster oven (mini oven), 60–90 seconds on each side, until sizzling and slightly softened. Take care not to cook too long, as you want the peppers to keep their integrity. Cut lengthwise into strips ½ inch (1 cm) wide. Cut the *yuba* crosswise into pieces ¾ inch (2 cm) wide.

In a small bowl, mix the shoyu and dashi together.

In a medium bowl, toss the peppers, *yuba*, and dressing together. Serve immediately as an elegant summer salad.

~~~~~~

焼きなす

GRILLED EGGPLANT IN DASHI

YAKINASU

Preparation time: 15 minutes, plus 2 hours chilling time
Cooking time: 15 minutes
Serves: 4

• 4 medium Japanese eggplants (aubergines), 10½ oz (300 g)
• 1⅔ cups (13½ fl oz/400 ml) Happo Dashi (page 25)
• 2 tablespoons usukuchi shoyu (see page 344)
• 2 teaspoons finely grated young ginger

Since ovens or built-in stovetop cooking surfaces are not standard equipment in many Japanese kitchens, urban grilling takes place in a fish broiler or toaster oven (mini oven). In the countryside, a Japanese brazier (*shichirin*, see page 354) or ash pit (*irori*, see page 194) would have traditionally been used, though less so now. Blackening eggplant (aubergine) over charcoal or an open flame makes it easy to peel and renders the flesh succulent and oil-free. This is a refreshing and delicious way to serve eggplant in the height of summer when eggplant is plentiful.
-
Set a wire-mesh grill over low-ember coals in a charcoal brazier (*shichirin*) or a medium gas flame and grill to blacken on all sides. (Alternatively, broil (grill) in the oven, 4 inches (10 cm) from the heat.) Peel the skin, wipe any lingering black flecks off, and slice off the tops. Quarter each eggplant crosswise into about ¾-inch (2 cm) pieces and place in a container with a lid. Stir the *happo dashi* and *usukuchi shoyu* together and pour over the eggplant. Refrigerate for 2 hours to chill.

To serve, spoon into small bowls with the dashi. Pinch a small mound of the ginger on top of the eggplant and serve as a light course in a summer menu.

OVEN-GRILLED PEPPERS WITH YUBA

なすの焼き蒸し

STEAM-GRILLED EGGPLANT

NASU NO YAKI-MUSHI

Preparation time: 30 minutes
Cooking time: 15 minutes
Serves: 4

- 4 small Japanese eggplants (aubergines), 10½ oz (300 g)
- 1 tablespoon canola (rapeseed) or unroasted sesame oil
- 2 teaspoons shoyu
- 3 tablespoons finely grated daikon, drained in a fine sieve
- 1 teaspoon finely grated fresh ginger
- 1 heaping teaspoon finely chopped negi or scallion (spring onion)

The method in this recipe was shared with me by Nancy Ukai Russell, a longtime friend of my late editor Kim Schuefftan. She learned it the year she spent as a live-in weaving apprentice at Kotokuji temple in Fukumitsu-machi, Toyama prefecture in the late 1970s. I had never eaten this style of eggplant (aubergine) but thought it sounded exactly like something I would love. I wrote and tested the recipe, and it was just as good as I thought it would be, even with winter eggplants!
-
Cut the calyxes off the eggplants (aubergines) and discard. Halve the eggplants lengthwise.

Place the eggplant halves cut side down, side by side, on a cutting board. Score the flesh, making 3 or 4 shallow, diagonal slices about ¼ inch (5 mm) apart in the middle of each eggplant. Rotate the board about 45 degrees counterclockwise (anticlockwise) and make a few shallow crosscuts through the first three cuts. (Be sure to cook the eggplants immediately after cutting, otherwise the flesh will discolor.)

Heat a large cast-iron skillet over medium-high heat. Once you can feel the heat rising from the pan, add ½ tablespoon of the oil. Place the eggplant halves flesh side down in the pan. Cook for 1 minute and add the remaining ½ tablespoon oil, lifting up the eggplants a little and tipping the pan to distribute. Cook for 1 more minute, until the flesh is golden, and a few brown speckles have appeared. Flip and cook 2 minutes on the skin side. Flip back to flesh side down, add a scant ⅓ cup (2½ fl oz/75 ml) water. The water will sizzle and bubble as it hits the pan. Cover partially to allow steam to escape, reduce the heat to low, and cook until cooked through and softened but not collapsed, 4–5 minutes.

Remove from the heat and place 2 eggplant halves, flesh side down, side by side, on each of four small plates. Lift up each eggplant half and drizzle ¼ teaspoon shoyu underneath it. Mound 1 teaspoon grated daikon in the center of the back of each eggplant half. Make a small divot in the center of the daikon and add ⅛ teaspoon ginger in a mound to each divot. Pinch a ⅛-teaspoon mound of chopped *negi* on top of the ginger, or sprinkle attractively over the tops, and serve as a vegetable side dish or starter to a summer meal.

STEAM-GRILLED EGGPLANT

柚子味噌なす

PAN-GRILLED EGGPLANT WITH YUZU MISO

YUZU MISO NASU

Preparation time: 35 minutes
Cooking time: 10 minutes
Serves: 4

- 2 smallish round Japanese eggplants (aubergines), 9 oz (250 g)
- 6 tablespoons lightly roasted white sesame oil or unroasted sesame oil
- Yuzu Miso (page 29)

Slowly frying the eggplant (aubergine) while pushing down evenly with a weight will bring out its velvety texture, and the sweet miso with fragrant citrus will soften the earthy flavor. This dish is compelling served warm, but also good at room temperature.

-

Cut the tops and bottoms off the eggplants (aubergines), peel, and halve the eggplant crosswise into rounds ¾ inch (2 cm) thick. Soak immediately in a bowl of cold water to cover for 5 minutes or until ready to proceed. Remove from the water, pat dry, and prick all over with a sharp fork.

In a medium frying pan, heat the oil over medium-low heat.

Once the oil is rippling, place the smaller of the cut sides down in the pan and allow them to soak up oil. Flip the eggplant rounds and place a foil-wrapped drop lid (*otoshibuta*, see page 354) or flat (not too heavy) pan lid on top of the eggplant. Press down gently as they cook. The idea is to encourage the middle area to soften, but not to squish the eggplant. Cook until golden on the bottom, about 5 minutes. Flip and cook the smaller side for about 5 minutes more to brown slightly.

Serve on four small plates and slather the exposed round surface of the eggplant generously with the yuzu miso.

~~~~~~

豆腐トマトグラタン

TOFU AND TOMATO GRATIN

TOUFU TOMATO GURATAN

Preparation time: 30 minutes, plus 2–8 hours tofu weighting time
Cooking time: 40 minutes
Serves: 4

- 5¼ oz (150 g) cotton tofu (momendofu, see page 352) or Japanese-style soft block tofu
- 1 medium potato (5¼ oz/150 g), scrubbed and unpeeled
- ½ small (3½ oz/100 g) Boiled Bamboo Shoot (page 34)
- ½ tablespoon (7.5 g) unsalted butter
- 1¾ oz (50 g) shimeji, torn apart and halved crosswise
- 1 cup (8 fl oz/250 ml) Tomato-Mushroom Sauce (page 31)
- 4½ oz (125 g) mozzarella cheese, grated

This is one of those surprising crossover dishes that may leave you wondering why you hadn't thought of it. Light and fresh, this is an extremely tasty gratin. The textures are remarkable with the creamy tofu, crunchy bamboo, and soft potato and mushroom. For a nondairy version, substitute vegan melting cheese, and mild olive oil for the butter.

-

Weight the tofu overnight in the fridge or for at least 2 hours. Halve lengthwise and slice crosswise into slabs ¼ inch (5 mm) thick.

In a small saucepan, combine the potato with cold water to cover generously, and bring to a boil over high heat. Cook until easily pierced with a bamboo skewer, 20–25 minutes. Drain and peel while still warm. Slice crosswise into rounds ¼ inch (5 mm) thick.

Quarter or halve the bamboo shoot lengthwise, depending on the shape, and cut crosswise into slices ¼ inch (5 mm) thick.

Position a rack in the center of the oven and preheat the oven to 350°F (180°C). Butter a 7 × 10½-inch (18 × 26 cm) oval gratin dish and line the bottom with the thinly sliced tofu. Arrange the potato rounds over the tofu in an even layer, followed by the bamboo. Strew the shimeji over the bamboo. Pour the tomato-mushroom sauce over the vegetables and sprinkle with the mozzarella. Transfer to the oven and bake until lightly browned and bubbling, 12–15 minutes.

TOFU AND TOMATO GRATIN

里芋の炒め物

STIR-FRIED TARO ROOT

SATO-IMO NO ITAME-MONO

Preparation time: 25 minutes,
plus cooling time
Cooking time: 20 minutes
Serves: 4

  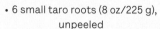

- 6 small taro roots (8 oz/225 g), unpeeled
- 1 tablespoon lightly roasted gold sesame oil or ½ tablespoon dark roasted and ½ tablespoon unroasted sesame oil
- 1 tablespoon slivered fresh ginger
- 2 tablespoons shoyu
- 1 tablespoon hon mirin
- ½ tablespoon finely slivered yuzu or Meyer lemon zest
- 1 tablespoon finely slivered green shiso leaves

Small Japanese taro roots become meltingly soft when simmered or roasted. The larger Pacific Island varieties aren't suitable for these Japanese taro dishes, because the over-sized varieties are starchy and don't cook into a silky consistency. Here, stir-frying the boiled taro root mitigates its natural viscous quality and gives it a pleasant caramelization. The pieces are crispy, creamy, and coated with sweet shoyu—irresistible!

-

In a medium saucepan, combine the taro roots with cold water to cover generously, and bring to a boil over high heat. Cook until soft in the center but not mushy, about 10 minutes. Drain and allow to cool in a wire-mesh sieve. Peel, pat dry, and cut into ¾-inch (2 cm) rounded triangular pieces (*rangiri*, see page 17).

In a medium frying pan, heat the sesame oil over medium heat and, once you can feel the heat rising, add the ginger. Stir once, then add the taro. Stir-fry gently, to avoid breaking, until the taro is golden on all sides, about 3 minutes. Swirl in the shoyu and mirin and stir-fry 1–2 minutes more to allow the liquids to reduce and the flavors to be absorbed— be careful not to burn the shoyu.

Spoon into a pretty serving bowl or individual saucers and serve hot, garnished with the slivered yuzu and shiso.

木の芽味噌のなす田楽

SANSHO LEAF MISO–GRILLED EGGPLANT

KINOME MISO NO NASU DENGAKU

Preparation time: 15 minutes
Cooking time: 15 minutes
Serves: 4

   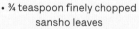

- ¾ teaspoon finely chopped sansho leaves
- 4 tablespoons white miso
- 4 tablespoons soy milk
- 2 tablespoons sake
- 2 tablespoons hon mirin
- 4 small Japanese eggplants (aubergines), 9 oz (250 g)
- 1 tablespoon dark roasted sesame oil

Dengaku sauce is usually made with a fermented miso such as brown rice or barley, but here the white miso and soy milk provide a light base so as not to eclipse the aromatic *sansho* leaves.

-

In a small saucepan, stir the *sansho* leaves, miso, soy milk, sake, and mirin together. Cook over low heat, stirring with a flat wooden spoon, for 3 minutes.

Position a rack about 4 inches (10 cm) from the top and preheat the broiler (grill).

Halve the eggplants (aubergines) lengthwise, leaving the stem and calyx. Make shallow diagonal cuts in the flesh about ¼ inch (5 mm) apart and place cut side up on a baking sheet. Brush lightly with the oil and broil (grill) for 5 minutes. Flip and cook 3 minutes, face down. Flip again, smear the *sansho* miso smoothly across the surfaces of each eggplant and broil again until bubbling, with browned spots, 3–4 minutes.

Serve hot, 2 halves per person, on individual small plates.

STIR-FRIED TARO ROOT

HON MIRIN

Historically, mirin was a naturally sweet alcohol fermented and brewed from steamed glutinous rice and rice koji. Today there are many categories of mirin, ranging from *hon mirin* ("true mirin"), to new mirin, salt mirin, *ni-kiri mirin* (boiled mirin), to ersatz mirin-style seasonings.

Selecting *hon mirin* is essential when building your Japanese pantry. Nonetheless, it is important to understand the wide gap between general purpose *hon mirin* and artisanal *hon mirin*. The general purpose *hon mirin*, though manufactured from steamed glutinous rice and rice koji (steamed rice inoculated with *Aspergillus oryzae* spores), also contains added alcohol and starch syrup (*mizuame*) to compensate for the short production period of two to three months. Artisanal *hon mirin*, on the other hand, ferments into alcohol and saccharifies naturally, before being pressed and aged further to develop flavor—a one- to two-year process. The mirin lees are called *kobore ume* ("spilled plums") because they are crumbly and resemble white plum blossoms. *Kobore ume* are used as a natural sweetener in local desserts.

Although *hon mirin* does have an alcohol content similar to sake at about 14 percent—calling mirin "sweet rice wine" is a misnomer. (Similarly, sake is often seen dubbed as "rice wine," despite being fermented and brewed in a process nothing akin to the wine making process.) This term "sweet rice wine" was applied to mirin after World War II, when Japanese products began finding their way out of Japan and onto the shelves abroad, and most likely was chosen for easy understanding rather than strict accuracy. A top-quality mirin (such as Mikawa Mirin) will be full and deep in the mouth—much like an aged sherry—but it will also have a complex sweetness. Drinkability

is the benchmark of judging mirin. Despite its 500-year history in Japan, *hon mirin* was used only by the aristocracy, samurai, and priests, and eventually restaurants serving high-end cuisine or river eel (*unagi*). Finally, in the 1930s, *hon mirin* use spread to Japanese homes, though still could only be sold by shops with a liquor license.

By the 1940s, *hon mirin* had become a thriving industry with over 200 producers. Post World War II, only a handful remained: Sumiya Bunjiro Brewery Co., Ltd., producer of Mikawa Mirin, was the most prominent, but a few tiny producers also stayed viable. As the economy of Japan improved and pride in Japanese cuisine returned, more small artisanal mirin companies began cropping up, and some have enough production to sell their mirin outside of Japan. Nonetheless, Mikawa Mirin is not only the most serious mirin made in Japan, but also the one most available abroad (often repackaged and found in proprietary organic seasoning lines).

Following the custom of my farmer husband, our house did not use much mirin until I started writing Japanese cookbooks and began delving more deeply into artisanal ingredients outside of our local area. One of the first trips I made in 2013 when filming with Fuji TV was to a barrel-maker in Kobe whom I had befriended, as well as Konanzuke a local *narazuke* and mirin-maker. (The actual name of the company is Takashima Liquor Foods Co., Ltd., but the shop name is Konanzuke.)

The company was founded in 1870 by Heisuke Takashima in the Nada ward of eastern Kobe in Hyogo prefecture. Originally, the founder bought sake lees from a nearby sake brewer and his business consisted of selling sake lees as well as making and selling *shochu* (distilled liquor). In 1896, Heisuke Takashima began manufacturing and selling *hon mirin*

made from *shochu*, and in 1904 he added *narazuke* (vegetables pickled with sake lees, mirin lees and mirin) to the line-up. According to Takashima family lore, their *narazuke* gift boxes sold well the following year, in 1905, due to the victorious end of the Russo-Japanese War and the resulting boost to the economy of Japan.

The current president, Zenpei Takashima, continues in this vein of creating products with higher added value from their specialty products: Such as from sake lees to *shochu*, *shochu* to *hon mirin*, and *hon mirin* to *narazuke*. While their main business is *narazuke* (which is sold nationwide), Konanzuke makes two top-notch mirins: Hakubishi Hon Mirin and Hakubishi three-year Aged Hon Mirin. There is a viewing room at the main Konanzuke shop where you can see the steps of how the mirin is aged in small wooden barrels—this was my first contact with artisanal mirin. Additionally, the Hakubishi Hon Mirin is pressed in the traditional way, by ladling into hemp bags, which are laid out in stacks in a large wooden pressing boat (*shiboribune*). They are weighted and allowed to drip out naturally, before pressure is applied slowly with a vice setup. Unfortunately, their production is too small to export.

Kawaishi Honke is a tiny 150-year-old brewery in Himeji, of Hyogo prefecture. Both times I visited, Kawaishi, the brewer, walked me through the process of his mirin making. Besides the hands-on approach of this small operation that uses local rice, equally impressive is the traditional wood *shiboribune* (pressing boat) that Kawaishi still uses to press the liquid mirin out of the solids (lees). He produces a wide range of mirin but of note are: Kawaishi Honke Hon Mirin, Tegarayama Hon Mirin, Junmaimoto Mirin "Enju," and Hon Mirin "Gokujo" and, luckily, recognition for his dedicated work and excellent products is growing in Japan.

Currently, there are two types of manufacturing methods for mirin: traditional and industrial. The traditional method uses high-quality glutinous rice steamed in a Japanese steaming vessel (*kama*). The rice is inoculated with koji spores (*Aspergillus orzyae*), allowed to saccharify, and then aged over a period of time to mellow and develop complexity. Sumiya Bunjiro includes rice *shochu* in their proprietary brewing method for Mikawa Mirin and the process takes a total of two years. Post World War II, industrial methods began to be used, such as pressure steaming for the rice as well as liquefaction of the rice at high temperatures to speed up the process of breaking down the starches and proteins.

As a luxury item, mirin was subject to a high liquor tax due to a rice shortage during World War II and in its aftermath, so besides *hon mirin,* other mirins were developed to avoid the tax. These new mirins were either made from miscellaneous grains (rather than rice) or were "salt mirins": alcohol fermented in salt water, then artificially sweetened. In 1975, the Fair Trade Commission further disallowed products that did not reach a standard to call themselves "mirin" and instead required that they be labeled "mirin-style seasonings." Mirin-style seasonings are made by mixing glucose or a starchy saccharified syrup (*mizuame*) with chemical seasonings such as MSG and amino acid liquid fragrances. Salt mirins are produced through alcoholic fermentation in salt water, then adjusted in taste by adding a sugar solution. New mirin or boiled mirin (*ni-kiri mirin*) is made from miscellaneous grains instead of rice, with MSG and chemical-based acids added. Mirin-style seasonings, salt mirins, new mirin, and boiled mirin all contain virtually no alcohol.

When choosing mirin, at the very least, always select *hon mirin* for optimal flavor and best results. Also, as a very strong rule of thumb, read the ingredient list on the back of the label to verify there is no added alcohol, starch syrup, or other. But if you are truly interested in researching a product, scroll through the company's website to learn production methods. Google Translate is an extremely useful tool when browsing through Japanese web pages. If exact key words are not included, such as "organic," "Japanese grown," or "barrel fermented," then you can assume the materials used are not organic, Japanese grown, or barrel fermented. Additionally, if there is no detailed explanation of the brewing method, I would doubt the underlying integrity of the product. A company that is actually following traditional methods will clearly detail their production process from beginning to end (you can find a fascinating visual chart of the brewing process on the Mikawa Mirin website).

Naturally saccharified, top-quality *hon mirin* leaves no lingering sweetness in the mouth. The alcohol content in mirin adds glossiness to grilled and simmered foods and brings out the richness in deeply flavored foods such as root vegetables. *Hon mirin* is particularly compatible with miso, shoyu, and rice vinegar and serves to soften salt or acidity.

Choosing *hon mirin* over sugar to soften salt or acid in Japanese dishes is a personal choice, but logically, since miso, shoyu, and rice vinegar are all fermented seasonings, it makes sense to balance their deeply rounded salt or acid profiles with another fermented seasoning: *hon mirin*. The only caveat here is that some *hon mirin*, such as *Aji no Haha*, contains salt (this allows it to be categorized as a seasoning not an alcohol for sales and export), so keep that in mind when pairing with miso or shoyu. And if you are growing your own vegetables or buying from the farmers' market, there is a strong case to be made for using artisanal Japanese seasonings on these full-flavored vegetables because they enhance each one and leave a memorable impression in your mouth as you taste their powerful harmony.

じゃが芋のクリーム煮

CREAMY POTATOES

JYAGAIMO NO KURI-MU NI

Preparation time: 30 minutes
Cooking time: 35 minutes
Serves: 4

• 1 lb (450 g) medium-small potatoes, peeled and quartered
• 2 cups (16 fl oz/500 ml) Konbu Dashi (page 22) or Shiitake Dashi (page 22)
• 2 teaspoons flaky sea salt
• ½ small bunch (3½ oz/100 g) spinach, preferably with roots intact
• 2½ tablespoons canola (rapeseed) oil
• 3½ tablespoons (35 g) unbleached all-purpose (plain) flour
• 1 cup (8 fl oz/250 ml) soy milk
• ½ cup (2¾ oz/75 g) fresh corn kernels, cut from 1 ear (optional)
• 2 tablespoons pine nuts
• ½ teaspoon freshly grated black pepper
• 1 teaspoon freshly squeezed lemon juice
• 1 handful Italian parsley, coarsely chopped
• 2 fresh green japones chiles, chopped (optional)
• Freshly cooked Japanese Rice (page 27), for serving

This appealingly creamy dish is quintessentially Japanese in mind-set but owes its origins to Western cooking. If fresh corn is available, it's a great addition.

–

In a medium saucepan, bring the potato quarters, dashi, and 1 teaspoon of the salt to a boil over high heat. Reduce to a brisk simmer, cover, and cook until the potato pieces are soft in the center, about 5 minutes. Reserving the cooking liquid, drain the potatoes. (You should have about 1 cup/8 fl oz/250 ml of cooking liquid; if not, add water.)

Bring a medium saucepan of water to a boil. Hold the spinach stems in the boiling water for 30 seconds. Push the leaves into the boiling water, cook 15 seconds more, then scoop out with a wire-mesh sieve. Refresh under cold running water to cool. Squeeze down the length of the leaves and stems. Cut the spinach bottoms, if you have them, into ½-inch (1 cm) pieces and stems and leaves crosswise into 1½-inch (4 cm) pieces.

In a heavy medium saucepan, heat the oil over medium heat. Add the flour and cook by spreading and scraping across the surface of the saucepan with a flat wooden spoon for about 1½ minutes, taking care not to color. Whisk the reserved potato cooking liquid and soy milk in gradually to form a smooth velouté. Simmer gently for 10 minutes, stirring occasionally to make sure it does not scorch.

Add the potatoes, spinach, corn (if using), pine nuts, pepper, lemon juice, parsley, chile (if using), and remaining 1 teaspoon salt and fold into the velouté. Serve over Japanese rice.

ピーマンのじゃが詰め

GRILLED POTATO-SALAD-STUFFED PEPPERS

PI-MAN NO JYAGA-ZUME

Preparation time: 20 minutes
Cooking time: 2 minutes
Serves: 4

• 4 medium Japanese green peppers (piman, see page 347) or sweet red and yellow peppers (4¼ oz/120 g)
• ¼ recipe Potato Salad (page 48)
• 2 teaspoons chopped Italian parsley
• 4 teaspoons grated or crumbled Parmesan-Style Vegan "Cheese" (page 38)

Potato salad equals summer in many countries, including Japan. Stuffing leftover potato salad into hollowed-out pepper halves is a genius instant stuffed-pepper method. Feel free to use a mild Parmesan or Romano cheese instead of the vegan version.

–

Halve the peppers lengthwise. Discard the seeds but leave the cores. Mound the potato salad into the pepper halves with a soup spoon. Flatten the surface

and sprinkle with the parsley followed by the "cheese." Make a "boat" with heavy-duty foil on a toaster oven (mini oven) tray and nestle the stuffed peppers into the "boat." Since their bottoms are curved, the peppers will be wobbly. Crumple up logs of foil and use them to keep the peppers propped up so the surfaces are upright. Broil (grill) for about 2 minutes, until the "cheese" is lightly browned. Best hot, but also good at room temperature.

GRILLED POTATO-SALAD-STUFFED PEPPERS

焼ききのこ柑橘あえ

CITRUS-DRESSED MUSHROOMS

YAKI-KINOKO KANKITSU-AE

Preparation time: 30 minutes
Cooking time: 10 minutes
Serves: 4

- 4 medium shiitake (2¼ oz/60 g), stems removed
- 2¾ oz (80 g) shimeji mushrooms, separated into chunks
- 2¼ oz (60 g) maitake mushrooms, separated into chunks
- 1 teaspoon flaky sea salt
- 1 small bunch (3½ oz/100 g) mizuna, connected bottom ends intact
- ⅔ cup (5½ fl oz/160 ml) Konbu Dashi (page 22)
- 2 tablespoons usukuchi shoyu (see page 344)
- 2 teaspoons shoyu
- 4–6 teaspoons sudachi, kobosu, or yuzu juice (or Meyer lemon juice with a touch of lime)

Earthy mushrooms benefit from a spritz of fragrant citrus such as *kabosu*, *sudachi*, or yuzu. If Japanese citrus is not available, add a little Key lime or conventional lime to Meyer lemon juice to give it some acid balance. The mushrooms, mizuna, and dressing can be prepared ahead of time, but be sure to add the citrus at the last minute so as not to lose brightness, and dress just before serving. This unusually compelling dish has lovely flavors and contrasting textures.

-

Heat a dry frying pan over low heat and add the shiitake (cap sides down), shimeji, and maitake. Roast for about 3 minutes on each side, flipping when the bottom is lightly colored. When slightly softened, transfer the mushrooms to a cutting board. When cool enough to handle, tear each shiitake cap with your hands into 6 thin strips and the shimeji and maitake into large bite-size pieces.

Bring a medium pot of water to a boil with the salt. Blanch the mizuna for 30 seconds in the salted water. Scoop out and refresh under cold running water until cool to the touch. Shake off and squeeze to express as much water as possible. Align the root ends on a cutting board. Slice off the ends and discard. Cut the stems and leaves crosswise into 1¼-inch (3 cm) pieces. Stack together and wrap in paper towels to press out moisture.

In a medium bowl, stir together the dashi, *usukuchi shoyu*, and shoyu. Right before serving, add 4 teaspoons of the citrus juice to the dressing and toss with the mushrooms. Taste and add 1 or 2 more teaspoons if needed. The citrus should enhance the dressing, but not overwhelm the mushrooms. Spoon into four shallow lacquer or ceramic bowls, place a small stack of mizuna alongside, and serve.

CITRUS-DRESSED MUSHROOMS

舞茸のほうらく焼き

DONABE-BAKED MAITAKE AND EGG

MAITAKE NO HOURAKU-YAKI

Preparation time: 30 minutes
Cooking time: 20 minutes
Serves: 4

- 5¼ oz (150 g) maitake, torn
into 6 chunks for grilling
- 1 heaping tablespoon finely
chopped fresh ginger
- 4 eggs, at room temperature
- 2 tablespoons lightly roasted white
sesame oil or unroasted sesame oil
- 2½ tablespoons white miso
- 4 tablespoons Konbu Dashi (page 22)
- 1 teaspoon usukuchi shoyu
(see page 344)

Earthenware pots (donabe, see page 353) are used for cooking one-pot dishes (nabe), rice, or horaku-style oven-baked dishes. Although here eggs and grilled mushrooms are the stars, horaku-style often includes a whole fish and various types of shellfish, and in those cases the ingredients are baked on a bed of pine needles. Either way, the ingredients bake together into a fragrant meal. A small, flat gratin dish substitutes well for this dish because there is no need for a top while baking.
-
Position a rack in the upper third of the oven and preheat the oven to 350°F (180°C).

Grill the maitake on a grate set directly over the flame for about 2 minutes on each side, until fragrant and the surface is starting to color, but don't cook them all the way through. When cool enough to handle, tear the maitake into pieces that are easily picked up with chopsticks and strew across the bottom of a shallow 7½-inch (19 cm) round earthenware pot (donabe) or a 7 × 10½-inch (18 × 26 cm) oval gratin pan. Sprinkle the ginger evenly across the maitake.

Separate the eggs, placing the yolks in one bowl and the whites in a second. Slowly whisk the sesame oil into the egg yolks to emulsify until all the oil has been added and the mixture has thickened like mayonnaise, then whisk in the miso.

Add the dashi to the egg whites and gently whisk to combine without agitating, so as not to create bubbles. Stir in the usukuchi shoyu and strain through a fine-mesh sieve to remove bubbles or non-amalgamated portions. Add to the egg yolk/miso mixture and pour into the donabe, making sure the egg mixture evenly covers the maitake.

Transfer to the oven and bake until puffed and browned in spots, 15–20 minutes.

DONABE-BAKED MAITAKE AND EGG

柿の山椒だれ焼き

GRILLED PERSIMMON WITH SANSHO

KAKI NO SANSHOU-DARE YAKI

Preparation time: 15 minutes
Cooking time: 25 minutes
Serves: 4

- ½ cup (4 fl oz/125 ml) sake
- Scant ⅓ cup (2 ½ fl oz/75 ml) hon mirin
- ¼ cup (2 fl oz/60 ml) shoyu
- 2 firm Fuyu persimmons (8¼ oz/235 g each)
- A few small pinches green sansho powder

This densely flavored sauce (*tare*) is often used to marinate meats or small birds, but persimmon makes sense as a vehicle for the sauce and for grilling, much in the same way that Westerners grill peaches. There will be left over *tare* that can be used for grilling peppers, eggplant (aubergines), or peaches.
-
In a small saucepan, bring the sake and mirin to a boil over high heat to cook off the alcohol for about 3 minutes, but watch that the liquids do not boil over. Once the alcohol aroma has dissipated, stir in the shoyu and cook down over medium-high heat for about 10 minutes to reduce the liquid by about one-third. The *tare* will keep for several months, if refrigerated.

Heat a toaster oven (mini oven) or a broiler (grill) with the rack positioned 4 inches (10 cm) from the top.

Remove the calyx of the persimmons, halve lengthwise, and pare out the core and seeds. Bevel the edges of the persimmon halves, then dip the halves in the *tare*. Grill on one side for about 2 minutes, brush with *tare*, and cook for 2 more minutes until caramelized. Brush with *tare* again, flip, and grill on the other side for another 4 minutes, brushing one more time with *tare* after cooking for 2 minutes.

Serve hot, sprinkled lightly with *sansho*.

GRILLED PERSIMMON WITH SANSHO

焼き椎茸

GRILLED SHIITAKE WITH GRATED DAIKON

YAKI SHIITAKE

Preparation time: 30 minutes
Cooking time: 5 minutes
Makes: 4

• 4 medium shiitake (3½ oz/100 g)
• ¼ teaspoon flaky sea salt
• 4 tablespoons finely grated daikon
• 2 medium green shiso leaves, finely chopped
• 2 teaspoons Konbu Dashi (page 22)
• 1 teaspoon usukuchi shoyu (see page 344)
• 1 teaspoon hon mirin

In the 1960s and '70s, grilled mushrooms stuffed with chopped stems, breadcrumbs, herbs, butter, and Parmesan cheese were a popular hors d'oeuvre in the United States. In this fresh, bright, and unusual Japanese version, no dairy is used, and grated daikon is added to the chopped stems instead of bread-crumbs, thus making them extra juicy. To achieve the finely grated consistency for the daikon, use a Japanese grater (*oroshiki*, see page 354) or *oroshigane* (see page 354).
-
Brush the shiitake and wipe them clean with a damp towel. Remove the stems and chop finely. Sprinkle the gill side of the caps with the salt. Heat a medium frying pan over medium heat and add the shiitake caps, gill side down, with the chopped stems. Pan-grill the caps for about 3 minutes, while stirring the stems, until their heady aroma lifts from the pan. Place the shiitake caps, gill side up, on a plate and scrape the chopped stems into a small bowl to cool.

Add the grated daikon and shiso to the cooled stems and toss together. Mound onto the shiitake caps, and place the shiitake on a pretty ceramic plate. In a small bowl, stir the dashi, *usukuchi shoyu*, and mirin together and drizzle over the shiitake. Serve immediately as a succulently textured bite before dinner.

大根の味噌 幽庵焼き

WHITE MISO–GRILLED DAIKON

DAIKON NO MISO YUUAN YAKI

Preparation time: 20 minutes, plus 2 hours marinating time
Cooking time: 15 minutes
Serves: 4

• Scant ½ cup (3½ fl oz/100 ml) sake
• 14 oz (400 g) daikon, cut crosswise into 1¼-inch (3 cm) rounds
• 3½ tablespoons white miso
• 1 teaspoon finely slivered yuzu zest
• ⅓ cup (2¾ fl oz/80 ml) hon mirin
• 3 tablespoons usukuchi shoyu (see page 344)
• 1 tablespoon shoyu

Yuuan yaki is a style of grilling used at yakitori shops that yields caramelized pieces of fish and meat. Here, the deeply flavored marinade infuses the daikon and is brought out in the grilling process. The citrus zest is a key point for the success of this dish, so substitute Meyer lemon if you do not have access to yuzu.
-
In a small saucepan, bring the sake to a boil to burn off the alcohol. Pour into a medium mixing bowl to cool. Peel the daikon rounds, halve each piece crosswise, and bevel the edges.

Once the sake has cooled to about room temperature, stir in the white miso and ½ teaspoon of the yuzu zest to form a smooth paste. Add the mirin, *usukuchi shoyu*, and shoyu and stir to blend. Slip in the daikon pieces and toss to distribute the marinade. Scrape into a 1-gallon (4-liter) resealable freezer bag, roll up to eliminate any air, and seal. Store in the refrigerator for 2 hours to absorb flavor.

Position a rack 6 inches (15 cm) from the heat source and preheat the broiler (grill).

Discard the marinating liquids. Pat the daikon pieces dry with paper towels. Arrange the daikon on a baking sheet. Broil (grill) for about 8 minutes each side, until well browned and caramelized, but take care not to burn. Serve hot or at room temperature with a pinch of the yuzu zest.

GRILLED SHIITAKE WITH GRATED DAIKON

大根の豆腐詰め

TOFU-STUFFED DAIKON WITH UME

DAIKON NO TOUFU-ZUME

Preparation time: 45 minutes,
plus 1 hour tofu weighting time
Cooking time: 10 minutes
Serves: 4

• 7 oz (200 g) cotton tofu (momendofu,
see page 352) or Japanese-style
soft block tofu
• 3 inches (8 cm) daikon, about
2¾ inches (7 cm) in diameter
• 2 teaspoons dried hijiki
(see page 349), soaked in cold water
for 20 minutes
• ½ teaspoon red shiso powder
(aka shiso, see page 350)
• 2 tablespoons potato starch,
plus more for dusting
• 2 tablespoons dark roasted
sesame oil
• 4 green shiso leaves, for serving
• 1 teaspoon sour "plum" paste
(bainiku, see page 350)
• ½ teaspoon finely grated fresh wasabi

The contrasting flavors and
textures in this dish are striking.
The crispy, seared daikon stuffed
with creamy tofu, finished with
puckery, fruity, dried sour "plum"
paste (bainiku, see page 350) and
spicy wasabi make this unusual
dish unforgettable.
-
Place the tofu on a plate and
weight with a small chopping
board for 1 hour.

Cut the daikon crosswise into
4 rounds and peel the circumference with a sharp knife. Bevel
the edges. Use a 2-inch (5 cm)
ring to punch out a daikon round
from the center of each piece.
Make 5 curved V-cuts around the
perimeter of the punched-out
rounds to create flower shapes
and bevel the petals. Reserve the
"flowers" and the daikon "rings."

Smash the tofu in a Japanese
grinding bowl (suribachi, see
page 354) until creamy. Drain
the hijiki, pat dry in a clean tea
towel, and fold into the tofu
with the shiso powder and
2 tablespoons potato starch.
Mix until the ingredients are

evenly incorporated. Lay the
daikon rings out on a cutting
board and stuff with the tofu
mixture so that it is flush or
rises slightly above the ring.
Wipe off any stuffing that might
have smeared on the daikon ring
surface. Dust the rings with a light
coating of potato starch using
a sifter or a fine-mesh sieve.

In a large frying pan, heat the
sesame oil over medium heat.
Sear the stuffed daikon rings and
daikon "flowers" until golden on
the bottom sides, 4–5 minutes.
Dust the tops of the daikon rings
lightly with potato starch, flip
all the pieces and cook until
the second sides are golden,
4–5 minutes longer.

Arrange a shiso leaf off-center
on each of four small plates and
set one stuffed daikon on top
of the stem ends of the shiso.
Position the daikon "flower" near
the stuffed daikon and squeeze
a small mound of bainiku onto
the shiso leaf or plate. Add a dab
of wasabi to the plate and serve
warm with a fork and knife.

TOFU-STUFFED DAIKON WITH UME

柚子田楽　　　　YUZU WITH SESAME MISO

YUZU DENGAKU

Preparation time: 30 minutes
Cooking time: 10 minutes
Serves: 4, as a small bite

- 2 small juicy yuzu or Meyer lemons (7 oz/200 g)
- 6 tablespoons white sesame seeds
- 2 tablespoons white miso
- 2 tablespoons sake
- Pinch of flaky sea salt

Dengaku sauce is a sweetened miso that is smeared on cooked vegetables (or meat) before grilling to caramelize. While often made with fermented miso such as brown rice or barley, here the white miso is mixed with delicate ground white sesame seeds and slathered on yuzu slices before grilling, resulting in juicy, bright textures. Serve this as a revitalizing bite in the middle of a full meal or before dinner to stimulate the appetite.
-
Wipe the yuzu and trim off the ends. Slice the yuzu crosswise into rounds ½ inch (1 cm) thick. Poke out the seeds and discard.

Set a bamboo steamer over a large wok filled one-third of the way with water and bring to a boil. Lay the yuzu slices directly in the steamer, cover, and steam for 5 minutes. Remove from the steamer and cool.

In a small dry frying pan, warm the sesame seeds until fragrant. Slide into a Japanese grinding bowl (*suribachi*, see page 354) and grind until completely broken down and the oils are coming out. (Alternatively, pulse in a spice grinder.) Mash the miso into the ground sesame to make a thick paste. Slowly stir or mash in the sake to thin.

Arrange the yuzu on a foil-lined toaster oven (mini oven) tray and smear each piece evenly with the sesame-miso. Broil (grill) in the toaster oven until caramelized, about 3 minutes.

Sprinkle with a tiny bit of salt and serve hot.

YUZU WITH SESAME MISO

納豆お好み焼き　NATTO OKONOMIYAKI

Preparation time: 15 minutes
Cooking time: 15 minutes
Serves: 4

- Scant ⅔ cup (5¼ fl oz/150 ml) whole milk
- ¾ cup (2¾ oz/80 g) all-purpose (plain) flour
- ¼ teaspoon flaky sea salt
- 2 packs (3 oz/85 g each) natto, finely chopped
- 2½ oz (75 g) coarsely grated mild cheddar cheese
- 2 teaspoons canola (rapeseed) or unroasted sesame oil
- Green nori powder (aonori, see page 349), for serving

American cheese slices have been popular in Japan for decades and appear often in recipes that call for cheese. I prefer a mild cheddar and have used it here, though feel free to use soy milk instead of dairy milk and vegan cheese for a nondairy version. On a historical side note: While not a proven theory, there is a common belief in the Japanese temple community that "natto" was given its name because the beans were traditionally fermented in a temple storage building called a *nassho*.

-

In a medium bowl, whisk the milk into the flour and salt. Drop in the natto and mix vigorously. Stir in the cheese until evenly incorporated.

In a large well-seasoned cast-iron skillet or nonstick frying pan, heat the oil over low heat.

Ladle out 4 equal scoops of the batter, cover, and cook slowly until bubbles appear across the entire surface of the pancakes, about 10 minutes. Flip and cook until the bottom side is golden, about 5 minutes longer.

Serve hot: one per person, sprinkled lightly with green nori.

~~~~~~~~~~~~~~~~~~~~~~~~~~~~~~~~~~~~~~~

精進お好み焼き　SHOJIN OKONOMIYAKI

Preparation time: 25 minutes
Cooking time: 15 minutes
Serves: 4

- 2¼ inches (6 cm) medium mountain yam (3½ oz/100 g), scrubbed
- 4 large cabbage leaves (9 oz/250 g), coarsely diced
- 3 inches (8 cm) takuan (5¼ oz/150 g), diced
- 1½ cups (12¾ fl oz/375 ml) soy milk
- 7 oz (200 g) all-purpose (plain) flour, whisked
- 4 tablespoons tenkasu (see recipe introduction), optional
- 2 tablespoons canola (rapeseed) or unroasted sesame oil
- Shoyu, for serving
- Green nori powder (aonori, see page 349), for serving

The beauty of this recipe is that you can use little bits and pieces of vegetables or pickles you have stashed in your fridge or hanging around on your counter as you cook. Also be sure to save the fried crumbs of tempura batter (*tenkasu*) after preparing any of the tempura dishes in this book. They keep well, stored in the freezer in an airtight container. While *tenkasu* is available commercially, it is almost impossible to find without MSG and other food additives. And although there is a recipe for making your own Takuan (page 316) in this book, this semidried daikon pickle is also available in health food stores and Japanese grocery stores.

-

Peel and finely grate the mountain yam on a sharp-toothed ceramic grater (*oroshiki*, see page 354) or metal grating plate (*oroshigane*, see page 354) and scrape into

a medium bowl. Add the cabbage, *takuan*, soy milk, flour, and *tenkasu* (if using) and toss lightly until the ingredients are well distributed.

Working with 2 large nonstick frying pans set over low heat, heat 1 tablespoon oil in each pan. Ladle in the batter to make 4 pancakes in each pan. Cook slowly for about 10 minutes, covered. Uncover every 3 minutes or so, wipe the water beaded up on the top, and press down the pancakes with the back of a spatula to compress. Flip and cook for 5 more minutes on the other side, pressing down once with the back of a spatula, until both sides are golden and the pancakes are well set.

Place 2 pancakes, overlapping, on each of four small plates. Drizzle with shoyu, sprinkle with green nori, and serve hot.

NATTO OKONOMIYAKI; SHOJIN OKONOMIYAKI

麻婆豆腐

MABODOFU WITH TERA NATTO

MA-BO-DOUFU

Preparation time: 30 minutes
Cooking time: 15 minutes
Serves: 4

• 1 lb 5 oz (600 g) cotton tofu
(momendofu, see page 352)
or Japanese-style soft block tofu,
cut into ¾-inch (2 cm) cubes
• 2 cups (16 fl oz/500 ml)
Konbu Dashi (page 22)
• 1 tablespoon barley miso
• 2 tablespoons tobanjan
• 2 tablespoons tenmenjan
2 tablespoons dark roasted
sesame oil
• 1 tablespoon unroasted sesame oil
• 1 teaspoon whole Sichuan pepper
• 1 tablespoon finely chopped garlic
• 1 tablespoon finely chopped
fresh ginger
• 5¼ oz (150 g) Simmered Soybeans
(page 32), finely chopped
• 2 tablespoons tera natto
(see page 350), finely chopped
• 1 teaspoon freshly ground
black pepper
• 1 tablespoon potato starch,
mixed with 2 tablespoons water
• 6 thick center portions of
napa cabbage (Chinese leaf)
leaves (10½ oz/ 300 g), cut into
¼-inch (5 mm) dice
• 4 thin scallions (spring onions)
or garlic chives (1 oz/30 g), cut
crosswise into ¾-inch (2 cm) pieces
• 1 teaspoon crushed Sichuan pepper
• 2 teaspoons shoyu

Mabodofu is a Sichuan dish introduced to Japan via NHK television by a Sichuan chef in the 1970s. The chef modified the traditional dish to be more universally appealing and Japan wholeheartedly adopted *mabodofu*, making it their own. Since *tera natto* is similar to Chinese fermented black beans, adding the *tera natto* into the dish makes it more authentic to its actual roots. This vegetarian version has textures and deep flavors similar to the original version with meat and retains a feeling of freshness. Be warned, this dish is spicy from the Chinese chile pastes: *tobanjan* and *tenmenjan*. And if you are not a fan of Sichuan pepper, halve the amount of crushed pepper added at the end or omit.

-

Bring a large saucepan of water to a boil and slide in the tofu. Simmer briskly, but not wildly, for 2 minutes. Carefully scoop out the tofu with a wire-mesh sieve and set aside to drain.

In a small bowl, stir 3 tablespoons of the dashi into the miso, *tobanjan*, and *tenmenjan* until smooth and emulsified.

Warm a large frying pan over medium heat and, once you can feel the heat rising from the surface of the pan, add 1 tablespoon of the dark sesame oil, the unroasted sesame oil, and the whole Sichuan pepper. Stir for 30 seconds, add the garlic, ginger, soybeans, and *tera natto*, and stir-fry for 30 seconds until fragrant.

Stir in the black pepper, remaining dashi, and the miso/*tobanjan*/*tenmenjan* mixture and bring to a brisk simmer over medium-high heat. Scrape in the potato starch slurry and cook over medium heat, stirring, for 5 minutes to thicken.

Add the napa cabbage (Chinese leaf), making sure it is well immersed in the sauce, and cook for 3 minutes more. Stir in the scallions (spring onions) or garlic chives and gently add the tofu. Separate each piece so they are not sticking to one another, and spoon sauce over to flavor. Drizzle with the remaining 1 tablespoon dark sesame oil, sprinkle with crushed Sichuan pepper and cook over medium-high heat for 2 minutes, without stirring, to heat through.

Swirl in the shoyu and serve, with or without rice, as a spicy midday meal or casual supper.

MABODOFU WITH TERA NATTO

野菜カレー

VEGETARIAN JAPANESE-STYLE CURRY

YASAI KARE-

Preparation time: 1 hour
Cooking time: 35 minutes
Serves: 4

- 4 medium potatoes (1 lb 5 oz/600 g)
- 2 medium carrots (10½ oz/300 g)
- 3 tablespoons canola (rapeseed) or unroasted sesame oil
- 2½ cups (20 fl oz/600 ml) Konbu Dashi (page 22)
- 1 lb 10 oz (600 g) canned tomatoes and their juices, diced
- 4 tablespoons mild curry powder
- 4 tablespoons Japanese white sesame paste
- 2 tablespoons Hatcho or soybean miso
- 1¾ oz (50 g) shimeji, separated
- 1¾ oz (50 g) maitake, torn into large bite-size pieces
- 7 oz (200 g) thick deep-fried tofu (atsuage, see page 350), cut into sixths
- Neutral oil, such as canola (rapeseed), peanut, or safflower, for deep-frying
- 4 medium Japanese eggplants (aubergines), 10½ oz (300 g)
- 8 medium okra, for serving
- 1 teaspoon flaky sea salt
- 1 tablespoon shoyu
- Freshly cooked Japanese Rice (page 27), for serving

Curry rice, along with ramen, might well be the Japanese national dish. The British style of making curry from a flour-based sauce flavored with a curry spice mix was introduced to Japan in the Meiji period (1868–1912) by British sailors. Originally it was made with a homemade roux until a commercial version of curry roux became available. Nowadays, most people just use one of the many brands readily available in the supermarket, the majority of which contain MSG. Typically, Japanese use pork in their curry rice, but with a combination of flavorful vegetables and mushrooms there is no need for meat. Also, the combination of tomatoes, miso, and sesame paste eliminates the need for making a curry roux with flour, so the resulting texture is silky and luscious, without the thickness of a flour-based sauce. If you cannot source atsuage, use medium tofu, but wait to add it until the last 5 minutes of cooking. Fresh corn kernels, briefly sautéed for 30 seconds, also make a beautiful, and tasty, garnish, in place of the okra.
-
Peel the potatoes and carrots and cut into rough, triangular bite-size chunks (rangiri, see page 17).

In a medium pot, heat 2 table-spoons of the oil over medium heat until starting to ripple. Add the potatoes and carrots and stir-fry to coat the pieces with oil. Add the dashi and bring to a boil over high heat. Reduce to a brisk simmer and cook until the potato and carrot pieces are soft, about 10 minutes.

In a medium frying pan, warm the remaining 1 tablespoon oil over medium-high heat. Add the tomatoes and curry powder and

bring to a lively simmer. Cook for 5 minutes, stirring, to take the raw edge off the curry powder and to concentrate the tomatoes.

In a small bowl, mix the sesame paste and miso together. Ladle in a small scoop of the cooking liquid from the potatoes and carrots and stir to emulsify. Scrape back into the pot with the vegetables and stir in the shimeji, maitake, tomato mixture, and atsuage. Bring to a simmer over medium heat and simmer for about 15 minutes more.

In a high-sided medium sauté pan, heat 1¼ inches (3 cm) oil over medium-high heat until the oil is starting to ripple.

Cut the eggplants (aubergines) into bite-size irregular chunks (rangiri, see page 17) and slip the pieces into the hot oil. Fry, turning with cooking chopsticks (saibashi, see page 354), until evenly burnished, about 3 minutes.

Bring a small saucepan of water to a boil over high heat. Pare the brown portions of the okra tops off and lay the okra horizontally to you on a cutting board. Sprinkle with ¼ teaspoon of the salt and roll in the salt with the flat of your palm to break down the fibrous skin a bit. Pick up the okra and drop into the boiling water for 30 seconds. Scoop out and set aside.

Brush the salt on the cutting board into the curry along with the remaining ¾ teaspoon salt. Stir in the shoyu.

Mound hot rice on the side of four plates and ladle some curry in beside the rice. Garnish with the okra and eggplant and serve hot for a casual meal.

VEGETARIAN JAPANESE-STYLE CURRY

汁物

Dashi is the underpinning of Japanese food and vegetarian dashi typically is prepared from konbu or a combination of shiitake and konbu, but can just as well be made from soaked or simmered beans, dried daikon, dried vegetables, etc. Azuki and black bean cooking liquids will lend an attractive hue to rice if used to replace the cooking water and can also be used as the dashi for miso soup. Also, using the cooking liquids from nonbitter vegetables or herbs, such as snow peas (mangetout) or *mitsuba* as a dashi will give a simmered dish more depth.

Taking less intense cooking juices and adding them to a slightly stronger simmered dish in a cycle gives a deeper and deeper taste to your vegetarian food and the variation enhances your enjoyment of the cooking process as well as the meal itself. If you are not preparing Japanese food every day, obviously it becomes more difficult to use all the leftover pieces, so forgive yourself and move on. Though if you have room in your freezer, you can always freeze for later use.

Given the crucial role that konbu plays in creating Japanese vegetarian food, be sure to use good-quality konbu. Most dried shiitake available abroad is grown in China, but if you put in some effort, it might be possible to find Japanese-grown shiitake. *Donko* (thick capped with deep fissures) is the commonly preferred variety of Japanese shiitake, though *koshin* (thin, wide, smooth caps) will also yield a flavorful broth. Dashi is the most important flavoring element so take your time on this.

It is fine to make the broth a little strong if you like but don't go overboard. You want to keep in mind the artifacts that you are creating—konbu expands almost fivefold, so you will need to think about how to use the soaked konbu. For instance, you can cut the konbu into a thin julienne and toss it with a small amount of vinegar and serve as a side dish; or toss it with curry powder, air-dry, then deep-fry slowly for a savory snack. Finely sliced shiitake and julienned konbu can be stir-fried with a little sesame oil and seasoned at the end with a splash each of shoyu and mirin (in a ratio of 2:1), simmered down to finish, and sprinkled with a little *sansho* or 7-spice powder (*shichimi togarashi*, see page 350) for serving.

Ichiju sansai (one soup, three dishes) is the classic Japanese meal format that consists of one soup and three side dishes (plus a bowl of rice and a small dish of pickles). This format can be modified to be less or more, but usually is modified in odd numbers, such as *ichiju issai* (one soup, one dish) or *ichiju gosai* (one soup, five dishes) and so on. Traditionally, Japanese drank soup at every meal and that served as the liquid. Tea was served after. This makes a good deal of sense since the taste of tea conflicts with the subtly salty soups. Although more people are drinking water in Japan, when I first arrived in 1988 it was very unusual. I was often offered a variety of drinks until I finally could convince my host that I truly just wanted water.

Restraint is essential in Japanese food. When constructing a bowl of clear soup or miso soup, keep in mind that less is more. Clear soups should be even more spare than miso soups, with only one or two ingredients and a simple garnish. Miso soups should never contain more than three main ingredients and a garnish or two such as sesame seeds, slivered ginger, chopped scallions (spring onions), or roughly chopped aromatic herbs: Japanese wild parsley (*seri*), *mitsuba*, or *sansho* leaves (see Building a Bowl of Miso Soup, page 264).

Typically cooked on a butane burner at the table, one-pot (*nabe*) meals are all-inclusive, so green vegetables such as napa cabbage (Chinese leaf) and *komatsuna* will be added in to konbu dashi with tofu and mushrooms to create a luscious, convivial repast. Once simmered, the ingredients and broth are ladled out into small bowls and seasoned with ponzu (citrus shoyu) or a sesame sauce. Alternatively, miso (or sake lees) can be added to the pot for seasoning. And soy milk can be combined with a base soup for a creamy-style *nabe* (see Tofu and Soy Milk Nabe, page 262). In these cases, the ingredients are ladled out and eaten as is. The use of small bowls that are replenished often keeps the broth hot and warming. A bowl of rice is served on the side as you eat the *nabe*. Otherwise, cooked rice or udon noodles can be stirred into the last simmering liquids and then served out to fill your tummy at the end of the meal.

SHIRUMONO

SOUP

竹の子のつみれ汁   # BAMBOO SHOOT DUMPLING SOUP

TAKENOKO NO TSUMIRE-JIRU

Preparation time: 45 minutes
Cooking time: 20 minutes
Serves: 4

• 2 rounds (2 inch/5 cm thick)
Boiled Bamboo Shoot
(page 34), 9 oz (250 g)
• 1 teaspoon flaky sea salt
• 4 tablespoons potato starch
• 1 tablespoon sansho leaves,
finely chopped
• Neutral oil, such as canola
• (rapeseed), peanut, or safflower,
for deep-frying
• 12 snow peas (mangetout),
stem ends and strings removed
• 2½ cups (20 fl oz/600 ml)
Konbu Dashi (page 22)
• 1 tablespoon usukuchi shoyu
(see page 344)
• 1 tablespoon sake

Bamboo shoots come and go quickly, but we were fortunate to have had an octogenarian citrus grower friend who would send us early bamboo shoots that she dug up in the forest, on the island where she lived in southern Japan. Making dumplings from these crunchy shoots requires extra steps, so perhaps organizing a dumpling-making party makes sense. Japanese dumplings are light and usually served in a brothy soup, so belie the image of heaviness that the word "dumpling" might evoke. If you cannot find sansho leaves, you can omit them, but they are worth the effort to source. These bamboo "balls" are also tasty served as is with a little salt.
-
Quarter the bamboo rounds, place in a medium saucepot, and add cold water to cover generously. Bring to a boil over medium-high heat, reduce to a brisk simmer, and cook until softened, about 10 minutes. Drain, shake off, and slide into a Japanese grinding bowl (suribachi, see page 354). Grind to a paste or finely pulse in a food processor.

Scrape the mixture onto a reusable cheesecloth (muslin), cinch up to form a tight package, and squeeze out excess water.

Drop back into the suribachi and mash in the salt and potato starch until well distributed. Fold in the sansho leaves and mix well. Form 8 small spheres by patting and rolling the mixture in between your palms.

In a large high-sided sauté pan, heat 1¼ inches (3 cm) oil over medium heat until hot and shimmering.

Slip the bamboo balls, one at a time, into the oil, taking care the oil does not bubble over. Fry, turning every 30 seconds, for 1½ minutes, until golden. Drain on a rack set over a pan to catch the drips.

Place 2 balls each in four deep soup bowls. In a small saucepan of boiling water, blanch the snow peas (mangetout) for 30 seconds. Scoop out and fan 3 peas attractively against the balls in each bowl.

In a small saucepan, combine the konbu dashi, usukuchi shoyu, and sake and bring to a boil over high heat. Ladle into the soup bowls and serve immediately as a delicate yet filling course.

BAMBOO SHOOT DUMPLING SOUP

翡翠そうめん　　　SLIPPERY GREEN "SOMEN"

HISUI SOUMEN

Preparation time: 30 minutes,
plus 1 hour chilling time
Cooking time: 5 minutes
Serves: 4

- Generous ¾ cup (6¾ fl oz/200 ml)
  Konbu Dashi (page 22)
- Generous ¾ cup (6¾ fl oz/200 ml)
  Shiitake Dashi (page 22)
- 2 tablespoons sake
- ¼ teaspoon green yuzu kosho
  (see page 350)
- 2 tablespoons usukuchi shoyu
  (see page 344)
- 2 medium okra (1¼ oz/35 g)
- A pinch of flaky sea salt
- 2 medium Japanese cucumbers
  (10½ oz/300 g)
- ⅓ cup (1¾ oz/50 g) potato starch, sifted

Here, finely julienned cucumber replaces somen, the ubiquitous summer noodles. Cutting the cucumbers will require a razor-sharp knife and a bit of time, but the result will be as gorgeous as it is light and delicious, so well worth the effort. Serve this in the hot summer when you are looking for a respite from the oppressive heat.

-

In a medium saucepan, bring the two dashis and the sake to an almost boil over medium-high heat. Transfer to a 2-cup (16 fl oz/500 ml) glass measuring cup. In a small bowl, stir a small spoonful of the dashi into the *yuzu kosho* to loosen, and scrape back into the dashi. Stir in the *usukuchi shoyu*, cool to room temperature, then refrigerate for about 1 hour to chill.

Bring a large saucepan of water to a boil over high heat. Set the okra horizontally to you on a cutting board and sprinkle with the salt. Roll in the salt with the flat of your hand (*itazuri*). Drop the okra into the water and blanch for 30 seconds. Scoop out with a small wire-mesh sieve and cool but keep the water on low heat. Lop off the tops and slice the okra into fine rounds ⅛ inch (3 mm) thick.

Cut the ends off the cucumbers and peel off wide lengthwise slices with a vegetable peeler. Stacking two slices at a time, carefully roll up (without breaking), and slice crosswise as finely as you can, about ⅟₁₆ inch (1 mm). Separate the threads into a loose pile of "noodles" and toss in a plastic bag with the potato starch. Shake off excess starch and set aside.

Set up a large bowl of ice and water. Increase the heat under the saucepan of water to high, drop in the cucumbers, and blanch for 30 seconds. Scoop out with a wire-mesh sieve and plunge immediately into the ice bath to chill instantly. Remove the sieve of cucumber from the bowl of ice water after a few seconds and shake off excess water.

Divide the cucumber "somen" among four small round soup bowls. Top with the okra, pour chilled dashi around the circumference of the bowl, and serve immediately. The cucumber is to be eaten with chopsticks and slurped up like noodles with the soup.

SLIPPERY GREEN "SOMEN"

そうめんとオクラ

SOMEN WITH OKRA

SOUMEN TO OKURA

Preparation time: 20 minutes
Cooking time: 1 minute
Serves: 4

• 6 small okra (2¼ oz/60 g)
• 2 bundles (1¾ oz/50 g each) somen
• 2½ cups (20 fl oz/600 ml)
Mori Tsuyu (page 25), chilled
• 1 tablespoon finely slivered
fresh ginger
• 1 small fresh green japones or
serrano chile, sliced into fine rings
• 4 small green shiso leaves,
finely slivered

Somen is eaten in the summertime all over Japan. There are myriad toppings: chopped green onion or garlic chives, slivered cucumber and or ginger, chopped okra, fine rounds of green or red chile . . . the possibilities are endless so long as they bring a fresh pop to the noodles and broth. Here the okra is the star, so the ginger and chile are understated and just there to complement.
-
Slice off the okra tops and discard. Finely chop the okra.

Set up a large bowl of ice and water. Bring a large saucepan three-quarters full of water to a boil over high heat. Remove the paper tabs from the somen bundles and drop the noodles into the water. Cook for 1 minute and scoop out quickly with a large wire-mesh sieve and a pair of cooking chopsticks to guide the noodles into the sieve. Drop into the ice water immediately to shock-cool for 1 or 2 minutes.

Ladle the cold broth into four large deep soup bowls (*donburi*, see page 354). Pick up handfuls of the noodles, shake off excess water, and add in swirls to each bowl until all the noodles have been added. Garnish with the okra, ginger, chile, and shiso and serve immediately.

グリーンスープ

GREEN SOUP

GURI-N SU-PU

Preparation time: 20 minutes
Cooking time: 2 minutes
Serves: 4

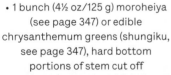

• 1 bunch (4½ oz/125 g) moroheiya
(see page 347) or edible
chrysanthemum greens (shungiku,
see page 347), hard bottom
portions of stem cut off
• ½ teaspoon fine sea salt
• 1½ cups (12 fl oz/350 ml)
Konbu Dashi (page 22)
• ¼ teaspoon flaky sea salt
• ½ teaspoon white sesame seeds,
warmed in a dry frying pan
until fragrant

Moroheiya (jute mallow) is a naturally viscous soft green that should be consumed (boiled or raw) soon after harvest. *Moroheiya* is eaten in the summer and is a rich source of vitamins and minerals. Substitute edible chrysanthemum greens (*shungiku*) or water spinach if you cannot find *moroheiya*, though the *moroheiya* will yield a more lusciously thick soup.
-
Cut the leaves off the stems of the greens and cut the stems cross-wise into 1¼-inch (3 cm) pieces.

Bring a medium saucepan of water to a boil with the fine salt. Drop in the stems and cook for 40 seconds before adding the leaves. Push the leaves down to submerge and cook an additional 20 seconds. Drain, refresh under cold running water, and shake off. Slide into a blender with the dashi and flaky salt and process until completely smooth and emulsified.

Scrape the soup into a small saucepan and bring to a simmer over medium heat. Ladle into four lacquer soup bowls, sprinkle with the sesame seeds, and serve hot.

GREEN SOUP

春キャベツスープ

SPRING CABBAGE SOUP

HARU KYABETSU SU-PU

Preparation time: 30 minutes
Cooking time: 20 minutes
Serves: 4

- 2 cups (16 fl oz/500 ml) Konbu Dashi (page 22)
- 1 cup (8 fl oz/250 ml) Shiitake Dashi (page 22)
- ½ cup (4 fl oz/125 ml) sake
- ¼ head cabbage (9 oz/250 g), cored and finely sliced
- 1 teaspoon fine sea salt
- ½ teaspoon freshly ground black pepper
- Neutral oil, such as canola (rapeseed), peanut, or safflower, for deep-frying
- 1 medium potato (5¼ oz/150 g), scrubbed
- 2 cups (16 fl oz/500 ml) soy milk
- ¾ cup (125 g) fresh corn kernels, cut from 2 ears corn
- 1 handful Italian parsley, finely chopped

Cabbage has been grown in Japan since the Edo period (1603–1868). A bit Western in flavor, this soup has its heart in Japan and makes a lovely late spring or early summer lunch, when corn and cabbage are just coinciding.

In a medium pot, bring the konbu dashi, shiitake dashi, and sake to a simmer over high heat. Add the sliced cabbage, salt, and pepper, reduce to a gentle simmer, and cook for 10 minutes.

While the soup is simmering, in a high-sided medium sauté pan, heat 1¼ inches (3 cm) oil over medium-high heat until the oil is rippling, but not smoking.

Dry the potato and cut into ½-inch (1 cm) cubes. Gently slip into the oil, taking care it does not bubble over, and cook until golden, 3–5 minutes. Skim out and drain briefly on paper towels.

Stir the soy milk and corn into the soup and warm over low heat, without simmering, for 5 minutes. (If the soy milk simmers it will separate.)

Ladle the soup into four large soup bowls and garnish with the fried potato and chopped parsley. Serve as a light, yet hearty lunch.

白みそ入り冷やしとろろ汁

CHILLED WHITE MISO SOUP

SHIRO MISO-IRI HIYASHI TORORO-JIRU

Preparation time: 30 minutes, plus 1–2 hours chilling time
Serves: 4

- 1⅔ cups (13½ fl oz/400 ml) Konbu Dashi (page 22)
- 4 tablespoons white miso
- 5¼ oz (150 g) mountain yam
- A few pinches green nori powder (aonori, see page 349)

Cold miso soup makes sense at the height of summer and this one is as elegant as it is refreshing. Serve as part of a special meal with other side vegetable dishes. Use a circular ceramic grater (*oroshiki*, see page 354) or metal grating plate (*oroshigane*, see page 354) for the correct creamy consistency when grating the mountain yam.

Stir a little konbu dashi into the white miso to loosen it. Scrape the loosened miso into the rest of the konbu dashi, stir to distribute evenly, and refrigerate.

Peel the mountain yam well and finely grate into a Japanese grinding bowl (*suribachi*, see page 354). Mash thoroughly to an ultrasmooth viscous consistency. Slowly mix in the chilled miso soup until evenly incorporated into the grated yam. Refrigerate until cold to the touch.

Serve in chilled glass or ceramic bowls with a small sprinkling of green nori powder.

SPRING CABBAGE SOUP

焼き味噌汁

CHILLED GRILLED MISO SOUP WITH MYOGA AND SOMEN

YAKI MISO SHIRU

Preparation time: 20 minutes,
plus 2 hours chilling time
Cooking time: 10 minutes
Serves: 4

- 4 tablespoons brown rice miso
  or barley miso
- 3⅓ cups (26½ fl oz/800 ml)
  Konbu Dashi (page 22)
- ½ deep-fried tofu pouch (usuage,
  see page 352)
- 1 bundle (1¾ oz/50 g) somen
- 3 medium myoga (see page 348),
  quartered lengthwise
- 3 medium shiso leaves,
  cut into fine threads
- 1 umeboshi (see page 350), pitted
  and finely chopped (optional)

Grilling miso before adding it to dashi brings out a bit of acid and gives an indescribable depth to this chilled summer soup. The soup amount is purposefully generous here because of its refreshing quality. While the *myoga* adds crunch and the somen a bit of body, the shiso and optional *umeboshi* contribute a bright finish.
-
Smear the miso in an even layer across a piece of heavy-duty foil into a rectangle about 5 × 6 inches (10 × 15.25 cm). Broil (grill) in a toaster oven (mini oven) or 4 inches (10 cm) from the heat source in a preheated oven broiler (grill) until fragrant and slightly dried around the edges, but not burned or browned, 3–4 minutes. Scrape into a 1-quart (1 liter) measuring cup.

In a small saucepan, heat a little of the konbu dashi over low heat. Slowly stir the dashi into the grilled miso. Once smoothly incorporated, add the remaining dashi, and refrigerate for at least 2 hours to chill.

Sear the *usuage* in a small dry frying pan for 1 minute on each side over high heat, until brown spots appear. Cut into quarters and set aside.

Set up a bowl of ice and water. Bring a medium pot of water to a boil over high heat. Drop in the somen and cook for 1 minute. Drain and immediately plunge into the ice bath to shock.

Pick up one-quarter of the somen, shake off, and swirl into a nest in the bottom of each of four rounded soup bowls. Rest 3 pieces of *myoga* standing up against the side of the bowl with their bottoms touching the nests of somen and ladle in the chilled miso soup. Float a square of *usuage* on top and garnish with the shiso. If desired, serve with the *umeboshi* on the side.

マスカットの冷汁

CHILLED MUSCAT AND GINGER SOUP

MASUKATTO NO HIYAJIRU

Preparation time: 20 minutes,
plus 2 hours cooling and chilling time
Cooking time: 5 minutes
Serves: 4

- 2½ cups (20 fl oz/600 ml)
  Konbu Dashi (page 22)
- ¼ teaspoon flaky sea salt
- 2 teaspoons usukuchi shoyu
  (see page 344)
- 4 tablespoons sake
- 4½ oz (125 g) muscat grapes
  (8–12 grapes), peeled
- ½ teaspoon finely slivered fresh ginger
- ½ teaspoon finely snipped nori threads

The dashi here is intentionally lightly salted to allow the flavor of the grapes to come through clearly. The ginger and nori are restrained for the same reason. This refreshing soup can be served at the beginning of a meal or in the middle as a palate cleanser. (Substitute another variety of seedless green grapes if you do not have access to muscats, but make sure you weigh them since the sizes vary considerably.)
-

In a small saucepan, bring the konbu dashi, salt, *usukuchi shoyu*, and sake to a simmer over medium heat for about 1 minute to dissolve the salt and burn off a bit of the alcohol. Transfer to a covered container, cool to room temperature, and refrigerate for 2 hours to chill.

Place 2 or 3 muscat grapes (or divide the amount you have) into each of four rounded small soup bowls. Ladle in the chilled broth and garnish with a small pinch each of ginger and nori threads. Serve immediately.

CHILLED MUSCAT AND GINGER SOUP

冷製トマトのスープ仕立て

CHILLED TOMATO IN CLEAR TOMATO BROTH

REISEI TOMATO NO SU-PU JITATE

Preparation time: 30 minutes,
plus 3 hours soaking and chilling time
Cooking time: 20 minutes
Serves: 4

- 7 oz (200 g) baby water lily buds (junsai, see page 349)
- 4 small "fruit tomatoes" or other round tomatoes (2 lb/900 g)
- Boiling water
- 3⅓ cups (26½ fl oz/800 ml) Konbu Dashi (page 22)
- 4 tablespoons sake
- 2 teaspoons flaky sea salt
- 1 tablespoon plus 1 teaspoon usukuchi shoyu (see page 344)
- Clear Tomato Broth (see below)

"Fruit tomatoes" have been popular in Japan for about ten years now—they are low in acid and have a sweet profile. Here, using clear tomato broth is both unusual and genius, and simmering the tomatoes in dashi lends a gentle note. If you cannot find the water lily buds (junsai), just omit, though they add a lovely slippery texture that cannot be duplicated.

-

Drain the water lily buds in a sieve and soak in plenty of cold water to cover for 1 hour. Scoop out with a sieve, rinse under cold running water, and shake off. Pat dry using paper towels and chill for about 1 hour.

Place the tomatoes in a medium bowl and add boiling water to cover. Leave for about 5 minutes to cool. Scoop out one tomato and check to see the skin has breaks in it and can be easily peeled. If not, allow to cool a little more in the hot water. Drain.

Set the tomatoes on a cutting board and wipe out the bowl. Working over the bowl, cut out and discard the core, and peel. Set the tomato inside the bowl and continue with the others. In a medium saucepan, bring the dashi, sake, 2 teaspoons of the salt, and the usukuchi shoyu to a boil over high heat. Reduce to a simmer, add the peeled tomatoes, and cook over low heat for 20 minutes to soften. Allow to cool to room temperature, then refrigerate in the cooking liquid for about 2 hours to chill.

Divide the clear tomato broth and water lily buds among four shallow bowls. Place 1 chilled, simmered tomato in the middle, core side down. (Discard the tomato cooking liquid.) Serve cold as a first course.

トマトの透明スープ

CLEAR TOMATO BROTH

TOMATO NO TOUMEI SU-PU

Preparation time: 30 minutes,
plus 2 hours dripping out
Makes: 2 cups (16 fl oz/500 ml)

- 8 medium tomatoes (3½ lb/1.6 kg)
- ¼ teaspoon fine sea salt

This broth is both restorative and refreshing. Serve during a meal to stimulate the appetite.

-

Roughly chop the tomatoes and drop into a blender with the salt. Blend until smooth. Line a wire-mesh sieve with several thicknesses of paper towels or a coffee filter, set over a bowl, and allow the tomato juice to drip out naturally for 2 hours in the refrigerator.

Serve chilled in a small glass or ceramic cup, or heat briefly before serving.

CHILLED TOMATO IN CLEAR TOMATO BROTH

じゃが芋のポタージュ寺納豆
ソース

POTATO SOUP WITH TERA NATTO

JYAGAIMO NO POTA-JYU TERA NATTOU SO-SU

Preparation time: 15 minutes
Cooking time: 25 minutes
Serves: 4

• 2 medium potatoes
(5¼ oz/150 g each), scrubbed
• ½ teaspoon flaky sea salt
• Generous 1¾ cups (15 fl oz/450 ml)
Konbu Dashi (page 22)
• 2 tablespoons Tera Natto–Sesame
Paste (page 30)
• Generous ¾ cup (6¾ fl oz/200 ml)
soy milk
• 1 teaspoon Japanese egoma oil
(see page 345) or unroasted sesame oil

Salting the potato boiling water, but not the soup itself, introduces an ever-so-imperceptible feeling of salt in the background. And the salty, earthy *tera natto* sauce dabbed on top provides the piquancy needed to raise this creamy soup up to be both unusually well balanced and surprisingly soothing.
-
Place the unpeeled potatoes into a medium saucepan with the salt and add cold water to generously cover. Cover the pan, bring to a boil over high heat, and cook until a bamboo skewer can be easily inserted into the centers, 20–25 minutes. Drain and peel while still hot. Allow to cool to room temperature.

In a small bowl, stir 2 tablespoons of the dashi into the *tera natto*-sesame paste and set aside.

Cut the potato into chunks and drop into a blender with the remaining dashi, the soy milk, and the *egoma* oil. Blend until smooth. Scrape the soup into a medium saucepan and bring to an almost boil over medium-high heat.

Ladle into four small rounded soup bowls and dab artfully with small drops of the *tera natto* sauce. Serve immediately.

ブロッコリーのポタージュ

CREAMY BROCCOLI STEM SOUP

BUROKKORI- NO POTA-JYU

Preparation time: 20 minutes
Cooking time: 10 minutes
Serves: 4

• 4 small broccoli florets,
for garnish
• 2 thick broccoli stems
(9 oz/250 g), peeled and
coarsely chopped
• 1⅔ cups (13½ fl oz/400 ml)
whole milk
• 2 teaspoons (10 g)
unsalted butter
• ½ teaspoon flaky sea salt
• ¼ teaspoon freshly ground
black pepper

When you prepare broccoli dishes, such as Asparagus and Broccoli Namul (page 93), that only use florets, this soup is an inspired way to use up the broccoli stems. And doing so leaves you with a warm feeling of accomplishment for having used the whole vegetable with no waste. The stems contain essential minerals and vitamins, so are nourishing as well. Unroasted sesame oil and soy milk can be substituted for the butter and milk, for a dairy-free version of this light and lovely soup.
-
Bring a medium saucepan of water to a boil over high heat. Add the florets and boil until just softened but not mushy, 30 seconds to 1 minute. Scoop out and drain in the sink in a small wire-mesh sieve.

Add the broccoli stems to the boiling water and cook until completely tender, about 5 minutes. Drain.

In a blender, pulse the drained broccoli stems and milk until smooth. Scrape into a medium saucepan, add the butter, and bring to an almost boil over medium-high heat. Season with the salt and pepper.

Ladle into 4 small bowls and garnish each with a floret of broccoli. Serve hot.

CREAMY BROCCOLI STEM SOUP

かぶのみぞれ汁

GRATED TURNIP MISO SOUP

KABU NO MIZORE-JIRU

Preparation time: 20 minutes
Cooking time: 5 minutes
Serves: 4

- 2 medium turnips
(7 oz/200 g), peeled
- 3 cups (24 fl oz/700 ml)
Konbu Dashi (page 22)
- 5¼ oz (150 g) cotton tofu (momendofu,
see page 352) or Japanese-style
soft block tofu
- 3 tablespoons brown rice
miso or barley miso
- 1 teaspoon black or white sesame
seeds, warmed in a dry frying
pan until fragrant
- 1 teaspoon finely slivered yuzu zest

Grated daikon is the classic grated root vegetable in *mizore-jiru*, but here the turnip adds a roundness to the soup and does not dilute the miso since it lacks the water content of daikon.
-
Finely grate the turnips on a ceramic grater (*oroshiki*, see page 354) or metal-toothed grating plate (*oroshigane*, see page 354) and divide among four small lacquer soup bowls.

In a medium saucepan, heat the dashi over low heat. Cut the tofu into ½-inch (1 cm) cubes and slide into the dashi to heat up for 1–2 minutes. In a small bowl, add a spoonful of the dashi to the miso and stir until well emulsified, then scrape back into the saucepan and stir to blend.

Ladle the tofu and soup into the bowls with the turnip. Garnish with the sesame seeds and yuzu and serve hot.

じゃが芋と枝豆の冷製
すり流し

COLD POTATO AND EDAMAME SOUP

JYAGAIMO TO EDAMAME NO REISEI SURI-NAGASHI

Preparation time: 30 minutes,
plus 1–2 hours chilling time
Cooking time: 25 minutes
Serves: 4

- 1½ oz (40 g) raw peanuts
- 9 oz (250 g) edamame pods
- 2 teaspoons flaky sea salt
- 2 medium potatoes
(10½ oz/300 g), peeled and
cut into ½-inch (1 cm) cubes
- 3 teaspoons olive oil
- 1¾ oz (50 g) shimeji, separated
into small clumps
- 1 cup (8 fl oz/250 ml) soy milk
- 2 teaspoons usukuchi shoyu
(see page 344)
- 1 teaspoon finely chopped
Italian parsley

This soup is low in fat, yet still has a creamy richness that is comforting when we want something a bit more substantial than a broth-based soup.
-
In a small dry frying pan, toast the peanuts over low heat until slightly colored, 5–7 minutes.

Bring a medium saucepan three-quarters full of water to a boil over high heat. Stir in the edamame and 1 teaspoon of the salt and cook for 8 minutes. Skim out and, when cool enough to handle, pop the edamame out of their pods. Peel off the thin skins and discard along with the pods.

In a medium frying pan, heat 1 teaspoon olive oil over medium heat. Add the potatoes and shimeji and stir-fry for 3 minutes, then add a scant ½ cup (3½ fl oz/ 100 ml) water. Simmer briskly until the potato is tender, 3–5 minutes. Scrape into a blender, add the peanuts, remaining salt, scant ⅔ cup (5¼ fl oz/150 ml) of the soy milk, and scant ⅔ cup (5¼ fl oz/150 ml) water. Process until smooth and scrape into a 1-quart (32 fl oz/ 1-liter) measuring cup. Rinse the blender container.

To the blender container, add the edamame, remaining scant ½ cup (3½ fl oz/100 ml) soy milk, scant ½ cup (3½ fl oz/100 ml) water, *usukuchi shoyu*, and remaining 2 teaspoons olive oil. Blend until smooth and scrape into a 2-cup (16 fl oz/500 ml) measuring cup.

Refrigerate the potato and edamame mixtures for 1–2 hours to chill, then divide the potato soup among 4 small rounded soup bowls. Swirl even amounts of the edamame soup into each bowl and garnish with the parsley.

GRATED TURNIP MISO SOUP

枝豆のすり流し

CREAMY EDAMAME SOUP

EDAMAME NO SURINAGASHI

Preparation time: 15 minutes,
plus 2 hours chilling time
Cooking time: 10 minutes
Serves: 4

- 14 oz (400 g) edamame pods
- 1⅔ cups (13½ fl oz/400 ml)
Konbu Dashi (page 22)
- 2 teaspoons sake
- ½ teaspoon flaky sea salt
- 1 teaspoon lightly roasted
white sesame oil or unroasted
sesame oil

Soybeans are grown from early summer into the fall, so we have several waves of edamame reaching well into September or October depending on the weather. Fresh edamame are full of natural sweetness and in a soup benefit from just a light touch of salt. This kind of purposefully underseasoned dish epitomizes Japanese vegetarian food.

-

Bring a medium pot of water to a boil over high heat. Drop in the edamame and cook for 10 minutes until soft. Drain and, when cool enough to handle, pop out the green soybeans. Set aside 12 beans for garnish.

Slide the remaining soybeans into a blender with ½ cup (4 fl oz/ 125 ml) of the dashi. Process for several minutes on high speed until smooth and homogenous. Add the remaining dashi and the sake and process for another 1 or 2 minutes until completely emulsified. (Alternatively, go old-school and smash the beans in a Japanese grinding bowl with a wooden pestle until broken down to a paste. Slowly mash in the dashi and sake until creamy.) Pass through a fine-mesh sieve to remove any remaining solids. Refrigerate for 2 hours to chill.

Ladle out into four soup bowls. Garnish each bowl with 3 edamame and a drizzle of sesame oil. This soup is also good hot, in which case skip the chilling step and warm over medium-high heat before serving without the oil drizzle.

まつたけ椀

MATSUTAKE IN BROTH

MATSUTAKE WAN

Preparation time: 25 minutes
Cooking time: 20 minutes
Serves: 4

- 2 matsutake mushrooms
(3 oz/80 g)
- 1 oz (25 g) mibuna (see page 346)
or Italian puntarelle
- 2½ cups (20 fl oz/600 ml)
Happo Dashi (page 25)
- 2½ teaspoons usukuchi shoyu
(see page 344)
- ¼ teaspoon flaky sea salt
- Finely slivered yuzu zest,
for garnish

Matsutake are extremely dear and perhaps out of reach— though there are areas around the world where they grow. Substitute a similarly fragrant thick-stemmed mushroom.

-

Brush gently and shave a teeny portion of the *matsutake* stem end off to clean and remove the hard portion. Fill a medium bowl halfway with water and dip the mushrooms in and out, rubbing off any dirt with your fingers or a paper towel. Halve lengthwise, then crosswise, if long. Make a few shallow cuts in the caps to allow the dashi to penetrate.

Bring a medium pot of water to a boil. Drop the *mibuna* in and push down to submerge, then immediately scoop out with a wire-mesh sieve. Cool under cold running water or in a bowl of ice water. Squeeze down the length of the greens to express excess water and cut crosswise into 1½-inch (4 cm) pieces.

In a small saucepan, combine the dashi and *matsutake* and slowly heat over medium-low heat, without boiling, for about 5 minutes. When it becomes fragrant, stir in the *usukuchi shoyu* and salt. Continue cooking until the *matsutake* has cooked through, about 10 minutes longer.

Divide the *matsutake* among four lidded bowls (o-wan, see page 354), and drape the *mibuna* across the center. Ladle in the hot soup around the circumference, garnish with a pinch of yuzu zest, cover, and serve hot as a warming middle course.

MATSUTAKE IN BROTH

GRATED DAIKON SOUP

大根のみぞれ汁

DAIKON NO MIZORE-JIRU

Preparation time: 15 minutes
Cooking time: 15 minutes
Serves: 4

- 8-inch (20 cm) small daikon with tender leaves (12¼ oz/350 g)
- 2 small turnips with leaves (5¼ oz/150 g)
- 2 pieces (1½ oz/40 g each) dried brown rice mochi
- 3⅓ cups (26½ fl oz/800 ml) Konbu Dashi (page 22)
- 7 oz (100 g) shimeji, ends trimmed off
- 1 teaspoon flaky sea salt
- 2 tablespoons shoyu

Soups with grated daikon are called *mizore-jiru*. They are particularly warming in the cold months and the daikon aids digestion. This seemingly plain soup is multi-layered and incredibly tasty, so not to be overlooked.

-

Bring a medium saucepot two-thirds full of water to a boil. Blanch the daikon leaves for 2 minutes, scoop out and refresh under cold running water. Chop crosswise into ¼-inch (5 mm) pieces and squeeze out excess water. Blanch the turnip leaves in the same pot for 2 minutes. Scoop out, refresh under cold running water, chop crosswise into ¼-inch (5 mm) pieces, and squeeze out the water.

Peel the daikon and grate on a circular ceramic grater (*oroshiki*, see page 354) or sharp-toothed metal grating plate (*oroshigane*, see page 354). Drain in a fine mesh sieve set over a bowl to catch the drips.

Peel the turnips and halve through the top to the tail. Lay cut side down on a cutting board and slice into half-moons ¼ inch (5 mm) thick.

Position a rack 4 inches (10 cm) from the heat source and preheat the broiler (grill). (Or preheat a toaster oven/mini oven.) Broil (grill) the mochi until puffed up and lightly browned on the top, about 3 minutes. Flip and repeat for the other side. Cut in half and place one piece in each of four rounded soup bowls.

While the mochi is grilling, in a medium saucepan, heat the dashi over medium heat. Once steaming, but not quite simmering, slide in the shimeji. Add the turnip pieces and simmer gently until the turnip is just cooked but not falling apart, about 2 minutes. Stir in the grated daikon, salt, and shoyu. Once the soup comes back to a simmer, scrape in the chopped daikon and turnip leaves, and remove from the heat.

Ladle over the mochi in the soup bowls and serve immediately.

GRATED DAIKON SOUP

CLEAR SOUP WITH TOFU, CARROT, AND DAIKON

無明碗

MUMYOU WAN

Preparation time: 35 minutes, plus 15 minutes tofu weighting time
Cooking time: 10 minutes
Serves: 4

• 5¼ oz (150 g) cotton tofu (momendofu, see page 352) or Japanese-style soft block tofu
• ¾ inch (2 cm) medium carrot, cut crosswise into ¼-inch (5 mm) rounds
• 4 cups (32 fl oz/1 liter) Konbu Dashi (page 22)
• 2 teaspoons shoyu
• 3 tablespoons sake
• 2 teaspoons hon mirin
• 4 thin round slices of medium daikon
• ¾ teaspoon flaky sea salt
• 2 teaspoons lightly roasted gold sesame oil

The carrot "shines" through the translucent daikon, hence the name 無明碗, which refers to Avidya, the Buddhist concept of ignorance or misconception. The Japanese characters for Avidya 無明 mean an absence of clarity, whereas 碗 is *wan*, the vessel in which the dish is served. Here, the carrot is hidden, yet not, thus mirroring this abstract notion.
-
Place the tofu on a small plate and set another plate on top but be careful not to break or crush the tofu. Leave for 15 minutes to lightly press out a bit of the water. Quarter and set aside.

Slide the carrot rounds into a small saucepan with a generous ¾ cup (6¾ fl oz/200 ml) dashi. Bring to a boil over medium-high heat. Add the shoyu, 1 tablespoon of the sake, and the mirin and simmer for 5 minutes more.

Bring a small saucepan of water to a boil over high heat and slip in the daikon. Boil for 1 minute, drain, and refresh under cold running water until cool to the touch. Drain.

In a medium saucepan, bring the remaining 3⅓ cups (26½ fl oz/800 ml) dashi, 2 tablespoons sake, and the salt to an almost simmer over medium-low heat.

In a small frying pan, heat the sesame oil over low heat. Add the tofu to the pan and sear slowly to color, 20–30 seconds per side.

Place a piece of tofu in the middle of each of four medium lacquer bowls with a lid (*o-wan*, see page 354). Place a drained carrot round on each piece of tofu, lay a piece of daikon on top. Ladle in the soup, cover, and serve hot.

GINGER-FLAVORED ROOT VEGETABLE PEEL SOUP

雲片汁

UNPEN-JIRU

Preparation time: 25 minutes
Cooking time: 10 minutes
Serves: 4

• 2 tablespoons dark roasted sesame oil
• 2 handfuls (1¾ oz /50 g) root vegetable peels (daikon, carrot), chopped
• ¼ teaspoon flaky sea salt
• 3¼ cups (26 fl oz/750 ml) Konbu Dashi (page 22)
• 2 teaspoons shoyu
• 2 squares (1½ inches/4 cm) softened konbu, finely diced
• 2 tablespoons hon kuzu (see page 352) mixed with 6 tablespoons water
• 4 teaspoons fresh ginger juice

This extremely flavorful, gingery soup gets a lovely silkiness from the *kuzu* and a richness from the sesame oil—on the surface modest, yet actually quite special. Make this when you have a mound of vegetable peels that you would like to repurpose.
-
In a medium saucepot, heat the sesame oil over medium-high heat. Scrape in the vegetable peels and stir-fry for about 1 minute, until fragrant. Add ⅛ teaspoon of the salt and stir-fry for 1 more minute over low heat. Stir in the dashi, shoyu, konbu,

and remaining ⅛ teaspoon salt. Swirl the *kuzu* slurry into the pot and continue stirring continuously over medium heat until slightly thickened, 2–3 minutes. Stir in the ginger juice.

Ladle into small lacquer bowls. Serve as a hearty soup to accompany a light meal: breakfast, lunch, or dinner.

CLEAR SOUP WITH TOFU, CARROT, AND DAIKON

一石三鳥精進鍋 "THREE BIRDS, ONE STONE" NABE

ISSEKI SANCHOU SHOUJIN NABE

Preparation time: 45 minutes
Cooking time: 10 minutes
Serves: 4, generously

- 1 small bunch (7 oz/200 g) spinach, preferably with roots intact
- 4 large leaves (9 oz/250 g) napa cabbage (Chinese leaf)
- 2¼ inches (6 cm) medium carrot (2⅔ oz/75 g), scrubbed
- 1 small burdock root (2⅔ oz/75 g), scrubbed
- 1 tablespoon rice vinegar
- 7 oz (200 g) shirataki (see page 353)
- Boiling water
- 3½ oz (100 g) white miso
- 3½ oz (100 g) brown rice miso or barley miso
- 2½ cups (20 fl oz/600 ml) Konbu Dashi (page 22)
- Generous ¾ cup (6¾ fl oz/200 ml) Soybean Dashi (page 23)
- 1⅔ cups (13½ fl oz/400 ml) Vegetable Peel Dashi (page 23)
- 10½ oz (300 g) cotton tofu (momendofu, see page 352) or Japanese-style soft block tofu, cut into 8 cubes
- 4 Tofu Croquettes (page 131)
- 1⅔ cups (13½ fl oz/400 ml) soy milk

The name of this unforgettably luscious winter *nabe* references the plethora of ingredients in this all-in-one meal: tofu in two forms, greens, root vegetables, and miso as well as the *konnyaku* noodles (*shirataki*) and soy milk for richness. The brightness of the konbu dashi marries well with the more earthy soybean and vegetable peel dashis, lending a lightness to the dish. Serve with small bowls of Japanese rice on the side if you like. Be aware: The salt content in the miso will cause the soy milk to separate a little so the soy milk is added just before serving.

-

Cut the spinach and napa cabbage (Chinese leaf) crosswise into 1¼-inch (3 cm) pieces. Cut the carrot and burdock diagonally into ¼-inch (5 mm) slices. Soak the burdock in cold water to cover with the vinegar until ready to use to avoid discoloration. Drain before adding to the *nabe*.

Drain the *shirataki* in a wire-mesh sieve and pour boiling water over for 10 seconds. Shake off and halve crosswise.

In a small bowl, mash the two misos together until evenly incorporated.

Add the three types of dashi to the *nabe* and place the cabbage, carrot, drained burdock, tofu cubes, and *shirataki* each in its own distinct area in the *nabe*. Bring to a simmer over medium heat and cook until the vegetables have softened, 5–7 minutes.

Stir a small amount of the hot dashi into the miso mixture and stir to loosen. Scrape the mixture into the *nabe*, mound the spinach in one corner and nestle the croquettes in another corner. Cover the *nabe* and just bring back to a simmer over medium heat. Reduce the heat to low, gently stir in the soy milk, and heat through briefly, without simmering.

Ladle into individual bowls and serve piping hot.

"THREE BIRDS, ONE STONE" NABE

豆腐の豆乳鍋

TOFU AND SOY MILK NABE

TOUFU NO TOUNYUU NABE

Preparation time: 20 minutes
Cooking time: 10 minutes
Serves: 4

• 10½ oz (300 g) cotton tofu
(momendofu, see page 352)
or Japanese-style soft block tofu
• ¼ head (7 oz/200 g) napa cabbage
(Chinese leaf)
• ½ bunch (4 oz /115 g) mizuna
• 1 medium carrot (5¼ oz/150 g),
peeled or scrubbed
• ½ bunch (4 oz/115 g) spinach
• 3½ oz (100 g) shimeji, separated
• 3⅓ cups (26½ fl oz/800 ml)
Konbu Dashi (page 22)
• Generous ¾ cup (6¾ fl oz/200 ml)
soy milk
• 3 tablespoons Japanese
white sesame paste
• 1 tablespoon usukuchi shoyu
(see page 344)
• 1 tablespoon hon mirin
• 1 teaspoon flaky sea salt

Using soy milk as the base for this incredibly well-balanced and vegetable-packed one-pot dish imparts a richness that is enhanced by the sesame paste. Be aware, soy milk has a tendency to separate a bit. But do not worry, the result will still be warming and satisfying. An added benefit is that this dish is quick to pull together for an instant supper.
-
Cut the tofu into 8 cubes and set aside on a small plate. Slice the napa cabbage (Chinese leaf) and mizuna crosswise into 1¼-inch (3 cm) pieces and place each in a separate mound on a dinner plate.

Bring a small pot of water to a boil. Cut the carrot crosswise into ¾-inch (2 cm) lengths, then slice thinly lengthwise (tanzaku-giri, see page 17). Add the carrot to the boiling water and blanch for 30 seconds in boiling water. Scoop out the carrot with a wire-mesh sieve and leave in the sink to drain. Shake off and mound on a dinner plate. Dip the spinach in and out of the boiling water, refresh under cold running water,

and squeeze into a ball. Cut the squeezed ball crosswise into 1¼-inch (3 cm) pieces. Place on the dinner plate along with the carrot and add the shimeji, each in a separate mound.

Cook on the stove or at the table: In an earthenware pot (donabe, see page 353), heat the konbu dashi and soy milk over low heat. In a small bowl, combine the sesame paste, usukuchi shoyu, mirin, and salt and stir together to make a smooth paste. Slowly whisk a generous ¾ cup (6¾ fl oz/ 200 ml) of the dashi into the sesame paste to loosen and emulsify. Scrape the contents of the bowl into the donabe. Bring to a simmer over medium heat, then add ingredients in this order: tofu, shimeji, carrot, napa cabbage, mizuna, and spinach, each in its own spot in the donabe. Simmer gently for about 5 minutes to cook the cabbage, mizuna, and shimeji and to heat the tofu through to the center.

Ladle out into deep bowls (donburi, see page 354) and eat as a light but protein-rich supper.

白みそ雑煮

WHITE MISO OZONI

SHIRO MISO ZOUNI

Preparation time: 45 minutes
Cooking time: 15 minutes
Serves: 4

- 2½ inches (6 cm) thin daikon, peeled and quartered crosswise into rounds
- 2½ inches (6 cm) medium carrot, peeled and quartered crosswise into rounds
- ½ small bunch (4 oz/115 g) komatsuna (see page 346)
- 5 cups (40 fl oz/1.2 liters) Konbu Dashi (page 22)
- 4 dried round mochi or dried brown mochi squares
- 3 tablespoons white miso
- 1 teaspoon brown rice miso or barley miso
- 1 teaspoon finely julienned yuzu or Meyer lemon zest

Served on New Year's Day, *ozoni* has many variations throughout Japan, but all contain mochi. The mochi fills your stomach and the simple, yet warming soup launches you on a healthy path for the new year. *Ozoni* can be seasoned with shoyu or any kind of miso, though here, in the Kansai (Western Japan) tradition, it is seasoned with white miso with a dab of darker miso for nuance. Although most people do not make mochi anymore in Japan, fresh mochi is widely available during the New Year season. But dried mochi is what is available outside Japan, so for practicality it is used in this recipe. And, while typically made on New Year's Day, there is no rule that it cannot be consumed during other times of the year. This version of *ozoni* is particularly light and lovely.
-
Cut the daikon and carrot into flower shapes (*hanagiri*, see page 17) with a vegetable cutter or paring knife. Slide into a medium saucepan, add cold water to cover, and bring to a boil over high heat. Reduce to a brisk simmer and cook until soft, about 3 minutes. Drain in a wire-mesh sieve.

Bring a medium pot of water to a boil over high heat. Hold the *komatsuna* stems in the boiling water to cook for 30 seconds.

Drop the *komatsuna* into the water, push down to submerge, and cook for 30 seconds more. Scoop out with a wire-mesh sieve, refresh under cold running water, and leave to drain in the kitchen sink. Squeeze to express excess liquid and cut crosswise into 2-inch (5 cm) pieces. Separate into 4 even piles.

In a medium saucepan, bring 2 cups (16 fl oz/500 ml) of the dashi to a simmer over medium-high heat and add the mochi. Cook for 10 minutes to soften.

In another medium saucepan, bring the remaining 3 cups (24 fl oz/700 ml) dashi to a simmer over medium-high heat. In a small bowl, combine the white miso and brown rice miso. Ladle some of the hot dashi into the miso mixture and whisk to emulsify. Scrape the mixture into the pan of dashi.

Scoop each mochi piece out with a slotted spoon and place in a deep lacquer soup bowl with a lid (*o-wan*, see page 354). Add one piece each daikon and carrot and one pile of *komatsuna*. Ladle the steaming hot miso dashi around the circumference of the mochi (so as not to disturb the daikon, carrot, and *komatsuna*). Garnish with yuzu zest, place the lids on the bowls, and serve.

BUILDING A BOWL OF MISO SOUP

~~~~~~

Four basic components make up the perfect bowl of miso soup: dashi, 1–3 seasonal ingredients, miso, and a sprinkled garnish (*yakumi*).

The ingredients are cut into one-bite pieces, easily eaten with chopsticks.

Finely sliced root vegetables and seasonal greens are simmered briefly in the dashi until softened. And the miso is stirred in at the end, off heat, so as not to destroy its lovely aroma and natural probiotic properties.

Garnishes (*yakumi*) such as slivered yuzu, ginger, and *myoga* are sprinkled in the bowl before serving.

~~~~~~

DASHI

• konbu
• dried shiitake + konbu
• vegetable peel + konbu

MISO

The Japan Federation of Miso Manufacturers Cooperatives recognizes three classifications of miso, according to the grain or pulse that has been inoculated with koji spores before adding to the steamed soybeans that form the main base for Japanese miso:

• *kome* (rice)
• *mugi* (barley)
• *mame* (soybean)

GARNISHES (*YAKUMI*)

• slivered yuzu, ginger, *myoga*, or green shiso
• finely chopped scallions (spring onions) or chives
• torn cress, *mitsuba*, or *sansho* leaves
• 7-spice powder (*shichimi togarashi*)
• red pepper powder (*ichimi togarashi*)
• black pepper
• green *sansho* powder
• roasted sesame seeds

SEASONAL INGREDIENTS

SPRING

• asparagus, young cabbage + *sansho* leaves
• new potato, snow pea + finely chopped scallion (spring onion) whites
• cabbage, onion + *shichimi togarashi*
• poached egg, sweet potato, spinach + *ichimi togarashi*
• tofu, egg + *shichimi togarashi*
• lettuce, enoki + black pepper
• celery, green bean + white sesame seeds
• tofu + cress

SUMMER

• Japanese eggplant (aubergine) + slivered *myoga*
• broiled Japanese eggplant + green shiso chiffonade
• okra, tomato + salt
• tomato, corn + *ichimi togarashi*
• tomato, zucchini (courgette) + white sesame seeds, chopped scallions (spring onions)
• kabocha, green bean + green shiso, black pepper
• kabocha, kimchi + chopped scallion (spring onion) greens and whites
• kabocha, wakame + finely sliced ginger
• potato balls + slivered *myoga*
• sweet potato, *koyadofu*, green bean + finely chopped scallion (spring onion) whites

FALL

• seasonal mushroom + pieces of yuzu peel
• shimeji, *komatsuna* + slivered yuzu, *shichimi togarashi*
• lotus balls, *konnyaku* + chopped *mitsuba*, *ichimi togarashi*
• mountain yam, chrysanthemum petals + black sesame seeds
• potato, cauliflower, spinach + unsalted butter

WINTER

• tofu, *komatsuna* + slivered yuzu
• cabbage, *atsuage* + slivered ginger, chopped chives
• kabocha + chives, slivered yuzu, *shichimi togarashi*
• shimeji, *komatsuna* + white sesame seeds
• tofu, lettuce + white sesame seeds
• daikon, hijiki, carrot + chopped *mitsuba*
• napa cabbage (Chinese leaf) kimchi, enoki mushrooms + chopped scallion (spring onion) greens and whites

~~~~~~

雪鍋

SNOW NABE

YUKI NABE

Preparation time: 15 minutes,
plus 30 minutes soaking time
Cooking time: 15 minutes
Serves: 4, generously

- 1½ inches (4 cm) konbu
- 6-inch (15 cm) medium daikon,
peeled and finely grated
- 1 lb (500 g) cotton tofu
(momendofu, see page 352)
or Japanese-style soft block tofu,
cut into ¾-inch (2 cm) cubes
- 3 tablespoons shoyu
- Ponzu, for serving
- Red pepper powder (ichimi togarashi,
see page 350), optional

Essentially a variation on *yudofu*
(a classic vegetarian *nabe* of
simmered tofu), here the *nabe* is
prepared with a good amount of
finely grated daikon, hence the
name "snow *nabe*." Spare, but
soothing on the tummy—make it
as a light, warm supper on a brisk
evening. And if you are looking for
a little spice, sprinkle in a little
ichimi togarashi when serving.

-

Place the konbu in the bottom of
a medium *nabe* and add 6 cups
(48 fl oz/1.4 liters) cold water.
Soak the konbu for 30 minutes.

Scrape in the grated daikon and
bring to a simmer over medium
heat. Reduce the heat to low
and cook until the daikon is
translucent, about 5 minutes.
Carefully spoon the tofu into
the *nabe* and swirl in the shoyu.
Continue cooking for an additional
5 minutes over low heat.

Ladle into individual bowls.
Drizzle with a little ponzu,
sprinkle with *ichimi togarashi* (if
using), and serve hot with a few
vegetable side dishes and some
rice, if you like.

~~~~~~

基本の味噌汁

BASIC MISO SOUP

KIHON NO MISO SHIRU

Preparation time: 15 minutes
Cooking time: 5 minutes
Serves: 4

- 1 small handful fresh wakame
(1¼ oz/35 g) or 1 tablespoon dried
wakame
- 5¼ oz (150 g) cotton tofu
(momendofu, see page 352) or
Japanese-style soft block tofu
- 3 cups (24 fl oz/700 ml)
Konbu Dashi (page 22)
- 3 tablespoons (1½ oz/40 g) miso
- 1 teaspoon white sesame seeds,
warmed in a dry frying pan
until fragrant

Less is more when it comes to
miso soup, and starting with
a clear, beautiful dashi is essential.
Keep it simple. And that goes for
the garnishes as well. Choose one
or two. Restraint is the key here.
While the suggested amount
of miso to dashi can be used
as a guideline for all your miso
soups, feel free to add more or
dial it back to taste. For a darker
flavor, use soybean miso or mix
soybean miso with rice miso or
barley miso to vary the nuances.
Serve with a bowl of rice and
a side dish of pickles, for a classic
Buddhist meal (*ichiju sansai*).

-

Bring a medium saucepan three-
quarters full of water to a boil
over high heat. Dip the wakame
in and out of the boiling water to
shock from black to green. Shake
off and cut into bite-size pieces.
(If using dried wakame, soak in
a medium bowl with plenty of
cold water to cover for 10 minutes
before draining.)

Divide the wakame among four
small bowls. Cut the tofu into
½-inch (1 cm) cubes and set aside.

In a medium saucepan, bring the
dashi to a boil over medium-high
heat. Immediately add the tofu
and bring back to a boil. Remove
from the heat. Spoon the miso
into a ladle and scoop a little of
the broth into the ladle. Stir the
miso into the broth in the ladle
until completely emulsified and
submerge all the way into the
broth, scraping out any lingering
miso coating the ladle. Stir once
with a spoon, carefully avoiding
breaking the delicate tofu, and
remove from the heat.

Ladle evenly into the bowls and
serve garnished with sesame seeds.

赤出汁の味噌汁　RED MISO SOUP

AKA DASHI NO MISO SHIRU

Preparation time: 15 minutes
Cooking time: 10 minutes
Serves: 4

(V) (DF) (GF) (NF) (<30)

• 5¼ oz (150 g) nameko (see page 348)
• Boiling water
• 5¼ oz (150 g) cotton tofu
(momendofu, see page 352) or
Japanese-style soft block tofu
• 2½ cups (20 fl oz/600 ml)
Konbu Dashi (page 22)
• 2 tablespoons sake
• 2 tablespoons soybean miso
• 2 tablespoons white miso
• 4 thin stalks mitsuba (see page 346),
stems cut crosswise into ½-inch (1 cm)
pieces and leaves torn in thirds

Aka dashi refers to dashi that has been flavored with aged, very dark, miso made from soybean koji, such as Hatcho miso. It is consumed most often in mountain areas and during the winter, when we are looking for a deep flavor to sustain us on cold days. Here, the sake gives this soup a brightness with a slight bit of acid to cut the rich miso. The *mitsuba* adds a piquant spark and the vibrant green leaves contrast well against the brown palette of the miso and mushrooms. Substitute chopped scallions (spring onions) if you cannot find *mitsuba*.

–

Trim any discoloration off the ends of the *nameko*, break them apart, and place in a wire-mesh sieve. Pour boiling water over for 10 seconds to remove some of their naturally sticky coating. Shake off and set aside.

Drain the tofu and cut into ½-inch (12 mm) cubes.

In a medium saucepan, bring the konbu dashi and sake to a simmer and drop in the *nameko*. Reduce the heat to low and spoon the two types of miso into a ladle. Dip the ladle into the pan to catch up a little of the broth and stir the broth into the miso with a pair of cooking chopsticks (*saibashi*, see page 354) until well emulsified. Dunk back into the pan and stir the miso into the broth. Gently stir in the tofu.

Divide among four miso soup bowls. Garnish with the *mitsuba* and serve immediately.

RED MISO SOUP

飯物

The character for *han* (飯) means "food" or "meal," but literally refers to cooked rice since rice is the meal. Most commonly seen written with the honorific *go* as in *gohan*, the character 飯 can also be read as *meshi*. *Gohan* and *meshi* are Japanese words that refer interchangeably to both cooked rice and the meal itself. Clearly, rice is the center of the family meal and the side dishes (*okazu*) exist to complement the rice. Keep in mind, however, that *okayu*, fried rice, and sushi are served with a minimal amount of side dishes as they are almost complete meals in themselves. Using an iron or earthenware pot will yield more compelling results than the oversteaming that can happen with a rice cooker.

Although rice can be seasoned when prepared into *okayu*, fried rice, or sushi dishes, rice is most often served without salt or shoyu because the side dishes are seasoned—some salty, some rich from sesame or walnuts, some crisp-fried, and some intensely flavored from shoyu- or miso-grilling. In more formal or restaurant meals, rice is typically served last.

And while noodles might take the place of rice, they would rarely co-mingle on the same menu. There are only a few noodle recipes in this book by design, because the vegetable dishes were so many and so wonderful, and the rice dishes included here were particularly complementary. Most vegetarian broth soups or *nabe* can be used as a base for udon, but ultimately no deep dive into hand-cut udon can be complete without including konbu and *katsuobushi* (smoked, fermented, sun-dried skipjack tuna) dashi, therefore not appropriate for a vegetarian cookbook. As for soba and ramen, since we live in Japan, those noodles are only eaten at soba or ramen shops.

A word about rice quality: I have collaborated with many restaurants around the world during this last decade-plus that I have been writing cookbooks. At the outset, I hand-carried from Japan multiple kilos of organic rice grown by my husband, Tadaaki, but it all became too much. I still hand-carry artisanal ingredients, but more and more, these ingredients are available abroad, so the suitcase weight has lessened. Sourcing Japanese rice, however, remains an issue. Just because a rice is packaged in Japan, does not mean it was grown in Japan. Outside of Japan, I have come across American and Chinese rice in Japanese packaging.

I have also encountered rice that is noticeably (and mysteriously) heavier than it should be, so I recommend following a 1:1 measuring system of rice to water using metric volume rather than by weight, which is why all the rice recipes include milliliters in addition to grams.

飯物

HANMONO

RICE

うどの桜飯

CHERRY BLOSSOM RICE WITH UDO

UDO NO SAKURA MESHI

Preparation time: 20 minutes, plus
30 minutes draining and soaking time
Cooking time: 15 minutes,
plus 5 minutes resting time
Serves: 4

• 1 small stalk udo (see page 346)
or celery (1 oz/25 g)
• 2 tablespoons loosely packed
Salt-Pickled Cherry Blossoms
(page 300), soaked in cold water
for 20 minutes
• Generous ⅔ cup
(200 ml/6¼ oz/175 g) rice
• Boiling water
• 1½ tablespoons Zakkoku (page 28)
• 1 teaspoon sour plum "vinegar"
(umesu, see page 345)

Cherry blossoms are as quietly
stunning as they are short-lived.
They begin to appear on the
trees in the early spring—but
timing is completely dependent
on weather, so nearly impossible
to predict exactly. *Udo* has a
lovely bitterness that cannot be
duplicated, but celery can be
substituted in a pinch. Also, if you
did not pickle your own blossoms
in the spring, good-quality ones
are available online.
-
Peel off a thick layer of the outer
skin of the *udo* and discard or
make Udo Peel Kinpira (page 30).
Cut the *udo* into ¼-inch (5 mm)
dice. Immediately place in a bowl
and fill with cold water. (If using
celery, de-string before dicing,
but no need to soak.) Drain the
cherry blossoms.

Wash and drain the rice according
to the directions for Japanese
Rice (page 27). Slide into a small
pot and add a generous ¾ cup
(6¾ fl oz/200 ml) cold water.
Soak for 20 minutes. Meanwhile,
pour boiling water over the
zakkoku in a small bowl and soak
for 20 minutes.

Drain the *zakkoku* and add to
the soaking rice. Cover, bring
to a boil over high heat (about
90 seconds), reduce the heat
to low, and cook for 12 minutes.

Remove from the heat and allow
to sit, covered, for 5 minutes. Turn
out into a wooden rice container
(*ohitsu*, see page 353) or wooden
bowl and fold in the *udo*, cherry
blossoms, and *umesu*. Mound into
small rice bowls and serve.

新生姜ご飯

YOUNG GINGER RICE

SHIN SHOUGA GOHAN

Preparation time: 15 minutes, plus
30 minutes draining and soaking time
Cooking time: 20 minutes,
plus 5 minutes resting time
Serves: 4

• 2 cups (16 fl oz/500 ml)
Konbu Dashi (page 22)
• 2 tablespoons sake
• 1 teaspoon fine sea salt
• 1 teaspoon usukuchi shoyu
(see page 344)
• 2¼ cups (540 ml/1 lb/450 g)
Japanese short-grain rice
• ¾ oz (50 g) young ginger, scrubbed
• 2 green shiso leaves, cut into
chiffonade

Young ginger is used to garnish
and flavor a wide range of dishes
from its first appearance in
the early summer. Cooking rice
with young ginger will soften
its hotness and lend a gentle
perfume to the rice. Be sure to
select a piece of ginger that is
both white and pink, since the
color contrast will add beauty to
the dish. A bonus: The kitchen
fills with a warm, enticing aroma
while the rice is cooking.
-
In a small saucepan, warm the
konbu dashi, sake, salt, and
usukuchi shoyu together over
medium heat for 1–2 minutes to
dissolve the salt and soften the
alcohol. Cool to room temperature
in a small bowl.

Wash and drain the rice according
to the directions for Japanese Rice
(page 27). Slide the rice into a small
cast-iron pot (*tetsu gama*, see page
354) or earthenware pot (*donabe*,
see page 353), add the cooled
dashi, and soak for 20 minutes.

Julienne the (unpeeled) ginger
and sprinkle over the rice. Cover
and bring the pot to a boil over
high heat. This will take about
5 minutes. Once you see bubbles
coming out the top, reduce the
heat to the lowest setting and
cook for 12 minutes. Allow to rest
for 5 minutes before aerating
with a rice paddle or cooking
chopsticks.

Mound into rice bowls and serve
hot, strewn with the shiso. It's
also good formed into rice balls.

CHERRY BLOSSOM RICE WITH UDO

たけのこご飯   # BAMBOO SHOOT RICE

TAKENOKO GOHAN

Preparation time: 25 minutes, plus
30 minutes draining and soaking time
Cooking time: 15 minutes,
plus 5 minutes resting time
Serves: 4

- 2¼ cups (540 ml/1 lb/450 g)
Japanese short-grain rice
- 5¼ oz (150 g) Boiled Bamboo
Shoot (page 34)
- 1 deep-fried tofu pouch (usuage,
see page 352)
- Boiling water
- 2½ cups (20 fl oz/600 ml)
Konbu Dashi (page 22)
- 1½ tablespoons usukuchi shoyu
(see page 344)
- ¼ teaspoon fine sea salt
- 1 tablespoon finely torn sansho
leaves, for garnish

Takenoko gohan is one of the
favorite ways of eating bamboo
in Japan. The rice absorbs the
subtle flavor of the seasonings,
and the bamboo shoot adds
a soft, resilient texture to the
cooked rice. *Takenoko gohan*
can also be shaped into plump
triangle-shaped rice balls
(*onigiri*), wrapped in nori, and
eaten. This version of bamboo
rice is elegantly understated
and good served as a side dish
to accompany other spring
vegetables.
-
Wash and drain the rice according
to the directions for Japanese
Rice (page 27).

Cut the bottom portion of the
bamboo into ½-inch (1 cm) cubes.
Quarter the tops lengthwise and
then crosswise into ¼-inch
(5 mm) pieces.

Quarter the *usuage* lengthwise,
stack, and cut crosswise into
½-inch (1 cm) cubes. Place in
a wire-mesh sieve and pour boiling
water over for 10 seconds to
remove oil. Shake off and pat
dry in a clean tea towel.

Slide the drained rice, bamboo,
and *usuage* into a heavy medium
pot and stir in the konbu dashi,
usukuchi shoyu, and salt. Cover
and let sit for 20 minutes to
absorb flavor.

Bring to a boil over high heat.
This will take about 5 minutes—
you should see some bubbling
around the lid of the pan. Reduce
the heat to low and cook for
15 minutes. Do not uncover at
any time during the cooking and
resting period. Remove from
the heat and let sit 5 minutes
before fluffing and serving in
small rice bowls, garnished with
the *sansho* leaves.

BAMBOO SHOOT RICE

菜の花ちらし

FLOWERING GREENS RICE

NANOHANA CHIRASHI

Preparation time: 30 minutes,
plus 1 hour draining, soaking,
and resting time
Cooking time: 20 minutes
Serves: 4, generously

• 2¼ cups (540 ml/1 lb/450 g)
Japanese short-grain rice
• 1 cup (8 fl oz/250 ml)
Konbu Dashi (page 22)
• 1 cup (8 fl oz/250 ml)
Shiitake Dashi (page 22)
• 2 tablespoons sake
• 4 tablespoons red vinegar
(akasu, see page 345)
• 3 tablespoons light brown
cane sugar (kibizato, see page 345)
• 3½ teaspoons fine sea salt
• 1 bunch flowering greens
or broccoli rabe (rapini)
with 2-inch (5 cm) of the thick
bottoms cut off (5¼ oz/150 g)
• 1 deep-fried tofu pouch
(usuage, see page 352)
• 4 reconstituted dried
shiitake (from making the
Shiitake Dashi, above)
• 1 small carrot (2½ oz/75 g)
• 1 teaspoon dark roasted sesame oil
• 1 teaspoon usukuchi shoyu
(see page 344)
• 2 green shiso leaves, finely chopped
• 1 teaspoon white
sesame seeds, warmed in a dry
frying pan until fragrant

Eating rice strewn with flavored ingredients on top became popular in the Muromachi period (1336–1573). And this particular style, with the quintessential spring flowering greens (nanohana, see page 347), has been enjoyed during the Peach Festival, also known as the Doll Festival, on March 3 since the Edo period (1603–1868). Although chirashi zushi (scattered sushi) is often seen with raw fish on top of sushi rice, this flowering greens version is very special and might be the best chirashi zushi I have ever tasted.
-
Wash and drain the rice according to the directions for Japanese Rice (page 27). Slide the rice into a heavy medium pot, add the konbu dashi, shiitake dashi, and sake and let soak for 20 minutes. Then cook according to the directions for Japanese Rice.

In a small bowl, combine the vinegar, sugar, and 1 teaspoon of the salt. As you are preparing the other ingredients, give the vinegar solution a stir when you think of it to encourage the sugar and salt to dissolve.

Bring a medium pot filled three-quarters with water and 2 teaspoons of the salt to a boil over high heat. Hold the stem ends of the flowering greens into the boiling water for 10 seconds, then drop into the water and cook for another 50 seconds. Scoop out with a wire-mesh sieve and refresh under cold running water to cool. Shake off and roll in a clean tea towel to blot off as much moisture as possible.

Align on a cutting board, matching up the stem ends. Cut off the stem portions and finely chop. Halve the budding portion crosswise and reserve separately.

Halve the usuage lengthwise and cut crosswise into fine strips. Finely slice the shiitake. Cut the carrot into thin rectangular pieces 1½ inches (4 cm) long (tanzaku-giri, see page 17).

Warm a medium frying pan over medium-low heat and add the oil. Drop in the usuage, shiitake, and carrot and stir once with a flat wooden spoon to distribute the oil. Add the usukuchi shoyu and remaining ½ teaspoon salt and stir-fry gently for about 3 minutes to soften the carrot and flavor the other ingredients. Remove from the heat and allow to cool in the pan.

Once the rice is cooked, immediately turn out and spread across a flat wooden tub (handai, see page 353) or large wooden cutting board. Give the vinegar solution one last stir and sprinkle evenly over the rice. Use one hand to fan the rice and the other to cut the rice and turn it over in portions so the grains can absorb the vinegar. There should be no visible wetness. Cover with a clean, damp tea towel and allow to rest for 30 minutes to develop flavor.

Fold the shiitake, usuage, carrot, and any pan juices into the rice along with the chopped flowering greens stems. Spread evenly in the handai or an ohitsu (see page 353) and top attractively with the flowering green tops. Sprinkle with the shiso and sesame seeds and serve as a light lunch dish.

FLOWERING GREENS RICE

菜飯

DAIKON LEAF RICE

NA-MESHI

Preparation time: 10 minutes, plus
30 minutes draining and soaking time
Cooking time: 15 minutes,
plus 5 minutes resting time
Serves: 4

• 1½ cups (360 ml/10½ oz/300 g)
Japanese short-grain rice
• 1 tablespoon sake
• 1 teaspoon fine sea salt
• 4 tender stalks daikon leaves
(3½ oz/100 g)
• 1 teaspoon dark roasted
gold sesame oil
• 1 tablespoon black sesame seeds

Bunches of tender daikon leaves show up on the farm stand tables beginning in the late spring or early summer when the farmers are thinning their daikon and are often sold with tiny little daikon roots attached. Here the delicate leaves are used to add liveliness to a simple bowl of rice. If you do not have tender daikon leaves, substitute turnip leaves or even mustard; this is one dish that should not be overlooked for lack of a main ingredient.

-

Wash and drain the rice according to the directions for Japanese Rice (page 27). Slide into a heavy medium pot and add scant 1½ cups (11½ fl oz/ 345 ml) water, the sake, and the salt. Cook, rest, and fluff according to the directions for Japanese Rice.

While the rice is cooking, bring a small saucepan of water to a boil over high heat. Add the daikon leaves and cook for 2 minutes. Scoop out with a wire-mesh sieve and refresh under cold running water to cool. Cut crosswise into ¼-inch (5 mm) pieces. Squeeze by small handfuls to express excess water.

In a medium frying pan, warm the sesame oil over medium-low heat. Drop in the chopped daikon leaves and stir-fry for 2 minutes to dry out a little and deepen the flavor. Fold into the fluffed rice, mound into small rice bowls, and sprinkle with the black sesame seeds.

DAIKON LEAF RICE

SWEET POTATO RICE

SATSUMA-IMO GOHAN

Preparation time: 30 minutes,
plus 1 hour soaking time
Cooking time: 15 minutes,
plus 5 minutes resting time
Serves: 4, generously

(V) (DF) (GF) (NF) (<5)

• 1⅔ cups (5¼ oz/150 g) cubed
(½-inch/1 cm) unpeeled sweet potato
• 2¼ cups (540 ml/1 lb/450 g)
Japanese short-grain rice
• ½ teaspoon flaky sea salt
• 1 tablespoon black sesame seeds

The most commonly available
Japanese sweet potatoes are
red skinned with yellow flesh that
turns fluffy when baked. They are
often served or cooked with black
sesame seeds because it makes
such a pretty palette.
–
Soak the sweet potato cubes in
cold water for about 1 hour. Drain
and rinse in clear water.

Wash, drain, and soak the rice
according to the directions

for Japanese Rice (page 27).
Stir in the rinsed sweet potato
cubes and salt. Cook and rest
according to the directions in
Japanese Rice. After resting, fold
in the black sesame seeds, by
sprinkling in evenly as you cut
the rice with a rice paddle.

Serve mounded in small bowls
to accompany a couple vegetable
side dishes.

~~~~~~

EDAMAME RICE

EDAMAME GOHAN

Preparation time: 30 minutes, plus
50 minutes draining and soaking time
Cooking time: 15 minutes,
plus 5 minutes resting time
Serves: 4

(V) (DF) (GF) (NF) (<5)

• 2-inch (5 cm) square piece konbu
• 2 teaspoons (9 g) flaky sea salt (2% of
water weight)
• 10½ oz (300 g) edamame pods, rinsed
well
• 2¼ cups (540 ml/1 lb/450 g) Japanese
short-grain rice

Edamame rice is a fresh and
pretty way to serve white rice
in the summer when soybeans
are growing. Edamame—green
soybeans—are harvested in
Japan from early June through
September, depending on
the soybean variety. Although
some farmers grow soybeans
exclusively to sell as edamame
(you pull the whole plants out
by the roots, when harvesting),
others sell only a small amount as
edamame but leave the majority
of the crop to mature into soybeans. For mature soybeans,
the pods are left on the plants in
the fields to dry naturally, then
harvested. The cooking method
in this recipe is a bit unusual
because it recycles the salty
edamame boiling water to subtly
flavor the rice.
–
In a bowl, soften the konbu in a
generous 1¾ cups (15 fl oz/450 ml)
water for 20 minutes.

Pluck out the konbu, julienne,
and set aside. Transfer the soaking
water to a medium saucepan,
add the salt and bring to a boil
over high heat. Drop in the rinsed
edamame, return to a boil, and
cook for 3 minutes. Reserving
the cooking water, scoop out the
edamame. Pour the hot cooking
water into a large measuring cup
and add enough cold water to
make 2¼ cups (18¼ fl oz/540 ml).
Cool to room temperature.

Wash and drain the rice
according to the directions for
Japanese Rice (page 27). Add
the cooled edamame cooking
water and konbu and soak for
20 minutes. Cook, rest, and fluff
according to the directions for
Japanese Rice.

Remove the edamame from the
pods, fold into the rice, and serve
immediately.

SWEET POTATO RICE

人参ピラフ

CARROT PILAF

NINJIN PIRAFU

Preparation time: 30 minutes
Cooking time: 15 minutes,
plus 5 minutes resting time
Serves: 4, generously

- 1½ cups (360 ml/10½ oz/300 g)
  Japanese short-grain rice
- 1¼-inch (3 cm) square piece konbu
- 1 deep-fried tofu pouch
  (usuage, see page 352)
- Boiling water
- Generous ¾ cup (6¾ fl oz/200 ml)
  finely grated carrot
- 1 tablespoon unroasted sesame oil
- ¼ teaspoon flaky sea salt
- 1 teaspoon usukuchi shoyu
  (see page 344)
- 1 tablespoon sake
- 1 handful soft destemmed
  carrot fronds

Carrot fronds contain a large amount of carotene and add a welcome pungency to this rice pilaf, so be sure to source carrots with their tops. Use a circular ceramic grating plate (*oroshiki*, see page 354) or metal grating plate (*oroshigane*, see page 354) to achieve the necessary texture for the finely grated carrot. This intentionally lightly salted pilaf integrates well with other bright dishes. Substitute chopped Italian parsley for garnish if carrot fronds are not available.

-

Wash, drain, and soak the rice with the konbu according to the directions in Japanese Rice (page 27), using only 1½ cups (12½ fl oz/360 ml) water for soaking. After soaking for 20 minutes, cut the konbu into thin strips (about 2 heaping tablespoons) with a sharp knife and drop back in with the rice.

Place the *usuage* in a wire-mesh sieve and pour boiling water over it for 10 seconds. Halve lengthwise and cut crosswise into ¼-inch (5 mm) strips. Stir the *usuage*, grated carrot, oil, salt, *usukuchi shoyu*, and sake into the rice, cover, bring to a boil over high heat (about 2 minutes), and cook for 12 minutes over low heat.

Meanwhile, in a small pot of boiling water, blanch the carrot fronds for 1 minute. Drain, refresh under cold running water, blot dry, and finely chop.

When the rice has cooked, let it rest for 5 minutes. Fluff, mound into rice bowls, and strew with the carrot fronds. Serve as a light supper or hearty lunch with two or three vegetable side dishes and a clear soup.

CARROT PILAF

とうもろこしご飯

CORN RICE

TOUMOROKOSHI GOHAN

Preparation time: 20 minutes, plus
30 minutes draining and soaking time
Cooking time: 15 minutes,
plus 20 minutes resting time
Serves: 4

• 1½ cups (360 ml/10½ oz/300 g)
Japanese short-grain rice
• 1 large ear corn (9 oz/250 g)
• 2 teaspoons (10 g) unsalted
butter (or unroasted sesame oil
for a dairy-free option)
• ½ teaspoon shoyu

Cooking the rice with a couple
pieces of corncob imparts a
slightly nutty background note
to the rice and is a bit genius.
Make this flavorful dish in the early
summer when corn is at its peak.
-
Wash, drain, and soak the rice
in a small heavy pot according
to the directions for Japanese
Rice (page 27), but use 1⅔ cups
(13½ fl oz/400 ml) water.

Stand the ear of corn in a bowl
and remove the kernels with a
sharp knife. Scrape the cob with

the back of the knife to express
any juicy bits of remaining kernels.
Cut two 1¼ inch (3 cm) thick rounds
of the cob and bury in the rice.
Cover, bring to a boil over high heat
(about 2 minutes), then reduce to
low heat and cook for 12 minutes.
Allow to rest for 20 minutes.

Heat a frying pan over medium
heat. Add the butter and melt.
Stir-fry the corn in the butter
until fragrant and slightly golden,
about 1 minute. Remove from the
heat and stir in the shoyu. Fold
into the rested rice and serve.

栗と銀杏のご飯

CHESTNUT AND GINKGO NUT RICE

KURI TO GINNAN NO GOHAN

Preparation time: 45 minutes,
plus 45 minutes draining and
soaking time
Cooking time: 20 minutes,
plus 10 minutes resting time
Serves: 4

• 2¼ cups (540 ml/1 lb/450 g)
Japanese short-grain rice
• 12 Shelled Whole Chestnuts (page 35)
• 12 ginkgo nuts
• 1½ teaspoons flaky sea salt

There is a magic moment in the
autumn when both chestnuts
and ginkgo nuts can be harvested
and enjoyed in myriad seasonal
dishes. One reason this is a magic
moment is that neither can be
enjoyed at any other time of
the year unless they are frozen
or vacuum packed—which is
not at all the same. Serve this
beautifully understated rice dish
as an elegant main meal with
a few vegetable side dishes.
-
Wash and drain the rice
according to the directions for
Japanese Rice (page 27).

Pare off the papery brown inner
skins of the chestnuts with a
sharp knife. Soak the chestnuts
in cold water to cover generously
for 15 minutes, then cut out any
brown spots. Halve or quarter the
chestnuts, depending on size.

Place the ginkgo nuts inside
a tea towel and rap with a rubber
mallet to crack. Remove the
shells and soak the nuts in a bowl
of cold water for 15 minutes.

Leave the ginkgo in the water and
remove one by one to peel off the
inside skin with your fingernail
or a sharp paring knife. Halve the
nuts crosswise and set aside.

Stir the salt into 2¾ cups (22 fl oz/
650 ml) water to dissolve—if you
dip your finger into the water,
you should taste the salt, but
it should not be overly salty.
Place the washed, drained rice
in an iron rice pot (*tetsu gama*,
see page 354) or earthenware
casserole (*donabe*, see page 353).
Add the salted water and flatten
the surface of the rice. Strew the
chestnuts across the rice evenly.
Place the top on the pot and soak
for 20 minutes.

Bring to an almost boil over
high heat, about 4 minutes.
Immediately (and quickly) strew
in the ginkgo, replace the top and
cook for 1 minute longer over high
heat. Reduce the heat to low and
cook for 12 minutes. Allow to sit,
covered, for 10 minutes, before
fluffing and serving.

CORN RICE

四種のきのこご飯 # FOUR-MUSHROOM RICE

YON-SHU NO KINOKO GOHAN

Preparation time: 30 minutes, plus
30 minutes draining and soaking time
Cooking time: 15 minutes,
plus 5 minutes resting time
Serves: 4

- 1⅔ cups (400 ml/12 oz/335 g)
Japanese short-grain rice
- 1 tablespoon sake
- ¼ teaspoon flaky sea salt
- 1 tablespoon shoyu
- Boiling water
- 2 tablespoons Zakkoku (page 28)
- 1 deep-fried tofu pouch
(usuage, see page 352), crisped
up on a dry frying pan
- 1¾ oz (50 g) maitake, roughly torn
- 1¾ oz (50 g) shimeji, separated
and halved crosswise
- 3 medium shiitake (1¾ oz/50 g),
stems removed, caps finely sliced
- 1¾ oz (50 g) enoki, spongy ends
cut off, quartered crosswise
- 12 fine stalks mitsuba
(see page 346), cut crosswise into
½-inch (1 cm) pieces

With virus-killing and anti-cholesterol components, shiitake could be called the most important health food in Japan. Regardless, dried and fresh shiitake are an essential flavoring mushroom in Japanese cuisine and appear in small quantities in many dishes. In the autumn, when mushrooms are especially plentiful, mushroom rice (*kinoko gohan*) is enjoyed the length and breadth of Japan. There is no need to source the exact Japanese mushrooms called for in this recipe; best to use ones that are found naturally in your own locale. Serve as a main course with vegetable side dishes.
-

Wash and drain the rice according to the directions for Japanese Rice (page 27). Add the rice to a heavy medium pot, stir in the sake, salt, shoyu, and 1⅔ cups (13½ fl oz/400 ml) water and soak for at least 20 minutes.

Meanwhile, pour boiling water over the *zakkoku* in a small bowl and soak for 20 minutes. Drain and add to the soaked rice.

Halve the *usuage* lengthwise and finely julienne crosswise. Stir the *usuage* into the soaking rice along with the maitake, shimeji, shiitake, and enoki. Cook, rest, and fluff according to the directions for Japanese Rice. Serve mounded into rice bowls, garnished with the *mitsuba*.

FOUR-MUSHROOM RICE

茗荷寿司　MYOGA SUSHI

MYOUGA ZUSHI

Preparation time: 1 hour, plus
30 minutes draining and soaking time
Cooking time: 12 minutes,
plus 30 minutes resting time
Makes: 12 pieces

- 4 large myoga (3½ oz/100 g)
(see page 348)
- 3 tablespoons sour plum "vinegar"
(umesu, see page 345)
- 1½ cups (360 ml/10½ oz/300 g)
Japanese short-grain rice
- 2-inch (5 cm) square piece konbu
- 2 tablespoons rice vinegar,
plus more for forming the sushi
- 1½ tablespoons hon mirin
- 1 teaspoon usukuchi shoyu
(see page 344)
- ½ teaspoon fine sea salt
- 12 thick stalks mitsuba
(see page 346), 6 inches (15 cm) long
- Boiling water
- 1 teaspoon freshly squeezed
lemon juice

Myoga is often incorrectly translated as "Japanese ginger." While *myoga* is part of the ginger family, we also grow ginger in Japan and myoga neither tastes nor looks anything like ginger. *Myoga* has an almost celery-like flavor and looks like a pinky-tan flame-shaped bud. The buds poke out of the ground at the base of the plant in the early summer and are used in salads and sashimi plates around this time. A natural foil to rice, here the *myoga* sits atop plump pillows of sushi. Depending on the size of your *myoga*, you could end up with a little leftover rice—in this case, chop up the centers of the myoga, fold into the rice remaining after making the sushi, and form into rounded triangles (*onigiri*). Enclose in plastic wrap (cling film) and eat within a day.

-

Drop the *myoga* into a resealable 1-quart (1-liter) plastic bag and add the *umesu*. Squeeze out the air and seal. Place inside a small bowl and set a weight on top while you proceed with preparing the sushi rice.

Wash, drain, and soak the rice with the konbu according to the directions for Japanese Rice (page 27), but only use 1½ cups (12½ fl oz/360 ml) cold water. After soaking, remove the konbu and cut into ¼-inch (5 mm) dice (about 2 heaping tablespoons). Stir into the rice, cover, and bring to a boil over high heat (about 2 minutes). Reduce to low heat and cook for 12 minutes.

In a small bowl, mix together the rice vinegar, mirin, *usukuchi shoyu*, and salt. Curl the *mitsuba* into a fine mesh sieve and pour boiling water over for 10 seconds. Drain in the kitchen sink. When cool, squeeze gently to express excess water.

As soon as the rice has finished cooking, turn out into a large shallow tub (*handai*, see page 353) or wooden cutting board and sprinkle with the lemon juice. Drizzle on the vinegar mixture and cut and turn the rice with a rice paddle to distribute and aid absorption of the vinegar into the rice. Wave a handheld fan or piece of cardboard over the rice to cool as you cut. Let rest covered with a damp cheesecloth (muslin) for 30 minutes to absorb the *umesu*.

Set up a small bowl of rice vinegar next to your workplace, wet your palm and fingers with a little of the vinegar, and pat together 12 oblong-shaped pieces of sushi rice.

Drain the *myoga* (reserving the *umesu* for salad dressings or quick pickling) and separate the layers—reserve the inner core portion to chop up and add to any rice that remains after forming the sushi. Stack into 12 even piles, curved sides up. Pick up one of the oblong rice pieces, nestle it in the flat of your palm and press a pile of *myoga*, curved sides down, cupping over the top of the rice. Tie with a *mitsuba* stem and place on a pretty dinner plate. Repeat with each piece of rice and serve immediately with green tea as a refreshing afternoon snack.

MYOGA SUSHI

キャベツのめはり寿司　　　# MEHARI-STYLE CABBAGE SUSHI

KYABETSU NO MEHARI-ZUSHI

Preparation time: 1 hour,
plus 1 hour macerating time and
2 hours weighting time
Cooking time: 25 minutes,
plus 5 minutes resting time
Makes: 8 large rice "balls"

• 1½ cups (360 ml/10½ oz/300 g)
Japanese short-grain rice
• 2 salted sour "plums"
(umeboshi, see page 350), pitted
and finely chopped
• 8 small leaves of cabbage (9 oz/250 g)
• 1 teaspoon flaky sea salt
• ½ teaspoon fine sea salt
• 4 tablespoons rice vinegar
• 4 tablespoons hon mirin
• 4 dried wood ear mushrooms
• Boiling water
• Scant ½ cup (3½ fl oz/100 ml)
Konbu Dashi (page 22)
• 2 tablespoons shoyu
• 2 inches (5 cm) medium carrot
(2¼ oz/60 g), peeled and finely diced
• 4 inches (10 cm) burdock root
(1 oz/30 g), scrubbed and finely diced

Mehari-zushi is traditionally prepared by wrapping sushi rice with pickled mustard leaves (takana) and is native to Wakayama and Mie prefectures. Here the flavor is softer due to the cabbage. And while vinegar and umeboshi (salted "sour" plum) do play a role in adding a puckery note, plain rice is used in this method instead of sushi rice. Also, the root vegetables are seasoned on the sweet side to give balance to the dish. These little sushi parcels are good for a bento box or airplane meal.
-
Wash, drain, and soak the rice according to the method for Japanese Rice (page 27), but only use 1½ cups (12½ fl oz/360 ml) cold water. Cover, bring to a boil over high heat (about 2½ minutes), and cook for 12 minutes over low heat. Rest for 5 minutes before fluffing and turning out into a flat wooden tub (handai, see page 353) or wooden bowl. Fold in the umeboshi and distribute well with a pair of cooking chopsticks (saibashi, see page 354). Cover with a damp tea towel as you proceed with the recipe.

Smash the tough stem ends of the cabbage with a Japanese pestle (surikogi, see page 354) or rolling pin. Massage the flaky salt into the leaves in a large bowl.

Bring a large wok one-third full of water to a boil. Line the leaves across the bottom of a bamboo steamer, cover, and set inside the wok of boiling water. Steam over high heat for 3 minutes until the leaves are pliable. Remove the steamer from the wok, uncover, and cool the cabbage to room temperature.

In a small bowl, stir the fine salt into the vinegar to dissolve. Sweeten with 2 tablespoons of the mirin to make amazu. Stack the cooled steamed cabbage leaves in a large bowl, pour the amazu over the leaves, and set a drop lid (otoshibuta, see page 354) or plate on top of the leaves so they are all in contact with the amazu. Leave to macerate for 1 hour.

Place the wood ear mushrooms in a heatproof medium bowl and fill to cover generously with boiling water. Let soften for 15 minutes before draining and finely dicing.

In a small saucepan, bring the dashi, shoyu, remaining 2 table-spoons mirin, carrot, burdock, and mushrooms to a simmer over medium heat. Cook at a brisk simmer for about 10 minutes, until the liquids are reduced and the ingredients have absorbed flavor. Cool to room temperature, drain, and fold the seasoned ingredients into the cooked rice with the umeboshi. Discard the cooking liquid.

Remove the cabbage from the amazu, blot dry on all sides, and spread the leaves out side by side on a clean sheet pan. Form 8 equal-size spheres of rice, by patting and compressing them gently between your palms (the rice should become a cohesive mass but should not be smashed). Set each one at the base of a cabbage leaf. Roll up one turn, fold the sides of the leaves in toward the middle and continue rolling up to form a neat little package. Arrange the cabbage balls in the middle of the sheet pan and set an inverted sheet pan on top. Weight evenly with a 2-pound (1 kg) object on each of the short sides of the pan—not directly on top of the rice balls. Weight for 2 hours.

Slice into rounds ¾ inch (2 cm) thick and serve. Keeps refrig-erated for a couple of days though the rice will harden a little.

MEHARI-STYLE CABBAGE SUSHI

椎茸寿司

SHIITAKE SUSHI

Preparation time: 45 minutes,
plus 30 minutes draining and soaking
time, and 30 minutes resting time
Cooking time: 15 minutes
Makes 8

• 1 cup (240 ml/7 oz/200 g)
Japanese short-grain rice
• 2-inch (5 cm) square piece konbu
• 2 tablespoons rice vinegar,
plus more for forming the sushi
• 2 tablespoons hon mirin
• ½ teaspoon fine sea salt
• 4 large thick-capped dried shiitake
(donko, see page 350), soaked in
boiling water for 30 minutes
• ½ tablespoon dark roasted sesame oil
• 1 tablespoon sake
• 1 teaspoon flaky sea salt
• 16–32 thin stalks mitsuba
(see page 346)
• Boiling water
• 1 teaspoon white sesame seeds,
warmed in a dry frying pan until
fragrant and slightly crushed

Japanese-grown *donko* are
exceptionally flavorful so
I recommend trying to find them.
They soak up the cooking liquid
yet retain their natural quality,
thus do not overpower the rice.
-
Wash, drain, soak, and cook the
rice according to the method on
page 27, but lay the konbu on top
of the rice before soaking and
only use 1 cup (8 fl oz/240 ml) cold
water and cook for only 12 minutes.

In a bowl, stir the rice vinegar and
1 tablespoon of the mirin with the
fine salt until dissolved.

Turn the rice out into a shallow
wooden tub (*handai*, see page
353) or onto a wooden cutting
board and remove the konbu,
scraping off any clinging rice
grains. Discard the konbu and
sprinkle the vinegar mixture over
the rice. Waft with a fan while
you fold the vinegar mixture into
the hot rice until it cools to body
temperature. Cover with a damp
cheesecloth (muslin) and allow
to absorb flavor for 30 minutes.

Drain the shiitake, gently squeeze
out excess water, and pare out
the stems. In a small frying pan,
heat the sesame oil over medium
heat. Add the shiitake, stir once,
then add the sake, flaky salt, and
remaining 1 tablespoon mirin.
Cook over low heat for about
3 minutes to flavor, flipping every
30 seconds or so with a spoon,
until the liquids have absorbed.
Set aside.

Curl the *mitsuba* into a wire-
mesh sieve and pour boiling
water over for 10 seconds. Shake
off and separate into 8 stacks
of 2 or 3 strands, ends aligned.
These stacks will be used as ties.

Set up a small bowl of rice vinegar
and dip your fingers in to wet.
Form 8 small oblong shapes
with the sushi rice and sprinkle
the top sides with the sesame
seeds. Cut the cooled, simmered
shiitake caps in half and top each
rice oblong with the shiitake. Tie
each shiitake-topped sushi piece
with a stack of *mitsuba* stalks
and serve at room temperature.

ゆばとごま塩ののり巻き

YUBA AND SESAME
SALT NORI ROLLS

YUBA TO GOMASHIO NO NORI-MAKI

Preparation time: 30 minutes
Serves: 4

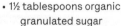

• 1½ tablespoons organic
granulated sugar
• 1 teaspoon fine sea salt
• 3 tablespoons rice vinegar
• 1⅔ cups (400 ml/10½ oz/300 g) freshly
cooked Japanese Rice (page 27)
• 2 sheets nori, halved lengthwise
• 2¼ oz (60 g) fresh yuba (see page 352)
• 4 teaspoons white or black
Sesame Salt (page 28)
• 4 sprigs nandina (nanten)
or small maple leaf, for garnish

The amount of uncooked rice
needed to make the cooked rice
called for in this recipe is 1-*go*
(1-合), which is equivalent to
¾ cup (180 ml/5¼ oz/150 g).
-
In a bowl, combine the sugar, salt,
and vinegar and stir to dissolve.

Turn the cooked rice into a shallow
wooden tub (*handai*, see page
353) or onto a wooden cutting
board. Sprinkle the vinegar
mixture over the rice while fanning
and turning the rice until the
vinegar has been absorbed.

Working with one at a time,
place the nori crosswise, shiny
side down, on a bamboo rolling
mat (*makisu*). Leaving ½–¾ inch
(1–2 cm) of nori free at the top,
spread one-quarter of the rice
evenly across the piece of nori.
Lay one-quarter of the *yuba*
across the middle of the rice and
sprinkle with one-quarter of the
sesame salt. Roll up the nori and
cut crosswise with a razor-sharp
knife into 6 rounds. Stand the
rolls in the middle of one of four
individual plates and garnish with
a sprig of nandina or maple leaf.

YUBA AND SESAME SALT NORI ROLLS

OKAYU: PORRIDGE TO HEAL YOUR BODY AND SOUL

In Japan, *okayu* is a rice porridge that has the reputation for being eaten when you are feeling poorly, or your tummy is tired. My husband used to prepare his version of *okayu* for himself or our sons when they were under the weather. Though years later, I learned his version was actually *ojiya* because he started with cooked rice. He stirred up the rice with water (or dashi) and simmered it over low heat with one *umeboshi* until the mixture was thick and creamy like risotto. Since my husband was a free-range egg farmer in those days, eggs were a big part of our family food. So, while not orthodox, he also broke a fresh egg inside the *ojiya* before spooning out into a bowl. The most common version of *ojiya*, also called *zosui*, is made from simmering cooked rice in the last savory juices of a *nabe* (one-pot dish).

Rice is the most fundamental component in a traditional Japanese diet. The first food fed to babies is called *rinyuu shoku* (離乳食)—the kanji characters for which mean "separation [from] milk food." After mother's milk, the very first food given to babies is made from rice and called *omoyu* (重湯), or "heavy hot water." Although generally made in the same way as *okayu*—from raw rice and water (or dashi for *okayu*)—*omoyu* starts with a much higher ratio of water to rice at 10 or 20 to 1. That said, we sometimes made our *omoyu* from cooked rice to speed up the process. And we never measured. After bringing to a boil over medium heat, the pan is stirred once to remove any grains of rice sticking to the bottom of the pan, partially covered, and left to simmer on low heat for about 30 minutes. The rice solids are strained out of the thick liquid while hot, and once cooled, the liquid is fed to the baby. (Adults should eat the strained-out rice.) The next step towards introducing "solid foods" is to mash or grind up the soupy rice liquid with the solids and feed that to the baby.

Given the importance of rice, buying random Japanese-grown rice might not be the best choice for people living outside of Japan, since much of the rice making its way to other countries can be subpar. If you have doubts about the quality of the Japanese rice available in your locale, I recommend searching out local growers producing Japanese rice. And in a pinch, Italian varieties such as Arborio or Carnaroli are good fallbacks for *okayu*, since they also are under the umbrella of japonica rice.

I did not appreciate *okayu* until I tested a recipe for my third book, *Japan: The Cookbook*. It was an incredibly simple *okayu* made from white rice, water, and sea salt. Japanese wild parsley (*seri*, see page 347) and grilled brown rice mochi were added right before serving. I passed around bites to various little kindergarten students who were hanging around in the afternoon with me while I cooked, and they all pronounced it "yummy." And I thought it was so good that we served it at a collaboration dinner I did at Reynard, a restaurant that used to be in the Wythe Hotel in Brooklyn, New York. We used organic rice from my husband's farm, Ohsawa brown rice mochi, Wajima no Kaien salt, and a peppery local cress. Here is a time when sourcing the ingredients made all the difference because the beauty is in the simplicity.

Morning *okayu*, either brown rice or white, is humble and unadorned, served only with some slivered *takuan* (preserved daikon) in the winter or *umeboshi* (sun-dried salted sour "plums") in the summer, and a small mound of sesame salt on the side. By dipping the tip of a spoonful of *okayu* into the sesame salt, the first taste of the powerful, salty, aromatic powder is immediately followed by the creamy unsalted *okayu*. It is impossible to imagine how eating the *okayu* with sesame salt in this way transforms it into a shockingly compelling dish. Likewise, pinching up a bit of *takuan* or *umeboshi*, in between spoonfuls of *okayu*, will provide an intensely flavorful foil to the humble bowl of porridge. Do not underestimate how good this can be.

Slowly simmering the rice in broth (or water) brings out the sweetness of the rice and at first bite your body will be immediately warmed and filled with a feeling of well-being. *Okayu* is deceptively simple, yet deeply nourishing in body and spirit. As a basic method: simmering uncooked rice in water, *okayu* provides a palette to which a minimal addition of greens or vegetables can enhance ever so slightly, thus elevate subtly. The key is how one eats *okayu*: never skip dipping each bite in sesame salt or pinching up a bit of salty pickle to chase an unseasoned bite.

Okayu is the ultimate symbol of all that is best about Japanese vegetarian food, and embodies the principle of gentle food that is seasoned with a light hand. Less is more.

山芋のお粥　MOUNTAIN YAM OKAYU

YAMA-IMO NO OKAYU

Preparation time: 40 minutes
Cooking time: 25 minutes
Serves: 4

- ¾ cup (180 ml/5¼ oz/150 g) Japanese short-grain rice
- ½ small (4½ oz/125 g) mountain yam, scrubbed
- ½ teaspoon flaky sea salt
- 1 teaspoon matcha
- 2 teaspoons black Sesame Salt (page 28)

Matcha is often used as a garnish for mountain yam dishes, but here it is stirred into the dish after cooking. This is a subtly flavored creamy rice dish that is particularly warming in the early morning yet is also a healthy bedtime snack after a late night out. Don't be tempted to stir the bitter matcha into the mild rice, because it is the contrast found in each bite that makes this dish so interesting and tasty.
-
Wash and drain the rice according to the directions for Japanese Rice (page 27). Slide into a heavy medium saucepan.

Peel the mountain yam and cut into ½-inch (1 cm) cubes. Add to the saucepan with the salt. (Wash your hands and forearms with warm, sudsy water to counteract the itchy properties of the yam.)

Add 2 quarts (2 liters) cold water to the rice and bring to a lively simmer over medium-high heat. Stir to dislodge any rice grains sticking to the bottom of the pan, reduce the heat to a controlled simmer, and continue cooking until the liquid has reduced and the rice has plumped and is cooked through, about 25 minutes.

Stir 2 teaspoons water into the matcha until smooth. Ladle the *okayu* into four bowls, drizzle with the matcha, and serve hot with a small saucer of sesame salt for each person. Dip the tip of a spoonful of *okayu* with a little matcha into the sesame salt before eating each bite. The contrasts of bitter, sweet, aromatic, and mild will surprise you.

五味粥

FIVE-FLAVOR OKAYU

GO-MI GAYU

Preparation time: 15 minutes,
plus 20 minutes soaking time
Cooking time: 30 minutes
Serves: 4

- ¾ cup (180 ml/5¼ oz/150 g)
Japanese short-grain rice
- Boiling water
- 4 tablespoons Zakkoku (page 28)
- 2 quarts (2 liters)
Konbu Dashi (page 22)
- ¼ bunch (2 oz/55 g) mizuna, cut
crosswise into 1¼-inch (3 cm) pieces
- 2 teaspoons white
Sesame Salt (page 28)

Zakkoku is a millet mix that is added to rice for texture, aroma, and healthful properties such as fiber. You can mix your own or purchase a commercial variety sold as a "grain mix for rice" at health food stores or Japanese grocery stores. The red and black rice included in these mixes gives this *okayu* a gorgeous lavender hue.

—

Wash and drain the rice according to the directions for Japanese Rice (page 27). Pour boiling water over the *zakkoku* and soak for 20 minutes.

Drain the *zakkoku* and add to a heavy medium pot with the rice. Stir in the dashi and cook uncovered over medium-low heat, keeping a close eye to make sure the rice does not boil over, until the rice has plumped and softened, 20–25 minutes.

Ladle into large deep bowls (*donburi*, see page 354), garnish with a healthy mound of aligned mizuna pieces, and serve as a hearty breakfast to start the day. Give each person a small saucer of sesame salt for dipping the tips of their spoonfuls of *okayu*.

餅入り七草粥

SEVEN GREENS OKAYU
WITH MOCHI

MOCHI-IRI NANAKUSA GAYU

Preparation time: 30 minutes
Cooking time: 25 minutes
Serves: 4

- ¾ cup (180 ml/5¼ oz/150 g)
Japanese short-grain rice
- 2 handfuls (1¾ oz/50 g) spring greens,
such as Japanese wild
parsley (seri, see page 347), turnip,
and mitsuba (see page 346),
roughly chopped
- 4 pieces (1½ oz/40 g each)
dried brown rice mochi
- 2 teaspoons white Sesame Salt
(page 28)

Okayu is a warming and satis-fying soupy rice dish that is a benchmark of simple vegetarian meals usually eaten for breakfast, but also for lunch. The creamy rice is intentionally unsalted, so serve with the sesame salt (or salty pickles) on the side. The brown rice mochi contrasts nicely with the white rice *okayu*, but you can substitute white rice mochi.

—

Wash and drain the rice according to the directions for Japanese Rice (page 27).

In a heavy medium saucepan, bring 2 quarts (2 liters) water to a boil. Stir in the rice and greens, adjust to a gentle simmer, and stir across the bottom once to dislodge any rice grains adhering. Cook for 20 minutes.

Once the *okayu* has simmered for 15 minutes, toast the mochi in a toaster oven (mini oven) for about 3 minutes to soften and puff up. Quarter each piece with a sharp knife (you will need a table knife to scrape the hot mochi pieces from the knife blade after each cut).

Stir the toasted mochi into the *okayu* and cook together for another 5 minutes, a total of 25 minutes.

Ladle out into four rice bowls and serve immediately with a small saucer of sesame salt per person. Dip the tip of each spoonful of *okayu* into the sesame salt to season as you eat.

FIVE-FLAVOR OKAYU

冷やし汁かけご飯

COLD MOUNTAIN YAM
AND OKRA SOUP ON RICE

HIYAJIRU-KAKE GOHAN

Preparation time: 1 hour,
plus 1 hour chilling time
Cooking time: 20 minutes,
plus 5 minutes resting time
Serves: 4

• 2½ cups (20 fl oz/600 ml)
Konbu Dashi (page 22)
• 1½ tablespoons shoyu
• 1¼ teaspoons flaky sea salt
• 1½ cups (360 ml/10½ oz/300 g)
Japanese short-grain rice
• Boiling water
• 2 tablespoons Zakkoku (page 28)
• 14 oz (400 g) mountain yam, scrubbed
• 5¼ oz (150 g) cotton tofu
(momendofu, see page 352) or
Japanese-style soft block tofu
• 8 small okra (2⅔ oz/75 g)
• ½ sheet nori, snipped
into fine threads
• 2 teaspoons grated fresh wasabi

Cold soups are a welcome relief to the often oppressive mugginess that envelops Japan during the height of summer. Both okra and mountain yam have a natural viscosity that is said to give one power, and they are often paired together. It is important not to pour the soup over the rice until you are ready to eat because the rice grains will become soggy. Also be sure to wash your hands and forearms with warm soapy water after grating the itchy mountain yam.
-
Set up a large bowl of ice. In a medium saucepan, warm the dashi with the shoyu and 1 teaspoon of the salt over medium heat to dissolve the salt. Remove from the heat and pour into a medium stainless steel bowl and set the bowl in the ice to cool. Transfer to the refrigerator for 1 hour to chill completely.

Wash and drain the rice according to the directions for Japanese Rice (page 27). Soak for 20 minutes in a small cast-iron pot with 1⅔ cups (13½ fl oz/400 ml) water. Meanwhile pour boiling water over the zakkoku in a small bowl and soak for 20 minutes.

Drain the zakkoku, add to the rice, and cover. Bring to a boil over high heat (this will take about 3 minutes), reduce the heat to low, and cook for 15 minutes. Rest for 5 minutes after cooking, then transfer to a medium bowl to cool.

Peel and finely grate the mountain yam on a circular ceramic grating plate (oroshiki, see page 354) or metal grating plate (oroshigane, see page 354). Scrape into a Japanese grinding bowl (suribachi, see page 354) and mash until smooth. Set aside.

Cut the tofu into ½-inch (1 cm) cubes and spoon into a small bowl.

Line the okra up horizontally to you on a cutting board and sprinkle with the remaining ¼ teaspoon salt. Roll the okra back and forth in the salt to soften (itazuri). Bring a small saucepan of water to a boil and drop in the okra. Cook for about 1 minute until brilliant green. Scoop out and refresh under cold running water. Pat dry. Slice off the tops and discard. Cut the okra crosswise into ¼-inch (5 mm) rounds.

Once the dashi has chilled sufficiently, mound a generous scoop of rice into a corner of four large soup bowls (donburi, see page 354) and spoon the grated mountain yam alongside in another corner. Mound the tofu and okra in the other two corners and add a generous pinch of nori threads on top of the mountain yam. Dab wasabi into the center of the nori and ladle the chilled soup around the perimeter. Serve immediately as a healthy and tasty lunch dish during the summer.

COLD MOUNTAIN YAM AND OKRA SOUP ON RICE

Tsukemono is typically translated into English as "pickles"—though in truth *tsukemono* means "put-upon things." In other words, things upon which you have put something salty: be it salt, miso, shoyu, *umesu*, fish sauce, etc. Japanese pickles might be naturally sour from lacto-fermentation or *umesu* (the salty, sour, fruity brine that results from salting and pressing sour "plums"), but generally do not include vinegar. Vinegared things are called *sunomono* (page 94) and were traditionally the Japanese version of salad. *Tsukemono* are mostly what we think of as quick pickles, however under the *tsukemono* umbrella are *hozonshoku* (preserved foods), such

as *umeboshi* (salted, sun-dried sour "plums"), *takuan* (rice bran- and miso-fermented semi-dried daikon), and *narazuke* (air-dried cucumbers or gourd melons preserved in sake lees and miso). Many types of *hozonshoku* are packed tightly in barrels or crocks, kept in a cool, dark place, and meant to last for several months or longer. But *hozonshoku* also includes sun-dried foods such as *hoshigaki* (dried whole persimmons) or *kiriboshi daikon* (dried daikon strands).

If you are new to Japanese cooking, I recommend starting with easy *tsukemono* dishes. Commercial Japanese pickles—including

so-called "traditional" ones sold in pickling barrels in department store basements (*depachika*) and Kyoto's famous Nishiki Market—are most likely made from imported vegetables, and certainly contain preservatives and MSG.

A notable exception to this rule of thumb are the organic, naturally pickled vegetables produced by Yamaki Jozo in our town of Kamikawa, in Saitama prefecture.

Serve your *tsukemono* or *hozonshoku* with a rice dish and a simple bowl of miso soup and you have created the quintessential Japanese meal.

TSUKEMONO & HOZONSHOKU

PICKLED & PRESERVED

桜の塩漬け

SALT-PICKLED CHERRY BLOSSOMS

SAKURA NO SHIO-ZUKE

Preparation time: 10 minutes
Pickling time: 1 week
Makes: About 4 tablespoons

• Flaky sea salt
• 2 handfuls cherry blossoms

Cherry blossoms are as quietly stunning as they are short-lived. They begin to show up on the trees in the early spring—but timing is completely dependent on the weather each year. Make these once the buds unfurl but before the flowers start falling like spring rain.

-

Add ¼ inch (5 mm) of salt to the bottom of a small crock or jar. Strew in some cherry blossoms to cover, then sprinkle with more salt. Keep layering blossoms and salt, ending with a last ¼ inch (5 mm) of salt at the top. Place a piece of food grade plastic wrap (cling film) on top of the salt and add a weight to compress. Leave for a week or so to salt preserve. Soak the salted blossoms in cold water to desalinate before using. Alternatively, soak the salted blossoms in plenty of cold water for about 20 minutes, then sun dry on neutral paper–lined flat baskets in the direct sun for 5–6 hours. Pack in a jar with sour plum "vinegar" (*umesu*, see page 345) and store in the refrigerator.

~~~~~~

スピード芝漬

QUICK SHIBAZUKE

SUPI-DO SHIBAZUKE

Preparation time: 30 minutes
Pickling time: 1–2 hours
Makes: 1 pound (450 g)

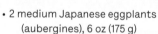

• 2 medium Japanese eggplants (aubergines), 6 oz (175 g)
• 2 medium Japanese cucumbers (7 oz/200 g)
• 1 teaspoon flaky sea salt
• 3 medium myoga (see page 348), halved lengthwise
• 8 green shiso leaves, cut into fine threads
• 4 tablespoons sour plum "vinegar" (umesu, see page 345)

Shibazuke is a traditional summer pickle that involves salting and weighting the vegetables for half a day, then pickling them in a red shiso solution for 2 more days to acquire flavor. Here red *umesu* is used to speed up the process to make these in a speedy 2 hours. The vegetables will not acquire as strong a red hue as the longer version, but they will be infused with the brightly tart fruity *umesu* and they will be compellingly delicious.

-

Cut the calyx off the eggplants (aubergines) and the ends off the cucumbers and slice into ½-inch (1 cm) rounds. Drop into a medium bowl and massage gently with ¾ teaspoon of the salt. Massage the *myoga* halves in a small bowl with the remaining ¼ teaspoon salt. Let sit for 10 minutes.

Squeeze the eggplant and cucumber by handfuls to express juice—avoiding the lingering salt at the bottom of the bowl—and place in a pickling press (*tsukemono yoki*, see page 354). (Alternatively, jerry-rig a rectangular container into which you can fit a smaller rectangular container and add weights to act as a press.)

Squeeze the *myoga* (avoiding the salt) and add in with the eggplant and cucumber. Toss with shiso leaves and *umesu* and screw down the press firmly but not enough to crush the vegetables. (Alternatively, place in a resealable plastic bag, roll up tight, and place a weight on top of the bag.) Leave for 1–2 hours before serving. It keeps for 1 week if stored in the fridge in an airtight container.

QUICK SHIBAZUKE

セロリの塩麹漬け

SHIO KOJI–PICKLED CELERY

SERORI NO SHIOKOJI-ZUKE

Preparation time: 10 minutes
Pickling time: 2–3 hours
Makes: ⅔ cup (6 oz/170 g)

- 2 medium stalks celery
(5¼ oz/150 g), with some
lingering leaves, but thick bottom
portions cut off
- 2 tablespoons shio koji

Shio koji has taken the world by storm thanks to Myoho Asari in Oita prefecture on the island of Kyushu. Myoho found a reference to *shio koji*-pickled sardines in a cookery book several hundred years old, and from this, she developed a method for producing *shio koji*. By pickling or marinating in *shio koji* you get the benefit of the salt, but also the gentle sweetness of the koji (*Aspergillus oryzae*), the fermenting spore used for making shoyu, miso, sake, and mirin.

-

Slice the celery crosswise at a diagonal into ¼-inch (5 mm) pieces. Drop into a heavy-duty resealable plastic bag and add the *shio koji*. Roll up the bag, while squeezing out the air and massaging the *shio koji* into the celery. Store in the fridge for 2 hours before spooning out into small dishes to serve. Keeps for 2 or 3 days, if refrigerated, but best the first day. If you find the dish too salty for your taste, blot off or squeeze the celery to remove excess *shio koji* before serving.

~~~~~~

荒布の時雨煮

SOUR PLUM–FLAVORED DRIED ARAME

ARAME NO SHIGURE-NI

Preparation time: 20 minutes,
plus overnight steeping and
1 day drying time
Cooking time: 15 minutes
Serves: 4

- Scant 1 oz (25 g) dried arame
(see page 349), soaked in cold
water for 20 minutes
- Scant ⅓ cup (2½ fl oz/75 ml)
sour plum "vinegar"
(umesu, see page 345)
- ½ cup (4 fl oz/125 ml) sake
- Scant ¼ cup (1¾ fl oz/50 ml) hon mirin
- ⅛ teaspoon fine sea salt
- ½ tablespoon finely julienned
organic sun-dried tangerine peel
(chinpi, see page 350)
- 1 teaspoon finely julienned
fresh ginger

Shigure ("November rain") is an ancient method of simmering, soaking, and sun-drying foods such as seaweed to preserve them. The tangy fruit elements introduced by the sour plum "vinegar" (*umesu*) and dried tangerine peel and the hot spark of ginger, make this *shigure* a bright and appealing bite in the cold dark winter and is delicious as an accompaniment to a cold beverage in the summertime. The ratio of *umesu* to sake to mirin is 3:5:2 for the cooking liquid.

-

Drain the *arame* well in a wire-mesh sieve for 10 minutes.

Slide the *arame* into a medium saucepan and add the *umesu*, sake, and mirin. Set a drop lid (*otoshibuta*, see page 354) or

piece of parchment paper on top and bring to a simmer over medium heat. Reduce the heat to a gentle simmer and cook until the liquid has reduced by half and the *arame* is meltingly soft, about 12 minutes.

Sprinkle in the salt, sun-dried tangerine peel, and ginger. Let sit overnight, stirring occasionally.

In the morning, bring to a simmer once again, then remove from the heat. Spread the *arame* on a bamboo basket or wire-net frame and dry in the sun for about 1 day, until 80 percent dried. Store in a plastic container in the fridge for several months. Use as a topping for cooked Japanese rice or as a sour-fruity snack.

SHIO KOJI–PICKLED CELERY

梅干し
UMEBOSHI

Preparation time: 1 hour (spread out),
plus overnight soaking time
Brining time: 2–3 weeks
Drying time: 3 days
Makes: 5½ lb (2½ kg)

- 11 lb (5 kg) ripe, but still hard,
green ume
- 14 oz (400 g) fine sea salt
(8% of the weight of the ume)

Given the steep price of good-quality *umeboshi*, making your own is probably worth the effort. There is not a lot of hands-on work, but you do have to stay vigilant to the process and keep an eye on the brining, since surface mold can form. Over the years, I have heard many chefs or fermenting enthusiasts relay their so-called *umeboshi* experiments with other fruits besides *ume*. The most common substitute are ripe plums, but plums aren't directly related to *ume*. If you are eager to make ersatz-*umeboshi*, find a farmer (or neighbor) who will pick you their apricots once the fruit has developed flavor, but not yet softened. *Ume*, which are related to apricots, are still rock hard when ripe enough to be picked and processed.

-

Rinse the *ume* in a large bucket and soak overnight in cold water. Drain and transfer the *ume* to a large crock or plastic pickling tub. Sprinkle in the salt, trying to distribute it evenly into the openings between the *ume*, as well as on top. Smooth a clean cheesecloth (muslin), large enough so that it can drape over the sides of the crock, across the surface of the *ume*. Place a drop lid (*otoshibuta*, see page 354) on top of the cloth with an 11-pound (5 kg) weight on top (if you do not have one large weight, use smaller ones but place them evenly).

Leave for 2–3 weeks in a sheltered spot at room temperature, but check daily to make sure the brine has come up and the *ume* are submerged, and no mold is forming. If mold forms, carefully lift it off and make sure no small pieces break off into the brine. If they do, you will have to drain out all the *ume*, wipe them carefully, and strain out any mold particles from the brine through a wire-mesh sieve lined with a clean cheesecloth (muslin). Wash and dry the crock, drop lid, and weight before putting the *ume* and brine back in the crock, laying a clean cheesecloth (muslin) on top, and replacing the drop lid and weight.

Remove the *ume* from the brine and save the brine (*umesu*) for pickling or tart dressings (stored in the fridge). Spread the *ume* out on a rattan mat that is suspended across a bamboo frame (or on large baskets) and set in the direct sunlight on a bright, sunny day. Dry from the morning to late afternoon, but bring in at night and pack (only half full) in large resealable plastic bags. Dry the *ume* 2 more sunny days, then store, well sealed, in the plastic bags in a cool dark place or the fridge.

梅味噌

UME MISO

Preparation time: 30 minutes,
plus daily turning
Pickling time: 1 month
Makes: 3 lb (1.3 kg)

• 1 lb 5 oz (600 g) organic sugar
• 2 lb (900 g) brown rice or inaka miso
• 2 lb (900 g) green ume

Catching green *ume* when they are ready to be harvested can be tricky since the window is only a matter of days . . . or sometimes only one day! Nonetheless, this preparation takes little work, just time, so it's definitely worth monitoring the *ume* harvest. Use as a flavoring for stir-fries, as a base for salad dressing, or dolloped onto cold tofu in the summer. Also take care to store in a container that is ventilated since the fermentation is fairly active. If you are using tiny *ume*, there is no need to soak or pierce. You can also make an approximate *ume* miso by mixing brown rice or *inaka* miso 1:1 with Ume Honey Syrup (page 307). Soak the *ume* overnight (or for at least 4 hours) in a large bowl. Drain and dry well. Pierce each *ume* around the circumference in two or three places with a fork.
-

In a large bowl, squish the sugar into the miso with your hands, until well incorporated. Spoon one-third of the miso mixture into the bottom of a large sterilized pickling jar or pot. (I used a stainless steel enameled pickling pot.) Drop the *ume* into the jar and spoon the rest of the miso on top. Shake side to side a little to settle and eliminate air pockets. Cover with a non-airtight lid or a double layer of cheesecloth (muslin) and secure with a rubber band or kitchen twine.

Leave in a cool, dark place for 1 month, but turn the contents gently with clean hands every day. The miso will keep, if stored in the refrigerator, for up to 2 years, by which time it will acquire the characteristics of *narazuke*, a pungent long-fermented sake lees pickle made in Nara prefecture.

オクラの煎り酒浸し

UMEBOSHI- AND SAKE-PICKLED OKRA

OKURA NO IRIZAKE BITASHI

Preparation time: 10 minutes
Cooking time: 5 minutes
Pickling time: 2–3 hours
Serves: 4

• 12 medium okra
(4 oz/115 g), brown portions
of tops pared off
• ¼ teaspoon flaky sea salt
• 1 salted sour "plum"
(umeboshi, see page 350)
• Generous ¾ cup
(6¾ fl oz/200 ml) sake

Pickling okra is a delicious way to make use of these crunchy little vegetables in the summer when they are abundant. Here, this quick okra pickle gets its refreshing fruity, salty, sour notes from the *umeboshi* and sweetness from the sake.
-
Arrange the okra horizontally to you on a large cutting board. Sprinkle with the salt and roll the okra with flattened palms to break down the fibers a little (*itazuri*).

Bring a medium saucepan of water to a boil. Add the okra and blanch for 20 seconds, scoop out with a wire-mesh sieve, and leave to cool.

Pit (destone) and finely chop the *umeboshi*. Save the pits. Add the *umeboshi* paste to a medium saucepan and stir in the sake. Drop in the pits as well and bring to a simmer over medium heat. Cook at a lively simmer for 3 minutes to burn off some of the alcohol (you will smell the aroma of alcohol waft up from the pan). This is called *irizake*.

Cool the *irizake* to room temperature in a medium bowl. Discard the pits and place the okra and the *irizake* in a heavy-duty resealable plastic bag. Roll up to squeeze out air and store in the fridge for 2–3 hours before serving as a pickle at the end of a meal.

SUN-DRIED VEGETABLES

One particularly scorching day in August I came upon my mother-in-law turning small rounds of Japanese eggplants (aubergines) as they dried under the sun on rattan mats. I had never seen her do that before, but possibly I just hadn't noticed. At the time, I was writing my first cookbook about life and food on the Japanese farm and had consulted Baachan (literally, "granny") about her country-style sushi recipes (*inaka-zushi* and *inari-zushi*). I am guessing that sharing her family recipe with me inspired her to revive the vegetable drying practice of a previous time. As the years go by, we lose energy, and Baachan was no longer making miso or pickles or even cooking much. She took great pleasure in eating the international meals that crossed our family table each evening and was content with the simpler fare she prepared for herself during the day. We lost Baachan in 2011, a year before my first book was published, but I will never forget her jaunty straw farm bonnet with the colorful sash and her wide smile as she turned the eggplant pieces and explained how she would store them in jars, then use them in simmered dishes throughout the year.

A few years later, while on the bullet train heading to Tokyo, I struck up a conversation with the elderly woman sitting next to me. I was writing my second Japanese cookbook, this time about pickling and preserving. We began talking about the subject and I brought up Baachan's eggplant drying. My companion's eyes lit up and she proceeded to tell me about all the fruits, vegetables, and fungi that she herself dried: carrots, daikon, turnips, shiitake, cucumbers, eggplant . . . tangerine peels on her urban veranda. I felt comforted to hear that despite urban living, she had not given up on this practice. Fading traditions can provide a backbone to Japanese society and are thankfully experiencing a comeback with young people interested in a more healthy, season-oriented life.

Vegetables are typically dried in late fall to early winter and mid to late summer in Japan. The method requires a string of sunny days, but otherwise is easy and not time-consuming. The sun-drying encourages natural sugars to intensify and the resulting dried pieces are mellow and nutritious and convenient to have around. With a high moisture content in the air year-round, the Japanese climate is ideal for gentle drying. If the sun is too intense, the vegetables will discolor and overdry.

There are many dried foods easily available in Japan, and countryside farm stands sell locally dried shiitake (sliced or whole), daikon threads (*kiriboshi daikon*), carrot threads (*kiriboshi ninjin*), and taro stems (*zuiki*). But supermarkets will only have the standard dried items such as shiitake, various kinds of seaweeds, gourd (*kampyo*), and perhaps daikon. Drying foods to preserve for the winter months has been a long tradition in Japan, but now that foods are readily available all-year-round, the custom is considerably less prevalent. As a preserving method, however, it is the simplest, and requires no extra ingredients, just the sun.

Dried steamed rice, a staple food carried to battle or on travels, is sung about in ancient songs. It was light and easy to store when dried, so conveniently portable. And in the Muromachi period (1336–1573) soldiers wrapped dried ropes of taro stems that had been simmered in miso (*imogara nawa*) around their waists before heading out to battle. They would tear off a piece as needed and simmer in water to make instant miso soup.

When vegetables are sun-dried, their sweetness is enhanced as the water content decreases—the taste is concentrated with the evaporation of the water. Additionally, as the vegetables warm under the sun, their natural enzymes are activated, thus producing umami-like components. Drying activates the enzyme amylase in vegetables, which breaks down the starches into sugars such as glucose and maltose, thus contributing sweetness. In addition, when reconstituted the dried vegetable will have a firmer texture than when raw and can give added texture to vinegared or simmered dishes.

The nutrients of some ingredients are altered by the power of the sun. An example of this is the marked taste difference between fresh and dried shiitake—dried shiitake acquire a completely unique aroma and depth of flavor from when fresh. Also, a compound called ergosterol contained in fresh shiitake is converted to vitamin D when exposed to the sun. Stored, however, sun-dried shiitake will lose half of their beneficial vitamin D in a month, so it is recommended to use them up quickly. To boost vitamin D in dried shiitake that have been stored, place in full sunlight for 30 minutes to 1 hour before using. (FYI: Most store-bought dried shiitake have been hot-air dried, rather than sun-dried. Always check the packaging.)

As for fresh daikon compared to dried daikon: Weight per weight, dried contains about fifteen times the calories and dietary fiber as fresh, and the calcium is more than twenty times. When dried (Kiriboshi Daikon, page 308), the intrinsic flavor of raw daikon becomes concentrated and also develops an appealing crunchy texture.

As a preserved food, dried vegetables are good for your health, so it's worth taking the time to spread them out in the sun and watch them dry.

梅のはちみつシロップ

UME HONEY SYRUP

UME NO HACHIMITSU SHIROPPU

Preparation time: 15 minutes
Pickling time: 1 month
Makes: 2 quarts (2 liters)

- 4 lb (1.8 kg) ripened ume
- 2 quarts (2 liters) honey

This versatile syrup is made from windfall and ripe *ume* once they have turned yellow and pink. Use as a cocktail mixer, dash into sparkling wine or water, or mix 1:1 with brown rice miso for instant *ume* miso for Ume Miso–Sautéed Summer Vegetables (page 202).
-
Wipe the *ume* and drop into a 4-quart (4-liter) sterilized jar or crock. Fill to cover with honey and place a double layer of cheesecloth (muslin) over the mouth of the jar. Secure tightly with twine or a heavy-duty rubber band and leave in a cool dark place for 1 month until effervescent. Strain out any pits (stones) or undissolved solids and store the syrup in jars or bottles in the refrigerator. Be careful when opening the containers because you will get a massive fizz-over if you do not release the compressed air out slowly. Keeps for at least 1 year.

~~~~~~

切り干しにんじん

KIRIBOSHI CARROTS

KIRIBOSHI NINJIN

Preparation time: 30 minutes
Drying time: 1–2 days
Makes: 1 oz (30 g)

- 2 medium carrots (10½ oz/300 g)

Although not as prevalent today, Japanese countrywomen have been drying vegetables for hundreds of years. Recently, *kiriboshi daikon* is common to see in the markets, but it is possible to dry many kinds of vegetables. Eggplant (aubergines) and cucumbers should be cut into rounds, while root vegetables should be sliced into thin strips. It is essential to dry vegetables when you are certain to have a good several days of bright sunshine since they tend to blacken if it takes too long for them to dry. In rainy Japan, this means most likely the end of summer or beginning of autumn.
-
Hold a carrot in your non-dominant hand and peel the exposed half of the carrot lengthwise with a vegetable peeler. Turn the carrot around so you're working on the other half periodically until you cannot peel any more without "peeling" your hand. Repeat with the second carrot. Lay out the peels on bamboo baskets in the direct sunlight for about 2 days, depending on the strength of your local sun. Bring in at night and cover with paper if 1 day is not enough. Store in an airtight container in a cool, dark spot and add to simmered dishes, miso soup, or stir-fried vegetable dishes.

切り干し大根　　KIRIBOSHI DAIKON

Preparation time: 1 hour
Drying time: 2–3 days
Makes: 3½ oz (100 g)

• 1 small daikon (2 lb/1 kg),
scrubbed or peeled

If you live outside of Japan and have access to winter daikon, I encourage you to dry your own *kiriboshi daikon*. You will need at least two or three sunny days in a row and some large baskets or rattan mats. And a mandoline will simplify the process immensely.
-
Slice the daikon lengthwise into strips ¼ inch (5 mm) wide with a Japanese mandoline (*benriner*, see page 353). (Alternatively, use a vegetable peeler—but you will need to roll the peels and cut into thin strips by hand—so this might take some time.)

Lay the strips out on bamboo baskets or a rattan mat in the direct sunlight for 2–3 days, to dry. The pieces should be dry enough that they will not mold when stored. Bring in at night and cover with paper before returning to the sunlight the following day. Store in an airtight container in a cool, dark spot. The *kiriboshi daikon* should keep for several months, if sufficiently dried. Reconstitute by rinsing well, then soaking for about 1 hour in plenty of cold water.

切り干し大根の針針漬け　　SPICY PICKLED KIRIBOSHI DAIKON

KIRIBOSHI DAIKON NO HARI-HARI ZUKE

Preparation time: 15 minutes,
plus 1 hour soaking time
Pickling time: 1 day
Makes: About 1 lb (450 g)

• 1¾ oz (50 g) dried daikon
(kiriboshi daikon)
• 2 (2-inch/5 cm) square
pieces konbu left over
from making konbu dashi
(or softened konbu)
• Scant ¼ cup (1¾ fl oz/50 ml) sake
• Scant ⅓ cup (2½ fl oz/75 ml)
rice vinegar
• Scant ¼ cup (1¾ fl oz/50 ml)
hon mirin
• Scant 2 tablespoons
(¾ fl oz/25 ml) shoyu
• 1 dried red japones chile

In the wintertime, when daikon is sweet and plentiful, it is cut down into julienne strips for *kiriboshi daikon* and sun-dried naturally, though machine-dried versions are available in the supermarket year-round. In cold areas with a bright winter sun, *kiriboshi daikon* is easy to make at home (see Kiriboshi Daikon, above), but is also sold all over Japan at farm stands. Natural versions of dried daikon are available outside of Japan through macrobiotic sources.
-
In a medium bowl set in the kitchen sink, scrub the dried daikon to remove any drying odors and rinse in several changes of cold water. Soak for 1 hour. (If you are in a hurry, soak with boiling water for 15 minutes.)

Drain, pat dry, and cut crosswise into roughly 2-inch (5 cm) lengths.

Cut the konbu into fine julienne strips and toss with the daikon. Pack into a sterilized glass jar.

In a small saucepan, bring the sake, vinegar, mirin, shoyu, and chile to a simmer over medium heat and immediately pour over the daikon and konbu. Cool to room temperature before screwing on the lid. Store in the refrigerator for 1 day before using. Keeps for several weeks.

SPICY PICKLED KIRIBOSHI DAIKON

なすの一夜漬け OVERNIGHT EGGPLANT PICKLES

NASU NO ICHIYA-ZUKE

Preparation time: 30 minutes,
plus 10 minutes salting time
Pickling time: overnight
Serves: 4

- 2 medium Japanese eggplants
  (aubergines), 7 oz (200 g)
- 2 teaspoons flaky sea salt
- ⅛ head small cabbage
  (4½ oz/125 g), cut into
  1¼-inch (3 cm) squares
- 1 tablespoon slivered
  young ginger, soaked in
  cold water for 10 minutes
- 1 small carrot (1¾ oz/50 g),
  finely julienned
- 1 tablespoon finely slivered
  green shiso

Quick salt pickles are a way of life in Japan. Most likely the mother or grandmother would put them together for the next day while the family was taking their nightly baths. Though mostly a phenomenon of the past, the wife of a farmer or fisherman would be the one whose days started first and ended last.
-
Slice the eggplant into ¼-inch (5 mm) rounds and drop into a medium bowl. Massage ½ teaspoon of the salt into the eggplant and let sit for 10 minutes. In another medium bowl, massage ½ teaspoon of the salt into the cabbage until its natural water comes out. Let sit for 10 minutes as well. Squeeze the eggplant slices and cabbage by small handfuls and drop into a clean bowl. Drain the ginger and blot dry.

Add the carrot to the bowl and massage everything with the remaining 1 teaspoon salt. Add the ginger and shiso and toss to combine. Pack into a 1-gallon (4-liter) resealable freezer bag. Roll up, squeezing out the air as you go, and refrigerate overnight before using. Keeps well for a few days but the vegetables will lose some of their perk as they leach out liquid.

OVERNIGHT EGGPLANT PICKLES

山芋の甘酢漬け

SWEET VINEGAR–PICKLED MOUNTAIN YAM

YAMA IMO NO AMAZU-ZUKE

Preparation time: 15 minutes
Pickling time: 1–2 days
Makes: 7 oz (200 g)

• 8 inches (20 cm) thin mountain yam
(9 oz/250 g), scrubbed
• 4 tablespoons rice vinegar
• 2 tablespoons hon mirin
• ¼ teaspoon flaky sea salt

Mountain yam is often shoyu- or miso-pickled, but here becomes almost like a salad in the slightly sweet vinegar solution. Mountain yam makes particularly satisfying pickles because, in raw form, it has a pleasing crunch that holds up to the pickling process.
-
Peel the mountain yam, rinse, and blot dry. (Wash your hands and forearms with warm sudsy water to prevent itchiness.) Cut the mountain yam crosswise into rounds ½ inch (1 cm) thick. Place in a resealable plastic freezer bag with the vinegar, mirin, and salt. Squeeze out air and roll up. Shake to distribute and store in the refrigerator to pickle for 1–2 days before using. Keeps for about 1 week.

山芋味噌漬け

MISO-PICKLED MOUNTAIN YAM

YAMA IMO MISO-ZUKE

Preparation time: 25 minutes
Pickling time: 1 day
Makes: 10½ ounces (300 g)

• 1 mountain yam (10½ oz/300 g),
3½ inches (9 cm) long and 2¼ inches
(6 cm) wide, scrubbed
• 2 tablespoons hon mirin
• 4 tablespoons brown rice miso
or barley miso

Hearty miso, such as barley or brown rice, imparts depth of flavor to the mild mountain yam. It makes an undeniably delicious pickle to bite into at the end of a meal.
-
Peel, rinse, and blot the mountain yam dry. (Wash your hands and forearms immediately in warm soapy water.) Quarter the mountain yam lengthwise and wrap each quarter in a piece of gauze-like cheesecloth (muslin).

In a small bowl, stir the mirin into the miso. Spread one-third on the bottom of a rectangular refrigerator container just large enough to hold the mountain yam side by side. Place the wrapped mountain yam on top of the miso and spread with the remaining two-thirds of the miso mixture. Place another rectangular container of the same size on top and add a can or two of tomatoes to weight. Refrigerate for 1 day to pickle.

Unwrap and slice the yam into half-moons ½ inch (1 cm) thick. Store in a clean container, wrapped in the cheesecloth, for about 1 week. The mountain yam will exude quite a bit of liquid, so the pickling bed cannot be used for making pickles, but it could be added to broth for a sweetly vegetal miso soup.

SWEET VINEGAR–PICKLED MOUNTAIN YAM; MISO-PICKLED MOUNTAIN YAM

白菜のスピード漬け QUICK PICKLED NAPA CABBAGE

HAKUSAI NO SUPI-DO ZUKE

Preparation time: 40 minutes
Cooking time: 5 minutes
Serves: 4

• 4 large leaves (9 oz/250 g) napa
cabbage (Chinese leaf)
• ½ teaspoon flaky sea salt
• 2 inches (5 cm) small carrot (1¾ oz/
50 g), peeled or scrubbed
• 1¼ inches (3 cm) small daikon
(2⅔ oz/75 g), peeled or scrubbed
• 1 deep-fried tofu pouch
(usuage, see page 352)
• 1 dried shiitake, soaked in boiling
water for 30 minutes
• Scant ⅓ cup (2½ fl oz/75 ml)
rice vinegar
• Scant ¼ cup (1¾ fl oz/50 ml) hon mirin
• ¼ teaspoon fine sea salt
• 1 teaspoon shoyu
• 1 small dried red japones chile,
finely chopped
• 2 teaspoons lightly roasted
gold sesame oil or 1 teaspoon
each dark roasted and unroasted
sesame oil
• 7-spice powder (shichimi togarashi,
see page 350), for serving (optional)

Napa cabbage (Chinese leaf) pickles are probably the easiest and most convenient to have in your repertoire and this version is no exception. The idea is to use the napa cabbage as a base, then add odds and ends of root vegetables such as carrot and/or daikon. The shiitake and usuage can be omitted for a more modern approach, but they ultimately add dimension to the overall dish.

-

Cut the cabbage leaves length-wise into strips 2 inches (5 cm) wide. Stack the pieces and slice into ¼-inch (5 mm) julienne. Massage ¼ teaspoon of the flaky salt in gently and leave for 10 minutes.

Julienne the carrot and daikon and place in two separate bowls. Massage ⅛ teaspoon of the flaky salt into the carrot and the remaining ⅛ teaspoon flaky salt into the daikon and leave for 10 minutes.

Squeeze as much liquid as you can from all of the vegetables, and drop into a medium bowl together. Toss lightly to distribute evenly.

Heat a small dry frying pan over medium-high heat. Add the usuage and sear for about 1 minute on each side to brown slightly. Halve lengthwise and cut crosswise into strips ¼ inch (5 mm) wide. Drop into the bowl of vegetables.

Drain the shiitake and squeeze gently. Cut off the stem and discard or recycle for dashi. Finely slice the cap and add to the bowl of vegetables.

In a small saucepan, heat the vinegar, mirin, fine salt, shoyu, chile, and oil over medium heat until steam rises from the pan and small bubbles form around the perimeter, about 5 minutes. Pour the dressing over all the ingredients in the medium bowl and toss well.

Serve in individual small dishes as a pickle or small salad course. And if anyone desires more heat, sprinkle with shichimi togarashi.

QUICK PICKLED NAPA CABBAGE

たくあん　TAKUAN

Preparation time: 1 hour
Drying time: 1 week
Pickling time: 1 month
Makes: 6 lb 10 oz (3 kg)

• 4 medium daikon with their
leaves (11 lb/5 kg), scrubbed
• 7 oz (200 g) flaky sea salt
• 17½ oz (495 g) rice bran (15% of
the weight of the dried daikon)
• 4 dried red japones chiles,
torn into pieces
• 2 handfuls dried persimmon peels
(from Dried Persimmons,
see right), optional
• Strips of zest peeled off
2 sour oranges or large yuzus

Takuan takes a bit of work, but in the end, the result is far superior to almost any commercially available *takuan*—in or outside of Japan. Most *takuan* not only contains MSG and yellow food coloring but also has not been sun-dried slowly to develop sweetness, nor properly fermented over time. It is important to dry the daikon until it has lost about 40 percent of its weight and the roots are quite flexible. Note: The rice bran is not parched as it is for rice bran pickles (*nukazuke*).
-
Tie the leaves of each of 2 daikons together and drape over a sheltered pole to air-dry in the indirect winter sun for about 1 week until dried down to about 60 percent of their original weight. You want the roots to be quite flexible, but you don't want them to yellow or shrivel (except at the ends).

Lop off the tops of the daikon, so the leaves are connected to a small disk of daikon root; reserve the leaves. Sprinkle a little salt in the bottom of a large crock or plastic pickling tub. Weigh the daikon so you know how much rice bran you need (15 percent of the weight of the daikon.) Add a ¾-inch (2 cm) layer of rice bran to the crock. Coil some daikon into the crock or tub (if need be, cut them into segments), making one layer. Gauging how much salt, rice bran, and aromatics you have, rub the daikon with salt, coil into the crock, and sprinkle each layer with (in this order)

chile, persimmon peel (if using), citrus zest, and rice bran. Before starting the next layer, stuff the dried daikon leaves into any empty spaces to eliminate air pockets where mold can form.

Be generous with the last layer of rice bran. Spread a clean cheesecloth (muslin) across the surface of the rice bran so that the cloth is draping down the sides of the crock. Place a drop lid (*otoshibuta*, see page 354) and a 22-lb (10 kg) weight on top. Cover with newspapers or a large cheesecloth (muslin), tie securely with twine, and leave in a cool, sheltered spot in the garden for 1 month to ferment.

After 1 week has elapsed, check the state of the rice bran. It should now be moist. If it is still dry and powdery, dissolve ¾ teaspoon fine sea salt into ½ cup (4 fl oz/125 ml) water and sprinkle over the top of the bran. Replace the cloth, drop lid, and weights. Cover and leave for 3 weeks, but check periodically if you have concerns. After 1 month, you can start eating the *takuan*. Remove a piece with some of the rice bran mash still clinging to it, and store in the fridge until ready to cut off a portion, wash, and slice into ¼-inch (5 mm) pieces. While the weather remains cold, it is fine to leave the *takuan* in the crock, but you can remove half of the weights, leaving 11 lb (5 kg).

干し柿

DRIED PERSIMMONS

HOSHIGAKI

Preparation time: 1½ hours
Drying time: About 1 month
Makes: 20

• 20 hard Hachiya (tannic) persimmons

It is hard to imagine anything more simple or more exquisite than *hoshigaki*. They are impossible to completely duplicate (though unsulfured apricots make a good substitute) and for some perplexing reason, the ones at the local farm stands are never as good as the ones dried at home. And as such, an excellent argument for taking the time to produce yourself. Although the method typically involves drying tannic persimmons under the eaves, I noticed in Yamanashi that one producer was drying the sweeter, round persimmons (Fuyu) in the direct sunlight. I have made *hoshigaki* successfully with both varieties, so don't give up if you cannot source the Hachiya persimmons. The most important point is that the persimmons need to be ripe, but still hard.

If possible, talk to the farmer before he or she cuts the persimmons off the tree: If the T-shaped stem section remains, your work will be much easier. You can still hang persimmons even if you can only use the calyx for gaining purchase—just use finer twine and poke it under the papery calyx that surrounds the top of the persimmon.
-
Bring a medium pot of water to a boil over high heat. Peel the persimmons but leave the calyx and stems. (Do not discard the peels.) Persimmons have a ½-inch (1 cm) portion of stem that juts out from the calyx to the thin branches of the tree—this enables the heavy fruit to remain attached to the tree during our windy autumn in Japan. Place each persimmon, one at a time, in a small fine-mesh sieve and dip in and out of the boiling water to "pasteurize." Drain immediately on a large, thick towel.

(Spread the persimmon peels out on large baskets and dry in the sun for about a week until the peels are completely dried. Store in resealable plastic bags in a cool, dark place and use in pickling operations, such as Takuan, see left).

If your persimmons still have their T-shaped stem sections, cut five 3-foot (1 meter) lengths of thin hemp rope. Poke the top of the "T" through at intervals of 4 inches (10 cm), alternating poking the stems in on either side of the rope so the persimmons are balanced. You want to get about five on each strand. Hang the top of the rope strands from a nail under the eaves for protection, but in direct sunlight. If you do not have such a spot, just hang in the sun. (Alternatively, if your persimmons no longer have T-shaped stem sections, use a thinner, light fiber twine and cut into 4-foot/1.25 meter lengths. Wrap each end snugly around the calyx of a persimmon, so that two are connected to the ends of one piece of twine and drape the two connected persimmons over the nail.)

Massage—daily if possible to gauge progress—by placing your fingers lengthwise up the fruit, with your palms cupping the bottoms. You are helping gravity elongate the persimmons, if they are round, as well as activating the softening and drying process. After about a month or so, the surface of the *hoshigaki* will be leather-like but not tough, and slightly whitened. Pack them in resealable plastic bags and store in a cool, dry place for a few months or freeze for longer storage. The *hoshigaki* will acquire additional white surface bloom as time goes by (created by the natural sugars exuding out to the surface).

巻き干し柿

ROLLED DRIED PERSIMMONS

MAKI HOSHIGAKI

Preparation time: 15 minutes
Pickling time: 1–2 days
Makes: 6

• 6 dried persimmons
(hoshigaki, see page 350)

Persimmons are harvested in the late autumn, then peeled and hung out to dry in the winter air. Dried persimmons (*hoshigaki*) are chewy, fruity, and unforgettable. Here they are rolled up, left to adhere together, then cut up and served in pretty, spiraled rounds. This might be the most enjoyable way to eat *hoshigaki* since the sticky inside portion is rolled into the dry outside portion, coming together in an extremely satisfying bite.
-
Slice off the tops and cut a vertical slit down the side of each *hoshigaki* and open them up like a book. Pry out any seeds and discard. Place 6 pieces of plastic wrap (cling film) lengthwise across your work surface and set each *hoshigaki* on a piece of wrap with a short side facing you. Roll up the *hoshigaki* and wrap tightly. Leave in a cool spot for 1–2 days to meld together. When ready to serve, unwrap and slice crosswise into 1⁄16-inch (1 mm) rounds. Use in a bento box or serve in a small bowl on the table as a palate refresher for a meal. Keeps for several weeks, if wrapped and uncut.

~~~~~~

にんじんの常備菜

"ALWAYS ON HAND" PICKLED CARROTS

NINJIN NO JOUBISAI

Preparation time: 15 minutes
Cooking time: 3 minutes
Makes: 13¼ ounces (375 g)

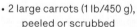

• 2 large carrots (1 lb/450 g),
peeled or scrubbed
• ½ tablespoon unroasted sesame oil
• Scant ½ cup (3½ fl oz/100 ml)
rice vinegar
• ⅓ cup (2¾ fl oz/80 ml) hon mirin
• ¼ teaspoon flaky salt
• 1 teaspoon shoyu
• 1 small dried red japones chile,
cut into fine rings

Stir-frying the carrots briefly before sousing in sweet vinegar gives a longer shelf life to these deliciously appealing quick pickles.
-
Quarter the thick parts of the carrot lengthwise and halve any thinner parts lengthwise. Cut into alternating diagonal, irregular pieces (*rangiri*, see page 17) about ¾ inch (2 cm) long.

In a medium frying pan, heat the oil over medium heat. Add the carrots and stir-fry until fragrant and the surfaces are slightly caramelized, about 3 minutes.

Slide into a sterilized jar large enough that the carrots only fill it to 75 percent. Add the vinegar, mirin, salt, shoyu, and chile. Cover, shake well, and store in the refrigerator as a convenient pickle to have on hand. Keeps for about 2 weeks.

ROLLED DRIED PERSIMMONS

ブロッコリーの茎の味噌漬け

MISO-PICKLED BROCCOLI STEMS

BUROKKORI- NO KUKI NO MISO-ZUKE

Preparation time: 25 minutes
Pickling time: 1–2 days
Makes: 5¼ ounces (150 g)

• 2 thick (2-inch/5 cm)
broccoli stems (6¼ oz/175 g)
• 6 tablespoons soybean miso
• 7-spice powder (shichimi togarashi,
see page 350), for serving

The outer layer of broccoli stems tends to be fibrous, but once pared off, the inner portion is flavorful and nicely textured. Pickling in miso for a couple of days transforms the stems into crunchy, savory bites to serve with drinks or tea. If your broccoli stems are thin (1¼ inches/3 cm), pickle for only 1 day and cut into rounds, rather than half-rounds for serving. For a lighter taste, use brown rice miso or barley miso.

-

Pare off about ⅛ inch (3 mm) around the outside of the stems. Drop the stems into a 1-quart (1-liter) resealable plastic bag and smear the miso around all surfaces of the stems to cover. Roll tightly, squeezing out all the air, and seal. Store in the refrigerator for 1–2 days to pickle.

When ready to use, remove the stems from the miso, scraping off the miso with your fingers. Wipe off any lingering miso from the stems. The miso can be reused once for pickling, for a broccoli-based miso soup with tofu and chopped *negi*, or dolloped into curry rice or *mabodofu* to add depth of flavor.

Cut the stems crosswise into ¾-inch (2 cm) pieces, arrange, cut side down on a cutting board and halve each piece but keep them together for serving. Arrange or stack several paired halves attractively on small individual plates. Sprinkle with *shichimi togarashi* and serve.

~~~~~~

シャキシャキ漬け

CRISPY CABBAGE AND CUCUMBER

SHAKISHAKI-ZUKE

Preparation time: 20 minutes
Serves: 4, generously

• ½ teaspoon flaky sea salt
• 2 medium Japanese cucumbers
(7 oz/200 g), cut into ¼-inch
(5 mm) rounds
• ¼ small head cabbage (9 oz/250 g),
sliced crosswise into thin shreds
• 4 green shiso leaves,
rolled and cut into thin tendrils
• 1 tablespoon unroasted sesame oil
• 1½ teaspoons usukuchi shoyu
(see page 344)

Not really a pickle, nor a salad, this treatment is reminiscent of *namul*, a beloved Korean dish in which raw vegetables or boiled greens are dressed with oil and salt.

-

Massage the salt lightly into the cucumber slices. Squeeze gently and toss with the cabbage, shiso, oil, and *usukuchi shoyu*. Serve as a side dish to a Japanese or Western meal. Keeps well for a few days in the fridge, though the cucumbers will give up some liquid.

MISO-PICKLED BROCCOLI STEMS

甘味

A piece of fruit is all you need at the end of a Japanese meal, but maybe you want something more—a sweet bite, perhaps. In such a case, think naturally sweet or fruit-based, or custards, ice cream, cakes made from buckwheat . . . or soy-based sweets using tofu, soy milk, or *okara* (page 352). It's fine to lean towards Western desserts if you are so inclined, but keep these guidelines in mind and avoid heavy treatments or elaborate creations involving clouds of whipped cream.

Formal Japanese meals traditionally did not include a dessert course. If anything, a perfect piece of seasonal fruit would have been served. Over time, however, Western food culture has influenced the way Japanese eat and that includes how formal menus are constructed.

Desserts served at the end of non-Western meals should be simple and tend toward a vegetal or fruit profile. They should not be overly sweet since the savory dishes often contain mirin or sugar. But for the most part, traditionally prepared sweets are served with tea in the afternoon as a pick-me-up interlude or when guests drop by for an impromptu visit.

Many of the sweets in this chapter are soy-based, so vegan—or can be if vegan whipped cream is substituted. Also feel free to pick up components of one dessert and use them paired with another dessert. Many of the pieces are interchangeable or complementary.

甘味

KANMI
———
SWEET

甘味

苺ババロア

STRAWBERRY RUM BABA

ICHIGO BABA ROA

Preparation time: 15 minutes,
plus 2 hours chilling time
Cooking time: 5 minutes
Makes: 8 small pieces

- 14 oz (400 g) strawberries, hulled
- 2 tablespoons (8 g) agar flakes
- Generous ¾ cup (6¾ fl oz/200 ml) Lightly Whipped Cream (page 37)
- A few sprigs of mint, for garnish

In Japan, greenhouse strawberries are seasonal in the winter, and this seems to have affected the June strawberries. We see fewer strawberries being grown outside, perhaps because of the rain. If possible, make an effort to find those gorgeous late-spring early-summer strawberries grown under the sun. They are exceptional.
-
Drop the strawberries into a blender and process on high speed to smoothly liquefy. Sprinkle in the agar and process on high for 30 seconds more.

Scrape into a small saucepan and stir for about 3 minutes over medium-low heat to completely melt the agar. Remove from the heat and pour into a 5½ × 4½ × 2-inch (14 × 11 × 4.5 cm) *nagashikan* mold (see page 353) or 4⅜ × 8½-inch (11.5 × 21 cm) loaf pan (bottom lined with parchment paper). Refrigerate for at least 2 hours to set.

Once set, cut into 8 pieces and serve on individual small dishes with a dollop of the whipped cream and a pretty sprig of mint.

~~~~~~

苺シャーベット

STRAWBERRY SORBET

ICHIGO SHA-BETTO

Preparation time: 20 minutes,
plus 2 hours chilling time
and 30 minutes churning time
Cooking time: 5 minutes
Makes: 1 quart (32 fl oz/1 liter)

- ⅔ cup (4½ oz/135 g) organic granulated sugar
- 1 basket (12 oz/340 g) small strawberries, hulled

Strawberries lend themselves to icy treatments because they are delicately sweet and don't take heat well. Serve this as a refreshing dessert at the end of a Japanese vegetarian meal. Use the most flavorful early-summer, sun-ripened strawberries you can find.
-
In a small saucepan, bring the sugar and ½ cup (4 fl oz/125 ml) water to a boil over high heat.

Reduce the heat to a brisk simmer and cook for 5 minutes. Cool the syrup to room temperature and refrigerate to chill.

In a food processor or blender, pulse the berries until smoothly puréed. Stir in the chilled syrup and freeze according to the directions on your ice cream maker.

STRAWBERRY RUM BABA

苺ジャム

STRAWBERRY JAM

ICHIGO JYAMU

Preparation time: 20 minutes
Cooking time: 5 minutes
Makes: Generous ¾ cup
(6¾ fl oz/200 ml)

• 10½ oz (300 g) small
  strawberries, hulled
• 2 thin slices lemon
• ½ cup (3½ oz/100 g) organic
  granulated sugar

Strawberry jam adds a stunning bright ruby red note to a dessert plate and can be used to liven up a simple cake or soy milk panna cotta.

-

Slice the strawberries and slide them into a medium saucepan with the lemon slices. Sprinkle with the sugar, massage in gently until the juices run out, and set aside to macerate for 10 minutes.

Place the saucepan over medium-high heat and bring to an active simmer. Cook, smashing the strawberries as they cook, until glossy and the sugar has completely melted, 3–5 minutes.

Sterilize a 1-cup (8 fl oz/250 ml) jar by boiling it and its lid for 1 minute. Fill the jar with the jam, screw on the lid, and turn upside down to cool completely. Store in the refrigerator. Use within a few weeks.

~~~~~~

すいか羹

GELÉED WATERMELON

SUIKA KAN

Preparation time: 30 minutes,
plus 2 hours setting time
Cooking time: 5 minutes
Makes: 8 small pieces

• 1⅔ cups (13½ fl oz/400 ml)
  Watermelon Juice (page 39)
• 2 tablespoons (8 g) agar flakes
• 8 small wedges of green yuzu,
  sudachi, kobosu, or Key lime

These naturally sweet squares are both mild and subtle and a spritz of citrus adds a welcome bit of acid balance. Serve as a palate cleanser during a meal or at the end as a light dessert.

-

Add the juice to a small saucepan and sprinkle with the agar. Leave for 3 minutes to soften.

Set over medium-low heat and bring to an almost simmer, stirring for about 3 minutes to melt the agar completely. Remove from the heat and pour into a 5½ × 4½ × 2-inch (14 × 11 × 4.5 cm) *nagashikan* mold (see page 353) or 4⅜ × 8½-inch (11.5 × 21 cm) loaf pan (bottom lined with parchment paper). Let cool to room temperature, then refrigerate for at least 2 hours to set.

Cut into 8 pieces and serve each with a small wedge of citrus.

GELÉED WATERMELON

かぼちゃと枝豆の二層羹

KABOCHA AND EDAMAME SQUARES

KABOCHA TO EDAMAME NO NISOUKAN

Preparation time: 30 minutes, plus 1 hour 15 minutes cooling time and 5 hours chilling time
Cooking time: 30 minutes
Makes: 12 small pieces

- 3½ oz (100 g) kabocha (see page 347)
- 3 tablespoons (6 g) agar flakes
- ½ cup (3½ oz/100 g) organic granulated sugar
- 7 oz (200 g) edamame pods

Sweetly vegetal, make this cooling dessert in the summer when kabocha and edamame are harvested.

-

Peel the kabocha well, so no green color remains, and cut into 2-inch (5 cm) chunks. Place in a small saucepan and add cold water to cover. Bring to a boil and cook at a brisk simmer until very soft, 8–10 minutes. Drain in a wire-mesh sieve.

Transfer the kabocha to a processor or blender, add a generous ¾ cup (6¾ fl oz/ 200 ml) water, 1½ tablespoons of the agar flakes, and ¼ cup (1¾ oz/50 g) of the sugar and process until well blended.

Pour into a small saucepan and cook over medium-low heat, stirring continuously for 5 minutes, to melt the sugar and agar. The mixture will want to simmer, but do not let it. Adjust the heat or pick up the pan and hold above the heat, stirring, until 5 full minutes have elapsed. Pour into a 6 × 5½ × 2-inch (15 × 14 × 4.5 cm) *nagashikan* mold (see page 353) or two 4⅜ × 8½-inch (11.5 × 21 cm) loaf pans (bottoms lined with parchment paper). Cool to room temperature, then refrigerate for 2 hours to set.

Bring a medium saucepan of water to a boil over high heat and drop in the edamame. Cook until very soft, about 15 minutes. Drain. When cool enough to handle, pop the beans out of the pods, then peel the skins from each bean. Add the peeled beans to a food processor or blender with the remaining 1½ tablespoons agar flakes, ¼ cup (1¾ oz/50 g) sugar, and a generous ¾ cup (6¾ fl oz/ 200 ml) water. Process well until completely smooth.

In a small saucepan, cook the edamame mixture over medium-low heat, stirring continuously for 5 minutes, but do not let the mixture simmer. Cool for 15 minutes, then pour over the chilled kabocha to form a second, distinct layer, and refrigerate for at least 3 more hours to set.

Cut into 12 small pieces and serve one or two per person on small saucers. Keeps for several days in the refrigerator, if well sealed.

KABOCHA AND EDAMAME SQUARES

りんごのおとし揚げ

DEEP-FRIED APPLE AND RAISIN FRITTERS

RINGO NO OTOSHI-AGE

Preparation time: 15 minutes
Cooking time: 5 minutes
Makes: 12 small fritters

• 1 medium apple (9 oz/250 g), peeled and cored
• 3 tablespoons unbleached cake flour
• 1 tablespoon potato starch
• Pinch of fine sea salt
• 2 teaspoons sake
• 2 tablespoons raisins
• Neutral oil, such as canola (rapeseed), safflower, or peanut, for deep-frying

Japanese vegetarian desserts rely mostly on natural sweetness rather than sugar, and apples and raisins pair up nicely for dessert-like dishes such as these fritters.
-
Cut the apple into roughly ½-inch (1 cm) cubes.

In a medium bowl, whisk the flour, potato starch, and salt together. Stir in 2 tablespoons plus 2 teaspoons water and the sake to make a batter. Fold in the apple cubes and raisins.

In a large high-sided sauté pan, heat 1¼ inches (3 cm) oil over medium heat until about 340°F (170°C). To check the oil temperature, flick a few drops of batter into the oil. The batter should sink to the bottom of the pan, then immediately bounce back up to the surface, and there will be a few medium-sized bubbles.

Frying in 2 batches, drop soup spoonfuls of the apple-raisin batter into the oil, taking care it does not overflow. Cook, turning occasionally with chopsticks, until the bubbles have quieted and the fritters are lightly golden, about 2 minutes. Drain on a rack set over a pan to catch the drips.

Serve hot at the end of a light meal.

りんごの葛湯

WARM APPLE CUPS

RINGO NO KUZU-YU

Preparation time: 15 minutes
Cooking time: 15 minutes
Serves: 4, generously

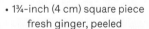

• 1¾-inch (4 cm) square piece fresh ginger, peeled
• 1 sweet medium apple (9 oz/250 g)
• ½ cup (3½ oz/100 g) organic granulated sugar
• 2 tablespoons hon kuzu (see page 352) mixed with 6 tablespoons water until smooth
• 4 lengthwise slivers of cinnamon stick

Since dessert is not really part of a traditional Japanese meal, fruit-based dishes work well if you want to serve something sweet. The ginger and cinnamon lend a subtle aromatic element to this light yet warming final bite.
-
Finely slice the ginger and cinch into a bundle in a piece of cheesecloth (muslin). Tie securely.

Peel and core the apple and cut into ½-inch (1 cm) cubes. Place in a small saucepan with 4 tablespoons of the sugar. Warm over low heat to melt the sugar. Once the sugar and apple liquids start to simmer, increase the heat to medium-low and cook, stirring with a flat wooden spoon, for 3 minutes. Add 3⅓ cups (26½ fl oz/800 ml) water, the remaining sugar, and the bundle of ginger, and bring to a simmer over medium heat. Remove from the heat and scrape in the *kuzu* slurry. Return to medium-low heat and cook, stirring continuously, until thickened, about 7 minutes.

Remove the ginger bundle and discard. Ladle into four glass dessert cups, add a piece of cinnamon in each as a "stirrer," and serve with a small spoon. (Alternatively, skip the stick and pinch in a small amount of freshly grated cinnamon.) This keeps well, if stored in the fridge, but reheat for serving.

WARM APPLE CUPS

おからパウンドケーキ

OKARA AND CHESTNUT POUND CAKE WITH TOFU "YOGURT"

OKARA PAUNDO KE-KI

Preparation time: 30 minutes,
plus 2 hours tofu weighting time
Cooking time: 20 minutes
Serves: 8

• 2½ oz (75 g) silken tofu
(kinugoshi dofu, see page 352)
• Canola (rapeseed) oil, for the pans
• ½ cup (4 fl oz/125 ml) soy milk
• 5 tablespoons organic
granulated sugar
• ½ cup (2¼ oz/60 g)
all-purpose (plain) flour, whisked
• 1½ teaspoons baking powder
• 1½ tablespoons Japanese
egoma oil (see page 345) or
unroasted gold sesame oil
• 5¼ oz (150 g) okara (see page 352)
• 3½ oz (100 g) Sweet-Simmered
Chestnuts (page 334), coarsely chopped
• 1 teaspoon fresh lemon juice
• ⅛ teaspoon apple cider vinegar

Okara is the pulp left over from making soy milk. It has a short shelf life and is sold very cheaply or given away by tofu shops in Japan. Typically, *okara* is used in a stir-fry dish called *unohana* but can also be made into a cake. The chestnuts give this an almost custard-like texture and an additional gentle sweetness, and the tofu "yogurt" makes a lovely nondairy topping.
-
Weight the tofu for 2 hours in the fridge to press out liquid.

Meanwhile, rub a little canola (rapeseed) oil on the inside surfaces of two 3⅛ × 5½-inch (8 × 14 cm) mini loaf pans and line the bottoms with parchment paper.

Position a rack in the center of the oven and preheat the oven to 350°F (180°C).

In a medium bowl, mix the soy milk, 3 tablespoons of the sugar, the flour, baking powder, and *egoma* oil together. Fold in the *okara* and chestnuts. Scrape into the prepared pans and smooth down the tops.

Transfer to the oven and bake until golden, about 20 minutes. Set the pans on a rack and cool until room temperature.

In a medium bowl, beat the tofu, lemon juice, remaining sugar, and vinegar with a wooden spoon until smooth to make tofu "yogurt."

Remove the cakes from the pans and cut each loaf into 8 slices. Serve 2 slices per person with a dollop of the tofu "yogurt" on top.

~~~~~~

蕎麦パウンド

SOBA POUND CAKE

SOBA PAUNDO

Preparation time: 15 minutes
Cooking time: 30 minutes
Makes: Two 3⅛ × 4½-inch (8 × 14 cm)
mini loaves

• Oil and flour, for the pans
• 1 cup (7 oz/200 g) organic
granulated sugar
• 3 eggs, at room temperature
• 5 tablespoons plus 2 teaspoons
grapeseed oil
• 1⅓ cups (5½ oz/160 g)
Japanese buckwheat flour
(sobako, see page 353)

Pound cake is quite dense, but if you whip the eggs and cream until they are frothy, the resulting texture is lighter—almost like a sponge cake. Substitute French or "light" buckwheat flour if you cannot find the Japanese.
-
Position a rack in the center of the oven and preheat the oven to 345°F (175°C). Rub the bottom and sides of two 3⅛ × 4½-inch (8 × 14 cm) mini loaf pans lightly with oil and dust with flour.

In a bowl, beat the sugar and eggs together with an electric mixer until lightly frothy. Add the oil and ⅓ cup (2¾ fl oz/80 ml) water and beat until emulsified.

Beat in the soba flour until incorporated and the batter is smooth. Scrape into the pans. Transfer to the oven and bake for 20 minutes. Increase the temperature to 350°F (180°C) and bake until nicely browned, about 10 minutes longer.

Let the cakes cool in the pans on a rack for 5 minutes, then carefully invert out of the pans onto the rack to cool to room temperature. Cut each cake into 6 slices and serve 1 or 2 slices per person. Once cooled, wrap well in plastic wrap (cling film) and store at room temperature in a resealable plastic bag. Eat within 2 or 3 days.

おからと小豆のパウンドケーキ

OKARA AND AZUKI POUND CAKE

OKARA TO AZUKI NO PAUNDO KE-KI

Preparation time: 15 minutes
Cooking time: 30 minutes
Makes: 1 small loaf

- Canola (rapeseed) oil, for the pan
- Scant ½ cup (2¼ oz/60 g) cake flour
- 6 tablespoons organic granulated sugar
- 1 teaspoon baking powder
- ¼ teaspoon fine sea salt
- Scant ½ cup (3½ fl oz/100 ml) soy milk
- 1 tablespoon plus 1 teaspoon canola (rapeseed) oil
- 5¼ oz (150 g) okara (see page 352)
- Scant ½ cup (3½ oz/100 g) Simmered Azuki Beans (page 32)
- Lightly Whipped Cream (page 37) or Vegan Whipped Cream (page 38), optional

Ovens were not standard in Japanese kitchens until after 2000, and most cakes or flour-based confections were cooked in a steamer. Pound cake was no exception, though today it is cooked in an oven. Nonetheless, many versions of pound cake exist because of its long history in Japan. During World War II, pound cake was often prepared with naturally sweet vegetables such as sweet potato, since sugar was scarce. Here the azuki beans lend a juicy sweetness to this cake and *okara*, the pulp by-product of the soy milk–making process, adds a moist, dense texture.

-

Position a rack in the center of the oven and preheat the oven to 350°F (180°C). Lightly oil a 3⅛ × 5 ½-inch (8 × 14 cm) mini loaf pan.

In a medium bowl, whisk the flour to lighten. Add the sugar, baking powder, and salt and whisk to incorporate evenly. Whisk in the soy milk and oil until well emulsified. Fold in the *okara* and azuki with a rubber spatula, until well combined. Smooth the batter into the pan, wipe the inner edges clean, and rap smartly against your workspace to settle the batter and eliminate any air bubbles.

Transfer to the oven and bake until golden brown, about 30 minutes. Let cool for 5 minutes in the pan, then turn out onto a rack to cool to room temperature before slicing and serving. Serve as is or with whipped cream.

渋皮煮

ASTRINGENT SKIN–SIMMERED CHESTNUTS

SHIBUKAWA-NI

Preparation time: 10 minutes
Cooking time: 45 minutes
Makes: 20

- 20 Shelled Whole Chestnuts (page 35), (10½ oz/300 g)
- ½ tablespoon baking soda
- ½ cup (3½ oz/100 g) Japanese refined light brown sugar (sanonto, see page 339) or organic granulated sugar
- ¼ teaspoon flaky sea salt
- ¼ cup (1¾ oz/50 g) Japanese black sugar (kurozato, see page 339)
- ½ teaspoon shoyu
- ½ tablespoon hon mirin

Bitterness is a well-appreciated flavor in Japanese cuisine and chestnuts boiled in their astringent skin are a classic preparation that reflects this appreciation. The bitterness is softened by multiple changes of water and reboilings. Serve these to complement other simple desserts such as Soy Milk Custard with Black Sugar Syrup (page 336).

-

Place the chestnuts (with their astringent skins intact) in a large saucepan with the baking soda and add cold water to cover generously. Bring to a boil over high heat, taking care not to boil over, and cook for 10 minutes, skimming off the scum that forms on the surface of the water. Drain, return the chestnuts to the pan, add fresh cold water to cover and bring to a boil over high heat. Cook 10 minutes, then drain. Repeat this step one more time for a total of three boilings.

Drain, add water to cover generously (the chestnuts need room to "dance" in the water), and stir in the light brown sugar and salt. Bring to a boil over high heat, reduce to a simmer, and cook for 10 minutes. Add the black sugar and shoyu and simmer for 5 more minutes. Stir in the mirin and allow to cool in the cooking liquid. These keep for about 2 weeks or more if refrigerated.

栗の甘露煮

SWEET-SIMMERED CHESTNUTS

KURI NO KANRO-NI

Preparation time: 1 hour, plus
30 minutes soaking time, 1 hour cooling
time, and 4 hours steeping time
Cooking time: 30 minutes
Makes: 20

- 20 Shelled Whole Chestnuts
  (page 35), (10½ oz/300 g)
- 1 small dried gardenia fruit pod
  (kuchinashi, see page 350),
  halved (optional)
- ½ cup (3½ oz/100 g) Japanese
  refined light brown sugar
  (sanonto, see page 339) or
  organic granulated sugar

Use these sweet chestnuts to garnish desserts or to punctuate a full meal as a rich bite to juxtapose beautifully against savory dishes. The *kuchinashi* (gardenia fruit pod) is primarily to lend color, so if you cannot source, omit. Also, if your chestnuts break apart in the cooking process, do not lose heart, they will still be delicious.
-
Working with one at a time, hold a chestnut in your nondominant hand and, starting from the butt of the chestnut, peel off the papery brown astringent skins with a sharp knife. Drop into a bowl of cold water to soak for 30 minutes or so. Drain.

In a medium saucepan, combine the chestnuts, *kuchinashi* (if using), and cold water to cover generously. Set a drop lid (*otoshibuta*, see page 354) on top and bring to a boil over high heat. Reduce to a brisk, but not overly wild, simmer and cook for 10 minutes. Remove from the heat and cool to room temperature.

In another medium saucepan, stir the sugar and a generous ¾ cup (6¾ fl oz/200 ml) water together over low heat. Once the sugar has dissolved, skim the chestnuts out of their cooking liquid and rinse under cold water. Gently lower into the syrup in the saucepan and bring to an almost simmer over medium heat. Adjust to a simmer and cook for 10 minutes. Remove from the heat and leave at room temperature for about 4 hours. Pack in sterilized jars. Stored in the refrigerator, the chestnuts keep for a few weeks. It is also possible to freeze the chestnuts, but they will lose some of their characteristic firm, yet soft texture.

かぼすとハーブのグラニタ

KABOSU AND APPLE MINT GRANITA

KABOSU TO HA-BU NO GURANITA

Preparation time: 15 minutes,
plus 20 minutes cooling time and
3 hours freezing time
Cooking time: 5 minutes
Serves: 4

- 3 tablespoons organic
  granulated sugar
  (4 tablespoons, if using lime)
- 1 small stalk lemongrass
- 4 large kabosu or round limes
- ½ teaspoon finely chopped
  apple mint leaves plus
  4 pretty sprigs, for garnish

Kabosu is a green Japanese citrus with a profile similar to lime. It is sweet and round, with beautifully floral citrus notes. Lime can be substituted, but you will need to add sugar to compensate for their tartness. This granita makes an elegant, yet tart palate cleanser.
-
Place a stainless steel medium bowl or rectangular container in the freezer.

In a medium saucepan, bring a generous ¾ cup (6¾ fl oz/ 200 ml) water, the sugar, and the lemongrass to a simmer over medium heat. Remove from the heat and let cool to room temperature. Strain the syrup into a bowl.

Juice the *kabosu* and strain through a fine-mesh sieve. You should have a generous ¾ cup (6¾ fl oz/200 ml) juice. Stir the juice and finely chopped apple mint into the cooled strained sugar syrup and add to the bowl in the freezer. Freeze for 1 hour.

Take out of the freezer to dislodge and stir in the crystals that have formed around the perimeter with a fork. Return to the freezer for 30 minutes before removing to stir in the crystals. Repeat 3 or 4 times until no liquid remains, only flaky ice crystals.

Scoop into pretty dessert coupes or bowls, garnish each with a sprig of apple mint and serve as a light dessert.

KABOSU AND APPLE MINT GRANITA

生姜豆乳グラニタ

GINGER-SOY MILK GRANITA

SHOUGA TOUNYUU GURANITA

Preparation time: 15 minutes,
plus 3 hours freezing time
Cooking time: 7 minutes
Serves: 4

• ½ cup (3½ oz/100 g) organic
granulated sugar
• 2-inch (5 cm) piece fresh ginger,
peeled and thinly sliced crosswise
• 1⅔ cups (13½ fl oz/400 ml) soy milk
• Mint leaves, for garnish

The addition of soy milk in this unusual milky granita lends body and richness to a normally spare, but nonetheless refreshing bite.
-
In a small saucepan, stir together the sugar and scant ½ cup (3½ fl oz/100 ml) water over low heat, to dissolve. Scrape in the ginger and cook gently for 5 minutes to flavor. Strain into a rectangular container large enough to hold 3⅓ cups (26½ fl oz/800 ml) and discard the ginger. Cool the syrup to room temperature. Once cool, stir in the soy milk and place, uncovered, in the freezer for 1 hour.

Remove from the freezer and stir the frozen perimeter into the wetter center with a fork. Repeat every 30 minutes for a total of about 2 hours more.

Mound into small glass coupes, garnish with mint, and serve as a light dessert.

GINGER GRANITA: In a medium saucepan, stir 3 quarts (3 liters) water into 3 cups (1⅓ lb/600 g) organic granulated sugar. Heat, stirring over high heat until the sugar has completely dissolved. Cool to room temperature, then add scant ⅔ cup (5¼ fl oz/150 ml) freshly squeezed ginger juice. Freeze, following the method for Ginger–Soy Milk Granita. Serve with a small squeeze of fresh lime and a sprig of mint.

黒蜜豆乳プリン

SOY MILK CUSTARD WITH BLACK SUGAR SYRUP

KUROMITSU TOUNYUU PURIN

Preparation time: 10 minutes
Cooking time: 12 minutes
Serves: 4

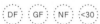

• 4 tablespoons hon kuzu
(see page 352)
• 3 cups (24 fl oz/700 ml) soy milk
• 1½ tablespoons (¾ oz/20 g)
Japanese black sugar (kurozato,
see page 339), well crushed
• 3 tablespoons (1½ oz/40 g)
Japanese refined light brown
sugar (sanonto, see page 345) or
organic granulated sugar
• Sweet-Simmered Black Beans
(page 33), for garnish (optional)

Japanese black sugar (kurozato) is dark and full of iron and minerals—a bit like crystalized molasses. If you cannot find Japanese kurozato, look for the darkest brown sugar available as a substitute. The soy milk is unsweetened so creates an interesting interplay against the black sugar syrup. And the kuzu powder in this custard contributes a lovely silkiness.
-
Add the kuzu powder to a medium saucepan and slowly stir in the soy milk. Heat, stirring, over low heat for 10 minutes until thickened and custard-like. Spoon into four attractive glass or ceramic handleless cups (chawan, see page 354) and allow to cool from hot to warm.

In a small saucepan, combine both sugars and stir 2½ tablespoons water into them. Set over low heat, stirring, to melt. Pour the syrup over the custard in the cups and top with simmered black beans, if using.

SOY MILK CUSTARD WITH BLACK SUGAR SYRUP

JAPANESE SUGAR

There are several types of sugar used in Japanese cuisine—most only slightly different than their Western counterparts. But two are truly native to Japan: *wasanbon* (fine artisanal sugar) and *kurozato* (black sugar), also known as *kokuto*. That said, I tend to use mirin when introducing sweet notes to Japanese dishes, and if using sugar, will usually turn to Brazilian organic cane sugar (locally sourced).

Wasanbon is a soft, ultrafine white or pale-colored sugar used in traditional Japanese sweets. It was developed in the Edo period (1603–1868) as a response to an implicit request for increased sugar production by the eighth shogun of the period, Yoshimune Tokugawa. At that time, sugar was only produced in Okinawa and Amami Oshima, the southernmost islands of Japan, and leaking the secrets of their sugar manufacturing methods was strictly forbidden. On the mainland of southern Japan, strife and hardships interfered with access to high quality sugarcane seeds, and it is said that the crucial seeds for initiating sugarcane cultivation on the mainland were smuggled off the island of Amami Oshima in a bento box. Sugarcane cultivation was eventually successful and spread throughout southwestern Japan (Satsuma, Kii, Sanuki, Awa, Izumi, Suruga, Totomi, Mikawa, etc.). Climate and terrain, however, impeded production of good-quality *kurozato* (black sugar) on Honshu, the mainland of Japan. As a result, a method for removing molasses was devised and *wasanbon* was born—warmly sweet with unique characteristics, it was completely unlike previous sugars.

Wasanbon begins with growing sugarcane, and the center for this limited production is in Kagawa Prefecture. After harvesting the cane before the first frost in December, it takes about one month to make *wasanbon*. First the sugarcane must be carefully ground up in a special grinding "car," before pressing out most of the liquid (it is essential not to press out too zealously because this will introduce sugarcane pulp into the liquid). At this point, the sugarcane juice is boiled in cauldrons until the impurities contained in the juice rise to the surface and are then skimmed off. Thorough removal of impurities is a testament to the skill of the craftsman. Next the sugar syrup is transferred to unglazed stoneware jars where it is left to crystallize. To remove molasses, the large sugar crystals are wrapped in cotton and hemp, placed in a weighting boat (*oshi-bune*) and pressed with heavy stones, of 110 pounds (50 kg) each, that have been passed down from generation to generation. As the weighting process continues over the course of a day and a night, four or five more stones may be added to increase pressure and encourage removal of molasses. The resulting sugar crystals are then ground, rewrapped, and reweighted for a total of five times. During the weighting process, fermentation progresses through naturally forming yeasts. Finally, the sugar is dried completely and packaged as is or pressed into wooden forms to create seasonal shapes. It is only through following these time-consuming, centuries-old methods that high-quality, traditional *wasanbon* can be made.

Kurozato/kokuto (black sugar) was introduced to Japan during the Genroku period (1688–1704), an era characterized by economic expansion and rapid growth of urban centers such as Edo (modernday Tokyo), Kyoto, and Osaka. It has been produced in the southernmost islands of Japan (primarily Okinawa and Amami Oshima) since the Edo period and, in Okinawa, it is called life medicine (*nuchi-gusui*, a colloquial form of *inochi gusuri*, which means "medicine for life" and "medicine for longevity"). Sugar's original use was as medicine, and if you taste artisanal black sugar from Okinawa (such as the one carried by The Japanese Pantry, see Resources, page 355) you will truly understand the concept of *nuchi-gusui*: Food that is effective enough to be a medicine.

Kurozato is made by boiling down sugarcane juice, and since unrefined, contains a lot of minerals. (White sugars are refined, so most minerals are removed during that process.) *Kurozato* consists of dark brownish-black lumps with a sugar content of 80–86 percent and is rich in calcium, iron, and various essential vitamins.

It was in the town of Edo (Tokyo) that sugar began being used for seasoning savory foods, not just sweets. Common sense presumes that people discovered that sugar enhanced the rich, dark soy sauce being made in the nearby areas of Noda and Choshi. Eventually, this practice shaped the profile of the cuisine of Kanto (Eastern Japan), as opposed to the light soy sauce and umami-rich, naturally sweet konbu used in the Kansai (Western Japan) surrounding Kyoto and Osaka.

Sugar itself was developed initially in India around the fourth century BCE, and cultivation of sugarcane in India was reported by an expedition with Alexander the Great (356–323 BCE). The soldiers were captivated by the "hard honey that was not made by bees." By the fifth century AD, sugarcane cultivation and sugar production methods were transported to neighboring countries such as Persia and Egypt, and eventually to China in the sixth century. Sugar production also spread rapidly through Islamic hands as their influences expanded throughout the Mediterranean regions. Christian crusaders brought sugarcane back from their expeditions during the eleventh through thirteenth centuries, further spreading sugarcane cultivation around the world. In the fifteenth century, Christopher Columbus transplanted sugarcane from the Mediterranean islands to the West Indies. By the sixteenth century, a global sugar trade was firmly in place and sugar had become an essential commodity.

Sugar was transmitted to Japan in the Nara period (710–794) from China and was first used as a precious medicine. By the Muromachi period (1336–1573), sugar had become more accessible, and the aristocracy and samurai enjoyed it as tea confections (*ocha gashi*) to accompany the tea ceremony or as gelled sweets (*yokan*) or steamed buns (*manju*). No longer strictly a luxury item, Japanese sweets using sugar were developed. Western-style cakes such as *castella* (inspired by similar Portuguese cakes) were developed and popularized during the mid-sixteenth century as a result of foreign (*nanban*) trade. As the *nanban* trade flourished, sugar trading also prospered and grew until the beginning of isolationism in 1614 in the early Edo period (1603–1868).

Yoshimune Tokugawa, the eighth shogun of the Tokugawa Shogunate that ruled during the Edo period, took measures to encourage domestic sugar production during the era of isolation, and the sugar industry spread throughout the country. Previously, sugar had been extremely dear. Imported in small quantities from China, sugar was used primarily for medicinal purposes, but also prized as a sweetener by the aristocracy. After the fall of the Tokugawa Shogunate and the end of isolationism, modern sugar manufacturing technology arrived from overseas and sugar finally spread to the general public in the Meiji period (1868–1912). Known as the Meiji Restoration, the Meiji era brought reforms that influenced major political, economic, and social change in Japan.

With the dramatic increase of sugar imports during Meiji came the devastation of the domestic sugar industry. With the exception of Okinawa and Amami Oshima, the small Japanese sugar industry was virtually destroyed. Large, mechanized factories were built overseas to process sugarcane into raw sugar and, conversely, modern sugar refining factories were built in Japan. Thus, Japan's sugar industry as we know it was established.

Raw sugar was shipped to Japan for refining until the Pacific War broke out and transporting became too difficult. As a result, Japan experienced severe sugar shortages. Strict rationing of sugar continued throughout World War II and until 1952. Due to the scarcity of sugar, sweetness became a longed-for and highly valued taste that still lingers in Japan today—especially among the older population.

Sugar is a source of sweetness to add a richer depth to savory foods, but depending on the type, lends different properties to dishes.

Johakuto (refined white cane sugar): The most common sugar used in Japanese households. *Johakuto* is a fine, slightly damp sugar and is 99 percent sucrose. It melts easily and has a pronounced sweetness but has no other intrinsic flavor characteristics.

Guranyu-to (granulated sugar): Used for sweetening beverages such as black tea, coffee, or cocktails.

Korizato (rock sugar): Large crystals of pure sugar that are good for steeped fruit liquors such as *umeshu*.

Kurozato/kokuto (black sugar): Rich in minerals such as potassium, iron, and zinc. The flavor profile is pronounced, but the sweetness is soft. Some would liken the relationship of white sugar to black

sugar much as one would white rice to brown rice. Black sugar is used for traditional country sweets such as *karinto* (a crispy cracker-like baked sweet) and when boiled with water, becomes the prized *kuromitsu* (black sugar syrup) that is often served with Japanese confections.

Sanonto (refined light brown sugar): Preferred for sweet shoyu-simmered dishes, such as *tsukudani* as well as lighter simmered dishes.

Kibizato (light brown cane sugar): Used when a more pronounced flavor with minerality is desired.

Zarame (coarse light brown sugar): Favored in pickling or added to azuki beans when simmering down to make sweet red bean paste (*anko*).

Wasanbon (artisanal Japanese sugar): Powdery, pale-colored or white native Japanese sugar produced in the southern islands, particularly Shikoku; most commonly used for high-level Japanese confectionery.

Originally prized as a rare medicine or luxury item, sugar is now an integral component in Japanese cuisine and daily life. Used in moderation, sugar can enhance other ingredients such as shoyu, miso, and rice vinegar when preparing Japanese food.

豆腐ケーキ

TOFU CAKE

TOUFU KE-KI

Preparation time: 25 minutes,
plus 4 hours chilling time
Cooking time: 10 minutes
Makes: 12 small pieces

• 10½ oz (300 g) silken tofu
(kinugoshi dofu, see page 352)
• 1 cup (8 fl oz/250 ml) plain yogurt
• ¼ teaspoon fine sea salt
• 2 tablespoons (8 g) agar flakes
• Generous ¾ cup (6¾ fl oz/200 ml)
Strawberry Jam (page 326)

Top-quality tofu is an exceptional
addition to desserts—rendering
them at once creamy and healthy.
-
In a food processor or blender,
pulse the tofu, yogurt, salt, and
agar to just emulsify—you don't
want to create too much foam.
Scrape into a medium saucepan,
and once any foam has subsided,
cook over low heat, without
simmering, for about 7 minutes,
stirring constantly.

Smooth the mixture into a
6 × 5½ × 2-inch (15 × 14 × 4.5 cm)
nagashikan mold (see page 353)
or two 4⅜ × 8½-inch (11½ × 21 cm)
loaf pans (lined with parchment
paper). Refrigerate for about
4 hours, until chilled and set.

Unmold carefully by running
a sharp knife around the outside
of the cake. Cut into 12 pieces,
top with a dollop of jam, and
serve with tea in the afternoon,
or at the end of a Japanese meal.

焼き蕎麦がきのみたらし団子

GRILLED SOBA GAKI WITH SWEET SOY SAUCE GLAZE

YAKI SOBA GAKI NO MITARASHI DANGO

Preparation time: 30 minutes
Cooking time: 15 minutes
Serves: 4

• 6 tablespoons organic sugar
• 4 tablespoons hon mirin
• 4 tablespoons shoyu
• 1 cup (4¼ oz/120 g) Japanese
buckwheat flour (sobako, see page 353)
• Boiling water
• 2 tablespoons potato starch

Soba gaki is similar to polenta, in
that it requires constant, vigorous
stirring. Though unlike polenta,
soba gaki hardens up almost
immediately after cooking, so
it's difficult to handle in large
quantities. Here it is formed into
dango balls, usually made from
glutinous rice flour, however the
texture and flavor of the soba
flour (sobako) gives these more
substance and depth. Substitute
French or "light" buckwheat flour
if you cannot source sobako.
-
Soak four 6-inch (15 cm) bamboo
skewers in water for 30 minutes.

In a small saucepan, stir the
sugar, mirin, and shoyu together
over medium heat. Once the
mixture reaches a simmer,
continue stirring for 1 minute to
allow the sugar to melt and the
mirin to burn off alcohol. Remove
from the heat and transfer the
sauce to a small bowl to cool.

Fill the bottom of a double boiler
halfway with water and bring to
a boil over high heat. Add the soba

flour to the top of the double
boiler and stir continuously
with a wooden spoon until hot
to the touch, about 5 minutes.
Remove the top of the double
boiler and add a generous ¾ cup
(6¼ fl oz/185 ml) boiling water.
Stir vigorously to incorporate
the flour into the water until
smooth. Roll into 12 small smooth
balls (dango).

In a small bowl, stir a generous
¾ cup (6¾ fl oz/200 ml) water
into the potato starch. Roll each
dango in the potato starch slurry
and thread three dango on each
skewer so that they go about
halfway onto the skewer and are
nudged up close to the tip end.

Prepare low ember charcoal
in a Japanese brazier (shichirin,
see page 354). Grill the dango,
turning once or twice, until lightly
speckled brown on all sides.
(Alternatively, grill the dango
using an oven broiler/grill.)

Place each skewer on a plate,
brush with the sauce and serve.

TOFU CAKE

GLOSSARY

~~~~~~

INGREDIENTS

SALTS

MISO (fermented soybean paste): In Japan, miso is made by fermenting steamed soybeans with koji-inoculated grains and salt. Koji (*Aspergillus orzyae*) is a spore used in fermenting Japanese traditional foods and drinks such as miso, shoyu, sake, *shochu*, and mirin. *Inaka* (country-style), *mugi* (barley), *genmai* (brown rice), and *mame* (soybean) miso are the most common misos in Japan besides the barely fermented, koji-prevalent white (*shiro*) miso. *Inaka* miso is often, but not always, made from white rice koji and is therefore slightly lighter in color than barley or brown rice miso (both a lovely, burnt ember–hued brown). Soybean miso (called Hatcho miso, if made in the area around Nagoya in Aichi prefecture following a specific ancient method) is deep, dark brown, almost black—though inexplicably called "red miso." Note: Due to misinformation and mislabeling in the initial export process, "red miso" has come to refer to almost all misos except white miso (or yellow miso, which I have never come across in Japan), including the lighter brown misos: *inaka*, *mugi*, *genmai*. Unfortunately, this is incorrect. The miso that I recommend wholeheartedly and without reservation is from Yamaki Jozo in Kamikawa-machi, Saitama prefecture. The excellent white miso I use is from Katayama Shoten in Kameoka-shi of Kyoto prefecture. In the United States, I recommend Aedan in San Francisco, Jorinji in Oregon, and South River in Massachusetts. Beware any miso-maker who claims to be harnessing koji spores from the air—this is barely possible even in Japan. I know of only one sake brewer, Terada Honke in Chiba, who has managed this feat and they have a 300-plus-year-old brewery where the spores live in the walls.

SHIO (salt): Japanese sea salt has been in a state of resurgence and renaissance since the end of the government salt monopoly in 1997. My favorite salt is Wajima no Kaien—it is very similar to the best *flore di sale* found in Trapani, Italy. Noto Salt is virtually identical and also highly recommended. Equally excellent, Nami No Hana salt made in Shodoshima has a finer grain and is extracted by slowly heating concentrated sea water over a wood-burning fire. Note: *Moshio* is a salt produced in the southern islands by boiling seawater with large bags of dried *hondawara* seaweed. The modern version of *moshio* is not extracted from the seaweed itself nor has it been for a few millennia.

SHIRO SHOYU (white soy sauce): This specialized, mainly restaurant-used "shoyu" fermented from koji-inoculated wheat, salt, and water, represents a tiny fraction of the shoyu market in Japan, though is found abroad. Caveat: Much of the *shiro shoyu* I have seen in foreign restaurant kitchens is of poor quality and contains various additives.

SHOYU (soy sauce): Technically, *koikuchi shoyu*, known colloquially as "shoyu," this is the everyday soy sauce made famous by Kikkoman, though nowadays, artisanal versions are readily available outside of Japan. I highly recommend Yamaki Jozo organic, Japanese bean shoyu bottled in Japan or rebottled by Ohsawa and sold as "Nama Shoyu." All other Japanese organic shoyus rebottled by large organic companies are made with Chinese soybeans (which are less expensive than Japanese conventional beans). Also available outside of Japan: Yamaroku Shoyu in Shodoshima makes boldly flavorful shoyu from organic Japanese soybeans and is doing inspiring work reviving the virtually extinct large barrel–making industry in Japan. Thanks to Yasuo Yamamoto, owner of Yamaroku, there are a growing number of projects around Japan to make new large barrels, and hopefully gain the skill to repair the old ones. One of those projects is supported by our local shoyu company, Yamaki Jozo, and includes my husband, Tadaaki, and Adam Zgola, a close Canadian friend based in Japan who has been a Japanese carpenter for over a decade.

TAMARI (low- or no-wheat soy sauce): Produced and consumed almost exclusively in Aichi prefecture, tamari is made in the same method and proportions as *koikuchi shoyu*, but (most of the time) no cracked wheat is added to the koji-inoculated soybeans, salt, and water, so it is usually gluten-free. Ito Shoten is the tamari I recommend. Though not organic, this small artisanal house uses only Japanese soybeans and puts a lot of heart into their tamari. It is available through The Japanese Pantry (see Resources, page 355) and can be substituted In equal proportions to shoyu for gluten-free.

USUKUCHI SHOYU (light-tasting soy sauce): After *koikuchi shoyu*, this is the second most used shoyu in Japan, although predominantly in Kansai (Western Japan). While it has been difficult to obtain artisanal *usukuchi shoyu* outside of Japan, as awareness and knowledge increases, the market is shifting. Suehiro Shoyu, outside of Himeji, in Hyogo prefecture, is highly recommended, especially their "Harima Kuni Tatsuno" *usukuchi shoyu*. For a gluten-free alternative, for every 1 teaspoon of *usukuchi shoyu*, substitute ½ teaspoon tamari plus ⅛ teaspoon sea salt.

VINEGARS

AKASU (red vinegar): Vinegar produced by fermenting sake lees (rice solids produced when pressing sake from the fermented rice mash) for at least one year. Akasu was the traditional vinegar used to make sushi since the Edo period and in the last decade has slowly regained momentum as the vinegar of choice for Edo-style sushi (what we know today simply as "sushi").

GENMAI SU (brown rice vinegar): Fermented from brown rice sake, hard to find, even in Japan (and can be confusingly labeled as "*kurosu*").

JUNMAI SU (pure rice vinegar): A beautiful all-purpose vinegar, worth seeking out for Japanese as well as Western vinegar treatments. Iio Jozo (Fujisu Vinegar) outside of Kyoto, Sennari (Oochi Vinegar) in Hiroshima, and Ohyama (Yamadai Vinegar) in Miyazaki prefecture are three of a small handful of companies in Japan that still ferment their vinegar from in-house brewed sake.

KAKISU (persimmon vinegar): A fruity, low-acid "vinegar" fermented for about 1 month from smashed persimmons in clay crocks set in the hot sun. This is one you can make yourself, and it is well worth the small effort.

KUROSU ("black" vinegar): Fermented for about one year in black earthenware pots in southern Japan from steamed brown rice, brown rice koji, and water, then aged for at least one year. This vinegar is found abroad, though is usually labeled as "Brown Rice Vinegar." Look for Kakuida aged brown rice vinegar at The Japanese Pantry (see Resources, page 355) or brown rice vinegar repackaged by macrobiotic or organic lines such as Eden, Spiral Foods, or Clearspring.

UMESU (sour plum "vinegar"): The brine that naturally occurs from salting and weighting sour "plums" (*ume*) when making *umeboshi*. Good-quality commercial versions can be found bottled as "Plum Vinegar" by some of the more prominent organic product lines in the world.

OILS & PASTES

EGOMA ABURA (perilla oil): *Egoma* is a sister plant to shiso but the leaves are darker, thicker, and more rounded. The seeds are pressed into a mild, yet aromatic oil used for adding flavor to soups or baked desserts. Available online.

GOMA ABURA (sesame oil): High-quality, lightly roasted sesame oil such as the ones made by Wadaman Sesame from white, black, and gold sesame seeds is a totally different product from the low-end, darkly roasted, sesame oil found in all Asian grocery stores. (Large production sesame oil companies often use hexane gas to extract the oil from sesame seeds, rather than pressing it out naturally.) For dark roasted sesame oil, Wadaman is the best of the best (though pricey). If budget is an issue, try an organic oil such as Ohsawa as a compromise from the poor-quality dark roasted sesame oils readily available. Unroasted sesame oil (*taihaku goma abura*) is often used as a mild oil in stir-fries or deep-frying tempura, and Maruhon is the most popular brand. Although I typically use an organic canola (rapeseed) oil (*natane abura*) for deep-frying, I can recommend the unroasted sesame oil from Maruhon without compunction.

NATANE ABURA (rapeseed oil): The universal oil of choice in Japan is rapeseed oil (commonly known as canola oil in many parts of the world). Treated with a centrifuge, it is clear and light, while freshly pressed virgin *natane abura* is a deep golden yellow and has a pronounced vegetality.

NERI GOMA (sesame paste): Roasted white, black, or gold sesame seeds that have been pulverized into a thickly rich paste. Much like organic peanut butter, naturally processed sesame paste will separate, so thoroughly mix the contents of the jar before using.

SUGARS

KIBIZATO (light brown cane sugar): A soft, fine-grain tan-colored sugar, with nuanced flavor and higher in minerals than refined sugar.

KUROZATO (black sugar): Found online or at Japanese grocery stores. Also known as *kokuto*, the best *kurozato* is minerally sweet in a round, deep, well-balanced way and so good you want to find ways to introduce it to dishes. The artisanal *kurozato* from Murakami Shoten in Okinawa is available through The Japanese Pantry (see Resources, page 355).

SANONTO (refined light brown sugar): A slightly damp mild sugar similar to American light brown sugar in texture and flavor that adds richness to a dish due to its caramelization during processing.

WASANBON (artisanal Japanese sugar): Up until the mid-Edo period (in the beginning of the 1800s) Japanese sugar was only produced in Okinawa and nearby Amami Oshima. However, in the early 1800s some secret houses in Shikoku developed a method to produce *wasanbon*, a fine, delicately textured sugar that was particularly well suited to Japanese tea sweets and confections. Making *wasanbon* involves a week-long process of extracting molasses from the boiled sugarcane juices while also allowing mild fermentation. Today, production remains small and in the hands of only a few houses.

LIQUORS

HON MIRIN (fermented sweet rice alcohol): There is no substitute for excellent mirin, so seek out the best if you can: Mikawa Mirin. Mikawa Mirin is fermented and matured for two years from koji-inoculated steamed glutinous rice combined with in-house brewed rice shochu.

SAKE (fermented rice alcohol): A mild, naturally sweet alcohol fermented from steamed rice combined with koji-inoculated steamed rice and pristine water. Calling sake "rice wine" is a misnomer since sake brewing shares nothing in common with the wine-making process.

SHOCHU (fermented and brewed alcohol): An initial fermented mash (typically from sweet potato, barley, or rice) is made using koji-inoculation in a way similar to producing sake. That mash is then distilled (and solids removed) to yield shochu, an aromatic liquor of 25 percent alcohol that is sipped over rocks, cut with cold or hot water, or mixed into cocktails.

UMESHU (sour "plum" liquor): White liquor steeped for a year with sugar and ripened (still hard) ume to develop a refreshing cordial most often served over ice in the summer.

WHITE LIQUOR (fermented and brewed alcohol): A generic liquor used for steeping fruit, made in the same way as shochu.

MOUNTAIN VEGETABLES

FUKI (butterbur): Long, fibrous stalks with an indescribable bitter, yet soft flavor that grow in the summer to fall and are used for simmered, stir-fried, deep-fried, and dressed dishes. Fuki will reseed in your garden so can be enjoyed over many years beginning each spring.

FUKI NO TO (butterbur buds): Large, yet soft and chewy buds from the fuki plant, that have the characteristic haunting flavor of fuki, so are used for flavoring miso, in dressed dishes, and as tempura.

ITADORI (Japanese knotwood): Long thin stalks and leaves harvested in the early spring. Typically itadori is soaked for half a day in cold water to remove bitterness and is often rubbed with salt to break down fibers and soften the stalks. However, the taste and texture of itadori is quite similar to rhubarb and can be used for compotes or a tart flavoring for ice cream (with the addition of sugar).

KOGOMI (ostrich ferns): Small, tightly curled, softly furry fiddlehead ferns with short stems. They are good simmered and dressed in dashi but need to be soaked in baking soda or fireplace ash to remove bitterness before using.

KOSHI ABURA (Araliaceae buds): Thin-stemmed buds with soft green leaves from the Chengiopanax sciadophylloides tree. Like tara no me (see below), koshi abura is mildly bitter and is said to have naturally restorative powers to aid our transition from the cold winter to the bright spring. Best as tempura, served with a sprinkling of salt.

TAKENOKO (bamboo shoot): Tender shoots that develop underground in the early spring at the base of bamboo stands. The trick is to dig out the shoots and cook them as soon as possible, to best enjoy their delicate flavor and texture.

TARA NO ME (Japanese angelica buds): Thick-stemmed, frilly, purple-tinged green buds of the angelica tree. Slightly bitter but extremely appealing as tempura, served with a sprinkling of salt.

UDO (herbal aralia): A bitter, yet almost licorice-flavored, white-stalked vegetable with pink and golden peels and curly tops. Peel before using and soak the stalks in water with a little vinegar until ready to cook to avoid discoloration.

WARABI (eagle ferns): Frilly fiddlehead ferns with long, thin stems that can be blanched and dressed as is.

GREENS & HERBS

KARASHINA (mustard greens): A prickly, naturally spicy green with wide jagged leaves and thick stems. Use in dressed dishes and nabe.

KOMATSUNA (Japanese mustard): One of the most versatile greens grown in Japan and available almost year-round. In the same family as bok choy, but the leaves and stems are thinner and more tender. Used like spinach in simmered dishes, soups, and dressed dishes—but without the lingering iron taste characteristic of spinach.

MIBUNA (mibuna mustard): A Kyoto green with long, thin, flat leaves that grow from a connected bunch of tender stems jutting off the root—thought to have been developed as a cross between mizuna and turnip in the early 1800s. Substitute mizuna or Italian puntarelle.

MITSUBA (trefoil): Unforgettably aromatic green (or sometimes purple) leaves with tender stems used as garnish for miso soup, in dressed dishes, or as a tie for various simmered rolls.

MIZUNA (spider mustard): Along with komatsuna, one of the two main traditional greens used in Japanese cuisine with long, thin, jagged leaves that grow from a connected bunch of tender stems jutting off the root. Use as a garnish, in soups, or as a dressed dish.

MOROHEIYA (jute mallow): A leafy summer green similar to water spinach with a natural viscosity that comes out after blanching.

NANOHANA (flowering brassicas): The flowering tops of any of the brassicas, but most commonly *komatsuna*, turnip, or mustard. Enjoyed in dressed dishes, stir-fries, and tempura.

SANSHO (prickly ash): Small green leaves that begin to renew in early spring. Best when young. Used most commonly as a garnish for bamboo shoot.

SERI (Japanese parsley): A bright peppery, cress-like green with small frilly leaves that appears in the early spring. Good for garnishing soups, simmered and dressed dishes, and as tempura.

SHISO (perilla leaves): Green and red shiso are used as garnish, though the red has a shorter season. Shiso reseeds in early summer so is a good candidate to grow in your garden. Avoid the dull colored leaves with slightly red undersides that look like shiso but are actually *egoma* (a plant used in Japan primarily for its seeds to make oil).

SHUNGIKU (edible chrysanthemum leaves): Also known as *kikuna*, *shungiku* has a lovely haunting flavor that is extremely aromatic, so is a great foil for rich treatments such as smashed sesame sauce (*goma-ae*) or smashed tofu (*shira-ae*). *Shungiku* also livens up one-pot dishes (*nabemono*) or soups (*shirumono*). Lavender or yellow petals from edible chrysanthemum flowers (*kikunohana*) make a pretty garnish for dressed dishes.

TADSAI (bok choy): Generally harvested when small and tender, then quartered lengthwise and steamed or blanched. Good in soups and simmered dishes or as is with a gently flavored dashi.

VEGETABLES

KABOCHA (Japanese winter squash): Grown in the summer in Japan and harvested in the autumn, kabocha stores well, so is enjoyed through the winter until the new year. Kabocha are squat and round. And while there are pinky-orange kabocha varieties, the most common kabocha has dark green skin with a deep orange, dense flesh that, when simmered, becomes soft and succulent but never watery like other winter squashes can be. Because of their dense flesh, kabocha lend themselves well to mashing and forming into croquettes after being steamed, simmered, or baked. Substitute acorn squash if kabocha is not available.

KYURI (Japanese cucumber): Thin, about 6 inches (15 cm) long, with few seeds and soft skin. Eaten raw, salt-massaged, or pickled, all without peeling. Substitute other small Asian or Persian (mini) cucumbers or pickling cucumbers.

NASU (Japanese eggplant/aubergine): Slender, about 4 inches (10 cm) long, with brilliant dark-purple skin and ivory flesh, often eaten with the skins intact. Good for stir-fries, tempura, steamed and dressed, or grilled. Substitute any other small Asian eggplant.

PIMAN (Japanese green pepper): Small, thin-skinned mild peppers (usually sold green, but later in the summer red ones can be found). Most often eaten raw in salads or as tempura. Substitute small red or yellow sweet peppers.

ROOTS, RHIZOMES & CORMS

DAIKON (large Japanese radish): Round, long, short, fat, thin, spicy, sweet, white, green, purple, black . . . daikon comes in myriad shapes, flavors, and colors. Most common, however, are the long white roots found in organic shops or Asian grocery stores. No matter the shape or color, the skin of the daikon should be taut, and not wrinkled.

EBI IMO ("shrimp potato"): Small teardrop-shaped taro about 2 inches long (5 cm) and 1¼ inches (3 cm) wide at its thickest portion. The flesh is creamy white and prized for simmered dishes.

GOBO (burdock): An extremely long, fibrous root ubiquitous to Japanese vegetarian soups, simmered dishes, and stir-fries. Found as early as prehistoric Japan, burdock has been an integral part of the Japanese diet since the Heian period (794–1185). It is sold year-round, but best in season: early winter (November–January) and early summer (June–July). Burdock is high in minerals and the skin is rich in chlorogenic acid, a polyphenol, so it is to be scrubbed, not peeled. To avoid discoloration, once cut, soak in cold water with a little vinegar until ready to use. Do not substitute with salsify.

KONNYAKU (konjac): A gnarled corm (rounded, underground plant stem), also known as devil's root, that grows under rigid stalks with canopied leaves. Harvested in the autumn and processed into gelatinous blocks, spheres, or noodles to add an appealing rubbery texture to a wide variety of Japanese soups, salads, and simmered or dressed dishes. Extremely high in fiber.

RENKON (lotus root): Lotus roots are actually rhizomes (subterranean plant stems), not roots. They form into a sort of "necklace" of connected segments about 4 inches (10 cm) long (though can be found much larger). Grown in muddy areas and harvested from autumn to early spring (October–March), store in a cool, dark place, packed in sawdust. Lotus root is peeled before using and should be soaked in cold water with a little vinegar if not cooking right away. The flesh is crisp and juicy and has striking Swiss cheese-like holes, all of which make lotus root ideal for stir-frying or stuffing.

Lotus root is also finely grated and mixed with other ingredients before forming into balls or patties for steaming or deep-frying.

SATO IMO (taro): Thick, brown-husked, small round corms that simmer up to a lovely creamy texture. Taro is usually grown in sunny, open fields, although in Amami Oshima, a small southern Japanese island, it is grown in water-filled rice fields, and the yield is said to be double. Sown after the last spring frost, taro loves water, so it should be grown in a rainy climate and harvested in early summer. Avoid oversized taro roots found outside of Japan because they are unpleasantly starchy and not suitable for Japanese cuisine. Young taro stems (*zuiki*), fresh or dried and rehydrated, are enjoyed in various vegetarian simmered dishes, though are not included in this book due to difficulty in sourcing.

SATSUMA IMO (sweet potato): Sometimes purple-skinned and purple-fleshed, but the most common Japanese sweet potatoes are red-skinned and yellow-fleshed. Select local sweet potatoes, keeping in mind the appearance of the dish might change, depending on skin or flesh color. Sweet potatoes are most often eaten with their skins intact.

YAMA IMO (mountain yam): A pristine, white-fleshed, semitropical rhizome with light tan, tufted skin that is peeled off before grating. Commercially available *yama imo* is cultivated, while wild *yama imo* (*jinenjo*) is foraged in the mountains in autumn. Prized for its flavor and creamy texture, the hairs on the skin of *jinenjo* are first singed off with a butane torch, before grating unpeeled. As a result, finely grated *jinenjo* is a delicate tan color (from the skin). *Jinenjo* is native to Japan and has been consumed since the Jomon period (c. 14,000–300 BCE). Most often finely grated into a gloriously viscous mass and eaten cold with shoyu and wasabi, in dipping soups, or as a binder for various steamed or fried foods, but also excellent pickled. *Yama imo* also replaces egg in dairy-free versions of fried foods that require a flour dusting, egg dip, and panko coating. Due to the calcium oxalate crystals found in the tufted skin, peeling or grating causes the crystals to break apart, which results in temporary itchiness. Therefore it is important to wash your hands and forearms with warm, soapy water right after handling these yams. Do not substitute orange-fleshed sweet potatoes (sometimes erroneously called "yams") for *yama imo*.

FRESH MUSHROOMS
See also DRIED & PICKLED for dried mushrooms.

ENOKI: Laboratory-cultivated slender white (and sometimes light brown) mushrooms with tiny caps that add texture to traditional dishes. Usually quick-blanched before adding to dressed dishes, though used raw for soups or tempura.

ERYNGII (king oyster mushroom): A thick, flat-capped cultivated mushroom with a slight musky flavor, used in stir-fries and tempura.

MAITAKE (hen of the woods): Gathered in the forests in large clumps, maitake have frilly, dark gray-brown tops and succulently spongy pale bottoms. Torn into large chunks, they are ideal for tempura or grilling.

NAMEKO: Harvested in the forests, naturally slimy with glossy, burnished caps. Most often added to miso soup right before serving or paired with finely grated daikon. Remove any clinging dirt with a mushroom brush or damp paper towel before using.

SHIITAKE: Grown on logs in the forest, look for dusky tan caps with deep fissures and avoid ones with damp caps, if possible. The stem ends should not be discolored, and the gills should be snowy and succinct, not smashed. Used in simmered dishes and *nabe* and, in small amounts, to add a deep flavor to dressed dishes.

SHIMEJI: Dusky, gray-tan mushrooms with creamy white stems. If possible, source *hon shimeji* because they are naturally grown. Used in dressed dishes, soups, and *nabe*.

AROMATIC RHIZOMES

MYOGA: Erroneously billed as "Japanese ginger," though there is nothing ginger-like about the taste or shape. The stems and leaves of the plant, however, resemble ginger in an uncanny way. Nonetheless, ginger grows in full sun in open fields, and *myoga* thrives under a canopy of trees. Harvested through-out the summer, the pinky-tan, pointed buds peek out of the soil as they develop at the base of the stem of the plant. *Myoga* is pickled whole or sliced and used raw as a garnish for tofu dishes, soups, and dressed dishes.

SHIN SHOGA (young ginger): In the early- to mid-summer when ginger plants start to grow tall, ivory-colored, pink-tinged young ginger is harvested to be pickled whole or enjoyed raw (swiped through miso) as a spicy snack with beer.

SHOGA (ginger): Harvested in the fall when the roots have fully matured, and its skin has thickened (similar to potatoes). Pack, buried in dirt, in a cardboard box and store in a cool, dark place.

WASABI (Japanese horseradish): Gathered in the wild by mountain streams or cultivated in marshy areas of Japan or around the world (UK, Iceland, Tasmania, North Carolina, Oregon, and California, to name a few). The taste of wasabi bears no relationship to Western horseradish (which is used to make tubed wasabi paste). Pleasantly "hot," grated wasabi is served as a garnish on raw or cured fish, as well as tofu and myriad dressed dishes.

SEAWEEDS

AONORI (green laver): Usually eaten in powdered form, green nori is sprinkled on *okonomiyaki* and various other casual Japanese foods to add an element of brightness and the taste of the sea.

ARAME (sea oak): A soft variety of brown kelp (even when blanched) that is extremely high in nutrients. Found in rocky reefs in most of the southern waters surrounding Japan and cultivated mainly in Mie prefecture. Harvest is from July to September. Easily available outside of Japan through sites selling macrobiotic products. Good for simmered, fried, and vinegared dishes.

HIJIKI: A wiry brown sea vegetable with long, chewy tendrils that has been consumed for centuries and is harvested from early spring to early summer. It is rich in dietary fiber and minerals such as calcium, iron, and magnesium, so it is often used in Japanese vegetarian dishes to further boost the overall healthy properties. When blanched before drying, hijiki turns jet black. Soak for 20 minutes in plenty of cold water before using.

KONBU (kelp): Wild and farmed kelp is harvested in Hokkaido during a strictly controlled period from late July to early September and is used as the essential base flavoring of most Japanese vegetarian broths (dashi). The most common type of konbu found outside of Japan (and in Japanese supermarkets) is Hidaka, although The Japanese Pantry (see Resources, page 355) imports *ma konbu* ("true" konbu) from Konbu Doi, a generations-old, konbu-aging shop in Osaka. *Ma konbu* is prized by Japanese chefs for its well-balanced and full flavor. Rishiri is beautifully subtle and Rausu has a lovely fragrance and flavor. All are threatened because of ocean pollution, so wild harvests have lately declined drastically.

NORI (laver): Nori was traditionally produced in a similar way to paper, by spreading thin layers on screens, but nowadays is dried on hot rollers. The range of quality is wide, so try to find a good-quality nori by seeking *ichiban zumi*—first harvest—if possible. The sheets should be glossy black or dark green, extremely crisp, and noticeably tasty.

TORORO KONBU: Sold in soft, fibrous sheets that are folded around each other like cheesecloth, *tororo konbu* is produced by soaking konbu in vinegar to soften, then finely shredding by machine into threads. *Oboro konbu* is a similar product but shaved by hand, so quite pricey. *Oboro konbu* is left in threads, while *tororo konbu* is pressed into cloth-like sheets. *Tororo konbu* is usually crisped up in a dry frying pan before being folded into dressed dishes, or added, as is, to soups. Also, *tororo konbu* can be used in place of nori for sushi and rice balls (*onigiri*).

WAKAME: A soft-textured, mild variety of kelp that is most often found dried. In fish stores you might be lucky to encounter salted wakame or even fresh wakame in the spring. Soaking 5–10 minutes in plenty of cold water is all that is needed for dried or salted wakame. "Fresh" wakame is sometimes sold, already blanched, and in this case it will be bright green and ready to use in soups, salads, or vinegared dishes. If the wakame is brown, that means it has been recently harvested and will need to be dipped in and out of boiling water to shock green.

SPROUTS & BUDS

JUNSAI (baby water lily buds): Also called water shields, naturally sour, thin green sprouts about ¼–½ inch (5 mm–1 cm) long encased in a gelatinous covering. Freshly harvested from mountain ponds, May to September, these are the most delicate little bites you can imagine. Sadly, there are fewer and fewer these days because of environmental degradation. Cultivated *junsai* are found in the cold vegetable section of Japanese supermarkets in vertically packed plastic bags. Add to cold dashi for various summer dishes.

KAIWARE DAIKON (daikon sprouts): Peppery, fine-stemmed sprouts sold on spongy bottoms. Used for garnish or salads—particularly mayonnaise-based ones.

MOYASHI (mung bean sprouts): Thick, crunchy, juicy sprouts that are good for stir-fries. Optionally remove the small yellow "beard root" from the ends, and, if using fresh in a dressed dish or salad, pour boiling water over for 10 seconds, cool, and pat dry first. They are found packed in plastic bags in the cold vegetable section of supermarkets in Japan.

YURINE (lily bulbs): Small white bulbs similar to garlic in appearance but without a papery skin, they are rich in nutrients such as iodine and potassium. Most often packed in rice bran, they are found in autumn in the root vegetable section of Japanese supermarkets. The scales are separated from the bulb cluster and used whole in *chawan mushi* or other steamed Japanese vegetarian dishes such as *shinjo*, to lend texture and a subtle flavor.

CITRUS

DAIDAI: A Japanese sour orange used as the base for ponzu (citrus-shoyu).

KABOSU: Small green citrus with a slightly lime-like flavor. Substitute Key limes.

SUDACHI: Bright, fresh citrus notes—used both in the young green stage and when the mature fruit yellows.

YUZU: The most commonly found Japanese citrus, with lovely, well-balanced round notes that go particularly well with Japanese dishes. Along with *sansho*, yuzu is the oldest seasoning recorded in Japanese culinary tomes. Tiny windfall yuzu can be added to clear soups for aroma, young green yuzu is used for its zest, and mature early-winter yuzu for its juice. Left on the tree, yuzu will become extremely pithy as spring approaches, but can still be used in a pinch.

DRIED & PICKLED

BAINIKU (sour "plum" paste): *Umeboshi* that have been pitted (destoned) and passed through a machine to create a homogenous paste. Convenient to have on hand, though a bit expensive. Sold in small plastic bags or jars online at sites selling macrobiotic products. Check the ingredients for additives if you buy at the Japanese grocery store.

BENISHOGA (pickled red ginger): *Beni* means "red" in Japanese and here refers to the red color of the red shiso–flavored *umesu* used to pickle the ginger. Most commercial *benishoga* contains additives, so seek an organic version like the one made by Ohsawa.

CHINPI (dried tangerine peel): Used for adding a bright note to vegetarian dishes, substitute dried orange peel such as the one from penzeys.com.

DONKO (dried shiitake): Japanese-grown, sun-dried, with deep fissured thick caps, *donko* are the most flavorful dried shiitake for extracting dashi. Available through the Natural Import Company and The Japanese Pantry (see Resources, page 355). They can be pricey, but well worth it.

HOSHIGAKI (dried persimmon): Easy to dry at home, these addictive, chewy, fruity, dried persimmons are eaten as is, or cut up and added to dressed dishes. Available online, often as "sun-dried" and "hand massaged." Substitute organic unsulfured apricots.

KIKURAGE (wood ear mushrooms): Sold fresh or dried (I have used dried in this book). *Kikurage* have a firm, slightly rubbery quality that adds texture to dishes. They are often simmered in sweetened shoyu to bring out their depth of flavor.

KIRIBOSHI DAIKON (dried daikon): Daikon is cut (*kiri*) into fine threads or thick, flat strips and sun-dried (*hoshi*). Rinse well to remove any natural off-odors from the daikon and soak for at least 30 minutes in warm water before using in salads or vinegared dishes. Available through the Natural Import Company (see Resources, page 355).

KOSHIN (dried shiitake): Wide, thin-capped sun-dried, Japanese-grown shiitake good for making a subtle mushroom-flavored dashi.

KUCHINASHI (dried gardenia fruit pod): Sold as a Chinese herbal medicine (*shan zhi zi*: 山栀子), these pods are used to lend a vibrant yellow hue to simmered dishes such as sweet potato or chestnut.

TERA NATTO (fermented and dried soybeans): The original fermented soybean (natto) was first produced at Daitoku-ji, a monastery in Kyoto (the technique having been first learned in China). *Tera natto*, also known as Daitokuji natto, is made commercially in Hamamatsu and sold as "*hama natto*." The soybeans are fermented with koji, then dried and aged for one year. The resulting flavor is similar to miso or shoyu. The natto we know today is fermented with natto bacteria and should be consumed soon after making. Outside of Japan, look for dried natto (or perhaps Chinese fermented black beans, but rinse off the salt).

UMEBOSHI (sun-dried sour "plums"): *Ume* are related to the apricot. Toxic when fresh, *ume* are always treated before using and the most common method involves salting, weighting, then sun-drying to produce *umeboshi*, a puckery, salty, fruity little morsel that is beloved in Japan as a morning bite with a bowl of rice. Due to their uniquely powerful flavors, *umeboshi* are common in Japanese vegetarian cuisine.

YUZU KOSHO: A salty, spicy, citrusy paste stone-ground from a combination of salt-fermented yellow peels of yuzu and salt-fermented red or green japones chiles. Red *yuzu kosho* has a warm, appealing profile that lends itself to mixing into mayonnaise for sandwiches, while green *yuzu kosho* is bright and compelling, so an ideal way to add kick to salt-based soups or fried foods.

AROMATIC POWDERS

AKA SHISO (red *shiso* powder): The best versions of this powder are made from sun-dried red shiso leaves that have been dipped in sour plum "vinegar" (*umesu*).

ICHIMI TOGARASHI (red pepper powder): Sun-dried japones chiles, ground into a powder.

KARASHI (mustard powder): Ground from yellow mustard seeds. Caveat: Do not substitute Western mustard powder since it is typically made from white and brown mustard.

SANSHO (prickly ash): Often brown, high-quality *sansho* powder is ground from dried green *sansho* berries and has notes of citrus, along with its characteristic tongue-numbing qualities.

SHICHIMI TOGARASHI (7-spice powder): A mixture of seven (or more) spices, that always includes *ichimi togarashi* as the base. Besides the *ichimi*, these are common additions: sesame seeds, citrus zest, hemp seeds, amaranth, green nori, and *sansho*.

SEEDS & NUTS

GINNAN (ginkgo nut): Pungent when raw, ginkgo nuts achieve an appealing rubbery texture after boiling. These nuts have a slight toxicity that can cause nausea or vomiting, so it is wise not to overindulge. Children should not eat more than five nuts per day and adults not more than eight.

GOMA (sesame seeds): Most often sold as *iri goma* (roasted sesame), the best sesame seeds in the world are roasted by Wadaman Sesame in Osaka and are available in many countries, including the United States from The Japanese Pantry (see Resources, page 355). Supermarket seeds are fine, but typically lower quality (broken, poorly roasted, etc.).

KURI (chestnuts): Small and sweetly nutty, Japanese chestnuts originally came from Korea and their botanical name is *Castanea crenata*.

ONIGURUMI (black walnuts): Small black walnuts with extremely hard shells and flavorful nut meat. The trees are found in mountainous areas of Japan.

GRAINS

AKAMAI (red rice): A reddish-brown, ancient rice grain commonly consumed in prehistoric Japan, and now used to add nutrition, color, and texture to white rice—usually 1 tablespoon (15 g) *akamai* for every 1-*go* (¾ cup/180 ml) white rice.

AWA (foxtail millet): A pale-yellow, small, round grain native to Asia that has been cultivated in Japan since the prehistoric Jomon period (c. 14,000–300 BCE) renowned for its healthy properties.

GENMAI (brown rice): Rice that has been run through a machine to remove dust (and a small amount of the bran in the process) after husking.

HIE (barnyard millet): A highly nutritious, small, tan-colored grain dating to prehistoric Japan.

KIBI (proso millet): Small, round, yellowish grains rich in minerals and dietary fiber, known to be originally from India or China, but brought to Japan across the Korean peninsula in prehistoric times.

KOME (Japanese short-grain rice): Japonica rice, prized for its luster and stickiness (from amylose), believed to have originated in China from Fujian rice grown in the middle to lower Yangtze River area and transported to Japan 3,000 years ago during the Jomon period.

KUROMAI (black rice): Antioxidant-rich purply-black, ancient grains, which are mixed into white rice before cooking to contribute texture, aroma and a lovely hue—usually 1 tablespoon (15 g) *kuromai* for every 1-*go* (¾ cup/180 ml) white rice.

MOCHIGOME (glutinous rice): An opaque, round rice grain, with a highly sticky starch component called amylopectin (rather than the sticky, but not viscous starch amylose as in japonica rice).

OSHI MUGI (flattened barley): Glutinous barley that has been flattened by large rollers to make it more easily able to absorb water. Usually added to white rice before cooking to contribute texture and healthy properties.

BEANS

AZUKI (adzuki beans): Small, (typically) red mung beans, thought to have originated in China in prehistoric times, now cultivated throughout East Asia. Commonly sweet-simmered in Japan, they are used as a filling for traditional sweets. If you are looking for an heirloom bean substitute, try Domingo Rojo Beans from Rancho Gordo (perhaps the best bean grower in the United States).

DAIZU (soybeans): Soybean varieties typically have three properties: starch, oil, and protein. The soybean in Japan is the green soybean, high in protein, therefore suitable for traditional culinary applications such as making tofu, miso, shoyu, and natto. Outside of Japan, yellow soybeans are most commonly grown. High in oil content, non-Japanese beans are best used for soy oil production.

KUROMAME (black soybeans): Round black soybeans, most often long simmered, then sweetened, and served as a condiment (Simmered Black Beans, see page 33). Substitute Ayocote Negro Beans from Rancho Gordo for an heirloom bean alternative.

NATTO (fermented soybeans): Steamed soybeans (small or large) that traditionally were fermented naturally in rice straw, but in modern times have been treated with natto spores (*Bacillus subtilis*) to encourage a funky, sticky mass of beans. They are typically aerated with chopsticks before eating, and often seasoned with shoyu and mustard. Rather than purchasing in Japanese grocery stores (shipped frozen from Japan), I recommend sourcing locally. In recent years, I have seen a number of excellent producers enter the market outside of Japan.

TOFU

ATSUAGE (deep-fried tofu): Pressed *momendofu* ("cotton" tofu) that has been deep-fried. Used for simmered dishes.

GANMODOKI (tofu croquettes): Croquettes made from pressed tofu and other binders such as finely grated mountain yam, potato starch, and sometimes, finely grated lotus root. Simmered ingredients such as shiitake, konbu, carrot, and burdock are folded into the base before forming into patties and deep-frying.

KINUGOSHI DOFU (silken tofu): Tofu made by adding a natural coagulant (*nigari*) to soy milk and leaving to form curds.

KOYADOFU (freeze-dried tofu): Historically, there were two methods for producing freeze-dried tofu, however, with modernization, only one basic method remains. It is said to have been named after Mt. Koya (Koyasan) where one form of frozen, dried tofu originated, and where subsequently *koyadofu* became a popular souvenir gift during the Edo period (1603–1868). Tofu is highly perishable, but *koyadofu* offered a way to preserve it, and also made it easily transportable. *Koyadofu* is sold in flat squares as light as balsa wood that need to be re-inflated by soaking in several changes of water. They become spongy pillows to be used as vehicles for soaking up precious broth in simmered foods. For superior taste, source organic *koyadofu*, if possible. Or, to make a gluten-free substitute for panko, coarsely grate unreconstituted *koyadofu*.

MOMENDOFU (cotton tofu): This tofu is made by slowly heating soy milk, then carefully stirring in a natural coagulant (*nigari*), pouring into cheesecloth- (muslin-) lined molds with holes to allow drainage, and pressing with weights. Medium tofu can be substituted for *momendofu* in various dishes. If using, skip the weighting of the tofu to press out water, and process until creamy with a food processor—the traditional method of using a Japanese grinding bowl (*suribachi*) will not be sufficient to obtain a creamy texture. Meiji Tofu in Gardena, California is the only place I have found in the world making tofu similar to the top-quality *momendofu* sold in Japan.

OKARA (soybean pulp): The by-product of extracting soy milk from soybeans. After soaking, soybeans are ground up with water to a mash, then slowly heated to allow the milk to develop. The mash is pressed in a large cheesecloth (muslin) to extract the soy milk and the resulting solids are *okara*, also called (*unohana*), often used in vegetable stir-fries.

USUAGE/ABURA-AGE (deep-fried tofu pouches): Thin slices of tofu that have been weighted then twice fried to encourage puffing up, creating a natural pocket for stuffing. Mostly sold frozen outside of Japan.

YUBA (soy milk skin): The skin skimmed off soy milk as it is slowly heated during the tofu-making process. Fresh yuba is similar to burrata in texture and highly perishable. Dried *yuba* is available through sites selling macrobiotic products, but be sure to buy flat dried *yuba* from Japan. Hodo Foods in Oakland, California, is an excellent source for both fresh and semidried skins.

STARCHES, THICKENERS & FLOURS

FU (wheat gluten): With an over 1,000-year-old history, *fu* has been used in Japanese temple food (*shojin ryori*) for a very long time. To make raw *fu* (*nama fu*), make a dough with 7½ ounces (210 g) all-purpose (plain) flour, a pinch of salt, and scant ⅔ cup (5¼ fl oz/150 ml) water and knead for 10–15 minutes until no longer sticky. Cover with plastic wrap (cling film) and refrigerate for 1 hour to rest. Remove from the fridge and "wash" in a large bowl of water, kneading to remove starch and changing the water whenever it gets cloudy. Gluten is not water-soluble, so once you have washed and kneaded the dough well, all that is left is the gluten. Leave au naturel, or add sesame, *ume*, miso, or any seasoning you like and form the dough into small shapes. Cook in boiling water for 2–3 minutes until it floats. Dried *fu* is available in many forms in Japan, but only a few are found outside the country. Reconstitute and use to add texture to soups or simmered dishes.

HAKURIKIKO (low-gluten flour): Used for making udon and tempura batter. Avoid the mainstream flours available at Japanese grocery stores since they are produced on a large scale and don't have any intrinsic flavor. Find a good-tasting unbleached pastry or cake flour, or alternatively use an excellent all-purpose (plain) flour. The most important point is flavor, especially when making udon since it is made only from flour and water.

HON KUZU (kudzu): A starch made from the root of the kudzu plant. Production in Japan is relatively small, therefore 100 percent *kuzu* starch can be expensive. Starches sold as "kudzu powder" (*kuzuko*) look like *hon kuzu*, in that they consist of snowy white chunks, but are made from sweet potato starch or a combination of starches (potato, sweet potato, or corn). Using 100 percent *kuzu* yields an appreciably smoother, more resilient texture. Avoid the brown kudzu powder often found at health food stores.

JOSHINKO (rice flour): Produced by pulverizing washed and dried japonica rice into a powder and used for Japanese traditional sweets, such as *dango*, *kusa mochi*, or *kashiwa mochi*.

MOCHIKO (glutinous rice flour): Made from ground glutinous rice and used to make sticky mochi confections. Also known as "sweet" rice flour outside of Japan.

KANTEN (agar): A starch used to produce geléed squares, such as molded desserts or savory bites in the summer. Chilled agar blocks can also be extruded through a wooden press to create noodles (*tokoroten*) that are usually eaten chilled as a salad. Natural seaweed agar is the recommended form of agar to use for the recipes in this book, but the more readily available agar flakes substitute well.

KATAKURIKO (potato starch): Originally made from the rhizome of the dogtooth violet (*katakuri*), but now mass-produced from potatoes. Used for thickening dashi or simmering liquids to make a silky sauce (*ankake*), as a dusting powder for sweets, and as a dredging agent before frying. A slurry of 2 tablespoons potato starch mixed with 6 tablespoons water can substitute for egg when making dairy-free deep-fried foods that call for dipping in egg.

KINAKO (roasted soybean flour): A nutritious, nutty powder made from roasted soybeans used for dusting Japanese sweets such as *warabi mochi*.

KOMEKO (rice flour): Made from pulverizing japonica rice into a powder. Seek out brown rice flour (*genmai komeko*) because the texture and flavor will be superior. *Komeko* makes an excellent substitute for wheat flour in tempura or other fried foods because it has an inherent light silkiness. Do not use "sweet" rice flour since that is *mochiko* and made from glutinous rice.

KYORIKIKO (all-purpose flour): Find a good-flavored flour such as King Arthur or Giusto's. Used for tempura and various dusting of fried dishes.

SOBAKO (buckwheat flour): Pale, white-gray Japanese buckwheat flour can be substituted with French buckwheat flour, but not with other coarse buckwheat flours.

SHIRATAMAKO (*dango* flour): Made from washed, dried, and powdered glutinous rice and commonly used for soft confections such as *dango* or *daifuku*. Recently *shiratamako* (technically translated as "white ball flour") is also found packaged as *dango no kona* (*dango* flour).

NOODLES

SHIRATAKI/ITO KONNYAKU (konnyaku noodles): White or gray noodles made from konjac (*konnyaku*), a corm that is also formed into blocks and used to add texture to many vegetarian dishes.

SOBA (buckwheat noodles): Soba noodles are made from 100 percent buckwheat or a combination of buckwheat and wheat flour, plus water. Look for a soba shop that makes their own noodles in-house.

SOMEN (fine wheat noodles): Made from Japanese wheat flour and water, the dough for high-grade somen is rubbed with oil and hand-stretched, then sun-dried. The excellence of high-grade somen noodles is remarkable—and they can be sourced from The Japanese Pantry (see Resources, page 355).

UDON (wheat noodles): These simple flour and water noodles are available dried, but they are much superior if homemade and hand-cut.

KITCHEN TOOLS

BENRINER (Japanese mandoline): An inexpensive plastic mandoline used in modern home kitchens for slicing thinly, shaving, and making fine julienne.

DONABE (earthenware pots): Lidded earthenware casseroles produced in many different sizes and designs. These pots are flameproof, so can be used directly on a burner for *nabe*, or even in the oven.

HANDAI (wooden tub): Round cedar "bucket" (low tub), used for cooling rice while incorporating sweetened vinegar when preparing sushi rice.

HOCHO (knife): Razor-sharp Japanese knives, each one designed and forged for a specific use, traditionally made of carbon steel.

KIBERA (wooden spatula): Flat wooden spoons for stirring or stir-frying.

KONABASHI (flour chopsticks): Thick wooden chopsticks used for handling battered vegetables when frying for tempura.

KONRO (gas burner): Butane-fueled burner for cooking *nabe* at the table.

MORIBASHI (plating chopsticks): Long, thin metal chopsticks with fine points used for plating food and removing tempura from hot oil.

MUSHIKI (steamer): Bamboo or wooden steaming vessel (round or square).

NAGASHIKAN (molds): Stainless steel rectangular or square pans with a removable insert, used for making *goma dofu*, *tamago dofu*, or geléed squares. Large sizes are available from toirokitchen.com or elsewhere online—but you will need to increase the amount you make for any of these recipes to match the size of the mold. The two sizes of pan called for in this book are medium and large. Made by Shimotori Works (*Shimotori Seisakusho*), the pans are available online when searching for "egg tofu mold." The medium pan (Color: 02: 中) #409 has a cubic volume of 2½ cups (20 fl oz/600 ml) and the measurements are 5½ × 4½ × 2-inch (14 × 11 × 4.5 cm). The large pan (Color: 03: 大) #408 has a cubic volume of 3⅓ cups (26½ fl oz/800 ml) and the measurements are 6 × 5½ × 2-inch (15 × 14 × 4.5 cm).

OHITSU (wooden rice serving tub): Traditionally, just-cooked rice was transferred to an *ohitsu* to rest. Typically *ohitsu* are high-sided tubs banded with copper rings and fitted with inverted wooden lids. This style of *ohitsu* is most often made from Japanese cyprus (*sugi*), which lends aroma as well as absorbing steam from the hot rice to prevent sogginess. Shallow lacquer ohitsu (with dome-shaped lids) are used for room-temperature rice dishes such as scattered sushi (*chirashi zushi*) or mixed rice (*maze gohan*).

OROSHIGANE (metal grating plate): Traditionally copper, but now most often found made of tin, these grating plates are essential for finely grating daikon, turnip, and mountain yam. (It can also be used for grating wasabi, though purists use a sharkskin grater.)

OROSHIKI (ceramic grating plate): A round grating plate (usually white) used to finely grate ginger, daikon, and mountain yam.

OTOSHIBUTA (drop lid): Wooden, metal, or plastic rounds used to keep food submerged in its liquids while simmering—I highly recommend.

SAIBASHI (cooking chopsticks): Invaluable long wooden chopsticks for cooking.

SHICHIRIN (tabletop brazier): A charcoal-fueled brazier made of diatomaceous earth (soft, porous earth consisting of fossilized remains of diatoms). They come in varying sizes, from a one-person round mini-size to a rectangular, extra-long restaurant-size. Used for low-fire grilling (*aburi*, *yakitori*, etc.).

SURIBACHI (grinding bowl): An extremely useful, grooved ceramic grinding bowl—the larger the better—it should be the size of a medium or large mixing bowl.

SURIKOGI (grinding pestle): A wooden pestle used for grinding foods in the *suribachi* and traditionally made from *sansho* (prickly ash) branch.

TETSU BASHI (iron chopsticks): Mostly used for moving pieces of charcoal, but smaller sizes can be used for cooking hot-fire grilled foods.

TETSU GAMA (iron rice pot): A rounded cast-iron pot made specifically for cooking rice and sold in increments of *go* (¾ cup/180 ml), the measurement for rice.

TETSU NABE (iron pot): A traditional handled iron pot, the inside usually coated in copper or tin.

TSUKEMONO YOKI (pickling press): A plastic vessel with a plate that screws down, acting as a weight for quick pickling vegetables.

YASAI KATTA‑ KEIJO (vegetable cutters): Very useful little cutters to punch seasonal shapes out of vegetables for adding whimsy to a dish—sold in small sets.

SERVING IMPLEMENTS

CHAWAN (tea "bowls"): Small ceramic cups or bowls for serving rice, soup, or matcha (powdered green tea) that are rounded or more cylindrical, sometimes with lids, but always without handles.

DONBURI (deep bowls): Large ceramic bowls for serving one-dish meals, such as a hearty soup, noodles and soup, or rice with vegetables on top.

HASHI (chopsticks): Typically wood, but also made from plastic, acrylic, or bone. Often the wood is lacquered.

GOZEN/O-ZEN (trays): Traditional legged trays that serve as a table when eating on tatami mats.

O-WAN (covered bowls): Lacquered bowls of various sizes for rice, small bites, soups, and grilled, steamed, or simmered foods.

SHOYU ZARA (soy sauce plates): Small saucer-like dishes used for dipping sauces such as shoyu. They can also be used to serve one-bite foods.

RESOURCES

~~~~~~

In general, I favor health food stores or sites selling macrobiotic products over Japanese grocery stores, but below is information to get you started for some of the better Japanese online purveyors. Large organic companies, such as Eden (United States), Clearspring (UK), and Spiral (Australia) are reliable sources and offer quite a few Japanese organic products in mainstream stores—though the shoyu and tamari they sell is made with soybeans from other countries. There is also Amazon.co.jp, which can be a helpful resource for global readers.

UNITED STATES

THE JAPANESE PANTRY (thejapanesepantry.com): An excellent online source for top Japanese artisanal seasonings, highlights of which are: almost the complete line of Iio Jozo Vinegars and Wadaman Sesame products (including green *sansho* powder and house-made 7-spice mixes from Japanese-sourced ingredients). Japan-bottled Yamaki Jozo Shoyu is also available here along with a number of other types of shoyu, notably *usukuchi shoyu* from Suehiro Shoyu and tamari from Ito Shoten. The Japanese Pantry is a one-stop shopping place for organic Japanese mustard powder and dried chiles, *hon kuzu*, and high-grade somen noodles. It is the exclusive importer of an incredible Okinawan artisanal black sugar (*kurozato*) that is not to be missed, as well as top-quality Rishiri and Rausu konbu, ma-konbu from Konbu Doi in Osaka, and Japan-grown *donko* shiitake.

GOLD MINE NATURAL FOOD COMPANY (goldminenaturalfoods.com): They sell macrobiotic products connected with Muso Co., Ltd. (the largest organic company in Japan), such as a wide range of Ohsawa organic products, including miso and shoyu ("Nama Shoyu") from our local company (Yamaki Jozo), as well as tamari, brown rice vinegar, sour plum "vinegar," salted sour "plums," sour "plum" paste, *takuan*, brown rice mochi, wakame, arame, konbu, agar, nori, *nigari*, Japan-grown dried *donko* shiitake, and *hon kuzu*. Gold Mine offers a wide range of essential Japanese ingredients.

NATURAL IMPORT COMPANY (naturalimport. com): They sell macrobiotic products, mostly those connected with Mitoku (the second largest organic company in Japan) featuring an exhaustive portfolio of essential organic ingredients such as Japan-grown dried *donko* shiitake, *hon kuzu*, *koyadofu* ("snow-dried tofu"), shoyu, miso, sea salt, mochi, *kanten* (agar), *fu* (wheat gluten), green nori, *kiriboshi daikon*, Japanese grains and beans, koji and natto spores, shoyu, miso, tamari, brown rice vinegar, and sour plum "vinegar."

NIHON ICHIBAN (anything-from-japan.com): This is a well-curated site including excellent information pages on the producers and their products. Here you will find a full range of Kakuida aged vinegars; Wadaman sesame (oils, pastes, seeds, etc); *hongare katsuobushi* (for pescatarians); a range of essential konbu (Hidaka, Rausu, Rishiri), including *tororo konbu* (listed on the site as OKUI Marble Kombu); good-quality rice bran; and Kanzuri, a one-punch red chile condiment, which was originally made by local grandmothers in Niigata, but is now sold through the Kanzuri company. The site also features a wide range of goods for the kitchen or table and various Japanese crafts, including a personal favorite from Niigata: *inden* (deerskin leather goods with designs painted in enamel) produced by Inden-ya.

KITAZAWA SEED CO. (kitazawaseed.com): Based in Oakland, California, specializing in Japanese seeds but also offering an extensive array of other seeds.

KORIN (korin.com): Primarily a vendor for the professional food industry, nonetheless this site has a complete selection of Japanese cookware and tableware, so it's an invaluable resource.

TOIRO KITCHEN (toirokitchen.com): A kitchenware (and online) shop in Los Angeles, specializing in Iga-yaki *donabe*. It is also an excellent source for other well-curated Japanese utensils and vessels. Essential ingredients sourced from The Japanese Pantry (see left) are also available.

HIDA TOOL & HARDWARE CO., INC. (hidatool. com): A small traditional Japanese hardware shop in Berkeley, California, packed with Japanese knives and kitchen tools. They seem extremely dedicated to giving Japanese-style, attentive and informative customer service.

BERNAL CUTLERY (bernalcutlery.com): A shop in the San Francisco Mission District dedicated to promoting excellent knives and their care. Their honest advice will serve you well when purchasing a knife that you can pass on to the next generation. Online purchase is also available.

COUTELIER (couteliernola.com): An online site with brick-and-mortar shops in New Orleans and Nashville in the United States that sell a wide range of gorgeous knives and some select Japanese kitchenware, plus a few items from The Japanese Pantry (see left). The owners are very supportive of the local communities and the food community at large, evidenced by their vast and well-curated library of food books and periodicals.

ME SPEAK DESIGN (mespeakdesign.com): A husband (artisan) and wife (designer) team creating "Japanese Inspired Housewares with Southern Roots." Their online catalog is an impressively well-curated source for eclectic and beautiful, yet absolutely utilitarian "objets."

CANADA

KNIFEWEAR (knifewear.com): A small scattering of high-quality knife shops located in Calgary, Vancouver, Ottawa, and Edmonton. Owner Kevin Kent is a dedicated educator and author of this highly recommended deep dive into knives: *The Knifewear Guide to Japanese Knives*. Knives and other products are also available online.

AUSTRALIA

FINO FOODS (finofoods.com.au): An expertly curated line of some of the best Japanese products. The line is currently only available to restaurants and shops. Full disclosure: I selected and vetted all the products.

CIBI (cibi.com.au): A Japanese café and kitchenware shop in Melbourne featuring an awe-inspiring collection of Japanese cooking and housewares with a small selection of Japanese foods. They also have periodic Japanese workshops.

KOJI AND CO. (kojiandco.com.au): An online source for miso and miso-making ingredients and tools, such as cedar barrels and koji-making trays and cloths, based in Melbourne. Run by an engaging young Japanese woman dedicated to organics and promoting authentic Japanese food culture, Koji and Co. also sells a variety of misos, *shio koji*, Demeter organic rice, barley, and soybeans, barley koji and rice koji for making miso, as well as koji spores (*tane koji*) for fermenters who want to make their own rice, barley, or soybean koji.

CHEF'S ARMOURY (chefsarmoury.com): Shops located in Sydney and Melbourne with an online shop as well. An excellent source for Japanese knives, grills (barbecues), Oigen cast-iron cookware, and small but essential kitchen utensils.

THE GOOD GRUB HUB (thegoodgrubhub.com): An eclectic collection of off-the-wall Japanese products, yet a useful source for Mikawa Mirin, *hon kuzu*, and green *sansho* powder.

UNITED KINGDOM

NATIVE & CO. (nativeandco.com): The best source for Oigen Nambu Tekki ironware and Iga-yaki *donabe* in the UK. The brick-and-mortar shop in London (and online shop) offers other well-curated Japanese artisanal cookware as well.

THE WASABI COMPANY (thewasabicompany. co.uk): The best source for fresh wasabi and Japanese citrus in the UK. Also highly recommended specifically for their Wadaman Sesame products and Mikawa Mirin.

CLEARSPRING (clearspring.co.uk): The largest organic supplier in the UK, also serving bio stores across Europe. A good one-stop shop for organic and macrobiotic foods, including Japanese. Very reliable.

FRANCE

NISHIKIDORI (nishikidori.com): A well-curated, brick-and-mortar shop in Paris, selling an extensive range of Japanese products as well as knives and cooking utensils. Their online site is more comprehensive. Here you can find Yamaki Shoyu, Wajima no Kaien Salt, Iio Jozo Vinegar (Fuji Su), and Mikawa Mirin.

UMAMI PARIS (umamiparis.com): An online source for the excellent organic Sennari vinegars (Oochi Vinegar) and a few Wadaman Sesame products.

KUROSHIO (kuroshio.fr): A chef-oriented site for sourcing Uji tea, Japanese citrus (and fish), and the full line of Wadaman Sesame products: white, gold, and black seeds, paste and oil.

ISSÉ JAPAN (issejapan.com): Sister site to Kuroshio, Issé Japan targets the home cook as well as chefs. Besides Wadaman Sesame, this site (and Kuroshio) features Kazita, an excellent shoyu made in Ehime, and a special small batch vinegar from Hanabisu in Kyoto. The owner of Kuroshio and Issé Japan is an expert on logistics and ships to anywhere in the EU and beyond in lightning speed. (I have personally experienced this so can attest to the astonishing delivery turn around time.) Issé Japan has offices in France, Spain, and Tokyo.

REFERENCES

Aoe, Kakuho, and Shoyo Yoshimura. *Temple Food: Recipes to Nourish Your Mind and Body*. Tokyo: NHK Publishing, 2014.

Aoe, Kakuho. *Temple Food*. Tokyo: Discover 21, Inc., 2012.

Honma, Gaku. *The Folk Art of Japanese Country Cooking: A Traditional Diet for Today's World*. Berkeley, CA: North Atlantic Books, 1991.

Ishige, Naomichi. *The History and Culture of Japanese Food*. Oxford, UK: Kegan Paul Ltd. and Routledge, 2001.

Ishiwada, Satoshi. *Koyasan Ichijoin's Shojin Ryori that Captures the Heart and Body*. Tokyo: Wani Books, 2012.

Kawaguchi, Harumi. *Dictionary of Healthy Food*. Tokyo: Tokyo Do Publisher, 1993.

Kawaguchi, Harumi. *Side Dishes to Purify the Body*. Tokyo: Shogakukan, 2003.

Kondo, Fumio. *All Elements of Tempura: The Skill and Flavor of Tempura Kondo*. Tokyo: Shibata Shoten, 2013.

Kondo, Fumio. *Tempura Kondo: Kindly Taught by the Master (Professional Taste You Can Make at Home)*. Tokyo: Sekai Bunka, 2017.

Koyasan Shingon Sect Headquarters Kongobuji Temple, eds. *Shojin Ryori of Koyasan*. Tokyo: Gakken Plus (new edition), 2015.

Rath, Eric C. and Stephanie Assmann, eds. *Japanese Foodways, Past and Present*. Urbana, Chicago, and Springfield, IL: University of Illinois Press, 2010.

Takahashi, Eichi and Yoshihiro. *Kyoto Hyotei: Four Seasons of Japanese Cuisine*. Tokyo: NHK Publishing, 2014.

Yoneda, Soei. *The Heart of Zen Cuisine*. Tokyo: Kodansha International, 1988.

Yoshimura, Shoyo. *If You Feel Tired, Eat Porridge: Zen Teachings to Eat Abundantly and Live Politely*. Tokyo: Gentosha, September, 2014.

Yoshimura, Shoyo. *Thoughts on Shojin Ryori*. Tokyo: Shunjusha Publishing, Co. Ltd, August, 2019.

Yoshimura, Shoyo. *Zen Monk's Weekend Food*. Tokyo: Shufu-to-Seikatsu, May, 2014.

RECIPE NOTES

Butter should always be unsalted, unless otherwise specified.

All herbs are fresh, unless otherwise specified.

Eggs are medium (UK small) unless otherwise specified.

Individual vegetables and fruits are assumed to be medium, unless otherwise specified.

All milk is whole (3% fat), homogenized, and lightly pasteurized, unless otherwise specified.

Where a nut-free icon is listed, ensure you select a nut-free base oil from the accompanying list.

Top-quality medium tofu can be substituted for *momendofu* or Japanese-style soft block tofu for *shira-ae* (smashed tofu) recipes. In that case, no need to weight and squeeze: process to a creamy texture in a food processor, rather than smashing in a *suribachi* (Japanese grinding bowl).

Exercise a high level of caution when following recipes involving any potentially hazardous activity, including the use of high temperatures, open flames, and when deep-frying. In particular, when deep-frying, add food carefully to avoid splashing, wear long sleeves and never leave the pan unattended.

Cooking times are for guidance only. If using a fan (convection) oven, follow the manufacturer's instructions concerning the oven temperatures.

All herbs, shoots, flowers and leaves should be picked fresh from a clean source. Exercise caution when foraging for ingredients, which should only be eaten if an expert has deemed them safe. In particular, do not gather wild mushrooms yourself before seeking the advice of an expert who has confirmed their suitability for human consumption. As some species of mushrooms have been known to cause allergic reaction and illness, do take extra care when cooking and eating mushrooms and do seek immediate medical help if you experience a reaction.

Exercise caution when making fermented products, ensuring all equipment is spotlessly clean, and seek expert advice if in any doubt.

When no quantity is specified, for example of oils, salts, and herbs used for finishing dishes, quantities are discretionary and flexible.

All spoon and cup measurements are level, unless otherwise stated. 1 teaspoon = 5 ml; 1 tablespoon = 15 ml. Australian standard tablespoons are 20 ml, so Australian readers are advised to use 3 teaspoons in place of 1 tablespoon when measuring small quantities.

INDEX